Shades of Grey – Domestic and Sexual Violence Against Women

Arguing that the law must be looked at holistically, this book investigates the 'hidden gender' of the so-called neutral or objective legal principles that structure the law addressing violence against women. Adopting an explicitly feminist perspective, it investigates how legal responses to violence against women presuppose, maintain and perpetuate a certain context that may not in fact reflect women's experiences.

Carline and Easteal draw upon relevant legislation, case law and secondary studies from a range of territories, including Australia, England and Wales, the United States, Canada and Europe, to contextualize and critique policy responses. They go on to examine the potential and limits of law, making recommendations for best practice models of policymaking and law reform.

Aiming to help improve government, community and legal responses to women who experience violence, *Shades of Grey – Domestic and Sexual Violence Against Women: Law Reform and Society* will assist law-makers, academics, policy-makers and a wider audience in understanding the complexities of violence against women.

Dr Anna Carline is a Senior Law Lecturer at the University of Leicester. She has researched and published extensively on the topic of violence against women.

Professor Patricia Easteal AM is a Law Professor at the University of Canberra. She was made a Member of the Order of Australia for service to the community, education and the law through promoting awareness and understanding of violence against women, discrimination and access to justice for minority groups.

Shades of Grey – Domestic and Sexual Violence Against Women

Law Reform and Society

Anna Carline and
Patricia Easteal AM

Routledge
Taylor & Francis Group
a GlassHouse Book

First published 2014
by Routledge
2 Park Square, Milton Park, Abingdon, Oxon, OX14 4RN

and by Routledge
711 Third Avenue, New York, NY 10017

a GlassHouse Book

Routledge is an imprint of the Taylor & Francis Group, an informa business

British Library Cataloguing in Publication Data
A catalogue record for this book is available from the British Library

Library of Congress Cataloging-in-Publication Data
Carline, Anna, author.
Shades of grey – domestic and sexual violence against women : law reform and society / Anna Carline, Patricia Easteal AM.
pages cm
"A GlassHouse Book."
ISBN 978-0-415-62217-2 (hardback)—ISBN 978-1-315-81795-8 (ebk) 1. Women—Crimes against. 2. Abused women—Legal status, laws, etc. 3. Women—Crimes against—England. 4. Abused women—Legal status, laws, etc.—England. 5. Women—Crimes against—Australia. 6. Abused women—Legal status, laws, etc.—Australia. I. Easteal, Patricia Weiser, author. II. Title.
K5191.W65C37 2014
344.03'28292—dc23 2014016355

ISBN: 978-0-415-62217-2 (hbk)
ISBN: 978-1-315-81795-8 (ebk)

Typeset in Bembo
by Keystroke, Station Road, Codsall, Wolverhampton

MIX
Paper from responsible sources
FSC® C013604

We would like to thank David Easteal LLB (Hons) (Melb) for his most valuable substantive copy-editing of at least three versions of each chapter. He also provided excellent research assistance through updating Australian case law and legislation.

Contents

Chapter 1

Introduction

Magnitude of the issues: our raison d'être

From crime victim surveys conducted globally, it would seem that violence against women remains a serious problem. For example, a 2013 prevalence study using data from 141 studies of intimate partner violence in 81 countries found that globally *30 per cent* of women aged over 15 had experienced violence from a partner – that means that almost one-third of women were survivors of domestic violence.[1] This is a disturbingly high proportion, yet the actual numbers are likely to be even higher. For instance, in the context of rape: 'It is generally accepted in sexual assault research that undercounting is much greater than over-counting . . . Therefore, any statistical data available are likely to be an underestimation'.[2]

There is no doubt that violence against women is a major global public health issue and a significant human rights concern. The impact is not only felt by individual women and families, but also by the state, and it has been estimated that violence against women costs the United Kingdom £37.6 billion each year.[3] However, only a minority of those victimised disclose or report.[4] For those who do report, as we see in the following pages, the response is often problematic. Using comparative material, and a feminist and contextual approach, our intention is to shed more light on the legal responses to domestic violence and sexual assault. By drawing upon a range of material primarily from Australia and England and Wales but also from the United States, Canada and

1 Australasia – 28.29 per cent, compared to 19.30 per cent in Western Europe, 16.30 per cent in East Asia and 65.64 per cent in Central Sub-Saharan Africa: K.M. Devries et al., 'The Global Prevalence of Intimate Partner Violence Against Women', *Science* 340(6140), 2013, 1527–1528, p. 1528.

2 C. Tarczon and A. Quadara, 'The Nature and Extent of Sexual Assault and Abuse in Australia', Resource Sheet, Melbourne: Australian Centre for the Study of Sexual Assault, 2012, p. 14. The reasons for underestimation of both rape and domestic violence might include low levels of disclosure, shame and an inability to self-identify. These are discussed in later chapters.

3 HM Government, *The Equality Strategy – Building a Fairer Britain*, 2010, p. 8.

4 Statistics are provided in Chs 4–10.

European countries, we explore the range of laws and reforms which have been introduced, and highlight the indeterminacy of legislation and how that translates into decision-making. This exploration of indeterminacy will demonstrate how legal discretion permits the continued circulation of myths, stereotypes and misconceptions regarding femininity and violence against women – a circulation which at times works to defeat the aims of legislation and policy to respond in an effective manner, whether in terms of reducing incidence or protecting and providing justice for victims.

The feminist and holistic perspective

Our critical analysis will be explicitly feminist. Throughout the book, we will draw upon a range of feminist theories in order to explore how the law has responded to violence against women. This will not only highlight the many successes of feminist activism in bringing about productive law reform, for example changes to the law of rape,[5] but also draw attention to and lament the law's inadequacy. Throughout this analysis, we adopt a coalitional and contingent approach to feminist theory, or, to borrow a phrase from Halley, 'a politics of theoretic incommensurability'.[6] Hence, we draw upon a wide variety of perspectives – from radical feminism to queer theory – in order to highlight and explore not only the law's failure, but also its productive potential.

Undoubtedly, many of the feminist theories we utilise cannot be harmonised. Significant contradictions and disagreements exist. However, the aim of the book is not to develop a unified feminist jurisprudence. Moreover, it is doubted whether such unity is either possible or desirable. Rather, we see disagreement and divergence as a potential ground for productive engagement. Butler notes:

> As a democratic enterprise, feminism has had to forfeit the presumption that at base we can all agree about some things or, equivalently, to embrace the notion that each of our most treasured values are under contestation and that they will remain contested zones of politics.[7]

In contrast to leading to an interminable cycle of internal self-reflection which prevents any 'active engagement in with the world',[8] Butler maintains that 'resisting the desire into unity is precisely what keeps the movement alive'.[9] Furthermore, we

5 See further the discussion by K. Cook and H. Jones, 'Surviving Victimhood: The Impact of Feminist Campaigns', in S. Walklate (ed.), *Handbook of Victims and Victimology*, Abingdon, Oxon: Routledge, 2nd edn, 2011, 125–145.

6 J. Halley, *Split Decisions: How and Why to Take a Break from Feminism*, Princeton: Princeton University Press, 2006, p. 2.

7 J. Butler, *Undoing Gender*, New York: Routledge, 2004, p. 175.

8 Ibid.

9 Ibid.

find that by adopting an eclectic approach to our feminist theory we are able to delve into the myriad ways in which law and policy construct the issue of violence against women and frequently work to exclude, silence and stereotype victims. This, in turn, allows an exploration of a diverse range of reforms and potential solutions. The issue of violence against women is complex; it therefore stands to reason that no one feminist perspective in and of itself will exhaust the field of possibilities.

In addition to the feminist approach, we are writing from an holistic perspective and consider violence against women, legal processes, the practitioners' actions and the substance of laws as both interrelated and as incomprehensible without an understanding of the cultural landscape. As we discuss at p. 6 and in Chapter 2, that socio-legal landscape is undulating. It presents obvious and obscured obstacles for women accessing legal remedies in general and even more so for survivors of violence. Hence, even if the letter of the law is reformed to respond more effectively to violence against women, other barriers frequently exist.

Even what is perceived of as violence against women is context dependent. As we will explore throughout the chapters, over the years feminist theory and activism have drawn attention to the impoverished manner in which the law has conceptualised violence against women. By engaging in a genealogy of law and reforms, we can see that the state and the judiciary have frequently failed to acknowledge a range of abusive behaviour as amounting to activity that should raise concern, and we will show how this has been challenged from a variety of feminist perspectives. Furthermore, there is an ongoing heterogeneity in what is defined within a culture as domestic violence and as rape. Accordingly, a cross-cultural analysis of 'wife beating' identified variation in derivation and definition.[10] Generally across cultures, a common denominator is evident though. Male domination translates into a higher incidence of violence against women; therefore 'high levels of female empowerment ... [are] protective against intimate partner violence'.[11] Male dominance is associated with a number of societal characteristics, such as a gendered division of labour in which activities undertaken by men are more valued, male control of resources and a separation between the public and the private spheres.[12]

In Chapter 2, we describe the persistence of these variables in western countries such as Australia and England and Wales. In Australia, for example, there is a strong historical basis to the subordination of women with some theorising that the culture has 'never outgrown the former attitude, and our women are still deeply,

10 J. Campbell, 'Beating of Wives: a Cross–Cultural Perspective', *Victimology* 10(1–4), 1985, 174–185.

11 R. Jewkes, 'Intimate Partner Violence: Causes and Prevention', *Lancet* 359(9315), 2002, 1423–1429, p. 1425.

12 L. Lindsey, *Gender Roles: A Sociological Perspective*, New Jersey: Pearson Higher Education, 5th edn, 2010.

if unconsciously, impoverished by this dominant cultural characteristic'.[13] Although there have undeniably been advances for women, as we will see the division of labour within the home remains largely gendered. We agree with Margaret Thornton who wrote that significant changes in 'sexual relations cannot take place without addressing the anomalies which exist in the private sphere in the sense of family'.[14]

A lot has been written about Australian mateship in the bush, with male dominance continuing to be normative.[15] However, such sexism (and misogyny)[16] is not confined to the bush:

> systemic beliefs and behaviour . . . are predicated on the view that women do not have the fundamental right to be part of society beyond the home . . . [T]he misogyny factor is that set of attitudes and entrenched practices that are embedded in most of our major institutions (business, politics, the military, the media, the church, academia) that stand in the way of women being included, treated equally and accorded respect . . .[17]

While space does not permit a detailed analysis of the causes of domestic violence, we would agree with analysis that identifies a range of factors – individual, cultural and structural.[18] Thus, it is important to recognise both the responsibility of individual men and that of the state. As we explore throughout this book, many legal and social factors are implicated in the abuse suffered by women at the hands of men. Consequently, focusing solely on the responsibility of perpetrators, while vital, is not sufficient to work towards eradicating violence against women. The state also has a responsibility and needs to be proactive in order to bring about more effective systematic change. Over and above reforming laws, changes in practices and the challenging of problematic beliefs are also essential, and throughout this book we will explicate and critique many of the pervasive myths and misconceptions.

13 M. Dixson, *The Real Matilda: Women and Identity in Australia 1788 to the Present*, Sydney: University of New South Wales Press, 4th edn, 1999, p. 12

14 M. Thornton, *The Liberal Promise Anti–Discrimination Legislation in Australia*, Melbourne: Oxford University Press, 1990, p. 102.

15 R. Hogg and K. Carrington, *Policing the Rural Crisis*, Sydney: Federation Press, 2006; S. Sharma and S. Rees, 'Consideration of the Determinants of Women's Mental Health in Remote Australian Mining Towns', *Australian Journal of Rural Health* 15(1), 2007, 1–7; S. Jamieson and S. Wendt, 'Exploring Men's Perpetrator Programs in Small Rural Communities', *Rural Society* 18(1), 2008, 39–50, p. 48.

16 'Sexism goes hand in hand with misogyny. Sexism provides the rationale for misogyny': A. Summers, *The Misogyny Factor*, Sydney: New South Publishing, 2013, p. 8.

17 Ibid., pp. 7–8.

18 R. Dobash and R. Dobash, *Violence Against Wives: A Case Against the Patriarchy*, New York: Free Press, 1979.

Law, gender and violence

Our analysis also proceeds from a perspective that recognises that the law plays a crucial role in the construction of ideal gender norms and identities.[19] We recognise that gender is socially constructed, as opposed to innate and natural. This in turn leads to an acknowledgement that both femininity and masculinity are not static and settled, but rather fluid, contingent and diverse. Indeed, it is more appropriate to refer to femininities and masculinities and also imperative to acknowledge the significance of other aspects of identity – such as class, race and sexuality.[20]

While the focus of the book is on the law's response to, and construction of, female victims of violence, we nevertheless acknowledge the importance of exploring masculinity and its complex interrelationship with patriarchy and crime, including violence against women.[21] As Heidensohn noted, in the absence of a study of masculinity, 'there will be no progress in understanding the violence women experience at the hands of men, or in exploring male criminality, which still remains a significant problem for criminology and society'.[22] Throughout the book, we work from the presumption that violence is gendered. To quote Hearn:

> In most societies men enact most 'domestic' and 'intimate partner violence', especially planned, repeated, heavy, physically damaging, non-defensive, pre-meditated, non-retaliatory and sexual forms of violence, along with most economic, collective, institutional, organized and military violence, which are themselves often interpersonal, sometimes 'domestic'.[23]

19 See, e.g., A. Carline, 'Women who Kill their Abusive Partners: From Sameness to Gender Construction', *Liverpool Law Review* 26(1), 2005, 13–44, pp. 36–39; J. Conaghan, 'Reassessing the Feminist Theoretical Project in Law', *Journal of Law and Society* 27(3), 2000, 351–385, p. 361; C. Smart, *Law, Crime and Sexuality: Essays in Feminism*, London: Sage Publications, 1995, p. 191.

20 In Ch. 11 we explore the issue of intersectionality, as developed by K. Crenshaw, 'Mapping the Margins: Intersectionality, Identity Politics, and Violence Against Women of Color', *Stanford Law Review* 43(6), 1991, 1241–1300.

21 On the issue of masculinities generally and masculinities and crime, including violence against women, see, e.g.: R. Collier, 'Masculinities and Violence', *Criminal Justice Matters* 42(1), 2000, 8–10; R.W. Connell, *Gender and Power*, Cambridge: Polity Press, 1985; R.W. Connell, *Masculinities*, Cambridge: Policy Press, 1997; D. Gadd, 'Masculinities and Violence Against Female Partners', *Social and Legal Studies* 11(1), 2002, 61–80; J. Hearn, *The Violences of Men*, London: Sage Publications, 1998; J. Messerschmidt, *Masculinities and Crime*, Lanham: Rowman and Littlefield, 1993.

22 F. Heidensohn, 'Feminist Perspectives and their Impact on Criminology and Criminal Justice in Britain', in N. Rafter and F. Heidensohn (eds), *International Feminist Perspectives*, Buckingham: Open University Press, 1995, 63–85, p. 81.

23 J. Hearn, 'A Multi-Faceted Power Analysis of Men's Violence to Known Women: From Hegemonic Masculinity to the Hegemony of Men', *Sociological Review* 60(4), 2012, 589–610, p. 590. See further the discussion in Ch. 2.

Invisible biases

Within the holistic construct of society, each person possesses biases that are a consequence of both socialisation and a need to categorise.[24] This can generate stereotypes and lead to myths – especially concerning those who are 'outsiders':

> With respect to prejudice, the implication of this research is that differences within groups will tend to be minimized and differences between groups will tend to be exaggerated. Moreover, if these differences are consistent with well-known stereotypes, the distortion in perception may be highly resistant to change.[25]

Not surprisingly then, within cultures like Australia and England and Wales, there are gendered assumptions that can translate into mythology concerning domestic violence and sexual assault. Accordingly, the most recent Australian survey of attitudes about violence against women found that a substantial proportion of males and females in the community continue to believe the following:

- Domestic violence can be excused if it results from temporary anger or results in genuine regret.
- Women may make up violence allegations if they are involved in a custody battle in family law proceedings.
- Rape is the outcome of men's uncontrollable libido.[26]

Although results were not directly comparable with attitudinal research conducted a decade earlier, there were some indications that over the ten-year period some changes in viewpoint had occurred. For instance, significantly more people identified certain emotional behaviours (criticism, control) and economic acts (denial of money) as violence.[27] However, there was a shift in the opposite direction with one-fifth of those surveyed in 2006 expressing the view that domestic violence was *equally* perpetrated by men and women, as compared to nine per cent in 1995.[28]

In the context of sexual violence, correlating with the myth about the irrepressible male libido, studies have found other beliefs that directly or implicitly blame rape

24 Discussed by P. Easteal, 'Setting the Stage: The Iceberg Jigsaw Puzzle', in P. Easteal (ed.), *Women and the Law in Australia*, Sydney: LexisNexis, 2010, p. 18.

25 S. Plous, 'The Psychology of Prejudice, Stereotyping and Discrimination: An Overview', in S. Plous (ed.), *Understanding Prejudice and Discrimination*, New York: McGraw Hill, 2003, 3–48, p. 9.

26 N. Taylor and J. Mouzos, *Community Attitudes to Violence Against Women Survey: A Full Technical Report*, Canberra: Australian Institute of Criminology, 2006, p. 67.

27 Ibid, p. 46.

28 Ibid, p. 62.

victims[29] and sexual harassment targets.[30] Women are seen as potential provocateurs: 'they must be careful lest their behaviour unwittingly inflames the desires of men'.[31]

These attitudes are conducive to both individual[32] and community denial.[33] For the victims of domestic violence, the 'bizarre' and abusive behaviours may become normalised and unnamed.[34] This is contributed to by their own socialisation within a culture pervasive with mythology, which tends to define violence in narrower terms than their own experiences.[35] With sexual harassment in the workplace just as with violence in the home, behaviours may become so 'routine or habitual that they too become functionally invisible'.[36]

Incidence

Within such a contextual tapestry, it is not surprising to find high levels of violence against women. One in four women in the United States is reported as having experienced domestic violence,[37] and in the United Kingdom it is estimated that in 2012 'around 1.2 million suffered domestic abuse'.[38] Prevalence rates for physical or sexual violence by a partner or former partner in Australian surveys remained at 17 per cent from 2005 to 2012.[39]

In relation to sexual assault victimisation, in one survey, ten per cent of Australian respondents reported that, over their lifetime, they had experienced

29 See H. Clark, 'Judging Rape: Public Attitudes and Sentencing', *Aware: Australian Centre for the Study of Sexual Assault Newsletter* 14, Melbourne: Australian Institute of Family Studies, 2007. See further Ch. 9 and P. Easteal and L. McOrmond-Plummer, *Real Rape, Real Pain*, Melbourne: Hybrid Publishers, 2006, who focus on partner rape.

30 S. Saunders and P. Easteal, '"I Just Think it all Comes Down to How the Girl Behaves as to How She is Treated": Sexual Harassment "Survival" Behaviours and Workplace Thinking in Rural Australia', in P. Easteal (ed.), *Justice Connections*, Newcastle: Cambridge Scholars Publishing, 2013, 106–128.

31 Smart, *Law, Crime and Sexuality*, above n. 19, p. 80.

32 K. Rhodes and W. Levinson, 'Interventions for Intimate Partner Violence Against Women: Clinical Applications', *Journal of the American Medical Association* 289(5), 2003, 601–605, p. 602.

33 L. McKie, *Families, Violence and Social Change*, Maidenhead: Open University Press, 2005, p. 152.

34 This process is described more fully in Ch. 4.

35 This is discussed fully in Ch. 4.

36 F. Wilson and P. Thompson, 'Sexual Harassment as an Exercise of Power', *Gender, Work and Organization* 8(1), 2001, 61–83, p. 61. See also Saunders and Easteal, '"I Just Think it all Comes Down to How the Girl Behaves"', above n. 30.

37 P. Tjaden and N. Thoennes, *Extent, Nature, and Consequences of Intimate Partner Violence*, Research Report, Washington: US Department of Justice, 2000, p. iii.

38 Home Office, *Policy: Ending Violence Against Women and Girls in the UK*, 2014. Available online at www.gov.uk/government/policies/ending-violence-against-women-and-girls-in-the-uk#issue.

39 Australian Bureau of Statistics, *Personal Safety Survey, Australia 2005*, Cat. No. 4906.0, 2006; Australian Bureau of Statistics, *Personal Safety Survey, Australia 2012*, Cat. No. 4906.0, 2013.

attempted forced sexual intercourse, with a further nine per cent reporting forced intercourse.[40] In a recent survey, 19 per cent of women reported having experienced sexual assault since the age of 15.[41] A 2007 Australian study of rape and related offences found that most victims knew their perpetrators and that the majority of offences were perpetrated in residential settings.[42] Only 12 per cent of respondents in another Australian survey who reported having experienced sexual assault identified a stranger as perpetrator.[43] Just over half (51 per cent) of the one in six women in the United States who were sexually assaulted[44] were raped by past or present partners.[45] These proportions are consistent with an England and Wales survey which found that close to five per cent of women reported that they had been raped since the age of 16; 45 per cent of all rapes were committed by present partners, with a further 11 per cent by ex-partners.[46]

While emphasising the endemic nature of sexual and domestic violence against women, this is not to conceptualise women as always already passive victims.[47] There is considerable debate among the feminist movement regarding the problematic use of the label 'victim', and we recognise that for some the term 'survivor' is preferred.[48] Furthermore, as research has amply documented, women frequently assert agency in various ways in response to violence.[49] Indeed, it is important to emphasise the diverse and unexpected ways in which women perform their gender, as this often causes difficulties in the legal sphere. Hence, women are frequently punished by

40 J. Mouzos and T. Makkai, *Women's Experiences of Male Violence: Findings from the Australian Component of the International Violence Against Women Survey*, Research and Public Policy Series No. 56, Canberra: Australian Institute of Criminology, 2004, p. 26.

41 Australian Bureau of Statistics, *Personal Safety Survey, Australia 2012*, above n. 39.

42 M. Borzyck, *Pilot Study on Sexual Assault and Related Offences in the ACT: Stage 3*, Research and Public Policy Series No. 79, Canberra: Australian Institute of Criminology, 2007, pp. viii–ix.

43 Australian Bureau of Statistics, *Personal Safety Survey, Australia 2012*, above n. 39.

44 Tjaden and Thoennes, *Extent, Nature, and Consequences of Intimate Partner Violence*, above n. 37.

45 M. Black et al., *National Intimate Partner and Sexual Violence Survey: 2010 Summary Report*, Atlanta: National Center for Injury Prevention and Control, Division of Violence Prevention, 2011.

46 A. Myhill and J. Allen, *Rape and Sexual Assault of Women: Findings from the British Crime Survey*, Findings No. 59, London: Home Office, 2002.

47 M.R. Mahoney, 'Victimization or Oppression? Women's Lives, Violence, and Agency', in M. Fineman and R. Mykitiuk (eds), *The Public Nature of Private Violence: The Discovering of Domestic Abuse*, Abingdon, Oxon: Routledge, 1994, 59–92.

48 See, e.g., the discussion in A. Gill, 'Narratives of Survival: South Asian Women's Experiences of Rape', in M. Horvath and J. Brown (eds), *Rape: Challenging Contemporary Thinking*, Portland: Willan Publishing, 2009, 161–183. We will use both terms throughout the book.

49 See, e.g., K. Cavanagh, 'Understanding Women's Responses to Domestic Violence', *Qualitative Social Work* 2(3), 2003, 229–249; S.M. Hage, 'Profiles of Women Survivors: The Development of Agency in Abusive Relationships', *Journal of Counselling and Development* 84(1), 2006, 83–94; S. Hamby, *Battered Women's Protective Strategies: Stronger than you Know*, Oxford: Oxford University Press, 2014; Mahoney, 'Victimization or Oppression?', above n. 47.

society and the criminal justice system for failing to conform to ideal notions of femininity.[50]

Law (reform) within a gendered context

All of the chapters that follow are based upon holistic constructions of violence against women and of the law. We look at how these are related to other parts of culture such as sex roles and sex stratification and form a veritable contextual jigsaw puzzle. Indeed, laws are neither constructed nor implemented in an ideological vacuum. On the contrary, even laws' underpinning liberalist framework, with emphases on individual rights, equality and free will (subtly and not so subtly), may affect the issues we are looking at in this book. A denial of power inequity may coincide with an imperviousness and insensitivity to gender-derived differences and thinking with 'the very construct of free will . . . illusory and paradoxical'.[51]

There have been a plentitude of laws enacted to address/remedy violence against women in the countries on which we are focusing. This is in part attributable to feminist lobbying and representation in governmental bureaucracies. In Australia, for example, both the Commonwealth and state/territory governments fund women-focused policy units, task forces and committees that spearhead reform.[52] However, it is the nature of legislation that it is drafted using language made up of ambiguous words and phrases, which allows for interpretation; this is an integral part of the judicial role (see Chapter 3). The explicit and implicit cultural gender assumptions and beliefs about violence against women described at p. 6 potentially permeate legal principles and constructs. We see these biases as cerebral filters through which the grey-coloured words of the law are understood.

At the same time, however, and as we discuss in Chapter 3, we recognise that a certain amount of interpretation and indeterminacy is inevitable, due to the nature of the law and legal reform, but also of language. There is always an element of an unknowability, an excitability,[53] as it is impossible to know in advance how a particular law will be interpreted and operate in practice. Both the meaning and the impact of law cannot be predetermined. From this premise we emphasise the following. First, the inevitable fluidity of the law and language places a fundamental ethical responsibility upon those involved in interpretation and implementation, in particular judges, but also a range of practitioners. This responsibility requires the recognition, and challenging, of the law's role in maintaining and perpetuating problematic stereotypes, along with its failure to respond effectively and at times

50 J. Butler, 'Performative Acts and Gender Constitution: An Essay in Phenomenology and Feminist Theory', in S.E. Case (ed.), *Performing Feminisms: Feminist Critical Theory and Theatre*, London: John Hopkins University Press, 1990, 207–282, p. 273.

51 P. Easteal, 'Setting the Stage: The Iceberg Jigsaw Puzzle', above n. 24, p. 19.

52 See, e.g., Women NSW, which has a Violence Prevention Co-ordination Unit and oversees that State's initiatives for women. Available online at www.women.nsw.gov.au/.

53 See J. Butler, *Excitable Speech: A Politics of the Performative*, London: Routledge, 1997.

condone – if not promote – violence against women.[54] Second, law and reforms must remain subject to constant scrutiny. The introduction of a law or a reform is only one element of the move towards improved responses to violence against women. Continual engagement and scrutiny is fundamental.

In Chapters 4 to 11, we provide ample examples of judicial heuristics that are formed and influenced in large part from the normative and invisible assumptions. In each of those chapters we also highlight at least some of the underlying institutional and individual biases. For instance, in Chapter 4 we look at the situations in which domestic violence may evoke a criminal law response. This includes breaching of restraining orders, assault charges and anti-stalking legislation. We see from studies in different countries how important police officers', magistrates' and judges' attitudes are about criminalising violence against women. In Chapter 5 we focus on non-criminal legislation: protection order laws. The mechanics of the orders – their provisions and process – as well as their efficacy are examined, along with police and magistrate powers and attitudes. By looking at models from different jurisdictions, we identify the indeterminacy of these laws and variability in how they have been applied.

A significant proportion of relationships that end include allegations of violence. Does this differ between Australia and England and Wales? In Chapter 6, we provide an overview of how the relevant legislation in the two jurisdictions has been amended to define and address violence. We also look at dispute-settlement process and outcome. Through analysis of the case law and the research literature, we identify differences in how the family law systems in the two jurisdictions practise and implement protection of women and children from violence.

What has been the outcome for women who kill violent partners? We examine laws of self-defence, provocation and diminished responsibility and how they have been amended, examining whether the concepts of 'reasonable' and 'immediate' continue to be interpreted in a gendered way. In Chapter 7, we explore women's reality of domestic violence and evaluate how laws have integrated or ignored their experiences. We identify how expert evidence is used in different jurisdictions.

Turning from domestic violence to sexual assault, in Chapter 8 we look more at the substance of rape and sexual assault provisions focusing on consent and corroboration. The chapter examines reform, common law and studies that have looked at how these laws are implemented by the gatekeepers. We also compare what has been found about reporting and prosecution in the different jurisdictions. As with the other chapters, material about rape law is presented holistically with consideration of myths and stereotypes that affect both the drafting of legislation and its implementation.

Chapter 9 focuses more on the legal processes and the victim witnesses' experiences in the courtroom. We identify the many laws enacted to better protect

54 This analysis of the ethical responsibility draws upon the work of Drucilla Cornell and is discussed in Ch. 3.

rape victim witnesses from re-trauma. Relevant legislation includes 'rape shield' laws, mandatory judicial intervention where a witness is asked inappropriate questions, and recent changes concerning: paper committals, a support person, the ability to be screened from the defendant and the right not to be cross-examined by a self-represented defendant. We contrast what is known in Australia and England and Wales about the court outcomes, i.e. conviction rates and sentences.

By some estimates, as many as 60 per cent of women who experience domestic violence are also sexually assaulted by their partners.[55] What legislation has been enacted that made spousal exemption from rape prosecution anachronistic? Is the license to rape still valid, given community and court attitudes about consent? Does the victim's construction of consent and its vitiation match up with police, prosecutor and court views? In Chapter 10, we answer these questions and seek to understand the interplay between culture, legal practice and best practice.

Our legal system is often insensitive not just to differences based on sex but also to variation connected to race, disability, ethnicity, sexual affinity and additional 'others'. In Chapter 11 we look at a number of these intersectionality issues including how ethnicity, disability and sexuality impact upon the members' vulnerability to abuse, their experiences of violence and their access to the legal system. We see why each group may be disadvantaged in accessing justice and in their use of legal remedies and the different ways in which Australia and England and Wales have worked to assist them.

In addition, both explicitly in our 'Conclusion' (Chapter 12) and implicitly in all chapters, we provide suggestions for best practice models for policymaking and law reform to improve the government, community and legal responses to women who experience violence. At the same time, we recognise the complexities involved in turning to the law to address the issue of violence against women. There remains an ongoing issue of whether the law is simply too patriarchal to be used as an effective tool in combating violence against women,[56] along with concerns regarding the problematic co-opting of feminist campaigns,[57] which may only work to expand and strengthen the criminal justice system, do little to protect vulnerable individuals[58] and may problematically engender reforms which are contrary to feminist aims.[59]

55 A. Howard et al., 'Counseling Services for Battered Women: A Comparison of Outcomes for Physical and Sexual Assault Survivors', *Journal of Interpersonal Violence* 18(7), 2003, 717–734.

56 M.D.A Freeman, 'Violence Against Women: Does the Legal System Provide Solutions or Itself Constitute the Problem?', *Canadian Journal of Family Law* 3(4), 1980, 374–401.

57 S. Walklate, 'What is to be Done about Violence Against Women? Gender, Violence, Cosmopolitanism and the Law', *British Journal of Criminology* 48(1), 2008, 39–54, p. 43.

58 See, e.g., K. Bumiller, *In An Abusive State: How Neoliberalism Appropriated the Feminist Argument Against Sexual Violence*, London: Duke University Press, 2008.

59 See, e.g., W. Larcombe, 'Falling Rape Conviction Rates: (Some) Feminist Aims and Measures for Rape Law', *Feminist Legal Studies* 19(1), 2001, 27–45. These issues are discussed further in Ch. 12.

Given the focus in the forthcoming chapters, it is clear though that we consider that it is vital to engage with the law, and that the potential for productive and effective reform exists. Although this is not a straightforward task, to do otherwise is to potentially 'cede ground to antifeminist institutions and practices'.[60] Moreover, to quote Carol Smart: 'law (especially at the levels of both formulating legislation and case law) provides a vital site for the contestation of ideas and values. It provides an opportunity to voice feminist values and concerns, and even possible alternatives'.[61]

Throughout this book, we endeavour to provide a space to explore these feminist values, concerns and alternatives.

60 V. Munro, *Law and Politics at the Perimeter: Re-Evaluating Key Debates in Feminist Theory*, Oxford: Hart Publishing, 2007, p. 69.

61 C. Smart, 'Reflection', *Feminist Legal Studies* 20(2), 2012, 161–165, p. 162.

Chapter 2

The cultural context

In this chapter we identify gender differences with regards to participation in the paid labour force and within the domestic sphere, and therefore the differences in income between the sexes in Australia and England and Wales. Division of labour by sex and the gender pay gap contribute to cultural landscapes that are redolent with both overt and hidden gendered obstacles.[1] The less visible, deeply embedded and often invisible normalised discrimination reflects the learned assumptions about reality/normalacy/'truth' that are the result of socialisation. Each part of culture, including the socialisation process itself, correlates with and contributes to countless other cultural structures, processes and institutions. Picture an interconnected, dynamic and holistic feedback system.[2] For example, gender stratification is evident in and reflected by the persistence of the public/private divide. This dichotomy affects how the culture defines 'work' and the relative low value ascribed to what is done primarily by women in the domestic sphere, in contrast to paid labour in the public domain.

The legal system must be seen as a part of this holistic model. As this chapter emphasises, when looking at law it is very important to understand the gendered context and its rippling effects. Most legislation is drafted in grey terms; both interpretation and application within legal systems must be understood contextually. We do that in this chapter. We assess how and why, within such a context, the voices of female victim witnesses become muted and/or are regarded as less credible than men. We see too how the societal setting influences what is seen as 'real' or serious harm. These beliefs affect perception of an act as rape and an action as family violence and, in conclusion, drawing upon the work of Nancy Fraser, we argue that women suffer injustice in the forms of misrepresentation, maldistribution and misrecognition. Accordingly, the chapter provides a crucial background for the book's examination of law's (in)ability to deal effectively with violence against women.

1 Some of the material and ideas in this chapter are drawn from P. Easteal, 'Setting the Stage: The Iceberg Jigsaw Puzzle', in P. Easteal (ed.), *Women and the Law in Australia*, Sydney: LexisNexis, 2010, 1–20.

2 Discussed in P. Easteal, *Less Than Equal: Women and the Australian Legal System*, Sydney: Butterworths, 2001, pp. 3–14.

The gendered landscape

Gendered horizontal segmentation continues in the Australian labour market. Indeed, despite a quarter of a century of equal opportunity legislation, there is a persistent failure on the part of Australian corporations to improve the proportion of females at the top end of their organisations. However, there has been some limited recent improvement at least in the gender composition of board membership. In 2012, women held 12.3 per cent of ASX 200 directorships – an increase from 8.4 per cent in 2010.[3] Further, almost 62 per cent of the companies have at least one female director compared to 46 per cent in 2010.[4] However, in 2012, a mere six of the chairs of boards in the ASX 200 were women (three per cent).[5] In the UK, there has been a recent improvement in the numbers of female board members. In 2014, 20.7 per cent of the FTSE 100 company directors were women, a significant rise from 12.5 per cent in 2011.[6] The benefits of diversifying company boards should also not be undervalued, with research indicating that increased numbers of women board members improves a company's business and financial performance and 'increases levels of corporate social responsibility'.[7]

The percentage of women at slightly less senior management ranks in Australia has not progressed as successfully:

> The number of women in senior executive positions has not undergone the same increase. It seems to have peaked at 12.0% in 2006 and since reduced to the 2012 level of 10.1%. This is an important finding. Although more women are finding their way onto boards, they are not increasing in the senior executive ranks.[8]

The 2012 Australian study also identified that female executive managers are more likely to be in support rather than line roles. This is an important distinction since 'experience in line positions, where the individual has direct responsibility for profit and loss or client service, is seen as essential for rising to the most powerful positions in the company'.[9]

Gender imbalance in senior levels of the Australian public domain is not limited to the corporate sector. Systemic biases impact on the proportion of women leaders in other types of workplaces. For instance, although women in the Commonwealth

3 Equal Opportunity for Women in the Workplace Agency, *2012 Australian Census of Women in Leadership*, 2012, p. 8.

4 Ibid.

5 Ibid.

6 S. Vinnicombe, E. Doldor and C. Tumar, The Female FTSE Board Report 2014, Crossing the Finish Line, 2014, p. 1.

7 Equality and Human Rights Commission, *Sex and Power 2011*, 2011, p. 7.

8 Equal Opportunity for Women in the Workplace Agency, *2012 Australian Census of Women in Leadership*, above n. 3, p. 10.

9 Ibid., p. 24.

Public Service outnumbered men at all junior classifications in 2012, they made up only 39 per cent of the Senior Executive Service.[10] In tertiary education:

> . . . women account for approximately 50 per cent of lecturing staff in Australian universities; however, similar to their corporate and public service sisters, numbers drop off significantly as the seniority rises. Women account for only 24.5 per cent of Academic staff above senior lecturer.[11]

In the legal profession, although more than half of law graduates have been female over the past two decades,[12] in 2012 just under eight per cent of senior counsel in Australia were women.[13] Females account for 17 per cent of equity partnerships[14] and make up just 19 per cent of partners at the top Australian law firms, despite comprising 53 per cent 'of all lawyers at the same firms'.[15] Women are also still very much a minority in the judiciary: 'currently comprising 30% overall. This percentage varies across different levels of court and in different states and territories, ranging from 39% in the Family Court to 13% in the Federal Court'.[16]

Similar concerns can be levelled towards the legal profession in England and Wales. Despite amounting to over 50 per cent of law students, women are under-represented at the top levels within firms, as Queens' Counsel and in the judiciary. On currents rates of process, it will take another 45 years before we have equal numbers of male and female senior judiciary.[17] Consequently, law continues to be practised, applied and interpreted from an overwhelming male perspective, despite the preponderance of female law students.

It would seem that despite some gains in securing better career advancement, women continue to encounter 'imperceptible' barriers, notably stereotypes relating

10 Australian Public Service Commission, *State of the Service Report: State of the Service Series 2011–12*, 2012, p. 149.

11 E. Broderick, 'Is There Merit in Quotas? The Australian Context' (paper presented at the Second Diversity on Boards Conference, Sheraton on the Park, Sydney, 2 September 2009). Available online at www.humanrights.gov.au/news/speeches/there-merit-quotas-australian-context.

12 F. McLeod and L. Kennedy, 'Women in Practice', in P. Easteal (ed.), *Women and the Law in Australia*, Sydney: LexisNexis, 2010, 350–369, p. 350.

13 Australian Women Lawyers, 'Only 7.92% of Female Senior Counsel Practising at the Independent Bar Are Female, Fifty Years After Australia's First Female Silk Appointed' (Media Release, 4 September 2012), p. 1.

14 A. Van Onselen, 'Women Still Fight For Equal Billing', *The Australian*, 7 December 2012. Available online at www.theaustralian.com.au/business/legal-affairs/women-still-fight-for-equal-billing/story-e6frg97x-1226531596187.

15 G. Dent, 'As Partners, Women Still Held Back', *Business Review Weekly*, 2 August 2012. Available online at www.brw.com.au/p/sections/features/as_partners_women_still_held_back_hsRan7YJUs2UFbH0Ewfh7M.

16 K. Mack and S. Anleu, 'Women in the Australian Judiciary', in P. Easteal (ed.), *Women and the Law in Australia*, Sydney: LexisNexis, 2010, 370–388, p. 370.

17 Equality and Human Rights Commission, *Sex and Power 2011*, above n. 7, p. 3.

to gender roles and duties.[18] This includes the gendered nature of the paid work women tend to undertake. As noted by Romero:

> . . . women's waged labor has not escaped the strong and pervasive ideological belief that women are naturally caregivers and domestic. Female dominated occupations are traditionally shaped around values and expectations that force women into caregiving and other domestic work in the labor market, commonly referred to as 'industrialized housework'.[19]

In addition, there is still a tendency for women to be held responsible for unpaid duties in the home, and for men to be associated with paid work. This remains the case to date although the proportion of women who were employed in the paid labour force in Australia increased markedly over time from 34 per cent in 1961 to 59 per cent to 2011.[20] However, when looking at actual time spent alone with the child(ren), Lyn Craig found that mothers in Australia spend much more of their child-caring time with sole responsibility of the child(ren) even if they are also in the paid workforce full time:[21] 'It's a woman's job and a man's hobby. And it stays basically the same regardless of the amount of work women do in the paid workforce'.[22]

This gendered division of labour exists within a cultural landscape in which the state and the market take for granted the reproductive labour conducted primarily by women within the family sphere.[23] Such an approach reinforces problematic conceptions of the public and private, with little consideration of how the spheres of the family, state and market are far from natural, discrete, self-sufficient and stable, but are, in reality, constructed, contingent, interdependent and symbiotic.[24] What is significant is that the state is constantly in a process of constructing not only itself, but also the family and the market.[25] Such insights

18 A. Valerio, *Developing Women Leaders*, London: Wiley Blackwell, 2009, pp. 28–29.

19 M. Romero, 'Bursting the Foundational Myths of Reproductive Labor Under Capitalism: A Call for Brave New Families or Brave New Villages?', *American University Journal of Gender Social Policy and Law* 8(1), 2000, 177–195, p. 184.

20 Australian Bureau of Statistics, *Australian Social Trends December 2011*, Cat No. 4102.0, 2011, p. 13.

21 L. Craig, 'Does Father Care Mean Fathers Share?', *Gender and Society* 20(2), 2006, 259–281.

22 S. Lunn, 'Dads Give Kids a Minute a Weekday', *The Australian*, 20 October 2008. Available at www.theaustralian.com.au/news/dads-give-kids-a-minute-a-weekday/story-e6frg6o6-1111117796759.

23 See: M. Fineman, 'Women, Marriage and Motherhood in the United States: Allocating Responsibility in a Changing World', *Singapore Journal of Legal Studies*, 2011, 1–17; M. Fineman, 'Cracking the Foundational Myths: Independence, Autonomy, and Self Sufficiency', *American University Journal of Gender, Social Policy and Law* 8(1), 2000, 13–29; Romero, 'Bursting the Foundational Myths', above n. 19.

24 Fineman, 'Women, Marriage and Motherhood in the United States', above n. 23.

25 M. Fineman, 'The Vulnerable Subject: Anchoring Equality in the Human Condition', *Yale Journal of Law and Feminism* 20(1), 2008, 1–23.

deconstruct notions of the public and private, recognising their interrelated and interdependent nature, and highlight the extent to which the state and the market are dependent upon the family to engage in reproductive labour. As noted by Fineman:

> The work that is done in the family – work that produces the citizen, the worker, the consumer, the solider, the student, the teacher and so on – is essential to the continuation and well-being of not only the state, but also the market and its institutions.[26]

Accordingly, Fineman calls for a reconceptualisation of the state, the family and the market, along with a deconstruction of the positive/negative dichotomies of independence/dependency and self-sufficiency/subsidy,[27] in order to foster an egalitarian cultural landscape. This approach requires both the state and the market to acknowledge and provide support and/or compensation for the reproductive labour that is conducted within the family.[28] As Fineman notes:

> We can impose all the gender equality aspirations we want in the family, but if the state and the market continue to operate in ways that conform to old gendered patterns, gender equality will be close to impossible to achieve, particularly for women who are mothers.[29]

Although family-friendly work provisions and conditions, like working part-time, are available at least in theory to some fathers to enable them to adopt a share of the parenting responsibilities,[30] there are a number of social and economic reasons that fewer men in Australia have opted to use them. Australia has particularly long paid working hours – more time at work means less time with family. As the person who works longer hours tends to earn the most, this pattern of work can exaggerate the traditional breadwinner model. Accordingly, when a child is born and one parent needs to take time off and/or work part time, it is logically the lower paid partner who does so, for financial reasons. Consequently, while women's paid employment declines following the birth of children, men's amount of time in paid work remains about the same.[31] Given their higher salaries, it is not generally

26 Fineman, 'Women, Marriage and Motherhood in the United States', above n. 23, p. 12
27 Fineman, 'Cracking the Foundational Myths', above n. 23. See also Romero, 'Bursting the Foundational Myths', above n. 19.
28 Fineman, 'Cracking the Foundational Myths', above n. 23.
29 Fineman, 'Women, Marriage and Motherhood in the United States', above n. 23, p. 6.
30 '[I]n 1993, the option to work extra hours in order to take time off was available to 36 per cent of fathers employed full-time with children under the age of 12 years. By 2002, this had increased to 45 per cent': Australian Bureau of Statistics, *Australian Social Trends 2006*, Cat. No. 4102.0, 2006, p. 43.
31 L. Craig, *The Hidden Cost of Parenthood: The Impact of Children on Adult Time*, Sydney: University of New South Wales, 2004.

economically viable for men to sacrifice their income.[32] This compels women to continue performing the unpaid work in the home, which offers no motivation to increase their participation in the workforce,[33] especially in full-time employment.

Research in the United States indicates the existence of a gendered pay disparity which seems to flow from parenthood, and has been labelled by some as 'The Motherhood Penalty'.[34] Some commentators have argued that any such pay discrepancy is due to individual decisions made by women once they become mothers, as opposed to some structural discrimination within the system.[35] However, as discussed by Fineman, further analysis indicates that 'even if some choices accounted for some of the gap, there would still be a pay penalty accruing for mothers, of roughly 3 per cent for every child she has'.[36] Furthermore, the research also suggests 'that fatherhood had the effect of *enhancing* a man's wages',[37] regardless of racial and ethnic background. Whereas there exists a 'motherhood penalty', there is also a 'fatherhood bonus', pointing to structural discrimination within employment. Moreover, as already mentioned, many of the 'choices' that women make post-childbirth take place in the culture of a gendered workforce and gendered expectations. As Fineman argues:

> I suggest that the real heart of the dilemma presented by the motherhood penalty is *not* found in such discrimination. Rather it is rooted in cultural and social legacies arising from historically gendered patterns of family formation and functioning that affect expectations and aspirations of and for women who are mothers on an individual level.[38]

Concomitantly, there are other variables that act to dissuade men from using family-friendly provisions. Employment sub-cultures may not be encouraging. There may also be a social perception that career breaks could have devastating effects on career progress, potentially threatening a man's self-image and

32 M. Bittman, S. Hoffman and D. Thompson, *Men's Uptake of Family-Friendly Employment Provisions*, Canberra: Australian Government Department of Family and Community Services, Policy Research Paper Number 22, 2004, p. 53.

33 Human Rights and Equal Opportunity Commission, *Striking the Balance: Women, Men, Work and Family*, Discussion Paper, 2005. On an international level, women's participation in the Australian workforce is considered to be below the current standard.

34 S.J Correll, S. Benard and I. Paik, 'Getting a Job: Is There a Motherhood Penalty?', *American Journal of Sociology* 112(5), 2007, 1297–1338. See Fineman, 'Women, Marriage and Motherhood in the United States', above n. 23, pp. 7–10.

35 See the discussion in Fineman, 'Women, Marriage and Motherhood in the United States', above n. 23, p. 8.

36 Ibid., p. 8, discussing the findings of M. Budig, *New Evidence on the Gender Pay Gap for Women and Mothers in Management*, Hearing Before the Congress of the United States, Joint Economic Committee, 111th Cong, 2010, pp. 9–10.

37 Fineman, 'Women, Marriage and Motherhood in the United States', above n. 23, p. 8 (emphasis in original).

38 Ibid., p. 9 (emphasis in original).

gender identity.[39] This is despite almost two-thirds of respondents in one study agreeing with the statement 'children do just as well if mother works and father cares'.[40] These concerns about the effects of such interruptions on career progress are well founded. Women's time out of the workforce and/or their returning to work part-time contributes further to pay inequities, as mentioned below, and to both reduced upward mobility opportunities and to lower retirement incomes:

> Because the current superannuation system is linked to paid work, it overwhelmingly disadvantages women who are more likely to move in and out of paid work to care for family members. Women continue to earn less than men and are more likely to be engaged in casual and part-time work, which are also contributing factors to the gender gap in retirement savings.[41]

Retired men aged 55 to 64 in Australia, for example, have 1.7 times the disposable weekly income of retired women in the same age bracket.[42]

In these ways, the division of labour within the domestic and public spheres contributes to a gender pay gap and to gender stratification. Australia Bureau of Statistics data indicate that Australian women's mean gross weekly earnings (ordinary time excluding overtime and other penalty rates) are lower than men's across all age groups and occupations.[43] In September 2013 the gender pay gap remained at about the same as it had been for the previous 20 years – 17.5 per cent.[44] For example, in 2012, the average male university graduate's starting salary in Australia was $55,000, compared to $50,000 for a woman.[45]

39 Discussed in Human Rights and Equal Opportunity Commission, *Striking the Balance*, above n. 33, pp. 116–119.

40 D. de Vaus, *Diversity and Change in Australian Families: Statistical Profiles*, Melbourne: Australian Institute of Family Studies, 2004, p. 311.

41 Australian Human Rights Commission, *The Gender Gap in Retirement Savings*. Available online at www.hreoc.gov.au/sex_discrimination/programs/gender_gap.html. See also Australian Human Rights Commission, *Accumulating Poverty? Women's Experiences of Inequality Over the Lifecycle*, 2009.

42 R. Cassells et al., *She Works Hard for the Money: Australian Women and the Gender Divide*, Canberra: Australian Mutual Provident Society and the National Centre for Social and Economic Modelling, Joint Income and Wealth Report No. 22, 2009, p. 28.

43 Australian Bureau of Statistics, *Yearbook Australia 2009–10*, Cat. No. 1301.1, 2010, pp. 262–264.

44 Workplace Gender Equality Agency, 'The Cost of Being Female: 64 Extra Days at Work' (Media Release, 2 September 2013). Available online at www.wgea.gov.au/news-and-media/cost-being-female-64-extra-days-work.

45 Graduate Careers Australia, *GradStats: Employment and Salary Outcomes of Recent Higher Education Graduates*, 2012, p. 2.

Similar concerns exist in England and Wales. As noted by Anna Bird, the Acting Chief Executive of the Fawcett Society:

> More than 40 years after the Dagenham machinists went on strike, in a move that triggered the Equal Pay Act, women can still expect to earn less than their male counterparts. . . . The average pay gap is virtually unchanging, with the mean earnings gap stuck at 15 per cent. For every hundred pounds men take home, women on average take home around £85.[46]

The pay gap is wider in the private sector (20.4 per cent) in comparison to the public sector (13.2 per cent),[47] which has ramifications given the UK Coalition Government's (so far unfulfilled) expectations that the private sector will create jobs to replace those lost in the public sector due to the austerity drive. The Fawcett Society expressed the concern that: 'with the government focus now on boosting enterprise and private sector growth, there is a real risk that the pay gap will widen in the years ahead unless there is concerted action to tackle pay inequality'.[48] Such concerns are far from academic, with research undertaken by the Chartered Management Institute ('CMI') demonstrating that while improvements have been made in relation to junior executive pay, major discrepancies remain at the senior level. It is estimated that using the scale of process achieved so far, it will be 98 years until senior female executives are paid the same as their male counterparts.[49] Petra Wilson, CMI's Director of Policy and Research, commented:

> While CMI is delighted that junior female executives have caught up with males at the same level, this year's Salary Survey demonstrates, yet again, that businesses are contributing to the persistent gender pay gap and alienating top female employees by continuing to pay men and women unequally. This kind of bad management is damaging UK businesses and must be addressed.[50]

The pay differential and differences in power between the sexes have a flow-on effect back into the gendered division of labour in the home and vertical and horizontal segmentation in paid employment. The failure by the market to recruit more women into leadership roles can be seen as part of a culture of normalised sex discrimination which sees women underpaid and under-represented across a variety

46 Fawcett Society, 'Pay Gap Stagnant as Women's Unemployment Continues to Rise' (Press Release, 23 November 2011). Available online at www.fawcettsociety.org.uk/pay-gap-stagnant-as-womens-unemployment-continues-to-rise/. See Office for National Statistics, *Labour Market Statistics: November 2011*, 2011.

47 Fawcett Society, 'Pay Gap Stagnant', above n. 46.

48 Ibid.

49 See M. Petrook, *Female Junior Execs Break Down Gender Pay Barrier*, Chartered Management Institute, 2011. Available online at www.managers.org.uk/news/female-junior-execs-break-down-gender-pay-barrier.

50 Ibid.

of industries.[51] The impact of this gender discrimination in terms of the market also needs to be acknowledged. As the Equality and Human Rights Commission noted: 'The squandering of [female] talent is coming at a cost. We are losing out on what women can contribute with the Women and Work Commission estimating that unlocking women's talent in the workplace could be worth £15 billion or more'.[52]

A dissonance exists in that women are continually outperforming men in terms of education, including at degree level, but are failing to reach the higher management ranks. While during their twenties British women are at a level pegging with men, over the years this equality dissipates and women either eventually leave the workforce 'or remain trapped in the "marzipan layer" below senior management, leaving the higher ranks to be dominated by men'.[53] Given the high educational achievement rates of women, one can postulate that this discrepancy is due to the uneven gendered landscape, as opposed to a lack of female ability.

Politics of austerity and the culture of gender discrimination

The under-representation of women within politics has long been a cause for concern, and indeed was debated in the UK Parliament in January 2012. As noted by Labour MP Dame Anne Begg:

> although this Parliament is more diverse than previous ones, we still have some way to go before the House of Commons reflects the population more closely. Only 22% of MPs are women and only 4% are from an ethnic minority, and the proportion of those who have a disability or are lesbian, gay, bisexual or transgender falls far short of the numbers in society.[54]

The lack of diversity in public office is disconcerting. This enables issues to be framed in very particular ways, allows specific perceptions to dominate and constructs problems and their solutions from homogenous standpoints. On the current rate of progress, it will take another '14 elections, or up to 70 years, to achieve an equal number of women MPs'.[55] Concerns regarding the construction of public office are heightened when one focuses on cabinet ministers, the majority of whom are from a very specific background class: white, male, upper class.

51 Easteal, *Less Than Equal*, above n. 2, pp. 8–10.
52 Equality and Human Rights Commission, *Sex and Power 2011*, above n. 7, p. 11, citing Women and Work Commission, *Shaping a Fairer Future*, 2006.
53 Equality and Human Rights Commission, *Sex and Power 2011*, above n. 7, p. 1.
54 United Kingdom, *Parliamentary Debates*, House of Commons, 12 January 2012, col. 404 (Anne Begg).
55 Equality and Human Rights Commission, *Sex and Power 2011*, above n. 7, p. 10.

At the time of writing, only three of the 22 cabinet ministers are women.[56] Moreover, there are more millionaires than women in the cabinet.[57] This has led to accusations (even from those within their own political party) that they are 'out-of touch' with the ordinary British citizen,[58] who struggles with frozen wages, if not redundancy, along with high levels of inflation and increases in the cost of living.

In particular, attention needs to be paid to the impact on women of the UK's austerity drive. It seems that women more than men are having to pay for a financial crash which arguably developed from a male-orientated, capitalist environment of finance and banking, which rewarded high risk strategies aimed at bringing about excessive monetary rewards, such as the exceptionally high bonuses for bankers. Success is measured solely in terms of income generation, as opposed to more caring and non-materialistic conceptions.

Concerns regarding the gendered impact of the austerity drive were highlighted shortly after the Coalition Government's 'emergency budget' in June 2010. House of Commons analysis demonstrated that disproportionately 72 per cent of the amount to be raised from cuts in 2014–2015 would come from women, with only 28 per cent from men.[59] This is because, as the Fawcett Society notes: 'many of the cuts are to the benefits that more women than men rely on and the changes to the tax system will benefit far more men than women'.[60] The immense ramifications for women of the austerity budget were summed up by Labour MP Yvette Cooper:

> I cannot recall any budget that has ever had such a severe attack on women in the history of the welfare state. It shows neither [David] Cameron nor [Nick] Clegg have any understanding of the reality of millions of women's lives. They simply don't get that things like the child tax credit help millions of women manage to balance work and family life.
>
> This Budget seems to be reaching back to a pre-war approach to families. They've cut support for children more savagely than anything else so far – with billions of pounds being cut from child benefit, child tax credits, maternity support and child trust funds. And this is ideological not economic.[61]

56 See UK Government, *Cabinet Ministers*, ND. Available online at www.gov.uk/government/ministers#cabinet-ministers.

57 See Unlock Democracy, *Counting Women In*, ND. Available online at www.unlockdemocracy.org.uk/pages/counting-women-in.

58 See 'MP Dorries Calls PM and Chancellor "Arrogant Posh Boys"', *BBC News*, 23 April 2012. Available online at www.bbc.co.uk/news/uk-politics-17815769.

59 House of Commons Library, *Gender Audit of the Budget*, London: House of Commons, 2010. See also Fawcett Society, *Twice as Many Women as Men Lost Their Job in the Last Quarter*, 2012. Available online at www.fawcettsociety.org.uk/twice-as-many-women-as-men-lost-their-jobs-in-last-quarter/.

60 Fawcett Society, *Twice as Many Women*, above n. 59.

61 Cited at Joan Walley MP for Stoke-on-Trent North, *Let's Celebrate International Women's Day*, 8 March 2011. Available online at www.joanwalleymp.org.uk/news/national-news/news.aspx?p=1021029, discussing House of Commons Library, *Gender Audit of the Budget*, above

The full impact of the austerity budget on women was considered in detail by the Fawcett Society in March 2012. Its report makes for disconcerting reading, as it sets out in detail the 'triple jeopardy' faced by women:

1. Women are being hit hardest by cuts to public sector jobs, wages and pensions.
2. Women are being hit hardest as the services and benefits they use more are cut.
3. Women will be left 'filling the gaps' as state services are withdrawn.[62]

The Fawcett Society details the key 'pull' and 'push' factors that operate to 'incentivise women to take on more informal and unpaid work' and 'disincentivise paid work'.[63] The two key 'pull' factors are the reforms and cuts in relation to childcare and to social care. In relation to childcare, the Fawcett Society highlights how reforms to the eligibility requirements for Working Tax Credit and the closure, or reduction in services, offered by Sure Start Centres,[64] impact disproportionately upon women. As household finances are strained and affordable state-supported childcare is reduced, women are more likely to be the ones to leave the labour force, as childcare becomes increasingly unaffordable. This will impact negatively upon women 'both in the short term by diminishing their personal agency and economic autonomy and in the long term by diminishing their future prospects in the labour market'.[65] The second pull factor relates to social care. Funding for such services will no longer be 'ring-fenced' and history demonstrates that 'when social care is not ring-fenced it tends to be eroded'.[66] In such situations, however, as with childcare, the extra caring responsibilities tend to fall upon women,[67] as opposed to being evenly distributed among family members. As state provision and support for child and social care diminishes, women are left to fill the gaps.

The key push factor arises from the creation of Universal Credit, the stated aim of which is to 'simplify the [welfare] system to make work pay and combat worklessness and poverty'.[68] However, the Fawcett Society expressed concern that

n. 59. See also A. Stratton, 'Women will Bear Brunt of Budget Cuts, says Yvette Cooper', *Guardian*, 4 July 2010. Available online at www.guardian.co.uk/politics/2010/jul/04/women-budget-cuts-yvette-cooper.

62 Fawcett Society, *The Impact of Austerity on Women*, Policy Briefing, 2012.

63 Ibid., p. 36.

64 Sure Start Centres provide a variety of advice and support for parents and carers. Services are available from pregnancy to primary school. See Department for Education, *Sure Start Children's Centres*, ND. Available online at www.education.gov.uk/childrenandyoungpeople/earlylearningandchildcare/delivery/surestart.

65 Fawcett Society, *The Impact of Austerity on Women*, above n. 62, p. 36.

66 Ibid., p. 37.

67 Ibid., p. 38.

68 Department for Work and Pensions, *Universal Credit: Welfare that Works*, 2010, p. 2. See Fawcett Society, *The Impact of Austerity on Women*, above n. 62, p. 38.

the introduction of this new system will '*actively discourage* mothers in couples from seeking paid employment where their partner is already working/seeking work'.[69] This is due to the underlying rationale of the Universal Credit, which aims to provide 'work incentives for the household, as opposed to individuals'.[70] The main priority of the reforms is to incentivise first earners to work, who tend to be men, over and above second earners, who are frequently women. Indeed, the Universal Credit impact assessment explicitly acknowledged that:

> In some families, second earners may choose to reduce or rebalance their hours or leave work. In these cases, the improved ability of the main earner to support his or her family will increase the options available for families to strike their preferred work/life balance.[71]

Unlike the current welfare system whereby benefits and tax credits are paid to individual family members (so, for example, child benefit would be paid directly to the mother and working tax credit to her husband/partner), under Universal Credit benefits are paid to one member of the couple – 'the main claimant'. This will have the disadvantage of rendering women more economically dependent upon their partners. Concerns along these lines were made to the Fawcett Society by Heidi:

> If we [Heidi and her husband] make decisions about things that are bought in the house ... it's a constant theme that it's his decision really, because I've lost my power base ... it's not all 'our' money ... I don't have access to the account. Yes, we have a joint account, but the point is ... that money comes from [him] ... money is power ...[72]

Subsequently, it has been argued that the reform to the welfare system, along with the austerity budget, 'seems more supportive of an out-dated "male breadwinner, dependent female carer" model of relations between women and men, than an egalitarian "dual earner, dual carer" model'.[73] Hence, the overall impact of the reforms will be to shore up the gendered nature of the public/private divide and further imbed gender discrimination and inequality within the work environment. As will be discussed in further detail at p. 36, such economic impacts work to maintain and perpetuate the subordinate and unequal position of women in society,

69 Fawcett Society, *The Impact of Austerity on Women*, above n. 62, p. 38 (emphasis in original).
70 Ibid.
71 Department for Work and Pensions, *Universal Credit*, Impact Assessment, 2011. See Fawcett Society, *The Impact of Austerity on Women*, above n. 62, p. 38.
72 Quoted in Fawcett Society, *The Impact of Austerity on Women*, above n. 62, p. 39.
73 UK Women's Budget Group, *A Gender Impact Assessment of the Coalition Government Budget, June 2010*, 2010, p. 2.

increase the vulnerability of abused women and render escaping from violent relationships even more difficult.

Beneath the surface

This uneven playing field is not simply the effect of gender differences and sexism but also arises from more covert, institutionalised discrimination. Gendered personalities, gender roles and the public/private divide are enmeshed with a complex three-way feedback system:

> Some would deny that we continue to have this continuum of ideal 'feminine' and 'masculine' personality, sexuality and roles despite their obvious presence in legal interpretation. Yet, if we look at the current generation of children and the powerful enculturators they are exposed to, it is hard to miss. First, they have their role models. The kitchen and laundry domains are dominated by women whilst women continue to work part-time or casually in lower paying sectors of the employment market ... They go off to school, where everything, from playground rhymes to fairy tales, mateship, teachers and toys teaches them that boys and girls are not the same and are expected to behave differently too.
>
> Still having doubts? Then take a few hours to watch, what is in many families a major socializer – children's television programming. Particularly in the advertising segments, one continues to see marked gender stereotyping. Boys go rmmmm rmmmmm with trucks and girls gently nurture their dolls. Girls learn to be more co-operative and sharing and think in terms of caretaking whilst boys' games involve more 'doing' and expression of aggression (or assertion?).[74]

Such 'below the surface' biases are ongoing but for the most part many of us are completely unaware of them because they are endemic and permeate our institutions, our subconscious and the lenses through which we regard 'reality'. An example is gendered speech styles with numerous differences between the vocabulary and syntax of males and females. 'Women-speak' or the female genderlect[75] has been described as socially constructed, 'appropriate' and a more indirect person/process orientation language style that promotes solidarity and social relationships.[76] It has a more collaborative, facilitative and conciliatory tone, in contrast to a masculine

74 Easteal, *Less Than Equal*, above n. 2, p. 239.

75 The term 'genderlect' was developed and described by Tannen. See, e.g.: D. Tannen, *You Just Don't Understand – Women and Men in Conversation*, Sydney: Random House Australia, 1990; D. Tannen, *Gender & Discourse*, New York: Oxford University Press, 1994.

76 R. Wardhaugh, *An Introduction to Sociolinguistics*, UK: Wiley-Blackwell Publishing, 6th edn, 2010.

style, which tends to promote autonomy, competitiveness and confrontation.[77] These communication differences may contribute to women appearing submissive and deferential.[78] Accordingly, their sentences are more likely to end with a question mark either by intonation or with a 'tag' question such as, 'Do you think so?'. Women tend to use terms such as 'we' to a greater extent. These conversational 'down-toners' minimise the impact of what women are saying,[79] as do '"hyper-polite circumlocutions" like, "It would be really nice if you could please leave me alone", and "semantically ambiguous adjectives and intensifiers" such as "I guess it was kind of OK"'.[80] The masculine interactional style is more direct and outcome-focused[81] with males more likely to assert their power by interrupting, challenging, disputing, ignoring and trying to control the topic of discussion.[82] There are also gender differences in response to aggression, with females frequently viewing it as personally directed and negative, and males seeing it as simply a way of organising a conversation.[83]

Speaking women-speak in institutions dominated by the male communication style may be detrimental to the speaker. Mullany, for instance, found that women in managerial roles frequently used language which was inconsistent with the language socially and culturally expected of good managers, using instead the language commonly used by women in everyday parlance. This occurred because their gendered language patterns were stronger than their workplace discourses.[84] Another example is negotiation.[85] An American study found that women of any age were much less likely than men to negotiate salaries and those who did consistently asked for less,[86] which no doubt plays a role in ongoing gender wage inequality. Interestingly, Babcock and Laschever found that women outperform men when negotiating on behalf of someone other than themselves, which could be an accoutrement of being raised to take care of others. Women's distaste for negotiation seems to be a product

77 J. Holmes, *Gendered Talk at Work*, Oxford: Blackwell, 2006, p. 9.

78 R. Lakoff, 'Language and Women's Place', in J. English (ed.), *Sex Equality*, New Jersey: Prentice-Hall Inc, 1977, 220–230.

79 P. Eckert and S. McConnell-Ginet, *Language and Gender*, Cambridge: Cambridge University Press, 2003, pp. 183–184.

80 L. White, 'Subordination, Rhetorical Survival Skills, and Sunday Shoes: Notes on the Hearing of Mrs. G', in K. Bartlett and R. Kennedy (eds), *Feminist Legal Theory: Readings in Law and Gender*, Boulder: Westview Press, 1991, 404–430, p. 406.

81 L. Coates, J.B. Bavelas and J. Gibson, 'Anomalous Language in Sexual Assault Trial Judgments', *Discourse & Society* 5, 1994, 189–206, p. 198.

82 E. Mesthrie et al., *Introducing Sociolingustics*, Edinburgh: Edinburgh University Press, 2nd edn, 2009; Wardhaugh, *An Introduction to Sociolinguistics*, above n. 76.

83 Z. Salzmann, *Language, Culture and Society: An Introduction to Linguistic Anthropology*, Cambridge: Westview Press, 3rd edn, 2004.

84 L. Mullany, 'Narrative Constructions of Gender and Professional Identites', in S. Johnson (ed.), *Advances in Sociolinguistics*, London: Continuum, 2006, 157–172.

85 G. Tillett, *Resolving Conflict: A Practical Approach*, Melbourne: Oxford University Press, 1999.

86 L. Babcock and S. Laschever, *Women Don't Ask: Negotiation and the Gender Divide*, Princeton: Princeton University Press, 2003.

of socialisation and gender role stereotypes rather than something inherently female.[87] Those women who negotiated assertively ran the risk of being seen as pushy and possibly negatively sanctioned, while men were more likely to be rewarded.[88]

Gendered differences in communicating may also correlate with and contribute to the low number of women on boards and in senior executive roles, discussed at p. 14. Board directors are typically drawn from a pool of retired or senior executives. Women find it difficult to break into the right networks.[89] The corporate sub-culture may contribute to restricting women and supporting gender stereotypes: 'men use speech to command and control ... women on the other hand are expected to listen and to be amused by men'.[90] Consequently, a self-perpetuating, dynamic (and fairly invisible) process occurs with the lack of diversity in leadership promoting gender stereotypes, which maintains the status quo:

> Gender disparity in Australian workplaces, such as the disparity between men and women in leadership roles, perpetuates existing stereotypes about the role of women, both at work and in wider society, and exacerbates gender pay inequity. Further, research has shown that having significant numbers of women in leadership positions encourages and sustains other women. This means that unless systemic change in gender diversity in leadership is achieved, there is limited chance of the disparity improving on its own.[91]

Indeterminacy of law within this gendered context

Law, like other cultural components, should be examined within the context of its historical antecedents and 'the political, social and economic conditions, which have given it form and shape'.[92] 'Procedural and evidential categories and subjects are not neutral and inevitable, but are constructed in cultural images of masculine and feminine'.[93] Take the construct of 'relevance', for instance: 'The concept of relevance does not exist in a legal vacuum; it is itself shaped by the discriminatory and stereotypical reasoning embedded in the substantive law'.[94]

87 Ibid., pp. 6, 68–83.
88 Ibid.
89 C. Pascoe, 'Women and Company Law', in P. Easteal (ed.), *Women and the Law in Australia*, Sydney: LexisNexis, 2010, 49–68, p. 65.
90 J. Baxter, *The Language of Female Leadership*, Basingstoke: Palgrave MacMillan, 2010, p. 24.
91 Australia Human Rights Commission, *Women in Leadership*, ND. Available online at www.hreoc.gov.au/sex_discrimination/programs/women_leadership.html.
92 S. Berns, *Concise Jurisprudence*, Sydney: Federation Press, 1993, p. 120.
93 R. Hunter and K. Mack, 'Exclusion and Silence', in N. Naffine and R. Owens (eds), *Sexing the Subject of Law*, Sydney: LBC Information Services, 1997, 171–192, p. 192.
94 S. Bronitt, 'No Records. No Time. No Reason', *Current Issues in Criminal Justice* 8(2), 1996, 130–143, p. 134.

Gendered ideas and constructs therefore may continue to affect judges' and jurors' thinking unconsciously, especially in their interpretation of nebulous terms like 'relevance' and concepts such as 'reasonable'. Accordingly, in looking at medical negligence, Hum states that 'the reasonable person test, although seemingly gender neutral, has also long since been criticized because of its inherent application of male norms that exclude women'.[95]

The legal test for harassment in the Australian Sex Discrimination Act 1984, s. 28 and in Australian state and territory equivalent laws is another example of how 'reasonable person' can be very open to diverse interpretation: 'Many commentators . . . argue that the reasonableness standard is itself gendered; that it is male experiences, views and perspectives that are embodied in the notion of reasonableness and how it is applied'.[96] Determining reasonableness is about assessing whether the behaviour being complained about was sexual and unwelcome and whether the complainant was in fact humiliated and, if so, the degree of distress experienced. It is often the identity, history and behaviour of the complainant that is put in the spotlight and evaluated. An Australian study found that some judicial officers considered the complainant's sexual history or her engaging in sexual jokes as pertinent in determining whether behaviour was unwelcome and/or caused distress.[97]

Such potential (biased) underlying subjectivity in what are often considered to be objective tests and/or neutral terms is emblematic of the indeterminacy of the law. It is evident from these examples and from the discussion about the gendered landscape that law may not in fact reflect women's experiences – instead seeing and treating women 'the way men see and treat women',[98] which has been described as irrational, illogical, emotional and erratic.[99] A male style of cognition seems to permeate the 'voice' of the law with its emphasis upon abstract rules instead of connectedness. In this way and others mentioned at p. 26, the law has been described aptly as speaking 'to men while it alienates and excludes women'.[100] As we have just seen in our example from sexual harassment law, this affects who is seen as credible and what is perceived as gradation of injury.

95 F. Hum, 'Medical and Tort Injuries Against Pregnant Women', in P. Easteal (ed.), *Women and the Law in Australia*, Sydney: LexisNexis, 2010, 311–327, p. 315.

96 F. Pace, 'Concepts of "Reasonableness" in Sexual Harassment Legislation: Did Queensland Get it Right?', *Queensland University of Technology Law and Justice Journal* 3(1), 2003, 189–209, p. 192.

97 P. Easteal and K. Judd, '"She Said, He Said": Credibility and Sexual Harassment Cases in Australia', *Women's Studies International Forum* 31(5), 2008, 336–344.

98 C. MacKinnon, 'Feminism, Marxism, Method and the State: Toward Feminist Jurisprudence', *Signs* 8(4), 1983, 635–658, p. 644.

99 N. Naffine, 'Sexing the Subject of Law', in M. Thornton (ed.), *Public and Private: Feminist Legal Debates*, Melbourne: Oxford University Press, 1995, 18–39.

100 M. Davies, *Asking the Law Question*, Sydney: The Law Book Company, 1994, p. 191.

The 'good victim' witness

The courts' adversarial system has a 'male' character, 'with its gladiatorial, combative features'.[101] It encapsulates the traits that we continue to associate as ideal for males, whereas women, in general socialised to be more cooperative and passive, may have more trouble dealing with such a system:

> The 'primacy of the oral tradition', within a culture of adversarialism, has produced entrenched patterns of testing oral evidence through leading questions that utilise complex vocabulary, sentence construction and syntax. Such techniques have been described as 'legitimated bullying'.[102]

There are additional issues within the adversarial system for female witnesses who have survived violence. We see in Chapters 8 and 9 how, for sexual assault victim witnesses:

> That humiliation involves their being forced to recount ... in minute detail the most humiliating and degrading experiences they have ever gone through and then to suffer under cross-examination the imputation and insinuation about the victim's own responsibility for the offence and against the victim's character and morals.[103]

Possibly re-traumatised by cross-examination, the victim may be asked numerous times about specific details with regard to the rape, in an apparent attempt to cause her confusion and create an impression of not being credible. In one Australian Capital Territory rape matter committal hearing, for example, the complainant was asked question after question about the exact details of the alleged assault. Where was her left hand? Where was her right hand? Where were his hands at each point in time?[104]

> Q: Do you say that you did suffer injury to your lips or you didn't?
> A: I'm sorry but I'm not sure because this kind of abuse, not as bad but it had happened.
> Q: I'm not asking you about other occasions which may or may not have happened, I'm asking you about ... this occasion?
> A: I don't understand.

101 R. Graycar and J. Morgan, *The Hidden Gender of the Law*, Sydney: Federation Press, 1990, p. 410.

102 A. Cossins, 'Cross–Examination in Child Sexual Assault Trials: Evidentiary Safeguard or an Opportunity to Confuse?', *Melbourne University Law Review* 33(1), 2009, 68–104, p. 68.

103 Criminal Justice Sexual Offences Taskforce, *Responding to Sexual Assault: The Way Forward*, NSW: Attorney General's Department, 2005, p. 53.

104 P. Easteal and C. Feerick, 'Sexual Assault by Male Partners: Is the License Still Valid?', *Flinders Journal of Law Reform* 8(2), 2005, 185–207, p. 202.

Q: When you say you're not, whether or not you suffered injury to your lips although you do recall saying that that had happened on a previous occasion?

A: Yes I do, but I'm not too sure.[105]

In ways like this, questions used in cross-examining rape victims are designed to result in the victim's evidence being perceived as weak or not credible.[106]

Moreover, women in such an adversarial system lack the credibility of men:

> To be a woman, whether as victim of crime or accused, is to be incredible in the context of the law ... Women have suffered from the failure of the legal system to take women seriously, to grant to women the same allowance that is extended to men: that of characters with full mental powers, with full human status, with the right to be regarded as credible human beings operating in this world.[107]

Indeed, women may be seen as *extra* incredible witnesses if their speech styles are judged against males, whose speech patterns are considered the 'norm'.[108]

How Robyn Kina (discussed in Chapters 7 and 11), arrested for killing her partner, presented to her lawyer is an apt example. The solicitor observed that Kina was 'very reluctant to make any negative comments about the deceased'.[109] In answering questions concerning her violent partner's assaults, Kina tagged her responses with statements such as: 'But I probably deserved that'; or, 'I probably caused him to do that by my behaviour'.[110] Some women – especially those who have been further subordinated through violence – tend to use hedging expressions like, 'Well, um. Looks as if probably'.[111] Indeed, victimisation and its accoutrements of low self-esteem, self-doubt, vulnerability, fragility and distrust may contribute to an exaggerated deferential speech style.

Such witnesses are likely not to be perceived as credible if credibility is defined as testifying with consistency, genuineness and trustworthiness. These are traits

105 Ibid.

106 See NSW Department for Women, *Heroines of Fortitude: The Experiences of Women in Court as Victims of Sexual Assault*, Summary Report, 1997; J. Scutt, 'The Incredible Woman: A Recurring Character in Criminal Law', in P. Easteal and S. McKillop (eds), *Women and the Law: Proceedings of a Conference*, Canberra: Australian Institute of Criminology, 9–20; S.C. Taylor and L. Gassner, 'Stemming the Flow: Challenges for Policing Adult Sexual Assault with Regard to Attrition Rates and Under-Reporting of Sexual Offences', *Police Practice and Research: An International Journal* 11(3), 2010, 240–255.

107 Scutt, 'The Incredible Woman', above n. 106, pp. 9, 20.

108 Wardhaugh, *An Introduction to Sociolinguistics*, above n. 76.

109 *R v Kina* [1993] QCA 480, [26].

110 P. Easteal and A. Hopkins, 'Women and Criminal Defences to Homicide', in P. Easteal (ed.), *Women and the Law in Australia*, Sydney: LexisNexis, 2010, 109–130, p. 112.

111 Holmes, *Gendered Talk at Work*, above n. 77, p. 9.

identified by Australian prosecutors in evaluating the credibility of sexual assault victim witnesses. The prosecutors also mentioned that demeanour is important and that the credible witness 'is not aggressive or "smart" or argumentative towards the defence . . . [is] confident and relaxed . . . [and] shows some distress but is not withdrawn or numbed . . .'.[112]

The construction of violence against women

Societal context influences what is seen as serious harm and what is perceived of as genuine rape or as real family violence. In later chapters we show how these perceptions may affect the victims' ability to disclose or to report and the type of police, prosecutorial and court response that they may receive.

Indeed, given the socioeconomic separation of the public and private spheres there has been a traditional reluctance to get involved in what is seen as the private domain of the home and a dichotomy between what is perceived of as 'real' criminal assault and violence in the family.

Cultural labelling of violence against women

As Howe discusses, the utilisation of the phrase 'domestic violence' was a strategic move adopted by feminists in order to get the state to acknowledge the issue of violence within the family home. She notes: 'the relatively benign term "domestic violence" was far more acceptable to a "masculinist state" prepared to "extend *noblesse oblige*" to battered women supplicants than the more confrontationalist descriptor: "criminal assault in the home"'.[113] However, the term 'domestic violence' understates the seriousness and criminality of violence within the home. 'Domestic' means private, or relatively unimportant, in contrast to the 'real' world outside of the home. By prefixing violence with the word 'domestic', as a general category of offence, it becomes less criminal and neutralises the role of the perpetrator. Other words trivialise violence within the home too. For instance, as we see in Chapter 7, to successfully argue self-defence, the battered woman defendant must show that she had a *reasonable* belief that her life was in danger. This can be problematic when judges use language that minimise histories of brutal violence, referring to assaults as 'spats', 'matrimonial discord', 'stormy relationship', 'marital problems' or 'difficulties'.[114]

Turning to sexual assault, we will see in Chapters 8 and 9 that a 'real rape' template persists in our criminal justice system. This is reflected in language, with

112 D. Lievore, 'Victim Credibility in Adult Sexual Assault Cases', *Trends and Issues in Crime and Criminal Justice* 288, Canberra: Australian Institute of Criminology, 2004, p. 4.

113 A. Howe, *Sex Violence and Crime: Foucault and the 'Man' Question*, New York: Routledge, 2009, p. 181.

114 P. Easteal, 'Violence Against Women in the Home: Kaleidoscopes on a Collision Course?', *Queensland University of Technology Law and Justice Journal* 3(2), 2003, 250–273, p. 264.

some examples provided in Chapter 9. The ingrained myths about rape, along with the lack of terms in the English vocabulary to describe physical and sexual acts, create a situation which has judges, jurors and police officers inappropriately using the same words to describe sexual acts that are forced as those that are consensual. For example, in a study of 563 Canadian sexual assault cases between 1986 and 1992, it was found that the language used by judges frequently failed to appropriately describe sexual assaults.[115] Terms such as 'engage in sexual intercourse', 'bout of intercourse' and 'a form of bondage' described forced vaginal penetration; non-consensual manual-genital contact was referred to as 'fondling', 'brief touching', 'hand beneath her panties' and 'advantage taken of a situation'; and a history of assaulting children was described using statements such as 'sexual appetite' and 'obvious sexual difficulty'.[116]

Gender-neutral framing of domestic and sexual violence

When family violence and the legal system intersect, a masculine model of violence (assault in the public domain) tends to be used as the comparator. The focus is on a single episode of physical assault (such as a singular punch or a pub brawl) without much, if any, contextual background. However, Chapters 4 to 7 make clear that domestic violence is not about a single strike of physical violence. Often the 'incident' that has resulted in legal intervention is in actuality just a small part of the myriad of physical and non-physical behaviours aimed at disempowering the victim. If the act which resulted in contact with the police or the courts is placed on a continuum of severity as determined for an assault in the public domain, it might appear to belong to the less serious end of the scale.

In addition to the problematic way in which judges within the criminal justice system construct family violence, is the manner in which such violence is frequently presented in gender-neutral terms. The adoption of the phrase 'domestic violence' or 'family violence', for example, erases the gendered nature of the violence that occurs within the home. Indeed, as Howe notes, such phrases are 'resisted by many working in the field as it de-genders the violence, implying that any family member could be a perpetrator'.[117] In her detailed analysis of the previous UK government's domestic violence policies, Howe explores how New Labour initially adopted an explicitly gendered approach, maintaining that it intended to end the '"culture of excuses" for men's violence against women'.[118] Harriet Harman, the then Home Secretary, argued that the new range of legal provisions would involve 'making her safe and bringing him to justice'.[119] However,

115 Coates, Bavelas and Gibson, 'Anomalous Language', above n. 81.

116 Ibid., pp. 192–193.

117 Howe, *Sex Violence and Crime*, above n. 113, p. 184.

118 Ibid., p. 189.

119 H. Harman, 'Key Note Address' (presented at Rights of Women: Challenges within the Law Conference, London, 3 July 2003), cited in Howe, *Sex Violence and Crime*, above n. 113, p. 189.

throughout the consultation and reform process a gender-specific discourse on domestic and sexual violence gradually evolved into a more generic law and order discourse which focused upon 'making Britain "a place where we can live our lives without fear"'.[120]

This gender-neutral perspective of domestic and sexual violence has emerged alongside a field of research which maintains that women are just as, if not more, violent than men, an approach which has its beginnings in North America.[121] Within the United Kingdom, consultation and policy documents frequently commence with the statistics that one in four women and one in six men are victims of domestic violence.[122] However, this 'symmetrical' and gender-neutral conceptualisation of domestic and sexual violence has been vigorously contested by researchers who adopt a 'violence against women' perspective.[123] Academics such as Dobash and Dobash have highlighted how those who maintain that domestic violence is symmetrical, i.e. women and men are equally violent, adopt a methodology which tends to rely upon an 'act-based'/'conflict tactic scale' approach to estimate the frequency of intimate partner violence.[124] This approach is problematic as it adopts a decontextualised counting methodology, whereby the circumstances, motivations and impact of the violence are not considered to be relevant.[125] What amounts to an act of violence varies enormously in scale and

120 Howe, *Sex Violence and Crime*, above n. 113, p. 190, citing Home Office, *Living Without Fear: An Integrated Approach to Tackling Violence Against Women*, 1999, p. 5.

121 See Howe, *Sex Violence and Crime*, above n. 113, p. 61. See, e.g.: M.A. Straus and R.J. Gelles, 'Societal Change and Change in Family Violence from 1975 to 1985 as Revealed by Two National Surveys', *Journal of Marriage and the Family* 48(3), 1986, 465–479; M.A. Straus and R.J. Gelles, 'Gender Differences in Reporting Marital Violence and its Medical and Psychological Consequences', in M.A. Straus and R.J. Gelles (eds), *Physical Violence in American Families*, New Brunswick: Transaction Publications, 1990, 151–166; B.J. Morse, 'Beyond the Conflict Tactics Scale: Assessing Gender Differences in Partner Violence', *Violence and Victims* 10(4), 1995, 251–272; T.E. Moffitt, R.W. Robins and A. Caspi, 'A Couples Analysis of Partner Abuse with Implications for Abuse-Prevention Policy', *Criminology and Public Policy* 1(1), 2001, 5–36.

122 Home Office, *Safety and Justice: The Government's Proposals on Domestic Violence*, 2003, p. 9. See also Howe, *Sex Violence and Crime*, above n. 113, p. 191.

123 See, e.g.: R.E. Dobash and R.P. Dobash, *Women, Violence and Social Change*, London: Routledge, 1992; E. Pleck, *Domestic Tyranny*, Oxford: Oxford University Press, 1987; L. Gordon, *Heroes of Their Own Lives: The Politics and History of Family Violence: Boston 1880–1960*, New York: Viking, 1988; D. Levinson, *Family Violence in Cross-Cultural Perspectives*, Newbury Park, California: Sage, 1989; R.P. Dobash et al., 'The Myth of Sexual Symmetry in Marital Violence', *Social Problems* 39(1), 1992, 71–91; M. Wilson and M. Daly, 'Who Kills Whom in Spouse Killings? On the Exceptional Sex Ratio of Spousal Homicides in the United States', *Criminology* 30(2), 1992, 189–215; R.P. Dobash and R.E. Dobash, 'Women's Violence to Men in Intimate Relationships: Working on a Puzzle', *British Journal of Criminology* 44(3), 2004, 324–349; M.P. Johnson, 'Domestic Violence: It's Not About Gender – Or Is It?', *Journal of Marriage and Family* 67(5), 2005, 1126–1130.

124 Dobash and Dobash, 'Women's Violence to Men in Intimate Relationships', above n. 123, pp. 327–329.

125 Ibid., p. 330.

therefore qualitatively different acts of violence are rendered equal. To borrow an example from Dobash and Dobash:

> the woman who admits she 'tried to hit her partner' is equated with the man who reports 'beating up' his partner – both have perpetrated an act of violence against their intimate partner. Using the conventional scoring method, both the man and the woman are deemed violent; thus it is concluded that there is 'symmetry' in the perpetration of violence by the woman and the man.[126]

Such an approach not only fails to acknowledge that much of women's violence towards men is conducted in self-defence or retaliation, but also problematically categorises threats to leave as amounting to an act of abuse. Given the expectation that women in abusive relationships should leave their partners, particularly in cases in which women have eventually killed their partners, 'it seems reasonable to ask how this act can be defined as "abuse"'.[127]

The strategies developed by those who adopt the symmetry approach are disconcerting. For example, Strauss proposed that in order to reduce intimate partner violence women should refrain from using violence and should never use violence against a male partner, regardless of the circumstances, because this may result in the escalation of the man's violence against the woman.[128] As Dobash and Dobash eloquently respond: 'perhaps a more positive strategy for preventing or reducing women's violence ... is to eliminate men's violence against women'.[129] The perspective of Straus is disturbing. It blames the woman and renders her responsible for the increased violence her partner inflicts upon her. Intimate partner violence would not be such a problem if women did not act in self-defence or retaliate. This presupposes that women should endure, manage, contain and not provoke men's violence, as opposed to recognising that the violent man has a choice and acts with agency.

Once one brings the domestic homicide statistics into the frame, the contestation that intimate partner violence is symmetrical, as opposed to asymmetrical, is further disputed. As we will discuss further in Chapter 7, domestic homicide is emphatically gendered. In the United Kingdom it is estimated that around 120 women per year are killed by a partner or ex-partner, while the equivalent figure for men is 30.[130]

126 Ibid.

127 Ibid, p. 331.

128 M.A. Straus, 'Physical Assaults by Wives: A Major Social Problem', in R.J. Gelles and D.R Loseke (eds), *Current Controversies on Family Violence*, Newbury Park, CA: Sage, 1993, 67–88, cited in Dobash and Dobash, 'Women's Violence to Men in Intimate Relationships', above n. 123, p. 345.

129 Dobash and Dobash, 'Women's Violence to Men in Intimate Relationships', above n. 123, p. 345.

130 See, e.g., the discussion in Howe, *Sex Violence and Crime*, above n. 113, p. 191.

In relation to both genders, the killing frequently occurs after long-term male-to-female domestic abuse.

Understanding political, policy and legal responses to violence against women

This discussion of the discursive framing and labelling of domestic and sexual violence is far from academic, but instead has significant strategic, policy and resource implications. If such abuse is overwhelmingly perpetrated by men against women, this needs to be properly understood and acknowledged in order for states to develop realistic and effective policies that protect victims and eradicate such behaviour. Throughout this book we adopt a feminist perspective in order to critique the law and policy reforms brought in to deal with domestic and sexual violence against women. Following the arguments presented by authors such as Dobash and Dobash, we adopt an explicitly asymmetrical 'violence against women' perspective. Subsequently, we will proceed with the contention that the cultural context within which violence against women is committed needs to be resolutely taken into account and challenged. The approach understands violence against women 'as a cause and consequence of gender inequality',[131] an inequality which is only becoming more entrenched due to the negative impact upon women of the welfare reforms and austerity budget.

In addition to this gendered cultural context, we will also keep in mind the political policy context within which strategies and reforms develop. In particular, the predominance of a law and order agenda is queried and the extent to which this can problematically be used against victims of domestic violence highlighted. For example, Snider has noted with concern the use of contempt of court charges in North America for those women who 'refuse to testify against violent partners'.[132] This law and order approach fails to adopt a nuanced understanding of the problems of abusive relationships and therefore does little to support the female victim. A more recent and disconcerting example in the United Kingdom of the implications of a strict law and order approach is evinced by the case of *A v R*.[133] In this case a woman's conviction for perverting the course of justice was upheld by the Court

131 S. Cerise and H. Dustin, 'We Need an Integrated Approach to Ending Violence', *Criminal Justice Matters* 85(1), 2011, 14–15, p. 15. See also: A. Ballinger, 'Lessons for the Coalition', *Criminal Justice Matters* 85(1), 2011, 16–17; A. Ballinger, 'New Labour and Responses to Violence Against Women', in A. Silvestri (ed.), *Lessons for the Coalition: An End of Term Report on New Labour and Criminal Justice*, London: Centre for Crime and Justice Studies, 2011, 38–42.

132 Howe, *Sex Violence and Crime*, above n. 113, p. 187, discussing L. Snider, 'Toward Safer Societies: Punishment, Masculinities and Violence Against Women', *British Journal of Criminology* 38(1), 1998, 1–39, pp. 9–12. See also: Cerise and Dustin, 'We Need an Integrated Approach to Ending Violence', above n. 131; Ballinger, 'Lessons for the Coalition', above n. 131; Ballinger, 'New Labour', above n. 131.

133 [2012] EWCA Crim 434.

of Appeal, after she falsely retracted an allegation of rape she had made against her abusive partner. A policy which truly recognised and understood the complexities of abusive relationships, and the cultural context in which they are situated, would not set about criminalising abused women due to such retractions.

The current UK Coalition Government, at the level of political rhetoric, appears to have acknowledged the asymmetrical nature of domestic and sexual violence. Theresa May, the Home Secretary at the time of writing, has stated: 'No level of violence against women and girls is acceptable in modern Britain or anywhere else in the world'.[134] She has further commented: 'As women and as a society we have made great strides but we need to do more to ensure that women and future generations are not held back. My ambition is nothing less than <u>ending</u> violence against women and girls'.[135]

These sentiments need to be placed within the cultural context of budgetary cuts which, as discussed at p. 22, appear to disproportionately impact upon women, problematically reversing 'progress made toward gender equality'[136] and reinforcing stereotypical gender roles for women. Such austerity measures have an implicit negative impact upon victims of domestic and sexual violence. As noted by Cerise and Dustin: 'women's economic inequality, which is even greater for marginalized groups of women such as Black and Minority Ethnic women, increases vulnerability to and creates barriers from escaping violence and sexual exploitation'.[137]

Political pronouncements which claim that violence against women and girls must be eradicated seem hollow in a cultural context in which budgetary cuts will only increase the economic inequality of women, rendering them more financially dependent upon male partners and less able to leave violent relationships. While on the one hand the Home Office seems to acknowledge the gendered nature of violence, on the other it fails to recognise the overall cultural context within which it persists.

Moreover, recent governmental cuts in the United Kingdom have significantly impacted upon funding for services to support victims of domestic and sexual violence, as explored by Towers and Walby.[138] Their report highlights the following: between 2010/11 and 2011/12 local authority funding for services was cut by 31 per cent, from £7.8 million to £5.4 million; on any one day in 2011, '230 women, just under 9% of those seeking refuge, were turned away by Women's

134 HM Government, *Call to End Violence Against Women and Girls*, 2010, p. 3.

135 HM Government, *Violence Against Women and Girls Newsletter*, September 2010, p. 1 (emphasis in original).

136 Women's Budget Group, *The Impact on Women of the Coalition Spending Review 2010*, 2010, p. 2.

137 Cerise and Dustin, 'We Need an Integrated Approach to Ending Violence', above n. 131, p. 14.

138 J. Towers and S. Walby, *Measuring the Impact of Cuts in Public Expenditure on the Provision of Services to Prevent Violence Against Women and Girls*, Report for Northern Rock Foundation and Trust for London, 2012.

Aid . . . due to lack of space';[139] significant reductions have occurred in the number of independent domestic violence advisors; and '23 specialist domestic violence courts are due to close as part of the planned closure of 142 courts by the Ministry of Justice over the next three years'.[140] These cuts need to be considered in the context of the development of a 'state of the art' new business court in London – the Rolls Building – which was estimated to cost £300 million.[141] Business, it seems, is more important than protecting women from violence. Once again the law is more concerned with protecting what is generally considered to be male interests, over and above those of women.

Conclusion: a cultural context of injustice

Drawing upon the work of Nancy Fraser, this gendered landscape, it is argued, maintains and perpetuates injustice for women as it fosters and supports an environment in which women are unable to participate equally in social life. For Fraser, the 'normative core' of justice is what she calls 'parity of participation',[142] which she describes as a 'radical-democratic interpretation of the principle of equal worth' under which 'justice requires social arrangements that permit all to participate as peers in social life'.[143] Injustice occurs when some people are denied the opportunity to participate fully in social life, and on this basis Fraser argues for a transformative approach, 'dismantling' those 'institutional obstacles' that impede full participation.[144] This notion of justice, we argue, resonates not only with the concerns expressed about the gendered landscape in this chapter, but also with the law's response to violence against women.

As originally developed, Fraser's theory of justice consisted of two dimensions: redistribution and recognition.[145] She argued that people were prevented from participating due to either 'economic structures that deny them the resources they need in order to interact with peers',[146] which relates to an injustice of maldistribution, and/or 'by insititutionalized hierarchies of cultural value that deny them the

139 Ibid., p. 3.

140 Ibid., p. 16.

141 O. Bowcott, 'Rolls Building Court Complex Can Make London "Global Legal Centre"', *Guardian*, 19 August 2011. Available at www.guardian.co.uk/law/2011/aug/19/rolls-building-court-complex-london.

142 N. Fraser, 'Social Justice in the Age of Identity Politics: Redistribution, Recognition, and Participation', in N. Fraser and A. Honnet, *Redistribution or Recognition? A Political–Philosophical Exchange*, London: Verso, 2003, 7–109, p. 36. See also N. Fraser, 'Rethinking the Public Sphere: A Contribution to the Critique of Actually Existing Democracy', *Social Text* 25/26, 1990, 56–80, pp. 56–58.

143 N. Fraser, *Scales of Justice: Reimagining Political Space in a Globalizing World*, New York: Columbia University Press, 2010, p. 16.

144 Ibid.

145 N. Fraser, *Justice Interruptus: Critical Reflections on the 'Postsocialist' Condition*, London: Routledge, 1997.

146 Fraser, *Scales of Justice*, above n. 143, p. 16.

requisite standing',[147] which translates to a politics of misrecognition. The 'and/or' is significant: not all groups will suffer both forms of injustice, but many do, in particular women. More recently, Fraser has further developed her theory of justice in order to bring in a third, explicitly political dimension, that of representation.[148] Misrepresentation and political injustice, she argues, operate on two levels. The first, 'ordinary-political misrepresentation', occurs when 'political decision rules wrongly deny some of the included the chance to participate fully'.[149] Within this realm we can situate the under-representation of women within parliaments around the world, as is clearly identified in this chapter. The second level is termed 'misframing', which 'concerns the boundary aspect of the political' and the recognition that national/state/territory-based forms of politics are frequently unable to deal with the 'structural causes of many injustices in a globalizing world'.[150] One example Fraser mentions is that of financial markets, and such can be demonstrated by the impact of the global financial crash of 2007. However, a state-territorial framed politic is unable to respond to such transnational events. While a detailed analysis of this second level is beyond the terms of this book, rethinking the frame of justice, especially when the ramifications of the financial crisis are being felt disproportionately by women, is undoubtedly important.

One of the main contentions of this book is that, in addition to the 'ordinary-political misrepresentation', women suffer injustice in the forms of maldistribution and misrecognition. Such injustice faced by women is heightened for those who are victims of domestic and sexual abuse. As emphatically demonstrated throughout this chapter, maldistribution occurs due to unequal pay and employment opportunities and, more recently, the gendered nature of the austerity policies. Women are prevented from fully participating in the social domain not only due to unequal pay, but also due to gendered expectations of women's role within the family. For example, state policies to reduce the support given to families is premised upon an expectation that reproductive labour should be privatised, and this tends to result in women engaging in increased forms of unpaid labour.

In relation to the injustice of misrecognition, Fraser moves away from identity politics, preferring to conceptualise recognition on the basis of status. Under this approach misrecognition refers not to the 'deprecation and deformation of group identity' but is concerned with 'social subordination'.[151] Such injustice is committed when some people are categorised as 'inferior, excluded, wholly other or simply invisible'.[152] Examples include the negative construction of women in 'social-welfare policies that stigmatize single mothers as sexually irresponsible

147 Ibid.
148 Ibid., p. 18.
149 Ibid., pp. 18–19.
150 Ibid., p. 23.
151 N. Fraser, 'Recognition without Ethics?', *Theory Culture Society* 18(2–3), 2001, 21–41, p. 24.
152 Ibid., p. 24.

scroungers'.[153] In such a situation, cultural value constructs 'male-headed households' as normative and correct, and 'female-headed households' as other.[154] As discussed throughout this chapter, the recent budgetary cuts and welfare reform appear to place significant value on traditional male/breadwinner, female/homemaker gendered roles. Hence, women suffer injustice in both senses of maldistribution and misrecognition. The policies reduce women's economic autonomy and ability to work, and valorise stereotypical gendered roles with regards to the family.

The disparity of participation faced by women reverberates throughout our 'public' institutions, which continue to be dominated by males. Additionally, cultural worth continues to be attached to masculine values and ethos in the substance and process of law and among legal practitioners and players, as expected within the cultural 'scenery':

> Built upon tradition, and as gleaned from these pages, conservative and resistant to change, there are numerous ubiquitous legal concepts that have achieved a status of immunity from intervention . . . At the core of the paradigm is the liberalist construct of the autonomous and rational individual. It is a male. And not just any bloke but an able-bodied (as defined by his peers) Anglo, middle class and certainly 'straight' type of fellow. Law's alleged objectivity and 'reasonable' or 'ordinary' person are embodied in that autonomous individual. With all of those supposed levellers on hand, the criminal justice playing field is constructed as a veritable flat terrain with equal access to justice for all.[155]

However, as we have seen in this chapter, the landscape is far from level, creating obvious obstacles in accessing justice for women:

> There is an inherent dilemma in engaging with legal constructs which claim to represent an 'objective universal truth' yet which continue to negate women's understandings of reality and which make no genuine attempt to integrate the full-ranged chorus of women's voices.[156]

If there is in fact a sort of 'tunnel' hearing that unconsciously filters out the sopranos and the altos, this is antithetical to neutrality and objectivity. The result is that the tenors and baritones are louder, producing systemic disadvantages to women and probably to women who have been violently victimised. These injustices of maldistribution and misrecognition extend further than women's ability to work and the expectations regarding the structuring of private/family life. Such injustice

153 Ibid., p. 25.

154 Ibid.

155 Easteal, *Less Than Equal*, above n. 2, p. 230.

156 G. Mason, 'Reforming the Law of Rape: Incursions into the Masculinist Sanctum', in D. Kirkby (ed.), *Sex Power and Justice: Historical Perspectives of Law in Australia*, Melbourne: Oxford University Press, 1995, 50–70, p. 66.

occurs when the criminal and family justice systems fail adequately to acknowledge and respond to the plight of abused women. For example, the construction of the rape victim in *R v A*[157] as a criminal involves a misrecognition which impedes on her ability to participate fully as a peer. As a victim of violence, the legal system should have responded with understanding and empathy, as opposed to demonising and othering her, while the real culprit remains unpunished.[158] Such responses feed into a culture in which women feel that they have no access to justice and no right to ask for protection when they suffer violence. As will be discussed throughout this book, women's claims are denied and their accusations frequently considered false and malicious. In forthcoming chapters we will look at examples of indeterminate laws and their implementation and interpretation in order to explicate the systematic disadvantages faced by abused women.

157 [2012] EWCA Crim 434.

158 Significantly, her conviction for perverting the course of justice was premised upon the assumption that the rape allegation was true.

Chapter 3

The indeterminacy and discretion of law (reform)

What is determined is decided and fixed; its meaning is *found* rather than created. What is indeterminate is not fixed; its meaning is interpreted in an act of *creation* rather than *location*.[1] Throughout this book, one of our aims is to highlight the sociocultural contributors and the creative processes germane to interpreting legislation concerning violence against women.

In this chapter we briefly overview some of the major theorists' explanations of the substantive and procedural 'greyness', or indeterminacy, of laws. As an example of 'grey' words and phrases, we deconstruct one piece of recent Australian rape law reform: the Sexual and Violent Offences Legislation Amendment Act 2008 (ACT).[2] This Act amended the Evidence (Miscellaneous Provisions) Act 1991 (ACT) ('Evidence Act') and the Magistrates Court Act 1930 (ACT) in relation to sexual and violent offences.[3] It would seem that, not unexpectedly, there are political machinations behind the scenes of law reform. In the area of violence against women, as well as other areas of law, in order to get reforms passed (with strong lobbyists on both sides), the law that is enacted may be a compromise, which ends up being particularly indeterminate.[4]

In the latter part of the chapter, however, we will adopt a more positive and utopian perspective, which envisions the possibility of an alternative feminist legal future, a future in which law is able to provide an effective response to violence against women. To this end we will draw upon the earlier work of Drucilla Cornell, specifically her theory of legal interpretation as 'recollective imagination', and

1 'Indeterminacy' as defined in T. Mann (ed.), *Australian Law Dictionary*, Melbourne: Oxford University Press, 2010.

2 This chapter, including the legislative deconstruction, is drawn from the work of J. Kennedy and P. Easteal, 'Shades of Grey: Indeterminacy and Sexual Assault Law Reform', *Flinders Law Journal* 13(2), 2011, 49–77.

3 Further changes were made to ensure that the Sexual and Violent Offences Legislation Amendment Act 2008 (ACT) operated as intended. See Revised Explanatory Statement, Crimes Legislation Amendment Bill 2009 (ACT), p. 2.

4 For an understanding of the 'politics' behind this piece of legislation, see J. Kennedy and P. Easteal, 'The Conception, Gestation and Birth of Legislation: The Sexual and Violent Offence Legislation Amendment Act 2008 (ACT)', *Canberra Law Review* 10(2), 2011, 8–29.

emphasise the responsibility of judges to remember the suffering of the other when they engage in legislative (re)interpretation.

Theoretical threads

Views about indeterminacy and law range between those formulated by different theoretical 'schools', such as legal formalism, positivism, realism and critical legal theory. Legal formalists believe that judicial officers find the law rather than make it, whereas legal realists postulate that judges make law, and their decisions can be affected by their personal views, but indeterminacy is found in individual cases rather than at the core of legal meaning.[5]

Hart, a legal positivist, conceded that a large proportion of the law is indeterminate, but that this indeterminacy is only a marginal part of our legal system. He stated that the indeterminacy of the law is generally a result of the 'open-texture' of natural language; the vagueness of language affects how the rules are interpreted.[6]

On the other hand, Dworkin implied that the inclusion of principles and ideals in the law resolves the problem of indeterminacy. He argued that legal principles take judicial officers 'past the point where it would be accurate to say that any test of pedigree exists'; that legal principles indicate the intended scope of the rules and resolve any conflict by signifying how the rule should apply to the legal problem at hand.[7]

Critical legal studies, including feminist legal theoreticians, argue that law can never reasonably induce determinate results on a case-by-case basis.[8] This perspective sees indeterminacy as inescapable and fundamentally affects the decisions made by judicial officers: 'the law is infused with irresolvably opposed principles and ideals'.[9]

All of these theories, although promulgating completely different arguments, are basically in agreement that at some stage, to some extent, a court must make a decision that is not dictated by law; that indeterminacy in the law exists. At its most extreme, the 'indeterminacy of law' perspective provides that as a result of the indeterminate nature of the law, judicial officers are free to arrive at a range of decisions according to their particular values and inclination.[10] The critical legal

5 See: J.P. McCormick, 'Max Weber and the Legal-Historical Ramifications of Social Democracy', *Canadian Journal of Law and Jurisprudence* 17(1), 2004, 143–184, p. 143; L. Solum, 'On the Indeterminacy Crisis: Critiquing Critical Dogma', *The University of Chicago Law Review* 54(2), 1987, 462–503.

6 H.L.A. Hart, *The Concept of Law*, London: Clarendon Press, 1961, p. 119.

7 R. Dworkin, *Taking Rights Seriously*, Boston: Harvard University Press, 1977, p. 67.

8 C. Yablon, 'The Indeterminacy of the Law: Critical Legal Studies and the Problem of Legal Explanation', *Cardozo Law Review* 6(4), 1985, 917–946.

9 A. Altman, 'Legal Realism, Critical Legal Studies, and Dworkin', *Philosophy and Public Affairs* 15(3), 1986, 205–235, p. 217.

10 See: McCormick, 'Max Weber and the Legal-Historical Ramifications of Social Democracy', above n. 5; Solum, 'On the Indeterminacy Crisis', above n. 5.

studies approach towards indeterminacy 'opened up the possibility of the infinite manipulation of legal principle and the consequent collapse of the rule of law'.[11] Thus, Dworkin's theory of incorporating principles and ideals to address these issues would fail from a critical legal theorist's point of view because 'we are divided, among ourselves and also within ourselves, between irreconcilable visions of humanity and society, and between radically different aspirations for our common future'.[12]

Deconstructing and identifying indeterminacy: the Sexual and Violent Offences Legislation Amendment Act 2008 (ACT)

These reforms, which took effect in mid-2009, were intended to 'achieve the dual objectives of treating complainants in sexual and violent offence proceedings and other vulnerable witnesses with respect and dignity during the prosecution process, and ensuring a fair trial for an accused'.[13] The special measures for the giving of evidence in court proceedings were 'designed to extract the "best" evidence possible from witnesses who may otherwise suffer a disadvantage'.[14] However, as we see in this chapter, many of the sections enacted were drafted using indeterminate language.

The Sexual and Violent Offences Legislation Amendment Act inserted s. 90AA into the Magistrates Court Act 1930 (ACT), which introduced the idea of a 'paper committal' for all sexual offence proceedings. This means that victims are no longer required to attend and give evidence in person at the committal hearing and the provision is mandatory for all victims of sexual assault in the Australian Capital Territory ('ACT'). There are no exclusions or exceptions to this rule, which means that no judicial discretion is required. Another change was drafted in black hues instead of grey. Section 38D(4) of the Evidence Act states that the 'witness must not be examined personally by the accused person'. The provision is compulsory, stating that in all sexual offence proceedings, regardless of the circumstances, an accused must never personally cross-examine the victim witness in sexual offence proceedings. The determinate language does not allow for discretion.

However, the same cannot be said for almost all of the other amended provisions. Under s. 38C(3) of the Evidence Act the court is not required to make an order that the witness be screened; it *may* order that the courtroom be arranged in a way

11 C. Stewart, 'The Rule of Law and the Tinkerbell Effect: Theoretical Considerations, Criticisms and Justifications for the Rule of Law', *Macquarie Law Journal* 4, 2004, 135–164, p. 150.

12 D. Kennedy, 'Form and Substance in Private Law Adjudication', *Harvard Law Review* 89(8), 1976, 1685–1778, p. 1685.

13 Revised Explanatory Statement, Sexual and Violent Offences Legislation Amendment Bill 2008 (ACT), p. 2.

14 Ibid.

that, while the witness is giving evidence, the witness cannot see either the accused or anyone else that the court considers should be screened from the witness. There are no guidelines in the legislation that indicate when this order may, or should, be made, or what should be considered when making the order.[15] Judicial officers may only make an order under this section if they believe that it is necessary for the victim. Unless the prosecution requests an order under this section, although judicial officers can make an order without such a request, they might not consider it.

Victims are also not provided with an *absolute* right to a support person under s. 38E of the Evidence Act. Although the section does not provide judicial officers with discretion as such,[16] it does rely on the fulfilment of another, separate requirement before the order can be made. Judicial officers can only make this order following an application from the prosecution.[17]

Additionally, the court may order that the court be closed to the public while all or part of the witness's evidence (including evidence given under cross-examination) is given. In making this decision, under s. 39 of the Evidence Act, 'the court must consider whether the witness wants to give evidence in open court'; and if it is in the *interests of justice* that the witness give evidence in open court. This provision makes it possible for the court to be closed to the public while the witness gives evidence; however, the court must first make an order to this effect. The decision to close the court is up to the judge on the day. Although required to consider the witness's opinion, the judicial officer may conclude that it is in the interests of justice that the evidence be given in an open court.

Section 40P of the Evidence Act defines the type of sexual assault victim witness who is eligible to participate in a pretrial hearing – a special hearing held before the actual trial, at which the witness's evidence is presented and the witness is cross-examined. This testimony is recorded and later played at the actual trial[18] as a substitute for the witness's oral testimony, which eliminates the need for the witness to attend the trial to give evidence.[19] Aside from children and adult witnesses with intellectual impairment, those whom the *court considers* must give evidence as soon as practicable are those deemed *as likely to* suffer severe emotional trauma

15 There are examples contained in s. 38C to aid judicial officers in applying s. 38C(1)(c)(ii); however, this subsection applies only to violent offences, not sexual offences, and hence is not relevant here.

16 Evidence Act, s. 38E(3) states: 'The court *must, on application by a party who intends to call a witness,* order that the witness have a person (a *support person*) in the court close to, and within the witness's sight, while the witness gives evidence' (first emphasis added).

17 Evidence Act, s. 38E(3) states: 'The court must, on application by a party who intends to call a witness, order that the witness have a person (a *support person*) . . .' (emphasis in original).

18 Note that under Evidence Act, s. 40S, if the order has been made and the victim is then deemed as likely to suffer further trauma or be intimidated or distressed, the audiovisual recording *must* be admitted into evidence and played as the victim's evidence at the actual hearing.

19 Revised Explanatory Statement, Sexual and Violent Offences Legislation Amendment Bill 2008 (ACT), p. 5.

or those adult victims most likely to be intimidated or distressed.[20] Colour in grey the potentially differing interpretations of who *is likely to* experience trauma or distress.

This means that only those adult, non-disabled victims who have had an application made for them by the prosecutor and who can convince the court that they are likely to suffer further trauma *may* be eligible to give their evidence at a pre-trial hearing.[21] When s. 40Q was first enacted, the wording made it non-discretionary, although its application was still subject to the definition of 'witness' contained in s. 40P. However, as a result of the amendments in 2009, the section is now discretionary in nature with the word 'must' replaced with 'may'. Therefore, even if a victim witness satisfies the definition of 'vulnerable' in s. 40P and the prosecutor both advises the witness of this option and then makes an application for a pre-trial, the witness might still not be able to give evidence at a pre-trial hearing. The legislation provides no guidance on the process preceding the making of an order under this section.

Evidence Act, s. 40R dictates exactly who is allowed to attend a pre-trial hearing. Judicial discretion is used in determining who, apart from the judge, lawyers and the accused, the *court considers* appropriate to be present at the pre-trial hearing, or with the victim while he/she gives evidence. Again, the way in which the term 'appropriate' is defined could differ greatly between victims and (different) judicial officers. Thus, in *R v SH*,[22] Justice Refshauge stated that:

> Accordingly, while I would not regard the paragraph as enabling a wide range of persons to be present, and almost certainly not parents of mature accused persons, but such persons as the spouse of an accused person or the parents of a younger accused person seem to me to be appropriate persons.[23]

The legislation is also indeterminate about whether a witness who has given his/her testimony via audiovisual recording *may be* required to attend the hearing if the accused applies for such an order and the court decides that it is in the *interests of justice* to make the order.[24] This section does not aim to further protect victim witnesses' safe speaking. Rather, it provides a protection to the accused and his/her right to a fair trial, which is an additional intended aim of the legislation.[25] It is an example of yet another way in which the aim of protecting victim witnesses could be undermined.

20 Evidence Act, s. 40P(1)(c).
21 Evidence Act, s. 40Q.
22 *R v SH; R v Vaughan; R v Chifuntwe (No. 1)* [2010] ACTSC 157, [9].
23 Ibid., [10] (Refshauge J).
24 Evidence Act, s. 40T.
25 Revised Explanatory Statement, Sexual and Violent Offences Legislation Amendment Bill 2008 (ACT), p. 2.

Protecting the accused (in addition to the victim) is also the aim of Evidence Act, s. 40U, which contains no indeterminate language. If an order has been made under Division 4.2B for a pre-trial hearing to be held, the section states that at the actual trial, if there is a jury, the court *must* direct the jury that the victim gave evidence at a pre-trial hearing and that this is usual practice in these cases. The jury is directed not to draw any inference against the accused person or to give the evidence more or less weight, because the evidence was given at the pre-trial hearing. It is a mandatory direction and there is no potential for judicial discretion in its interpretation and application.

If there are any related proceedings,[26] the admissibility of evidence recorded at a pre-trial hearing is subject to acceptance by the court. Although there are statutory considerations that must be made by the court when determining whether the victim should be recalled to give further evidence (including, again, whether it is in the interests of justice),[27] there are no considerations, apart from those under the general law of evidence,[28] that must be taken into account when deciding to refuse to admit all or part of the victim's recorded evidence – a refusal which would result in the victim having to attend the trial anyway.

Section 43 provides for the use of closed-circuit television ('CCTV') for all victims of sexual assault to give their evidence at a pre-trial hearing or at the actual trial. Although there is an assumption that victims will give evidence via CCTV unless they otherwise wish, the court still has the power to order that the evidence not be given in this manner in certain circumstances – if the proceeding would be *unreasonably* delayed or there is a *substantial* risk that the proceeding would be conducted unfairly. Both 'unreasonably' and 'substantial' are grey-coloured words susceptible to interpretation.

Given these examples of substantive indeterminacy and thus the opportunity for the exercise of prosecutorial and judicial discretion (the latter is discussed next), it is possible that the legislative aims of sparing victim witnesses from the humiliation of open court, the trauma of having to be in the same room as the accused, having to give evidence multiple times or being unsupported, may not be fully actualised.

Judicial (and prosecutorial) discretion

One correlate of laws' substantive greyness is interpretation by judges. Given such indeterminacy, the individual gatekeeper becomes very important, as identified by

26 For the purposes of this section, a 'related proceeding' is defined as: '(a) a re-hearing or re-trial of, or appeal from, the hearing of the proceeding; or (b) another proceeding in the same court as the proceeding for the offence, or another offence arising from the same, or the same set of, circumstances; or (c) a civil proceeding arising from the offence': Evidence Act, s. 40V(6).

27 Evidence Act, s. 40V(5)(c).

28 For example, the evidence must be relevant, must not invite propensity reasoning, must not contain hearsay, must not be prejudicial and must have a probative value. See Evidence Act 2011 (ACT); Evidence Act 1995 (Cth).

Easteal in several research projects. For example, particular conventions in different Australian Family Court registries appear to affect what is weighted most heavily 'with some judges stressing a variable (e.g. a child's expressed wishes) as crucial and others acknowledging its existence but pointing to other factors that outweigh it'.[29] It is evident that family law relocation determinations involve a great deal of judicial discretion, with individual federal magistrates and judges interpreting the provisions and key terms with substantial diversity.[30] Similarly, an analysis of sexual harassment judgments and conciliations by different federal magistrates, federal court judges and the Discrimination Commissioner in the ACT showed a varied adherence to myths relating to credibility.[31]

Judicial discretion in interpreting legislation usually occurs because the legislation is unclear or ambiguous.[32] However, the ability of judges to exercise discretion is also an aspect of judicial independence under the doctrine of the separation of powers. In the legal sense of the term, judicial discretion is defined as 'the ability of a judge to exercise autonomy in making decisions in the absence of determinate rules, using individual judgement or assessment to arrive at a just and fair result'.[33] More broadly, Pound describes discretion as the power conferred by law to act on the official's own judgement and morality in certain cases.[34] Pound also introduces the idea that discretion integrates moralities into the law: discretion 'is an idea of morals, belonging to the twilight zone between law and morals'.[35]

Although judicial discretion is open to abuse, and decisions made using discretion may differ depending on the individual beliefs of the judge, it is argued that this is 'a lesser risk than attempting to shackle the judge's power within a straitjacket';[36] and that 'discretion is the lesser evil'.[37] Therefore, in order for a legal system to achieve justice, there needs to be an appropriate balance between the rules of law and the use of judicial discretion: rules must be comprehensive and judicial discretion must be limited.

As rationalised by Justice Brennan in *Norbis v Norbis*, 'an unfettered discretion is a versatile means of doing justice in particular cases, but unevenness in its exercise

29 P. Easteal, J. Behrens and L. Young, 'Relocation Decisions in Canberra and Perth: A Blurry Snapshot', *Australian Journal of Family Law* 14(3), 2000, 234–258, p. 245.

30 P. Easteal and K. Harkins, 'Are We There Yet? An Analysis of Relocation Judgments in Light of Changes to the *Family Law Act*', *Australian Journal of Family Law* 22(3), 2008, 259–278.

31 P. Easteal and K. Judd, '"She Said, He Said": Credibility and Sexual Harassment Cases in Australia', *Women's Studies International Forum* 31(5), 2008, 336–344.

32 N. Otakpor, 'On Indeterminacy in Law', *Journal of African Law* 32(1), 1988, 112–122, p. 114.

33 'Judicial discretion', as defined in Mann, *Australian Law Dictionary*, above n. 1.

34 R. Pound, 'Discretion, Dispensation and Mitigation: The Problem of the Individual Special Case', *New York University Law Review* 35(4), 1960, 925–938, p. 926.

35 Ibid.

36 *Selvey v Director of Public Prosecutions* [1968] 2 WLR 1494, 1524G (Lord Guest).

37 R. Pattenden, *Judicial Discretion and Criminal Litigation*, New York: Oxford University Press, 1990, p. 14.

diminishes confidence in the legal process'.[38] This means that discretionary power is usually limited by guidelines or principles, or by reference to other factors that must be considered when coming to a decision.[39] For example, as we saw above with the Evidence Act, s. 39:

> in deciding whether to order that the court be closed to the public, the court must consider whether the witness wants to give evidence in open court; and [whether] it is in the interests of justice that the witness give evidence in open court.[40]

In their survey of a sample of those who had experienced the Act in operation, Kennedy and Easteal[41] noted that judges provided mixed responses as to how they interpreted the meaning of this section. One stated that he/she would allow the court to be closed '[i]f the vulnerability test is satisfied and it is otherwise fair to allow the evidence to be given'.[42] Another judicial officer took a slightly different viewpoint on the meaning of 'interests of justice':

> The interest is the need for complainants especially not being deterred from making complaints by the fear that some very personal details of their interaction with the accused will become public property because of the evidence that they give.[43]

When asked what he/she would do if there was a conflict between the victim's wishes and the interests of justice, this same judge stated that he/she 'would mostly accept the wishes of the witness; ... [he/she could] see little justice in not doing so'.[44] However, the other two judicial officers did not agree, with one saying that he/she could not give either consideration more weight overall and that the 'decision would depend on the details of each competing consideration'.[45] This judge also stated: 'I would need to consider why the witness was so keen to give evidence in open court, and the nature and degree of the impact of that on the interests of justice'.[46]

38 *Norbis v Norbis* (1986) 161 CLR 513, 536 (Brennan J).
39 W. Lacey, 'Judicial Discretion and Human Rights: Expanding the Role of International Law in the Domestic Sphere', *Melbourne Journal of International Law* 5(1), 2004, 108–132, p. 110.
40 Evidence Act, ss 39(4)(a)–(b).
41 The following findings are drawn from J. Kennedy and P. Easteal, 'Colour "Black Letter" Sexual Assault Law Reform Grey: An Australian Example' in J. Sagade, V. Jivan and C. Forster (eds), *Feminism in the Subcontiment and Beyond: Challenging Laws, Changing Laws*, Lucknow, India: Eastern Book Company, 2014.
42 Survey of participant no. 1, judicial officer (1 June 2011).
43 Survey of participant no. 3, judicial officer (7 April 2011).
44 Ibid.
45 Survey of participant no. 2, judicial officer (27 April 2011).
46 Ibid.

Although judicial officers said that they would make an equal assessment of victim and offender rights when determining whether to close the court, lawyer respondents reported that orders to close the court were 'rarely sought and rarely made', but that an order might be 'requested if a complainant particularly wants the court to be closed during their evidence'.[47] One victim support worker believed that the '[p]ublic interest always trumps a victim's wishes or concerns. The victim is often treated as an afterthought or like an annoyance, despite the rhetoric that is heard in court'.[48] Indeed, all victim support personnel reported that most victims would prefer the court to be closed to the public, and that a closed court improved their experience:

> They do not like that others can hear their evidence and are particularly concerned about the defendant's supporters being able to hear the evidence. They find the open court very intimidating.[49]
>
> [K]nowing that their personal life is not being portrayed to those who may not know them is definitely a confidence booster.[50]

The two victim witnesses in the sample supported this view. Although both victim participants gave evidence in an open court, each stated that she would have preferred the court to be closed to the public. In one of the victim participant's cases, the prosecutor said that it was not in the interests of justice for the court to be closed, so did not even apply for an order. As a result, the victim reported feeling distracted and abused.[51] She felt that it was her story, not a story for the public – that she was talking about such personal things (including her own body) that she would rather not have talked about in public.[52]

Kennedy and Easteal found that although some of the sections, such as those concerning CCTV and support people, were strictly applied and working well,[53] a few provisions (in addition to closing the court) were being applied differentially by prosecutors and/or interpreted differently by different judicial officers.[54] For instance, the provisions providing for the use of screens in court were reportedly rarely used in practice, despite the reported benefit to victims, and, in one case, screens were not available even though the victim did specifically request them. One victim did not have her evidence pre-recorded because she was not made aware of the process at all and stated that she did not 'think it was available',[55]

47 Survey of participant no. 6, legal practitioner (11 May 2011).
48 Survey of participant no. 12, victim support (31 May 2011).
49 Ibid.
50 Survey of participant no. 11, victim support (31 May 2011).
51 Interview with participant no. 13, victim witness (28 October 2010).
52 Ibid.
53 Some legal practitioners and victim support personnel reported that witnesses who wished to have a support person almost inevitably had one.
54 Kennedy and Easteal, 'Colour "Black Letter" Sexual Assault Reform Grey', above n. 41.
55 Survey of participant no. 14, victim witness (26 July 2011).

despite her trial being held almost four months after the introduction of the reforms. In another matter, the prosecutor offered to pre-record the victim's evidence, but the victim declined because she had her 'mind set on giving evidence in court'.[56] This was because the police officer that she had spoken to had told her that she would appear to be a strong witness if she gave evidence in the courtroom, and despite the fact that the victim support worker had told her that she should not give evidence in court. As such, although this victim was aware of the reforms and that her evidence could be pre-recorded, an application was not made.[57]

Indeterminacy and the feminist perspective

The dilemma with law reform lies in the reality that substantive indeterminacy of its provisions may translate into discretion that is susceptible to interpretation in an unconsciously biased way. Such discretion is evidently an essential part of the Australian and England and Wales legal systems to some extent. However, its use 'dilutes the advantages of rules and creates the risk that discretion may be abused'.[58] In this book, we further explore legal indeterminacy and discretion in sexual assault and domestic violence provisions, in particular what Dworkin refers to as 'weak' discretion.[59] 'Weak' or 'concealed'[60] discretion is used to describe rules that leave the judicial officer with considerable freedom of choice because the provisions 'contain value-qualified precepts which require a personal assessment of the circumstances'.[61] Provisions which contain vague standards such as 'reasonable', 'just', 'necessary', 'fair', or which allow the judge to choose whether to follow a statutory requirement (e.g. the court 'may' order that the court be closed to the public) are all examples of weak or concealed discretion.

It is argued that the judicial nature of the exercise means that discretion is not a matter of personal conscience or inclination; that 'limitations on discretion are as inevitable and abundant as the sources of discretion . . . [and] discretionary decisions are rarely as unfettered as they look'.[62] However, although discretionary powers are never absolute, they are exercised within a broader legal and social context that is susceptible to influence by common societal and legal beliefs. This means that the 'guidelines', 'principles' and legal concept signposts do not exist in a legal vacuum and that judicial discretion in interpreting them could be seen as 'shaped by the discriminatory and stereotypical reasoning embedded in the substantive law', as

56 Interview with participant no. 13, above n. 51.

57 Ibid.

58 C. Schneider, 'Discretion and Rules: A Lawyer's View', in K. Hawkins (ed.), *The Uses of Discretion*, London: Clarendon Press, 1992, 47–88, p. 47.

59 R. Dworkin, 'Judicial Discretion', *The Journal of Philosophy* 60(21), 1963, 623–638, p. 624.

60 Pattenden, *Judicial Discretion and Criminal Litigation*, above n. 37.

61 Ibid., p. 2.

62 Schneider, 'Discretion and Rules', above n. 58, p. 79.

discussed in Chapter 2.[63] From this vantage point, discretion can be seen as taking place in a legal arena in which these so-called objective standards are in reality 'not neutral and inevitable, but are constructed in cultural images of masculine and feminine'.[64]

It has been theorised that in rape trials, for instance, judges must choose 'between conflicting moral imperatives' and the 'central, indeed overriding, importance attached to the fair trial principle', which means that one of these is potentially weighted more heavily.[65] Arguably, if orders under the new provisions of the Evidence Act are made to protect those who are perceived by the prosecution and judicial officers to be victims of 'real' rape and who are vulnerable and require protection, perceptual differences could result in the provisions, in practice, not protecting some victims from increased trauma. Further, grey language in the law could disadvantage victim witnesses by denying them access to special measures such as closing the court, CCTV and support people.

Drucilla Cornell's 'recollective imagination': towards feminist utopian futures

While acknowledging the problematics of indeterminacy and discretion, we nevertheless remain hopeful about using the law to deal with violence against women. To this end we turn to the earlier work of Drucilla Cornell and her insight that 'the invitation to think again and to see the world differently always remains'.[66] Indeed, the recent 'feminist judgment' work that has taken in place in Canada and England and Wales[67] amply illustrates how the inherent instability of legal rules, principles and precedent provides the space for the development of very different decisions, which are focused on 'asking the woman question'.[68] What is novel about this area of work is that these feminist judgments were rewritten/resignified within largely the same constraints (i.e. issues of precedent, available sources, writing style) as those judges who presided over the cases. As Hunter et al. explain,

63 S. Bronitt, 'No Records. No Time. No Reason', *Current Issues in Criminal Justice* 8(2), 1996, 130–143, p. 134.

64 R. Hunter and K. Mack, 'Exclusion and Silence', in N. Naffine and R. Owens (eds), *Sexing the Subject of Law*, Sydney: LBC Information Services, 1997, 171–192, p. 192.

65 S. Bronitt, 'Comparative Perspectives on the Fair Trial Principle: A Flawed Balance?' (paper presented at the National Forum, 'Peaceful Coexistence: Victims' Rights In A Human Rights Framework', Canberra, 16 November 2005).

66 D. Cornell, 'Institutionalization of Meaning, Recollective Imagination and the Potential for Transformative Legal Interpretation', *University of Pennsylvania Law Review* 136(4), 1988, 1135–1229, p. 1145.

67 'Special Issue: Rewriting Equality', *Canadian Journal of Women and the Law* 18(1), 2006; R. Hunter, C. McGlynn and E. Rackley (eds), *Feminist Judgments: From Theory to Practice*, Oxford: Hart Publishing, 2010.

68 R. Hunter, 'An Account of Feminist Judging', in Hunter, McGlynn and Rackley, *Feminist Judgments*, above n. 67, 30–43, p. 35; see also K.T. Bartlett, 'Feminist Legal Methods', *Harvard Law Review* 103(4), 1990, 829–888.

'these feminist academics dressed up as judges powerfully denaturalize existing judicial and doctrinal norms, exposing them as contingent, and as themselves (the product of) performances'.[69] The potential for auspicious transformation and resignifications inheres within the very structure of the law. While we are careful not to overstate the possibility of positive transformation due to the indeterminate nature of law and language, it nevertheless provides a moment and space of optimism for legal feminist academics and the utopian dream of a different (legal) world. Hence, Lacey has argued that the 'utopian moment within the critical project . . . points to the project of attempting to reimagine legal categories, legal worlds which either transcend or reconfigure sexual difference in less hierarchical and more heterogeneous ways'.[70] It is this potential for reimagining the law that this book endeavours to address.

In the development of her conceptualisation of indeterminacy and legal interpretation, Cornell commences with a critique of the work of Dworkin.[71] Cornell postulates that despite Dworkin's critique of Hart's positivism, he fails to break completely from legal positivism due to his reliance on 'a mythical individual [Hercules] whose legal proclamations stand in for communal ethics'.[72] While Dworkin acknowledges 'that law is essentially an interpretive enterprise',[73] he nevertheless posits that judges, in their interpretation, are uncovering the 'is' or the 'was' of the law, and are not involved in a critical reflection upon what it 'ought to be' or '*what it might have been*'.[74] Dworkin retains this distinction due to his concerns with 'legal pragmatism' – otherwise known as critical legal studies. Thus, as Cornell explains, Dworkin:

> wants to insist that there is enough conceptual determination of established legal principle to preserve the divide between the reliance on the 'is' of law as the basis of reinterpretation and an appeal to the impermissible 'should be' of the pragmatic vision.[75]

At the same time, however, Cornell argues that Dworkin identifies a reconstructive potential within the law through the notion of 'rose colored glasses'[76] and also due to the fact that social practices and their purposes change over time. Dworkin postulates that when a judge engages in interpretation, he/she 'construct[s] the best

69 R. Hunter, C. McGlynn and E. Rackley, 'Feminist Judgments: An Introduction', in Hunter, McGlynn and Rackley, *Feminist Judgments*, above n. 67, 3–29, p. 8.

70 N. Lacey, 'On the Subject of "Sexing" the Subject', in N. Naffine and R. J. Owens (eds), *Sexing the Subject of Law*, London: Sweet & Maxwell, 1997, 65–76, p. 68.

71 See Cornell, 'Institutionalization of Meaning', above n. 66. Cornell focuses in particular on R. Dworkin, *Law's Empire*, Cambridge: Belknap Press, 1989.

72 Cornell, 'Institutionalization of Meaning', above n. 66, p. 1141.

73 Ibid., p. 1146.

74 Ibid., p. 1164 (emphasis in the original).

75 Ibid.

76 Ibid., p. 1142.

possible reading in light of what would most fully realize the implied purpose of the practice'.[77] As a judge cannot uncover the author's intent, he/she must postulate what was intended, and do so in the best possible light. When purposes and social practices change, so do interpretations, and thus we have the space for the reconstruction of legal principle. For Dworkin, this reconstruction is still concerned with the uncovering the 'is' or 'was' of law: given the changes in practices and purposes, what 'is' the relevant legal principle? From this perspective, '[w]hen we reconstruct, we do so from within the practice, not by imposing outside principles upon it'.[78] Fundamental to Dworkin's theory of legal interpretation are the concepts of 'law as integrity'[79] and the 'group novel',[80] which ensure consistency of principle and impose constraints on interpretation; judges do not have a free rein to engage in radical reinterpretation; rather they work to maintain consistency and follow the development of the story in the 'group novel' which has been authored by previous judges.

Any reconstruction is thus necessarily constrained and does not provide the discursive space for a more radical and auspicious transformation of the law. In contrast, Cornell argues that 'we can only make sense of the reconstructive potential of the "is" of law if we understand how the indeterminacy of legal principle unleashes the "should be" in the "might have been"'.[81] Moreover, in a critique of Dworkin, she argues:

> if we accept Dworkin's central insight that legal interpretation always involves an elaboration of principle, then, whenever we enunciate what the law is, we are also implicitly stating that this is the way it *should be*, based on an evaluation or a reevaluation of what *might have been* as well as of *what has been*.[82]

Cornell reconceptualises legal interpretation as 'recollective imagination',[83] and in the development of this theory she turns to the work of Hegel and Peirce. While Peirce is more pertinent to our discussion, we will commence with a very brief overview of Cornell's reading of Hegel.

77 Ibid., p. 1153.
78 Ibid., p. 1154.
79 Dworkin, *Law's Empire*, above n. 71, pp. 226–227. See Cornell's discussion in Cornell, 'Institutionalization of Meaning', above n. 66, pp. 1157–1158.
80 Dworkin, *Law's Empire*, above n. 71, p. 229. See Cornell's discussion in Cornell, 'Institutionalization of Meaning', above n. 66, pp. 1160–1161.
81 Cornell, 'Institutionalization of Meaning', above n. 66, p. 1155.
82 Ibid., p. 1166 (emphasis in original).
83 Ibid., p. 1144.

Legal interpretation as recollective imagination

Cornell draws upon the work of Hegel in order to acknowledge the 'the inherent sociality of subjectivity',[84] and to develop a notion of collective ethics. She re-envisions the law 'as collective ethics which embody, if imperfectly, the "should be" of expressed ethical ideals'.[85] Cornell emphasises that Hegel's conceptualisation of law as collective ethics is important, as it highlights that interpretation is not necessarily 'simply in the individual subjective vision of the judge', but rather provides 'an actualized interpretative framework'.[86] Nevertheless, she remains critical of Hegel, noting that his 'move to totality' leaves no space for indeterminacy, and that his notion of 'Absolute Knowledge' involves 'closure as the exclusion of otherness and potential'.[87]

Additionally, Hegel's time frame provides no space for 'a prospective construction of legal principle', and thus his theory is 'inherently conservative in that this ties us to the rock of the past'.[88] In order to bring in an element of openness and prospectiveness, Cornell turns to the work of Peirce, to highlight that the '"truth" of legal indeterminacy is that social reality is never fully present to itself but always contains potential, or what Peirce calls the "would be"'.[89]

For Peirce, a sign can never finally signify that which it represents because the sign 'is always in a referential relation to some other sign or interpretant'.[90] Accordingly, any one sign exists only in its relationship to another and therefore 'there can be no closure of the process of interpretation'.[91] We can never refer directly to the object; rather, we can appeal only to its representative sign, which in turn contains meaning only due to its relationship with another sign. Such perspectives resonate with postmodern and poststructuralist insights that meaning is never determined, but open and fluid. This is not to say that meaning cannot be stabilised, and Cornell acknowledges that the meaning of the law is frequently 'stabilised' by 'conditional resolutions',[92] among which we can situate judgments. In Focauldian parlance we can perhaps see these conditional resolutions as hegemonic discourses that produce dominant versions of reality and meaning, of which law is a very powerful discourse. Judicial pronouncements can work to stabilise meaning, but at the same time any such stabilisations are conditional. They are not settled and fixed, but dependent and necessarily open. Good examples are the definitions of 'family' and 'spouse' within family law. Such notions have undoubtedly developed significantly over the years, moving from a complete rejection of

84 Ibid., p. 1178.
85 Ibid., p. 1142.
86 Ibid.
87 Ibid., p. 1195. As Cornell explains, 'by the achievement of Absolute Knowledge, I mean to indicate the achievement of the revelation of the truth of the essence of being': ibid., p. 1193.
88 Ibid., pp. 1144–1145.
89 Ibid., p. 1144.
90 Ibid., p. 1198.
91 Ibid.
92 Ibid., p. 1202.

same-sex unions to a gradual acknowledgement that such unions are equivalent to 'spouses'.[93] Along this evolutionary journey we can identify key judicial pronouncements which have operated over the years to stabilise meaning, but yet have always failed to close off future (re)interpretations. Significantly, however, acknowledging evolution is not to dispute that such 'conditional resolutions' have significant material effects which need to be remembered.

Through the concept of 'Secondness', Peirce maintains that there is always an 'excess' to a sign: 'that which cannot be fully captured in any system of signs',[94] a 'past that cannot be wiped out',[95] an experience that cannot be symbolised, or 'the real that resists'.[96] Herein we can acknowledge the material effects of conditional resolutions. As an example Cornell refers to the 'irreducible exteriority of suffering'.[97] The delineation of terms such as 'family', 'spouse' and 'battered woman' have real material effects – individuals are excluded from claiming a range of legal rights and state support, protection and benefits. Furthermore, any process of (re)signification can never fully capture and represent the suffering of another. Emotions, pain and feelings can never be completely expressed through signs, nor can such material effects be reinterpreted through resignification. Hence, there will always remain an outside, that which cannot be symbolised, 'a past that cannot be wiped out',[98] and it is this which Cornell draws upon in order to critique Dworkin's notion of 'rose colored glasses'.

From Dworkin's perspective, as the judge is not involved in a critique of the law that draws upon perspectives external to the law, he/she must interpret that law in the best light possible, given that the conscious intent of any author is unknowable. The difficulty with this approach, however, is that while the past may only be brought into the present through interpretation, and therefore is fundamentally open to positive reinterpretation, there is nevertheless a 'Secondness' which cannot simply be reinterpreted through any positive spin. As Cornell notes, although judges may don 'rose-colored glasses' in order to 'reinterpret' past unjust laws, such as the 'separate but equal' doctrine that was used to justify racial segregation, this will do little to erase the suffering of those who have been subjected to the law.[99] Similarly, while the House of Lords in *R v R*[100] may have reinterpreted the law relating to marital rape, this does little for those women who were raped and had no right to legal redress. Hence, when judges engage in interpretation they

93 See cases such as *Sefton Holdings v Cairns* [1988] 2 FLR 109; *Harrogate Borough Council v Simpson* [1986] 2 FLR 91; *Fitzpatrick v Sterling Housing Association Ltd* [2001] 1 AC 27; *Mendoza v Ghaidan* [2002] EWCA Civ 1533, [2003] 1 FLR 468; *Ghaidan v Godin-Mendoza* [2004] UKHL 30, [2004] 3 WLR 113.

94 Cornell, 'Institutionalization of Meaning', above n. 66, p. 1199.

95 Ibid., p. 1198

96 Ibid.

97 Ibid., pp. 1166–1170.

98 Ibid., p. 1198.

99 Ibid., pp. 1166–1170.

100 [1992] 1 AC 599.

have a responsibility to remember the suffering of others, a point to which we will return shortly.

Whereas for Peirce the concept of Secondness relates predominately to the past, his notion of 'Thirdness' relates to the future, in that '[n]o matter how far specification has gone, it can be carried further',[101] and herein we see the existence of what is called 'would be's'.[102] No specification is once and for all complete, totalised and finished. There always remains an 'openness to the future',[103] which can never be overcome. Cornell explains this further with reference to a quote by Bernstein, who notes that '[t]o say that a person or a thing has a habit means that it "*would* behave (or usually behave) in a certain way *whenever* a certain occasion should arise"'.[104] However, 'no agglomeration of actual happenings can ever completely fill up the meaning of a "would be"'.[105] That which has been could always have been different, and the range of potentialities remains despite any specific instance of signification. The infinite field of potentialities can never be exhausted by a 'conditional resolution'.[106] This is what Cornell refers to, drawing upon Derrida, as the 'might have been' in that 'which never was present'.[107] From this perspective we can see how each actualisation of the law is always contracted from a field of potentialities. However, the actualisation could never give effect to the infinite potentials. That which it did not actualise is the 'never was', and within that 'never was' remains the 'could have been' and the 'ought to have been'. These could be's/would be's/should be's remain despite the actualisation.

When a judge (re)interprets the law, he/she falls back into the realm of potentialities, in that he/she gives new meaning to the actualisation, as the meaning of such is not there simply to be revealed. Cornell notes that: 'when we reinterpret or reconstruct a line of precedent, we are recovering what "might have been" if we had understood the embodied principles or norms differently'.[108] This reconceptualisation, she argues, 'is not to accept the proposition that we simply pick the countervailing norms out of a hat'.[109] Rather, it is to recognise that 'the future of meaning arises out of the reinterpretation of the past; the "might have

101 C.S. Peirce, 'Triads', in C. Hartshorne and P. Weiss (eds), *Collected Papers of C.S. Peirce*, Cambridge MA: Harvard University Press, 1960, p. 475, cited in Cornell, 'Institutionalization of Meaning', above n. 66, p. 1199.

102 Peirce, 'Triads', above n. 101, p. 380; Cornell, 'Institutionalization of Meaning', above n. 66, p. 1200.

103 Cornell, 'Institutionalization of Meaning', above n. 66, p. 1200.

104 R. Bernstein, 'Action, Conduct, and Self-Control', in R. Bernstein (ed.), *Perspectives on Peirce*, New Haven: Yale University Press, 1965, 77–78, cited in Cornell, 'Institutionalization of Meaning', above n. 66, p. 1200 (emphasis in original).

105 Ibid.

106 Cornell, 'Institutionalization of Meaning', above n. 66, p. 1202.

107 D. Cornell, 'Time, Deconstruction, and the Challenge to Legal Positivism: The Call for Judicial Responsibility', *Yale Journal of Law and the Humanities* 2(2), 1990, 267–297.

108 Cornell, 'Institutionalization of Meaning', above n. 66, p. 1165.

109 Ibid.

been" is what supplies the "should be"'.[110] Herein lies the dramatic and radical potential of the law. That which is actualised, which is signified, requires (re) interpretation and this (re)interpretation brings about a return to the realm of the potential – that which never was – and hence a return to that which might have been. Within the legal principle resides a different future, another possibility – the 'would be's'. Accordingly, the 'ought to be'/'should be' for Cornell does not emanate from a transcendental evaluative viewpoint, but is instead inherent in the law itself as the 'might have been'.[111] The law might always have been different and it always retains the possibility to be different; however, '[n]one of us is free to step outside of our historical context and just make things up as we go along'.[112] Thus, '[u]topians may be dreamers, but the dream is within the social world that has been given to them'.[113] To point to the possibility of utopian future is not to adopt a 'view from nowhere', but to engage in immanent critique – a critique which is concerned with the potentialities that exist within social and legal structures. To quote Grosz, Cornell calls for us to:

> look more carefully at the *virtuality* laden within the present, its possibilities for being otherwise, in other words, the unactualized latencies in any situation which could be, may have been, instrumental in the generation of the new or the unforeseen.[114]

Judicial responsibility and remembering the future

Cornell, in her theorising of 'recollective imagination', strongly emphasises the responsibility of the judge, a perspective we take with us throughout these pages. (Re)interpretation is both prospective as well as retrospective, 'in that it implies a promise to guide our conduct in the future in accordance with the re-evaluation of the "should be" inherent in the "might have been"'.[115] Accordingly, 'imagination is memory' and when a judge engages in (re)interpretation he/she is 'remembering the future':[116]

> the judge can never be reduced to the instrument of the system who simply re-collects precedent. Her subjective role is not merely one of re-collecting what is there in the origin. She also cannot just do what comes naturally, that is, follow the rules as if such a following were a form of automatic writing.

110 Ibid.
111 Ibid., p. 1166.
112 Ibid., p. 1172.
113 Ibid.
114 E. Grosz, *Time Travels: Feminism, Nature, Power*, London: Duke University Press, 2005, p. 77.
115 Cornell, 'Institutionalization of Meaning', above n. 66, p. 1171.
116 Ibid., p. 1171.

She is responsible for her memory and the future which she promotes in the act of remembrance itself.[117]

Cornell develops this notion of judicial responsibility through a close reading of *Rowe v Wade*,[118] and closely linked to her discussion of the 'irreducible exteriority of suffering' is the importance of genealogy. When judges engage in (re)interpretation, their responsibility to the future requires an exercise in genealogy, whereby '[t]he tradition is called to remember its own exclusions and prejudices', and the suffering of the other. In relation to *Rowe v Wade*, Cornell notes how the judges involved had a responsibility to 'remember what the general conditions of women were during those times in history in which abortion was disallowed'.[119] A responsible judge recalls the suffering caused to women who were denied safe legal abortions, when they remember the future through his/her act of (re)interpretation. Genealogy, Cornell explains, 'is crucial to the integrity of justice that demands that we also examine the existing limits of actualized concepts of justice, particularly as these exist in, and perpetuate, the patriarchal order of society'.[120] Thus, judges, along with other lawmakers, have a responsibility to remember the suffering of the other – of women – and how such suffering has been maintained and perpetuated by patriarchal actualisations of the law, when they engage in legal (re)interpretation.

Conclusion

This chapter has engaged in a critical analysis of the problematics of the indeterminacy within the law and the level of discretion provided to judges. By engaging in a close reading of the law reforms in Australia relating to special measures, we have demonstrated how indeterminacy and discretion tends to leave many victims of violence without the protection they require in court in order for their voices to be heard and for them to seek justice. In the second part of the chapter, by drawing upon the work of Drucilla Cornell, we began to develop an immanent normative framework by which to critique the actualisations of law, which tend to maintain and perpetuate patriarchal systems and male violence against women. By adopting such a stance we indicate how the law still remains a useful tool in the fight against violence against women, but we charge judges (along with legislators) with a responsibility to 'remember the future' when they engage in interpretation (or law-making) and exercise discretion. In particular,

117 Cornell, 'Time, Deconstruction, and the Challenge to Legal Positivism', above n. 107, p. 291.

118 410 US 113 (1973). See Cornell, 'Time, Deconstruction, and the Challenge to Legal Positivism', above n. 107, pp. 289–297.

119 Cornell, 'Time, Deconstruction, and the Challenge to Legal Positivism', above n. 107, p. 292.

120 Ibid.

we emphasise the responsibility of judges and lawmakers to remember the history of violence women have suffered at the hands of men and the legal system, and we will refer to this responsibility in remaining chapters.

In Chapter 2, we explored the gendered societal landscape and the cultural images of masculine and feminine in which these legal constructs fit holistically. The rest of the book will illustrate that although dis-cretionary powers are never absolute, they are exercised within this broader legal and social context and, from a feminist perspective, are susceptible to influence by unconscious gender biases.

Chapter 4

Domestic violence and criminal law response

The family as a private place is a continuing theme in all areas of law. This contributes to a perceived dichotomy between 'real' criminal assault and what takes place in the home. There continues to be a mismatch between what victims experience as violence and what players in the criminal justice system tend to conceptualise as a criminal act. In this chapter, we look at the criminal justice system's response to domestic violence, and in particular we examine possible criminal charges in family violence matters, including contravention of civil protection orders, assault and stalking.[1] We identify the indeterminacy of the relevant laws and their ambivalent application by police, prosecutors and judicial officers, and argue for the creation of a specific domestic violence offence. At present, '[d]omestic violence continues to be dealt with primarily as a civil matter through domestic violence domestic order legislation'.[2] We examine that pathway in more detail in Chapter 5.

Mismatch: what constitutes violence?

From the victim's perspective domestic violence is insidious and unpredictable. The perpetrator's need to control, which is at the core of the violence, generally gets worse over time and manifests in a myriad of ways aside from physical abuse. None of the manifestations necessarily stop after estrangement; in fact, violence can escalate then.[3] One type of violence is sexual; it is examined in Chapter 10. There may be economic abuses with the abuser taking absolute control of the finances

1 Three Australian jurisdictions have separate domestic violence offence legislation: Domestic Violence and Protection Orders Act 2008 (ACT); Crimes (Domestic and Personal Violence) Act 2007 (NSW); and Family Violence Act 2004 (Tas). South Australia and Western Australia both have laws that make provision for aggravated offences that are committed in a family violence context.

2 H. Douglas, 'The Criminal Law's Response to Domestic Violence: What's Going On?', *Sydney Law Review* 30(3), 2008, 439–469, p. 443.

3 T. Altobelli, 'Family Violence and Parenting: Future Directions in Practice', *Australian Journal of Family Law* 23(3), 2009, 194–221, p. 194.

and allocating little or no money to his partner.[4] Economic violence can also include exploitation.

Ongoing emotional degradation generally precedes and accompanies other types of abuse:

> He started to say things like: 'I don't like that on you'.
> 'You're fat, and you're putting weight on', which I wasn't. 'What did you do to your hair?' 'You can't spell. You're stupid'.[5]

> And he'd make me feel stupid. Like every time we argued he'd say, 'Oh fix it yourself. You're a cow.'
> He was verbally abusive. He used to put me down too, like I wasn't worth anything as a person.[6]

The sub-text of control is evident. It may appear first as possessiveness:

> The relationship started out okay and then he started to control. 'Where am I going?' 'Who am I seeing?' 'What time am I going home?' 'What am I wearing?'[7]

The violent partner may begin to restrict whom the woman sees, diminishing her support system:

> I was never allowed a credit card or bank account. I wasn't allowed friends or phone calls. I wasn't allowed to go out. I was put down constantly. . . . My problem was that I didn't see it for what it was. And I was in an extremely violent situation before I realised it.[8]

Many victims, like the one who wrote the following poem, agree that the most serious and longest lasting injuries are those that result from emotional violence:

> Women once bruised and broken. But the bruises heal, the bones mend . . . don't they?
> Maybe . . . those that you see

4 This may be more common for immigrant women who lack any knowledge about their rights to government payments. See P. Easteal, *Shattered Dreams: Marital Violence and the Overseas-born in Australia*, Melbourne: Bureau of Immigration, Multicultural and Population Research, 1996.

5 'Tiffany', as cited in P. Easteal and L. McOrmond Plummer, *Real Rape, Real Pain*, Melbourne: Hybrid Press, 2006, p. 91.

6 'Shefali', as cited in ibid.

7 'Tiffany', as cited in ibid.

8 'Shefali', as cited in ibid, p. 90.

> What about the bruises inside?
> The broken confidence, the lack of esteem, the degradation of self?
> The guilt?
> The shame!
> The lack, complete and total, of trust?
> What about the loss of belief in oneself – as a worthwhile human being?
> The wounds the world can't see
> Are the wounds most devastating, the wounds most destructive.[9]

During a recent consultation process regarding the definition of domestic violence in England and Wales,[10] concerns were expressed that the previous definition failed to adequately acknowledge the role of coercive control in an abusive relationship and also the plight of victims between the ages of 16 and 18, who tended to be too old to fall within the ambit of child protection agencies, but at the same time were too young to be recognised as victims of domestic violence.[11] The new definition formulated through the consultation process therefore extends to cover both these issues:

> Any incident or pattern of incidents of controlling, coercive, threatening behaviour, violence or abuse between those aged 16 or over who are or have been intimate partners or family members regardless of gender or sexuality. The abuse can encompass but is not limited to: psychological, physical, sexual, financial, emotional.[12]

The new definition continues further to elaborate on the meanings of 'controlling' and 'coercive':

> Controlling behaviour is: a range of acts designed to make a person subordinate and/or dependent by isolating them from sources of support, exploiting their resources and capacities for personal gain, depriving them of the means needed for independence, resistance and escape and regulating their everyday behaviour.[13]
>
> Coercive behaviour is: an act or a pattern of acts of assault, threats, humiliation and intimidation or other abuse that is used to harm, punish, or frighten their victim.[14]

9 P. Easteal, *Less Than Equal: Women and the Australian Legal System*, Sydney: Butterworths, 2001, p. 107.

10 Home Office, *Cross-Government Definition of Domestic Violence: A Consultation*, 2011; Home Office, *Cross-Government Definition of Domestic Violence – A Consultation: Summary of Responses*, 2012.

11 Home Office, *Cross-Government Definition of Domestic Violence: A Consultation*, above n. 10.

12 Home Office, *Cross-Government Definition of Domestic Violence – A Consultation: Summary of Responses*, above n. 10, p. 19.

13 Ibid.

14 Ibid.

This acknowledgement of controlling and coercive control is indeed significant. It emphasises the importance, impact and range of non-physical abusive tactics which frequently play a large part in abusive relationships, activities which tend not to be recognised as amounting to abuse by many perpetrators and victims.[15] However, while this is undoubtedly an improvement, concern may be expressed that no thought was given to the possibility of introducing a specific domestic violence offence, a suggestion that was rejected by the previous government on the basis that it would not necessarily help victims.[16] Although it may be argued that creating a specific domestic violence offence may problematically perpetuate a culture in which such criminal activity is not considered to be as serious as stranger violence, a distinguishing element of domestic violence is that the abuse occurs over a period of time. The single incident-based approach of the majority of non-fatal offences against the person fails to encapsulate the ongoing nature of domestic violence. Within the criminal justice system there is a tendency to ignore this context:

> isolating specific incidents from a victim's broader history of violence can damage the credibility of his or her evidence in respect of the offences prosecuted. It is said that a break in the 'natural sequence of narrative evidence', can render the victim's account of specific incidents 'incoherent' and 'unpersuasive'.[17]

Criminal justice practitioners may focus on a 'one-off' physical assault:

> When [the police] took a statement from me, they only wanted to know about the last time he had assaulted me, which had probably been the most minor assault he'd ever carried out. I wanted to tell them about the years of serious abuse, but they only wanted to know about the one instance. . . . My first statement was one page long, whereas my second one took two to three weeks to do. It was 14 double sided pages long.[18]

This example reflects the 'phallocentric' construction of the criminal law – the law has developed and responds to situations in which men tend to find themselves.[19] Recent research suggests that men are more vulnerable to isolated stranger assaults, whereas women are more likely to be assaulted by someone known to them, be it

15 Ibid., p. 20.

16 Home Office, *Safety and Justice: The Government's Proposals on Domestic Violence*, 2003, p. 30.

17 Australian Law Reform Commission, *Family Violence: A National Legal Response*, Report No. 114, 2010, p. 564.

18 Victorian Law Reform Commission, *Review of Family Violence Laws*, 2006, p. 118.

19 C. Smart, *Feminism and The Power of Law*, London: Routledge, 1989, p. 27. See also C. Smart, *Law, Crime and Sexuality*, London and Thousand Oaks, Sage Publications: 1995.

an (ex)partner or an acquaintance, and this tends not to be a one-off event.[20] This correlates to the manner in which stranger violence is constructed and treated as a more serious form of violence. Indeed, an American study found that many police officers have rigid definitions of what constitutes assault and do not define anything that takes place in the domestic sphere as assault.[21] They may see violence in the home as mutual and are therefore not able to identify a victim.[22] This is probably in part due to an equation of harm with *physical* injury and limited state recognition of other forms of injury:

> Tasmania is the only Australian jurisdiction with specific offences in respect of economic and emotional abuse in the context of family violence. In respect of economic abuse, the *Family Violence Act 2004* (Tas) requires the offender to have an intention to unreasonably control or intimidate his or her spouse or partner (the victim), or cause mental harm, apprehension or fear in committing certain acts of economic abuse.[23]

Thus, to some extent the misconception that public violence is more serious than violence perpetrated in the home is still adhered to.[24] If there are *physical* injuries, the offender could be charged with criminal assault.[25] For instance, in the Australian Capital Territory ('ACT'):

- 'reckless wounding' – maximum penalty of seven years' imprisonment;[26] or
- 'assault occasioning actual bodily harm' ('ABH') – maximum penalty of five years' imprisonment.[27]

Traditionally, the police do not like to charge male partners in domestic violence situations with assault.[28] While some problems and unhelpful attitudes are products of particular officers or court personnel, others are systemic – rooted in the

20 For recent statistics, see Ministry of Justice, *Statistics on Women and the Criminal Justice System 2011*, 2012.

21 M. Finn and P. Bettis, 'Punitive Action or Gentle Persuasion: Exploring Police Officers' Justifications for Using Dual Arrest in Domestic Violence Cases', *Violence Against Women* 12(3), 2006, 268–287, p. 283.

22 J. Worrall, J. Ross and E. McCord, 'Modeling Prosecutors' Charging Decisions in Domestic Violence Cases', *Crime and Delinquency* 52(3), 2006, 472–503.

23 Australian Law Reform Commission, *Family Violence*, above n. 17, p. 573.

24 L. Mitchell, 'Domestic Violence in Australia – an Overview of the Issues', Background Note, Parliamentary Library, Parliament of Australia, 2011, p. 17.

25 R. Alexander, 'Women and Domestic Violence', in P. Easteal (ed.), *Women and the Law in Australia*, Sydney: LexisNexis, 2010, 152–173, p. 159.

26 Crimes Act 1900 (ACT), s. 35.

27 Ibid., s. 25. Grievous bodily harm is defined as any permanent or serious disfigurement.

28 K. Rollings and N. Taylor, *Measuring Police Performance in Domestic and Family Violence*, Canberra: Australian Institute of Criminology, 2008.

foundations of the criminal justice system.[29] Victim interviewees in Queensland reported that police appeared more willing to charge if there was a third party victim.[30] Of respondents in a New South Wales ('NSW') survey of victims, 7.4 per cent of those who did not report felt that the police would not act, while an additional one in ten had experienced 'a bad or disappointing experience with the police' previously.[31]

Once it is accepted that the structure of the key criminal offences is inadequate to capture the harm inflicted in an abusive relationship, the importance of adopting a specific domestic violence offence becomes evident. Moreover, as noted by Tadros, it can be argued that there is a certain moral distinctiveness to domestic violence, which further augments the need for a dedicated offence.[32] Specifically, Tadros highlights two key factors: the context of an intimate relationship and the systematic nature of the abuse.[33] These elements 'have the tendency to erode a distinctive kind of freedom that individuals ought to have',[34] which occurs due to the abuser's controlling behaviour, as he 'deprives the victim of the kind of perceptual and evaluative control over her options that is required for true freedom'.[35] In a further interesting development of the conceptualisation of domestic violence, Madden Dempsey maintains that domestic violence in 'its strong sense' encompasses not only violence and domesticity (which characterise domestic violence in its weak sense),[36] but also 'patriarchal power and control'.[37] To this end Madden Dempsey maintains that prosecutors can work towards the development of a 'feminist State' by concentrating efforts on those cases which involve domestic violence in its strong sense.[38] Such an approach would enable prosecutors to 'habitually isolate patriarchy' and by virtue of such 'habituated actions, prosecutors can thereby reconstitute the character of the State as less patriarchal'.[39] While Madden Dempsey develops this argument in the context of a discussion relating to the effectiveness of

29 J. Stewart, *Specialist Domestic/Family Violence Courts Within the Australian Context*, Australian Domestic and Family Violence Clearinghouse, Issues Paper No. 10, 2005, p. 3.

30 H. Douglas and T. Stark, *Stories from Survivors: Domestic Violence and Criminal Justice Interventions*, Queensland: T.C. Beire School of Law, The University of Queensland, 2010, p. 62.

31 E. Birdsey and L. Snowball, *Reporting Violence to Police: a Survey of Victims Attending Domestic Violence Services*, NSW Bureau of Crime Statistics and Research Crime and Justice Statistic, Issue Paper No. 91, 2013, pp. 5–6.

32 V. Tadros, 'The Distinctiveness of Domestic Abuse: A Freedom Based Account', *Louisiana Law Review* 65(3), 2005, 989–1014.

33 Ibid., p. 990.

34 Ibid.

35 Ibid., p. 998.

36 M. Madden Dempsey, 'What Counts as Domestic Violence? A Conceptual Analysis', *William and Mary Journal of Women and the Law* 12(2), 2006, 301–333, p. 318.

37 Ibid.; M. Madden Dempsey, 'Toward a Feminist State: What Does "Effective" Prosecution of Domestic Violence Mean?', *Modern Law Review* 70(6), 2007, 908–935, p. 917.

38 Madden Dempsey, 'Toward a Feminist State', above n. 37, pp. 925–929.

39 Ibid., p. 928.

prosecution,[40] such insights resonate with a move towards the development of a specific domestic violence offence.

Thus, it is maintained that states should continue to develop a domestic violence 'course of conduct' offence which encapsulates controlling and coercive behaviour, as well as activities which are more generally recognised as violent behaviour, such as ABH. Such an example can be seen in Tasmania, where it is an offence for a person to 'pursue a course of conduct that he or she knows, or ought to know is likely to have the effect of unreasonably controlling or intimidating or causing mental harm, apprehension or fear in, his or her spouse of partner'.[41] It is disconcerting that while the government in England and Wales has dedicated time to developing a non-statutory definition of domestic violence, along with a new crime of stalking (discussed at p. 71), it has failed to contemplate the introduction of a specific domestic violence offence. It is only with the introduction of a dedicated domestic violence offence that the state can be said to truly recognise the serious nature of domestic abuse, and move towards a 'feminist State'.[42]

Mismatch: minimising the harm

Douglas has called the legal intersection with domestic violence a 'ruthless contest' whereby '[r]espondents, police, lawyers and magistrates collude in the minimisation and trivialisation of violence'.[43] For example, in an analysis of trial decisions in England and Wales, Cammiss noted the tendency among prosecutors to adopt various discursive techniques in order to minimise the violence that occurred in the domestic setting.[44] Consequently, whereas 66 per cent of cases involving violence or public order offences were transferred to the Crown Court, 76 per cent of domestic violence cases remained in the magistrates' court.[45]

In Australian jurisdictions, the breaching or contravention of a domestic violence order is a criminal offence which may attract a potential penalty of 20 to 400 penalty units[46] and/or a term of imprisonment from one to five years.

40 Ibid.

41 Family Violence Act 2004 (Tas), s. 9. See also D. Tuerkheimer, 'Recognizing and Remedying the Harm of Battering: A Call to Criminalize Domestic Violence', *Journal of Criminal Law and Criminology* 94(4), 2004, 959–1032; D. Tuerkheimer, 'Renewing the Call to Criminalize Domestic Violence: An Assessment Three Years Later', *The George Washington Law Review* 75(3), 2007, 613–626.

42 Madden Dempsey, 'Toward a Feminist State', above n. 37, pp. 925–929.

43 Douglas, 'The Criminal Law's Response to Domestic Violence', above n. 2, pp. 439–40.

44 S. Cammiss, 'The Management of Domestic Violence Cases in the Mode of Trial Hearing: Prosecutorial Control and Marginalizing Victims', *British Journal of Criminology* 46(4), 2006, 704–718.

45 Ibid., p. 709.

46 The value of a penalty unit varies from state to state in Australia. Value is fixed each financial year around $100–$110.

However, the police can be slow in preparing and serving protection orders.[47] This can cause problems because in some jurisdictions (ACT, NSW and Victoria) a person cannot be found guilty of breaching an order unless he was present in court when the order was made or was served with a copy of the order.[48] If the order is made ex parte, as with many interim orders, there is no protection until the respondent has been served.[49] In the Northern Territory and Queensland an order is served if a police officer merely tells the respondent that an order exists.[50] This approach is realistic and practical given police resources.

The move towards criminalising a breach of a protective order is a relatively recent phenomenon in England and Wales. The Domestic Violence Crimes and Victims Act 2004 ('DVCVA') criminalised the breach of a non-molestation order,[51] the maximum punishment for which is five years and/or a fine. Prior to this reform, such orders could only be enforced via contempt of court and police could only make an arrest for breach of an order without a warrant if the court had attached a power to do so.[52] This reform has generally been supported by practitioners and domestic violence victims/survivors,[53] with it being noted that previously a non-molestation order without an attached power of arrest order was meaningless.[54] While the law already criminalised a breach of a restraining order under the Protection of Harassment Act 1997, until 2004 such orders could only be made on conviction for harassment. Hence, initially their reach was limited, a point which will be explored further in Chapter 5.

During the DVCVA reform process, New Labour also proposed criminalising a breach of an occupation order (which regulates the occupation of the family home); however, it did not do so on the basis that a 'history of violence or molestation is

47 NSW Ombudsman, *Domestic Violence: Improving Police Practice*, Special Report to Parliament Under s. 31 of the Ombudsman Act 1974, 2006.

48 Alexander, 'Women and Domestic Violence', above n. 25, p. 168; Domestic Violence and Protection Orders Act 2008 (ACT), s. 90; Crimes (Domestic and Personal Violence) Act 2007 (NSW), s. 14(2); Family Violence Protection Act 2008 (Vic), s. 123.

49 Alexander, 'Women and Domestic Violence', above n. 25.

50 Domestic and Family Violence Act 2009 (NT), s. 119; Domestic and Family Violence Protection Act 1989 (Qld), s. 80.

51 'A non-molestation order is aimed at preventing your partner or ex-partner from using or threatening violence against you or your child, or intimidating, harassing or pestering you, in order to ensure the health, safety and well-being of yourself and your children': Women's Aid, *Women's Aid Briefing: Domestic Violence Crime and Victims Act 2004*, 2007. Available online at www.womensaid.org.uk/domestic-violence-articles.asp?section=00010001002200070001&itemid=1257&itemTitle=Women%27s+Aid+briefing%3A+Domestic+Violence+Crime+and+Victims+Act+2004.

52 See Family Law Act 1996 (E/W), ss 42, 58.

53 M. Hester et al., *Early Evaluation of the Domestic Violence, Crime and Victims Act 2004*, London: Home Office, 2008.

54 J. Barron, *Not Worth the Paper . . .? The Effectiveness of Legal Protection for Women and Children Experiencing Domestic Violence*, Bristol: Women's Aid, 1990, cited in Hester et al., above n. 53, p. 19.

not a prerequisite for the grant of an [occupation] order'[55] and further stipulated that the reforms require a court 'to consider granting a non-molestation order when it considers making an occupation order'.[56] This justification can, however, be queried. When deciding whether or not to make a non-molestation order, the court is concerned with 'the need to protect the health, safety and well being' of the applicant (and any relevant child), and thus is more forward looking in nature, as opposed to focusing specifically upon on the behaviour of the respondent.[57] In contrast, with an occupation order, while evidence of molestation is not essential, courts are nevertheless required to take into account the 'conduct of the parties in relation to each other and otherwise'.[58] Indeed, it is generally accepted that occupation orders are more restrictive in nature than non-molestation orders[59] because they are considered to be 'draconian',[60] in that they can (for a short period of time at least) interfere with property rights. In addition, as Women's Aid notes, the current structure of the law could require a domestic violence victim to 'attend two separate courts on two separate occasions' if a perpetrator is served with and breaches both orders, which is a common occurrence.[61] Arguably a more coherent response would be to criminalise a breach of both orders, and the case for this is particularly strong in the absence of a nationwide implementation of an integrated domestic violence court.[62]

In voicing their support for the criminalisation of a breach of a non-molestation order, victims/survivors in England and Wales were, however, keen to stress that this was premised upon the presumption that the orders would be effectively enforced – i.e. the punishment would be significant, not just a 'little fine'.[63] Despite the fact that, in all jurisdictions, police are authorised to arrest without a warrant a person who breaches or contravenes a protection order, evidence from Australia

55 Domestic Violence, Crime and Victims Bill (E/W), Explanatory Notes, para. 17. Available online at www.publications.parliament.uk/pa/cm200304/cmbills/083/en/04083x—.htm. According to Women's Aid, *Women's Aid Briefing*, above n. 51, 'An occupation order regulates who can live in the family home, and can also restrict your abuser from entering the surrounding area. If you do not feel safe continuing to live with your partner, or if you have left home because of violence, but want to return and exclude your abuser, you may want to apply for an occupation order'.

56 Domestic Violence, Crime and Victims Bill (E/W), Explanatory Notes, para. 27.

57 Law Commission, *Family Law, Domestic Violence, and Occupation of the Family Home*, Report No. 207, 1992, para. 3.3–3.7.

58 Family Law Act 1996 (E/W), s. 33(6)(d).

59 J. Herring, *Family Law*, Essex: Pearson Education Ltd, 2011, p. 238.

60 *Davis v Johnson* [1979] AC 264, 302–303.

61 Women's Aid, *Women's Aid Briefing*, above n. 51.

62 An integrated domestic violence court was piloted in Croydon, as well as other locations in England and Wales. However, the court was not as effective as hoped, dealing with only five cases in an 18-month period. See M. Hester, J. Pearce and N. Westmarland, *Early Evaluation of the Integrated Domestic Violence Court, Croydon*, UK: Ministry of Justice, 2008.

63 Ibid., p. 23.

illustrates that enforcement of protection orders is notoriously lax.[64] This may be coupled with a lack of explanation concerning the criminality of the act(s) or the range of options available: victims may be deterred from pursuing charges.[65] Three studies of police and breaches (one in Victoria[66] and two in NSW[67]) found a high rate of non-action with officers not charging if the breach did not include physical assault or property damage.[68] Even the latter may not prompt arrest:

> A woman in the ACT . . . had five different domestic violence orders over an eight-year period. She rang the police more than 20 times for breaches of those orders. Her estranged partner was convicted of breaching once and was only kept in custody one night. A police officer told her, 'The reason men hit women is that you've got the gift of gab and you overpower men in an argument'. One evening her ex-husband came over, ripped her phone out of the wall and smashed every front window of the house. He was not charged with breach of bail or breach of the order or criminal assault of the woman but with damaging government property (the house) and damaging Telecom property (the telephone). The police were either regarding the property as more valuable than the woman or they were using the charges that they believed had the best potential for getting him locked up.[69]

Officers may even witness breaches at police stations during court-ordered contact handovers but justify inaction by labelling the incident as a family matter or parental conflict.[70]

There is a presumption against bail in certain family violence circumstances (e.g. where there is a record of violence) in the ACT, NSW, Northern Territory and Victoria. Bail is only to be granted in Tasmania if the court is satisfied that the affected person's safety, well-being and interests would not likely be adversely affected.[71] Note, however, that bail determinations can be based on a perception of the violence as a one-off incident, minimising the threat of future harm.[72] This may

64 Stewart, *Specialist Domestic/Family Violence Courts*, above n. 29, p. 3.

65 NSW Ombudsman, *Domestic Violence: Improving Police Practice*, above n. 47, p. 2. See also H. Katzen, 'It's a Family Matter, Not a Police Matter: The Enforcement of Protection Orders', *Australian Family Law Journal* 14(2), 2000, 119–141, pp. 138–139.

66 Victorian Law Reform Commission, *Review of Family Violence Laws*, above n. 18, p. 56.

67 L. Trimboli and R. Bonney, *An Evaluation of the NSW Apprehended Violence Order Scheme*, NSW Bureau of Crime Statistics and Research, 1997, p. 59; Katzen, 'It's a Family Matter, Not a Police Matter', above n. 65.

68 H. Katzen and L. Kelly, *'How Do I Prove I Saw His Shadow?' Responses to Breaches of Apprehended Violence Orders: A Consultation With Women and Police in the Richmond Local Area Command of NSW*, Lismore: Northern Rivers Community Legal Centre, 2000.

69 Easteal, *Less Than Equal*, above n. 9, p. 113.

70 Katzen, 'It's a Family Matter, Not a Police Matter', above n. 65, p. 119.

71 See Australian Law Reform Commission, above n. 17, p. 414.

72 Stewart, *Specialist Domestic/Family Violence Courts*, above n. 29.

not be just minimising per se but actually a lack of understanding of the 'big picture' through the victim's perception and experience.

The failure of police to use their powers could be, at least in part, a consequence of what they perceive of as a less than punitive approach by the courts on breaches. Judicial responses differ widely[73] and can range from sympathetic and understanding to condescending and inappropriate.[74] Women in one Queensland study identified that magistrates were failing to either penalise or direct offenders to programmes.[75] Thus, although breaching an order is a criminal offence (in NSW, for instance, such breach can attract fines of up to $5,500 and/or two years' imprisonment,[76] and in the ACT five years' imprisonment and or $55,000)[77] the usual result is no conviction.[78] If convicted, a custodial sentence is unlikely,[79] with a fine more likely to be issued.[80] For example, in Victoria between July 2004 and June 2007, 37.2 per cent of those sentenced for breaching an order were fined $500 to $1,000 with no custodial term.[81] In NSW, between January 2008 and July 2009, only 16.9 per cent of those convicted of breaching an apprehended violence order received a sentence of imprisonment.[82]

In England and Wales, the Sentencing Council has issued definitive guidelines in relation to sentencing a breach of a protective order (such as a non-molestation and restraining order)[83] and the sentencing of domestic violence cases.[84] While the latter guidelines contain numerous positive aspects, particularly the recognition that the domestic setting can operate as an *aggravating* factor,[85] some disconcerting

73 K. Warner, 'Sentencing the Violent Spouse', *Psychiatry, Psychology and the Law* 3(2), 1996, 107–117, p. 107.

74 Alexander, 'Women and Domestic Violence', above n. 25, pp. 164–65.

75 Queensland Government, *The Taskforce Report on Women and the Criminal Code*, 2000, pp. 11–112. One suggested solution was to enact a specific domestic violence assault offence.

76 LawAccess, *Consequences of Breaching an Apprehended Violence Order*, NSW Government: Attorney General and Justice. Available online at www.lawassist.lawaccess.nsw.gov.au/lawassist/lawassist_avo/lawassist_defendingavo_home/lawassist_defendantaftercourt_avo/lawassist_breach_def.html.

77 Legislation Act 2001 (ACT), s. 133: (1 penalty unit = $110 for an individual).

78 H. Douglas, 'Not a Crime Like Any Other: Sentencing Breaches of Domestic Violence Protection Orders', *Criminal Law Journal* 31(4), 2007, 200–233, p. 230.

79 Department of Justice, Courts and Tribunals Unit, *Statistics of the Magistrates' Courts and Children's Courts of Victoria: Intervention Order Statistics 2002/03–2006/07*, p. 124.

80 N. Taylor, *Analysis of Family Violence Incidents: July 2003 – June 2004: Final Report*, ACT: Australian Institute of Criminology, 2006; for Queensland, see Douglas, 'The Criminal Law's Response to Domestic Violence, above n. 2, p. 439.

81 Sentencing Advisory Council, *Sentencing Practices for Breaches of Intervention Orders: Final Report*, 2009, p. viii.

82 C. Ringland and J. Fitzgerald, 'Factors which Influence the Sentencing of Domestic Violence Offenders', Sydney: NSW Bureau of Crime Statistics and Research, 2010, p. 2.

83 Sentencing Council, *Breach of a Protective Order: Definitive Guideline*, 2006. The different orders are examined in detail in Ch. 5.

84 Sentencing Council, *Overarching Principles: Domestic Violence – Definitive Guideline*, 2006.

85 Ibid., p. i.

elements remain. Concern has been expressed that the defendant's 'positive good character' and provocation may, in certain circumstances, operate as mitigating factors. In relation to the former, as noted by the Women's National Commission, 'perpetrators regularly appear charming and in control and often win over officials in the system when compared with women'.[86] With regards to provocation, the courts have frequently constructed 'unwifely' conduct as sufficient to justifiably provoke a woman's demise.[87] Burton further notes that 'the courts will need to be very sensitive in their handling of the criterion if to free themselves from criticism that alleged "nagging" of a low-level nature is regarded as provocation for serious domestic violence'.[88] Both of these 'mitigating' factors maintain and perpetuate stereotypes about domestic violence. It is disconcerting that official policy explicitly states that domestic violence can be provoked, a notion that supports contentions that women are in some way to blame for the harm they suffer. A research project which examined the opinions of magistrates in relation to sentencing various ABH offences, some of which were of a domestic nature and others that involved stranger assaults, illustrates this point.[89] Disquieting comments include: 'Are there any courses the woman can attend to learn how to avoid being hit?'; 'If a woman knows what is going to happen, why does she carry on winding up the man?'; 'I would say that the husband [is] justified in being aggrieved at things not being ready'; 'The man was under stress'.[90]

As can be seen, the minimisation of harm continues to be an issue for the criminal justice system. As demonstrated by Cretney and Davis in the 1990s,[91] domestic violence offences tended to be downgraded and subject to more lenient penalties. Despite the plethora of policy and legislative changes over the years, disconcerting practices still remain.

Mismatch: stalking offences and the apprehension of harm

Stalking has been recognised in England and Wales as 'one of the most common types of intimate violence'[92] with the most common perpetrator being a 'partner

86 Women's National Commission, *Unlocking the Secret: Women Open the Door on Domestic Violence*, 2003, cited in M. Burton, *Legal Responses to Domestic Violence*, London: Routledge-Cavendish, 2008, p. 64.

87 S. Edwards, 'Provoking Her Own Demise: From Common Assault to Homicide', in J. Hamner and M. Maynard (eds), *Women, Violence and Social Control*, London: Macmillan, 1987, 152–168, cited in Burton, *Legal Responses to Domestic Violence*, above n. 86, p. 64.

88 Burton, *Legal Responses to Domestic Violence*, above n. 86, p. 64.

89 E. Gilchrist and J. Blissett, 'Magistrates' Attitudes to Domestic Violence and Sentencing Options', *British Journal of Criminology* 41(4), 2002, 348–363.

90 Ibid., p. 359.

91 A. Cretney and G. Davis, 'Prosecuting Domestic Assault: Victims Failing Courts, or Courts Failing Victims?', *Howard Journal of Criminal Justice* 36(2), 1997, 146–157.

92 Home Office, *Consultation on Stalking*, 2011, p. 5.

or ex-partner' – 39 per cent.[93] Until very recently victims had to rely on the Protection from Harassment Act 1997 ('PHA'); however an independent inquiry amply illustrated the failings of this law, noting that 'too many perpetrators fall through the net'.[94] The key aim of the PHA was to deal with stalking and the concept of harassment was not defined.[95] This definitional void, however, subsequently led to a wide range of disparate behaviour falling within the ambit of the Act, varying from disputes between neighbours to domestic violence.[96] In the inquiry, victims argued that stalking should be 'treated distinctly from other forms of harassment'.[97] Furthermore, problems arose due to the PHA's differentiation between two offences. The first, 'less' serious offence, is contained in s. 2, under which it is an offence to engage in a course of conduct which amounts to harassment. This is a summary offence and thus can only be tried at a magistrates' court. In contrast, s. 4 introduced a more serious, triable either way offence, of engaging in a course of conduct which causes another person to fear that violence will be used against them. Evidence submitted to the independent inquiry, however, demonstrated that the s. 4 offence was 'rarely used and when it was short custodial sentences were the norm, which were not long enough for treatment'.[98] Respondents to the Home Office's consultation on stalking commented upon the tendency of the Crown Prosecution Service ('CPS') to downgrade prosecutions 'to a lesser offence in order to increase chances of obtaining a conviction',[99] as difficulties existed in proving that the victim feared that violence would be used against him/her. As noted by Baroness Royall: 'The overwhelming evidence from the independent inquiry showed that the law is currently a barrier to just sentencing because the evidence required for stalking to be tried as an indictable offence is, in practice, too difficult to prove'.[100] Consequently, '[b]ecause of the near impossibility of proving fear of violence, perpetrator after perpetrator has been given ludicrously lenient sentences in the Magistrates' Court and has consistently broken restraining orders'.[101] The independent inquiry therefore proposed the following: to render PHA, s. 2 a triable either way offence; to abolish s. 4; and to introduce a new stalking offence

93 Ibid., p. 5, citing K. Smith et al., *Homicides, Firearm Offences and Intimate Violence 2009/10*, Home Office Statistical Bulletin 01/11, 2011.

94 Justice Unions' Parliamentary Group, *Independent Parliamentary Inquiry into Stalking Law Reform: Main Recommendations and Findings*, 2012, p. 4.

95 J. Harris, *An Evaluation of the Use and Effectiveness of the Protection from Harassment Act 1997*, London: Home Office, 2000, p. 1.

96 Justice Unions' Parliamentary Group, *Independent Parliamentary Inquiry into Stalking Law Reform*, above n. 94, p. 15.

97 Ibid.

98 Ibid., p. 12.

99 Home Office, *Review of the Protection from Harassment Act 1997: Improving Protection for Victims of Stalking – Summary of Consultation Responses and Conclusions*, 2012, p. 10.

100 Protection of Freedoms Bill, House of Lords, Third Reading, 12 March 2012, col. 21.

101 Ibid., col. 22.

which contains a non-exhaustive list of stalking behaviour.[102] Such an approach would replicate the law in Scotland.[103]

Explicit stalking offences, along with examples of what amounts to stalking,[104] were subsequently introduced by s. 111 of the Protection of Freedoms Act 2012. However, in significant ways the reforms reflect the PHA offences, in particular the divide between the summary and triable either way offences.[105] Thus, the Act brings in a 'lower level' stalking offence (s. 2A), which tautologically states that a 'course of conduct amounts to stalking if . . . it amounts to harassment',[106] and a triable either way offence (s. 4A), which is concerned with further impact upon the victim. As initially phrased, in order to fall within the more serious offence a victim was once again required to demonstrate that she suffered a fear of violence. This was eventually changed during the reform process to encompass stalking behaviour which causes the victim 'serious alarm or distress which has a substantial adverse effect on [the victim's] usual day to day activities', in addition to fearing violence.[107] Nevertheless, concerns remain, particularly in relation to the fact that the new s. 2A stalking offence is summary. Replicating this problematic divide in the PHA may potentially send out the message that stalking is not a serious issue, and also fails to deal with concerns that the police and CPS may more readily go for the summary offence in order to secure a conviction, which will consequently impact upon the sentence. Moreover, in order to achieve a conviction for the serious offence a victim must change her daily routine. However, as queried by Labour Member of Parliament, Stella Creasy, 'we . . . should reflect upon whether we would ask the victims to have their lives altered as a marker of seriousness'.[108] The focus thus becomes how the victim *responds* to the stalking conduct, as opposed to the nature of the conduct itself. Given the manner in which the behaviour of an abused woman is frequently judged against problematic notions of 'ideal victim types', these concerns are indeed justified.

In Australia, anti-stalking laws were introduced in an attempt to bridge the (perceived) gap between civil domestic violence orders and the criminal

102 Justice Unions' Parliamentary Group, *Independent Parliamentary Inquiry into Stalking Law Reform*, above n. 94, pp. 30–31.

103 See Criminal Justice and Licensing (Scotland) Act 2010 (Scot), s. 39.

104 This includes: (a) following a person; (b) contacting, or attempting to contact, a person by any means; (c) publishing any statement or other material – (i) relating or purporting to relate to a person, or (ii) purporting to originate from a person; (d) monitoring the use by a person of the internet, email or any other form of electronic communication; (e) loitering in any place (whether public or private); (f) interfering with any property in the possession of a person; (g) watching or spying on a person. See PHA, s. 2A, as introduced by the Protection of Freedoms Act 2012 (E/W), s. 111.

105 Section 111 introduces into the PHA, s. 2A (the offence of stalking) and s. 4A (the offence of stalking involving fear of violence or serious alarm or distress).

106 PHA, s. 2A(2)(a). See Protection of Freedoms Act 2012 (E/W), s. 111.

107 PHA, s. 4A(1)(a)(ii). See Protection of Freedoms Act 2012 (E/W), s. 111.

108 Protection of Freedoms Bill, House of Commons, 19 March 2012, col. 542.

law.[109] Compared to other countries, including England and Wales, Australian jurisdictions have defined stalking stringently, focusing on 'extreme examples of stalking behaviour' and relying 'upon predominantly subjective understandings of offenders needing to intend to cause harm'.[110] South Australian law, for instance, requires that there be acts on more than one occasion that could be *reasonably* expected to have intended to cause *serious* fear or apprehension.[111] That wording is illustrative of an attempt to include an objective element in the test of intent. Other examples include the following: in NSW, stalking is a crime if there was intention to cause fear of physical or mental harm if the stalker *knows that the conduct is likely to cause fear* in the other person;[112] the ACT in 2000 added the requirement of the offender's knowledge or *recklessness to the possibility*, that the other person was likely to be placed in apprehension or fear of harm, as a result of his stalking behaviour;[113] Victorian law requires a similar knowledge, or that the offender *ought to have understood* that engaging in a course of conduct of that kind would be likely to cause such harm or arouse such apprehension or fear and it actually did have that result.[114] Similarly, although the Criminal Code Act 1899 (Qld), s. 359B introduced intent under s. 359B(d)(i) in 1993, it involves looking at whether the behaviour 'would cause the stalked person apprehension or fear, *reasonably arising in all the circumstances*, of violence to, or against property of, the stalked person or another person'.[115]

An objective standard ideally grounds liability in what the stalker (reasonably) *ought to have known* given the 'particular circumstances' or context of the stalker's conduct.[116] Thus, charging and prosecution require an interpretation of the stalker's actions that reflects the context, complexities and control of domestic violence. For example, given the unpredictability and variety of abuses, the survivor develops a hyper-vigilance and a state of chronic tension that affects what she would sense as

109 NSW Law Reform Commission, *Apprehended Violence Orders*, Report No. 103, 2003, Ch. 12. Only NSW limited the range of application to domestic situations. Sanctions vary across jurisdictions, with offenders from NSW and the Northern Territory liable to two years' imprisonment, while a three-year maximum sentence has been mandated in Queensland and South Australia.

110 E. Ogilvie, 'Stalking: Criminal Justice Responses in Australia' (paper presented at Stalking: Criminal Justice Responses Conference, Australian Institute of Criminology, Sydney, 7–8 December 2000), p. 2. For an overview of the legislation, see The National Council to Reduce Violence Again Women and their Children, *Domestic Violence Laws In Australia: June 2009*, 2009.

111 Criminal Law Consolidation Act 1935 (SA), s. 19AA.

112 Crimes (Domestic and Personal Violence) Act 2007 (NSW), s. 13.

113 Crimes Act 1900 (ACT), s. 35(4).

114 Crimes Act 1958 (Vic), s. 21A.

115 Emphasis added. Tasmania also includes 'acting in another way that could *reasonably* be expected to cause the other person to be apprehensive or fearful': Criminal Code Act 1924 (Tas), Sch. 1, s. 192(1)(j) (emphasis added).

116 This is the wording in Criminal Code Act 1924 (Tas), Sch. 1, s. 192(3).

conduct that arouses apprehension.[117] Perhaps because this is not understood by the police, stalking within the 'domestic' sphere appears to engender, at best, a tepid response. One study found that few individuals had been charged; instead, officers opted for the civil legislation path.[118] They felt unable to gather sufficient evidence to prove the requirement of *intent* to cause fear, harm or apprehension.[119]

Of the matters that do proceed to prosecution, a 2010 NSW study found that just over one-third of those convicted of domestic stalking received a bond with supervision, with 11.9 per cent receiving a gaol sentence.[120]

Mismatch: battered women and beyond a *reasonable* doubt

Battered women generally are not the best witnesses. As we noted in Chapter 2, the female genderlect may become exaggerated due to the effects of victimisation and its accoutrement of low self-esteem. Numerous psychological defence mechanisms are also at play, which contribute to arguably weak evidence:

> I suppose it was partly because there was no one to validate my reality since I couldn't tell any of my friends what was going on in our house. Consequently, there's always this self-doubt; that maybe it really isn't as bad as it seems. And, there were the periods when he was charming and loving, which contributed to that type of denial. On the outside I looked like I had it all together. I never stopped functioning so you see no one knew. No one had a clue. But, on the inside, each time that I failed to follow up on a threat to leave him, the self-hatred grew. It expanded within like a malignancy until I totally lost a sense of myself.[121]

Minimising, rationalising and disassociation, which can make disclosure and testimony problematic, are other normal psychological mechanisms triggered by ongoing abuse:

> Abuses become so normative that its victims may trivialise or normalise it to the point of invisibility. The bizarre becomes normal. Narrow definitions of

117 Easteal, *Less Than Equal*, above n. 9.

118 According to ACT Director of Public Prosecutions statistics, only three family violence charges were finalised under the stalking legislation from June to December 1998. Another 174 were finalised during that time period under other legislation.

119 Police officers surveyed by A. Pearce and P. Easteal in 'The Domestic in Stalking', *Alternative Law Journal* 24(4), 1999, 165–169, p. 168.

120 C. Ringland and J. Fitzgerald, 'Factors which Influence the Sentencing of Domestic Violence Offenders', above n. 82, pp. 2, 7.

121 Partner rape survivor cited in Easteal and McOrmond-Plummer, *Real Rape, Real Pain*, above n. 5, p. 49.

> violence and the power of words to construct reality may help to obscure the violence from the victim's own vision.[122]

These 'blinders' were illustrated in the record of interview between the police and the battered woman defendant of a homicide case.[123] She was asked specific questions by the police about violent antecedents: 'Were you hit?'; 'Were you bashed?'. 'No', she responded.

Physical violence was in fact a fairly routine part of her life. If she slept later than her partner, he would pinch her breasts and nipples hard enough to bruise. In addition, it was not uncommon for him to jump on her with his full weight when she was lying down. These were not however acts that she constructed as 'hitting' or 'bashing'. They had become like a background drone and illustrate the need to correctly frame questions that reflect an understanding of the complex dynamics and effects of violence from the victim's perspective.

As a consequence, victims may be compelled by the prosecution to withdraw or lessen the charges.[124] Like the police, some prosecutors may have little understanding of these effects of violence, ignore the context and not ask the right questions.[125]

If a criminal charge is laid it must be proved beyond a reasonable doubt[126] – a higher standard than in civil matters:

> Of course, criminal law cases are harder to run because of the higher standard of proof of 'beyond a reasonable doubt' and the frequent absence of corroborating evidence from witnesses and/or other evidence such as medical reports or photographs.[127]

Victim witnesses must be prepared for cross-examination since, in all Australian jurisdictions, a spouse (and in some cases a de facto spouse) is not immune from giving evidence against her violent partner, and a similar approach is adopted in England and Wales.[128] However, in some jurisdictions, like NSW, South Australia and Victoria, a spouse can still be exempted from giving evidence by the presiding judicial officer according to certain prescribed criteria.[129]

122 P. Easteal, 'Violence Against Women in the Home: Kaleidoscopes on a Collision Course?', *Queensland University of Technology Law and Justice Journal* 3(2), 2003, 250–273, p. 250.

123 Described in Easteal, *Less Than Equal*, above n. 9, p. 42.

124 H. Douglas and L. Godden, 'The Decriminalisation of Domestic Violence', *Criminal Law Journal* 27(1), 2003, 32–43.

125 Stewart, *Specialist Domestic/Family Violence Courts*, above n. 29, p. 3.

126 Criminal Code 2002 (ACT), s. 57.

127 Alexander, 'Women and Domestic Violence', above n. 25, p. 160; *Woolmington v DPP* [1935] AC 462.

128 See Police and Criminal Evidence Act 1984 (E/W), s. 80. Generally, a spouse or civil partner is not compellable unless the case involves a specified offence, one of which is assault, injury or threat of injury to the spouse.

129 Alexander, 'Women and Domestic Violence', above n. 25, p. 160 summarises, for Australian jurisdictions: 'In the ACT, generally a spouse is not compellable in a prosecution but domestic

Conclusion – mismatch: tragedy and solutions

The result of the 'mismatch' between the victims' reality of violence in the home and the view of the criminal justice system can be tragic. Over 20 years ago, one of the authors did research on intimate homicide in Australia and found that in almost all cases in which a man killed his partner, the homicide was the last act in a lengthy history of battering; in over half of these homicides, the woman had left the relationship.[130] Roughly 20 years later, in July 2012, the Australian Broadcasting Corporation ran a documentary which followed two battered women's futile attempts to find legal sanctuary from a violent partner.[131] Ultimately, both died at the hands of their estranged partners despite having sought police assistance numerous times. Both had taken out domestic violence orders in an attempt to protect themselves. The orders had been repeatedly breached and the police had failed to act, perhaps not comprehending the men's need to control and inability to accept their partners' departure from the relationship. Both women's very serious apprehension about their estranged partners' stalking-like actions was not enough to have either man charged for stalking or for breaching an order.

Such tragedy seems to be almost an inevitable outcome of a persistent blindness by the police, courts (and community) to the seriousness of spousal violence. Legislation to protect victims of family violence, some enacted over the past two decades, is of negligible value if arrests, prosecutions and convictions do not take place. Also of concern are the relatively lenient sentences given, which are of little deterrent value.[132] Similarly, in England and Wales, ample evidence is available from the Independent Police Complaints Commission which demonstrates the devastating and fatal consequences which flow from the failure of the authorities to

violence is an exception. In a domestic violence prosecution, a victim/spouse is compellable (s 66(3)(e) *Evidence Act 1971*). In NSW, a spouse may object to giving evidence in any criminal prosecution (including a domestic violence prosecution) and the court must look at certain criteria to decide (ss 18(6) and (7) *Evidence Act 1995*). In the Northern Territory, a spouse is compellable for the prosecution in all criminal cases without the consent of the accused) (s 9(5) *Evidence Act 1939*). In Queensland, a spouse is a compellable witness for the prosecution and there are no special provisions for domestic violence cases where the compellable spouse is the victim (s 8(5) *Evidence Act 1977*). In South Australia, a spouse is compellable but can be granted an exemption. Various factors are set out (s 21 *Evidence Act 1929*). In Tasmania, a spouse is compellable in domestic violence cases (s 85A *Evidence Act 1910*). In Victoria, a spouse is compellable but can be exempted depending on various prescribed considerations (s 400 *Evidence Act 1995*). In Western Australia, the spouse of a defendant is compellable if charged with certain listed offences (s 9(1) *Evidence Act 1906*)'.

130 P. Easteal, *Killing the Beloved*, Canberra: Australian Institute of Criminology, 1993.

131 Australian Broadcasting Corporation, 'A Matter of Life and Death', *Four Corners*, 30 July 2012.

132 In Victoria, half of those who received a fine at their first sentence date also received a fine at the second sentencing: Sentencing Advisory Council, *Breaches of Intervention Orders*, above n. 81, p. 134.

take seriously, and respond adequately to, women's complaints of domestic violence.[133]

There is no mandatory arrest policy in England and Wales or Australia, unlike some parts of the United States and Canada, nor is there a 'no drop' prosecution policy.[134] Rates of charging and prosecution appear to vary depending on staffing and resources, police culture and attitudes, police powers and internal priorities and codes of practice.[135] For example, since 2004, Victoria police officers follow the Code of Practice for the Investigation of Family Violence, which is similar to the model in England and Wales and is based on a pro-arrest and pro-prosecution framework. This appears to have increased the arrest rate.[136] NSW,[137] Tasmania[138] and the ACT[139] have similar Codes of Practice.

Interestingly, although the ACT began a coordinated criminal justice and community response to family violence matters in 1998 – the Family Violence Intervention Program ('FVIP') – there was initially a lack of increase in the number of these matters coming into the criminal justice system, and the predominant view was that the police were not consistently applying a pro-arrest policy.[140] This was despite the expectation that, with an integrated model, police will deal with domestic violence as a crime, having been trained to gather prosecutorial evidence that would stand without the testimony of the victim.[141] It was not until six years

133 See, e.g., Independent Police Complaints Commission, *Learning the Lessons: Gender and Domestic Abuse*, Bulletin 11, 2010. Available online at www.learningthelessons.org.uk/Pages/bulletin11.aspx.

134 Discussed in Victorian Law Reform Commission, *Review of Family Violence Laws*, above n. 18, pp. 123, 127. Note that NSW is considering such a policy, which has resulted in concerns expressed by women's groups and family violence experts that this may make victims reluctant to testify. See A. Patty, 'Domestic Violence: Mandatory Sentencing Laws may Make Victims Reluctant to Give Evidence', *Sydney Morning Herald*, 25 February 2014. Available online at www.smh.com.au/nsw/domestic-violence-mandatory-sentencing-laws-may-make-victims-reluctant-to-give-evidence-20140224-33d4u.html.

135 In 2008, police forces in all states and territories endorsed the Australian Policing Strategy on the Prevention of Family Violence which promotes a national approach to active policing: Australasian Police Leaders, *Australasian Policing Strategy on the Prevention of Family Violence*, 2008.

136 Victorian Law Reform Commission, *Review of Family Violence Laws*, above n. 18, p. 56.

137 See NSW Police Force, *Code of Practice: NSW Police Force Response to Domestic and Family Violence*, 2009.

138 This pro-arrest strategy was enunciated by Tasmania Police, *Safe At Home*, 2004. Available online at www.police.tas.gov.au/programs/safe-at-home/.

139 The ACT police are part of the ACT integrated response to family violence – the Family Violence Intervention Project.

140 Keys Young (Firm), *Evaluation of Interagency Family Violence Intervention Program*, ACT: Department of Justice and Community Safety, 2000.

141 The issue of compelling domestic violence victims to testify is thoroughly scrutinised by J. Munstermann, 'Rescinding the Hitting Licence: Compelling Victims of Domestic Violence to Testify', *Current Issues in Criminal Justice* 7(3), 1998, 356–367, who looks at the Evidence Act 1995 (Cth) and the Evidence Act 1995 (NSW).

after the commencement of the FVIP that the Australian Federal Police endorsed a more active policing strategy.[142] Two years later, increases in the arrest rate for domestic violence and in the volume of family violence defendants began.[143]

Integrated models include education of key practitioners and the provision of specialist prosecutors and judicial officers. One would hope that these practitioners are better trained to understand the victims' reality of domestic violence. In these specialist courts, the judicial officer role is more inquisitorial, and in Canada and the United States may include 'monitoring [the] progress of the defendant'.[144] Successful family violence convictions in the ACT, with its specialist court, 'increased from 76 per cent in 2003–04 to 85 per cent in 2007–08' according to the Department for Public Prosecution annual reports.[145] Similarly, the specialist domestic violence courts have been championed in England and Wales as a beacon of good practice.[146] Without a doubt the utilisation of such courts help towards the production of a 'feminist State', which is concerned with eradicating both violence against women and patriarchy.[147] Arguably, however, increasing the provision of specialist integrated courts, which deal with both criminal and civil remedies, would provide a more effective model, as this will not only ease access to justice, but also enable a judge to garner an overview of the case. Opinions to this effect were made by Lord Justice Thorpe in *Lomas v Parle*:

> This appeal shows the unsatisfactory nature of the present interface between the criminal and family courts in such cases. It is expensive, wasteful of resources and time-consuming. It is stressful for the victim to move from court to court in order to obtain redress and protection from the perpetrator.[148]

Another approach recently piloted in England and Wales was a 'Domestic Violence Disclosure Scheme', under which individuals had a 'right to know' and 'a right to ask' about another person's history of domestic violence.[149] The rationale behind

142 Australasian Police Leaders, *Australasian Policing Strategy*, above n. 135.

143 R. Holder and J. Caruana, *Criminal Justice Intervention in Family Violence in the ACT: The Family Violence Intervention Program/1998–2006*, Canberra: Office of the Victims of Crime Coordinator, 2006, pp. 2–3.

144 Stewart, *Specialist Domestic/Family Violence Courts*, above n. 29, provides an overview of specialist programmes around the world.

145 As cited in Rollings and Taylor, *Measuring Police Performance in Domestic and Family Violence*, above n. 28.

146 D. Cook et al., *Evaluation of Specialist Domestic Violence Courts/Fast Track Systems*, London: Crown Prosecution Service, 2004, p. 144.

147 Madden Dempsey, 'Toward a Feminist State', above n. 37.

148 [2003] EWCA Civ 1804, [42]. See M. Burton, 'Lomas v Parle – Coherent and Effective Remedies for Victims of Domestic Violence: Time for an Integrated Domestic Violence Court?', *Child and Family Law Quarterly* 16(3), 2004, 317–330.

149 Home Office, *Domestic Violence Disclosure Scheme – A Consultation*, 2011; Home Office, *Domestic Violence Disclosure Scheme – A Consultation: Summary of Responses*, 2012; Home Office, *Domestic Violence Disclosure Scheme (DVDS) Pilot Assessment*, 2013. Under

these schemes focused upon enabling 'a potential victim to make choices about her safety and that of her children'.[150] To this end, the scheme introduced a 'recognised and consistent procedure'[151] for the police to exercise their existing common law powers to 'disclose information relating to previous convictions or charges to A where there is a pressing need for disclosure of the information concerning B's history in order to prevent further crime'.[152] Prima facie, such an approach appears to have much to recommend it and received support from the police and partner agencies that participated in the pilot.[153] However, there was a wide variation in disclosure rates among the pilot areas. This, the assessment suggests, may have been a result of the different interpretations given to the phrase 'pressing need', which was considered by practitioners to be unclear and too subjective.[154]

As is well documented, many violent men are initially very loving and charming – the abuse does not occur at the start of the relationship – and thus many women may be unaware of the violent tendencies of a new partner. However, concerns need to be noted. The move towards the introduction of such a scheme followed the murder of Clare Wood, who was killed by her ex-partner, George Appleton, who had a history of domestic violence.[155] Clare's family commented that she would not have become involved with Appleton had she been aware of his record. However, the Independent Police Complaints Commission report clearly highlights numerous failures in the Greater Manchester Police in their dealings with both Clare Wood and George Appleton.[156] Arguably, what needs to be improved is the state's response to domestic violence. More needs to be done to protect those who are at risk.

Indeed, the importance of providing sufficient support for potential victims was highlighted by police and support workers in the assessment of the pilot scheme, with concerns expressed as to whether 'an appropriate level of support could always be provided if the scheme was rolled out'.[157] As one support worker noted: 'If we

a 'Right to Ask' scheme: 'person (A) could ask the police about a person's (B) previous history of domestic violence or violent acts', whereas under the 'Right to Know' scheme 'the police would proactively disclose information to a person (A) about the previous violence behaviour of another person (B)': *Domestic Violence Disclosure Scheme – A Consultation: Summary of Responses*, pp. 8, 10.

150 Association of Chief Police Officers, *Tackling Perpetrators of Violence against Women and Girls*, 2009, para. 2.1.5; see Home Office, *Domestic Violence Disclosure Scheme – A Consultation: Summary of Responses*, above n. 149, p. 3.

151 Home Office, *Domestic Violence Disclosure Scheme (DVDS) Pilot Assessment*, above n. 149, p. 9.

152 Home Office, *Domestic Violence Disclosure Scheme – A Consultation*, above n. 149, p. 6.

153 Home Office, *Domestic Violence Disclosure Scheme (DVDS) Pilot Assessment*, above n. 149.

154 Ibid., pp. 18–20.

155 See Independent Police Complaints Commission, *IPCC Independent Investigation: Greater Manchester Police Contact With Clare Wood Prior to Her Death*, 2010.

156 Ibid.

157 Home Office, *Domestic Violence Disclosure Scheme (DVDS) Pilot Assessment*, above n. 149, p. 15.

delivered a disclosure without a support worker there, we would be "setting the potential victim up to fail"'.[158] It is interesting to note that some of the pilot areas 'chose not to actively publicise the scheme as they were concerned that they would not have the resources to deal with large number of applicants'.[159] Furthermore, the pilot assessment highlights the problematic that a result of a non-disclosure – i.e. where there is no information available to disclose – does not necessarily translate into the absence of risk.[160] Thus, it was also felt important to ensure the provision of support services to individuals in cases of non-disclosure.[161] An additional caution noted was that while the scheme was potentially 'another important "tool in the box" for professionals' it should not be considered to be a '"catch-all" for domestic abuse protection work'.[162]

The adoption of a disclosure scheme, it can be argued, falls within what has been termed a 'policy of responsibilisation', which is, as noted by Scoular and O'Neill, 'one of the distinctive techniques of governing in the neo-liberal welfare state'.[163] Scoular and O'Neill further explain that '[k]ey to this form of governance are active citizens who are required to self-regulate according to the norms of risk management'.[164] Accordingly, citizenship and state protection are afforded to those who engage in what is considered to be 'responsible' practices, while those who do not are 'othered' and excluded. This approach also individualises problems and does not address the many ways in which the state frequently fails to deal with male violence against women.[165] Thus, a concern may be expressed that women will be placed under increasing pressure to personally manage domestic violence, and those who fail to engage in 'a right to know', or adopt what is considered to be an inappropriate response to any information they may receive, may find themselves increasingly judged and consequently rendered more at risk, in a system which is already prone to victim-blaming.

158 Support Worker, Gwent, as cited in ibid.
159 Home Office, *Domestic Violence Disclosure Scheme (DVDS) Pilot Assessment*, above n. 149, p. 22.
160 Ibid., p. 19.
161 Ibid., pp. 20–21.
162 Ibid., p. 15.
163 J. Scoular and M. O'Neill, 'Regulating Prostitution: Social Inclusion, Responsibilization and the Politics of Prostitution Reform', *British Journal of Criminology* 47(5), 2007, 764–778, p. 771.
164 Ibid., p. 772.
165 Ibid.

Chapter 5

Domestic violence civil legislation

In Australia, family violence orders have been described as 'the strategic lynchpin in the states' and territories' system-based response to domestic violence'.[1] Indeed, orders are more commonly issued in Australia compared to Canada, the United States or the United Kingdom because in Australia 'they have been central to the development of responses by activists and reformers . . . and the crucial role of police (and hence the state) in the protection order application process'.[2] Each Australian state and territory enacted specific domestic violence civil legislation through the 1980s to provide for the issuing of family violence orders:[3] these are called protection orders in the Australian Capital Territory ('ACT') and in Queensland, apprehended domestic violence orders in New South Wales ('NSW'), intervention orders in Victoria, restraining orders in the Northern Territory, South Australia and Western Australia and restraint orders in Tasmania. The legislation was intended to provide victims with a protective remedy in civil law, as the criminal law was failing adequately to protect them. This lack of criminal protection fits within the well-established 'principle of non-intervention in the private sphere of family life':[4]

> The idea that we should distinguish between public and private spheres of life has been a central one in liberal political philosophy since the seventeenth

1 K. Wilcox, *Recent Innovations in Australian Protection Order Law – A Comparative Discussion*, Australian Domestic and Family Violence Clearinghouse, Topic Paper No. 19, 2010, p. 22. The different terms used for orders tend to be used interchangeably in the academic literature; this chapter is no exception.

2 Ibid.

3 The most current legislation is as follows: Domestic Violence and Protection Orders Act 2008 (ACT); Crimes (Domestic and Personal Violence) Act 2007 (NSW); Domestic and Family Violence Act 2007 (NT); Domestic and Family Violence Protection Act 1989 (Qld); Domestic Violence Act 1994 (SA); Family Violence Act 2004 (Tas); Family Violence Protection Act 2008 (Vic); Restraining Orders Act 1997 (WA). Criminal law is still evoked, at least in theory, if an order is breached, as discussed in Ch. 4.

4 Australian Law Reform Commission, *Family Violence: A National Legal Response*, Report No. 114, 2010, p. 167.

> century, although the roots of the idea can be traced back to Aristotle. In classical liberalism, the notion of a private sphere was a crucial part of the belief in limited government. There were certain parts of civil society in which the state had no business. And at the epicentre of the private sphere was the family; more specifically, the patriarchal family.[5]

In a sense, then, enacting civil legislation could be seen as perpetuating this differentiation by separating violence in private from that in public:

> the effect of domestic violence legislation has been to separate 'intimate partner' violence out from other forms of assault. The repositioning of violence between intimate partners within the private, less publicly accountable sphere has been to subtly construct it against the 'more serious' categories of criminally vilified violence. Violence between intimates can now be legitimately examined in a different light to criminal matters and different assumptions and rules are applied to the way it is dealt with. The construction of domestic violence as a counter poise to 'more serious' forms of violence illustrates the continuing relevance of gender to the issue.[6]

In addition to looking at the orders available under these domestic violence civil laws, we also examine injunctions[7] available under the Family Law Act 1975 (Cth) ('FLA') and remedies available in England and Wales under the Family Law Act 1996 ('FLA 1996') and the Protection from Harassment Act 1997.

The legislation: diverse, indeterminate and fluid

Essentially all the jurisdictions' family violence laws[8] include a response to the following questions, but each is distinctive in its approach:[9]

5 S. Parker, 'Rights and Utility in Anglo-Australian Family Law', *Modern Law Review* 55(3), 1992, 311–330, pp. 325–326.

6 H. Douglas and L. Godden, 'The Decriminalisation of Domestic Violence', *Criminal Law Journal* 27(1), 2003, 32–43, p. 32.

7 An injunction is a type of court order that can be obtained from the Family Court of Australia for personal protection. As discussed later, in Australia, family violence orders are generally preferred.

8 R. Alexander, 'Women and Domestic Violence', in P. Easteal (ed.), *Women and the Law in Australia*, Sydney: LexisNexis, 2010, 152–173, pp. 162–163 provides a table of the relevant legislation for each state and territory of Australia, and notes that all states have reciprocating provisions for enforcing the protection orders of other states. For a fairly up-to-date overview of the laws, see The National Council to Reduce Violence Against Women and their Children, *Domestic Violence Laws In Australia: June 2009*, 2009.

9 One example: NSW provides for the mandatory inclusion of children of the protected person and the offender if the protected person obtains an apprehended domestic violence order for herself, whether or not the children were exposed to domestic violence (Crimes (Domestic and Personal Violence) Act 2007 (NSW), s. 38(2)). The 2007 Act was a new 'stand–alone Act for

- Who can apply for an order?[10]
- What types of orders are available?[11]
- What relationships are covered?
- What are police powers if an application is made?
- What is the application process?
- What behaviours constitute domestic violence?
- Must the violence already have been committed?
- Are there additional considerations for the court in relation to exclusion orders?
- Are there cases in which a court is required to make an order?
- What specifics might be included?[12]
- What is the law concerning breaches?[13]
- Are there provisions for perpetrator programmes?

We look at examples of legislative responses to most of these questions in the following pages and note that the substance of the laws has been very fluid, with frequent amendments, particularly in responding to what behaviours constitute domestic violence. For instance, under the Family Violence Act 2004 (Tas), economic abuse[14] and emotional abuse or intimidation[15] are included, with the test

apprehended violence orders and associated domestic and personal violence issues': New South Wales, *Parliamentary Debates*, Legislative Assembly, 16 November 2007, 4327 (Tanya Gadiel, Parliamentary Secretary).

10 See Wilcox, *Recent Innovations in Australian Protection Order Law*, above n. 1, p. 5 for an excellent table, which shows the types of relationships covered by protection orders cross-jurisdictionally.

11 Orders can be emergency, temporary, interim or final orders. Their duration varies depending upon jurisdiction; for example, in NSW, an apprehended domestic violence order can be granted for up to two years.

12 Alexander, 'Women and Domestic Violence', above n. 8, p. 167: 'Different conditions or restrictions can be attached including: prohibiting the respondent from assaulting or threatening the protected person; prohibiting the respondent from being on premises where the protected person lives or works; prohibiting the respondent from exposing any children to domestic violence; suspending or cancelling a firearms licence; directing the use or return of personal belongings; counselling (optional or mandatory depending on the statute) and other prohibitions to restrain the respondent from engaging in conduct that constitutes family violence'.

13 This varies across jurisdictions but the Family Violence Protection Act 2008 (Vic), s. 125 specifically provides that a protected person cannot be charged with aiding or abetting offences if she invites or allows a respondent to contravene an intervention order. This is particularly useful where a protected person allows the respondent to access the family home or to spend time with a child pursuant to a private agreement or Family Law Act 1975 (Cth) orders. The person requiring protection cannot be charged in NSW or the Northern Territory.

14 Family Violence Act 2004 (Tas), s. 8 defines economic violence as including coercion to relinquish control over assets or income, disposing of property (owned or jointly owned) without consent, preventing access to joint financial assets and participation in decisions about household expenditure, or withholding (or threatening to withhold) reasonable, necessary financial support.

15 Emotional abuse is defined in Family Violence Act 2004 (Tas), s. 9 as prohibiting a person from pursuing conduct to have the effect of unreasonably controlling, intimidating, causing mental harm, apprehension or fear in his or her spouse or partner.

being whether the behaviour is calculated to unreasonably control or intimidate the victim. In addition to broadening the definition, given the intention of making the law more effective, other amendments have included increasing the range of relationships covered, providing for more emergency protection, an increased focus on children's need for safety and the addition of exclusion and tenancy orders.[16]

Such reforms were the result of numerous reviews by both the states and the Commonwealth that assessed the efficacy of domestic violence laws.[17] Three examples of the latter were *Time for Action: The National Council's Plan for Australia to Reduce Violence Against Women and their Children 2009–2021*;[18] the Australian Law Reform Commission's major report, *Family Violence – A National Legal Response*;[19] and the Model Criminal Code Committee ('MCCOC'), *Model Domestic Violence Laws: Discussion Paper.*[20] The last of these suggested a uniform law for all Australian jurisdictions. However, the MCCOC's suggested uniform legislation was criticised as including too narrow a definition of domestic violence, a requirement of a precipitating or 'trigger' incident and a requirement of proof that the defendant was likely to perpetrate another violent act.[21] The idea of having domestic violence law applied uniformly across the country continues to be discussed periodically. However, 'one major criticism is that this would cater to the lowest common denominator and be largely ineffective'.[22] The weakest of the legislative provisions would prevail. Thus, in Australia, the legislated approach continues to vary depending upon the jurisdiction. An example of this variation is in the test applied by the courts.

Diversity in tests

There are, broadly speaking, two different areas of concern in the various tests for granting intervention orders. One focuses on past and/or future conduct. Two states require both past domestic violence and a likelihood that domestic violence will

16 Wilcox, *Recent Innovations in Australian Protection Order Law*, above n. 1.

17 State-level examples include: Victorian Law Reform Commission, *Review of Family Violence Laws*, 2006; New South Wales Department of Attorney General and Justice, *Statutory Review of Crimes (Domestic and Personal Violence) Act 2007: Discussion Paper*, 2011.

18 The National Council to Reduce Violence Against Women and their Children, *Time For Action: The National Council's Plan for Australia to Reduce Violence Against Women and their Children 2009–2021*, 2009.

19 Australian Law Reform Commission, *Family Violence: A National Legal Response*, above n. 4. See also Australian Law Reform Commission, *Family Violence and Commonwealth Laws – Improving Legal Frameworks*, Report No. 117, 2011.

20 Domestic Violence Legislation Working Group, *Model Domestic Violence Laws: Discussion Paper*, 1997.

21 R. Hunter and J. Stubbs, 'Model Laws or Missed Opportunity?', *Alternative Law Journal* 24(1), 1999, 12–16.

22 Alexander, 'Women and Domestic Violence', above n. 8, p. 162.

recur in the future (Tasmania[23] and Victoria[24]). In these jurisdictions, indeterminacy is omnipresent since a 'one-off' incident may not suffice unless the court is satisfied that abusive behaviour is likely to happen again or that a past threat will be carried out in the future. The ACT simply requires that the respondent has engaged in domestic violence and there is no requirement to establish future likelihood. Therefore, in the ACT, a final domestic violence order ('DVO') will be granted if it is found that domestic violence has occurred,[25] while in Queensland, legislation prescribes either that a person has committed domestic violence or is likely to commit domestic violence.[26]

The other approach focuses on the effect on the victim ('fear' in NSW, Western Australia and the Northern Territory[27] or 'reasonable apprehension' that domestic violence will be committed in South Australia[28]) or the protection and safety of the victim (sufficient to obtain interim orders in ACT[29] and Victoria[30]). In Western Australia the test includes either past conduct and future likelihood or 'reasonable fear' that an act of abuse will be committed.[31] New South Wales allows for an exception that even if no fear is expressed, an order can be made if there is a likelihood of future violence.[32] Varying standards apply when determining whether to impose a subjective or objective test:[33] 'In NSW, victims are required to demonstrate what the "reasonable grounds" for their fears are and, in practice, the evidence presented tends to rest on the perpetrator's previous behaviour'.[34]

Diversity in types of orders

In addition to obtaining orders under the Australian domestic violence legislation just described, under FLA, ss 68C[35] and 114[36] the Family Court of Australia is able

23 Family Violence Act 2004 (Tas), ss 16(1)(a)–(b).
24 Family Violence Protection Act 2008 (Vic), s. 74(1).
25 Domestic Violence and Protection Orders Act 2008 (ACT), s. 46(1).
26 Domestic and Family Violence Protection Act 1989 (Qld), ss 20(1)(a)–(b).
27 Crimes (Domestic and Personal Violence) Act 2007 (NSW), s. 19(1); Domestic and Family Violence Act 2009 (NT), s. 18(1); Restraining Orders Act 1997 (WA), s. 12(1)(b).
28 Domestic Violence Act 1994 (SA), s. 4(1)(a).
29 Domestic Violence and Protection Orders Act 2008 (ACT), s. 7(1)(a).
30 Family Violence Protection Act 2008 (Vic), s. 53.
31 Restraining Orders Act 1997 (WA), ss 11A(a)–(b).
32 Crimes (Domestic and Personal Violence) Act 2007 (NSW), s. 16(2)(c)(ii).
33 Alexander, 'Women and Domestic Violence', above n. 8, p. 164, notes that where the impact on the victim is 'determinative', the results can also depend on the presiding magistrate, as well as the communication and advocacy skills of both the applicant (where self-representing) and the lawyer.
34 Wilcox, *Recent Innovations in Australian Protection Order Law*, above n. 1, p. 8.
35 '. . . to protect the welfare of a child'.
36 '. . . in circumstances arising out of the marital relationship'.

to grant injunctions.[37] A person who has already been granted a state or territory family violence order can also apply for an injunction under the FLA; the converse is not true. Further, a state or territory court can only 'revive, vary, discharge or suspend an injunction granted under [the FLA], to the extent to which it *expressly or impliedly requires or authorises a person to spend time with a child*'.[38] Thus, 'Family Law Act injunctions will prevail over a protection order made under state or territory family violence legislation to the extent of any inconsistency'.[39]

It has been suggested that reform is necessary to allow a state or territory court to amend an FLA injunction when making a protection order. This would address any inconsistencies and remove the need for the person to return to a federal family court to revoke an injunction before applying for a protection order under state or territory legislation.[40]

FLA injunctions are second choice for someone seeking protection.[41] As Alexander asserts, '[s]uch injunctions are difficult to obtain'.[42] Indeed: 'The processes for seeking a protection order under state and territory family violence legislation are generally quicker and cheaper than an application for an injunction under the Family Law Act'.[43]

Further, unlike the state and territory remedy, police do not assist in serving documents in relation to FLA injunctions; applicants will usually employ a commercial process server to effect service.[44] In addition, if the injunction is breached, the onus of responsibility falls on the victim:

> Breach of a FLA injunction is not a criminal offence of itself. Police do not institute breach proceedings: the victim has to go back to court to do so. In this regard . . . [an] injunction is not as effective as an intervention order.[45]

37 FLA, s. 68B: 'for the personal protection of the child, the child's parent, a person with a parenting order in respect of the child, or a person who has parental responsibility for the child'. Section 114(2) specifies injunctions available in relation to de facto relationships.

38 FLA, s. 68R(1)(c) (emphasis added).

39 Australian Law Reform Commission, *Family Violence: Improving Legal Frameworks*, Consultation Summary Paper 1, 2010, p. 104.

40 This and other recommendations to make injunctions more effective have been suggested by the Australian Law Reform Commission's 2010 Report, *Family Violence: A National Legal Response*, above n. 4.

41 L. Young and G. Monahan, *Family Law in Australia*, Sydney: LexisNexis, 2009, [16.8].

42 R. Alexander, 'Injunctions Under the Family Law Act (Commonwealth Law)', *Fitzroy Legal Service: The Law Handbook*, 2010.

43 Australian Law Reform Commission, *Family Violence: A National Legal Response*, above n. 4, 800.

44 R. Alexander, 'Family Violence', *Springvale Legal Centre: Lawyers Practice Manual Victoria*, 2009, [2.8.803], cited in Australian Law Reform Commission, *Family Violence: A National Legal Response*, above n. 4, p. 801.

45 Alexander, 'Injunctions Under the Family Law Act', above n. 42.

It is interesting that FLA, s. 114(2) contains what one might hope is an anachronistic provision. Under this section, the court is able to 'make an order relieving a party to a marriage from any obligation to perform marital services or render conjugal rights'. This implies that there is a continuing obligation to render conjugal rights and provide marital services. However, as discussed in Chapter 10, this has not been true in the legal sense in Australia for over 30 years.

In England and Wales the two key domestic violence remedies are non-molestation and occupation orders, which are contained in the FLA 1996. With regards to non-molestation orders, the court's approach is more forward looking, as it is entitled to take into account all circumstances, including 'the need to secure the health, safety and well-being' of the applicant or any relevant child, with health encompassing both physical and mental health, and thus potentially covering emotional and psychological abuse. Accordingly, it appears that evidence of physical violence is not a prerequisite for the making of an order. As Burton notes, 'the rationale behind this provision is victim focused; the emphasis is on the victim's need for protection and the needs of children, rather than the nature of the respondent's conduct'.[46]

In order to apply for a non-molestation order an applicant must fall within the scope of 'associated persons'.[47] However, as noted by Reece, it is difficult to identify a coherent justification for the construction of this category.[48] As initially structured, it was, paradoxically, both at once too wide and too narrow. While a large range of 'relatives' amounted to an associated person, same-sex couples and couples or ex-couples who had not lived together were excluded. Amendments to include such persons were contained in the Domestic Violence Crimes and Victims Act 2004 ('DVCVA'),[49] and while this is to be commended, the rationale behind the formulation of 'associated persons' appears to be ideologically concerned with 'intimacy and equality', as opposed to 'isolation and inequality', which, as Reece notes, are at the core of domestic violence.[50] Domestic violence is constructed as something that occurs in a broad range of relationships. However, this broadness, peculiarly, operates in a way that reenforces the minimisation of domestic violence. As Reece argues:

> The claim that domestic violence occurs in every type of relationship seems to be the reverse of minimising domestic violence, but in fact it is another method, because if domestic violence occurs everywhere then domestic violence occurs nowhere.[51]

46 M. Burton, *Legal Response to Domestic Violence*, Oxon: Routledge-Cavendish, 2008, p. 19.
47 FLA 1996, s. 62(3).
48 H. Reece, 'The End of Domestic Violence', *Modern Law Review* 69(5), 2006, 770–791.
49 DVCVA, ss 3–4.
50 Reece, 'The End of Domestic Violence', above n. 48, p. 791.
51 Ibid.

Consequently, the specificity and asymmetry of domestic violence is erased. Such an approach fails to recognise that domestic violence is a gendered phenomenon, which occurs within, and maintains and perpetuates conditions of, female inequality. This broad, sweeping approach fails to fulfil the requirements of a 'feminist State', which is concerned with effectively tackling domestic violence in 'its strong sense', in particular challenging patriarchy.[52]

The provisions relating to occupation orders in FLA 1996, ss 33–36 are more complex. The legislation draws a distinction between those who have a pre-existing right to occupy the family home – entitled applicants – and those who do not – non-entitled applicants. Whereas the former can obtain an occupation order against an associated person, the latter may only apply for an order against a current or former spouse, civil partner or cohabitant. The FLA 1996 in England and Wales distinguishes between five different categories of people, dependent upon entitlements to occupy and the relationship between the parties, and appoints each a separate section.[53] For reasons of space, this discussion will focus on s. 33, which relates to 'those entitled to occupy the property'.

Under ss 33(6)–(7) the court has a mandatory and a discretionary duty to grant an order. Section 33(6) states that the court has a discretion to grant an order taking into account all the circumstances, including the housing needs and resources of the parties and any relevant child; the financial resources of the parties; the likely effect of the court's decision to grant/not grant an order on the health, safety or well-being of the parties and of any relevant child; and the conduct of the parties in relation to each other. Section 33(7), however, goes further, and stipulates that the court *shall* grant an order 'if it appears to the court that the applicant or any relevant child is likely to suffer significant harm attributable to the respondent if an order . . . is not made . . .'. However, the section continues that this is *unless* 'the respondent or any relevant child is likely to suffer significant harm . . . [which] is as great as, or greater than' that suffered by the applicant or relevant child if an order is not made. This is known as the 'balance of harm' test, and it is now well established that the two tests in ss 33(6) and 33(7) are separate.[54] Consequently, the court will initially decide whether an order must be made under s. 33(7). If the answer is no, the court will then move on to decide whether to exercise its discretion under s. 33(6).[55]

52 M. Madden Dempsey, 'Toward a Feminist State: What Does "Effective" Prosecution of Domestic Violence Mean?', *Modern Law Review* 70(6), 2007, 908–935, p. 917.

53 Section 33 – those entitled to occupy the property; s. 35 – a former spouse/civil partner with no existing rights of occupation in the property where the other former spouse is so entitled; s. 36 – a cohabitant or former cohabitant with no existing rights of occupation in the property where the other partner/former partner is so entitled; s. 37 – a spouse or civil partner who has no existing right to occupy the property where the other spouse/civil partner also has no entitlement to remain in occupation; s. 38 – a cohabitant or former cohabitant who has no existing right to occupy the property where the other former cohabitant also has no entitlement to remain in occupation.

54 *Chalmers v Johns* [1999] 1 FLR 392; *Dolan v Corby* [2011] EWCA Civ 1664, [2012] 2 FLR 1031.

55 *Chalmers v Johns* [1999] 1 FLR 392, 396.

On initial examination this approach appears to restrict the court's discretion; as such, there are concerns regarding the phrasing and application of the balance of harm test. As discussed by Kaganas, it was anticipated by the Law Commission that the test 'would focus on the need for a remedy rather than on conduct and so avert the problems associated with a scheme emphasising conduct'.[56] Not only does the wording of s. 33(7) make it clear that the harm potentially suffered by an applicant is to be attributable to the conduct of the respondent, thus re-establishing a link, but commentators have also noted that the section may, at the same time, have an effect of minimising, if not rendering irrelevant, any *previous* violence suffered at the hands of the respondent.[57] After a close reading of two key Court of Appeal cases, *B v B*[58] and *Chalmers v Johns*,[59] Kaganas argues that:

> It may be that it is in the focus on the need for a remedy and in the future-oriented nature of the significant harm test that the potential for de-emphasising violence in such cases lies. If the victim and her children are beyond the reach of the abuser, then, the argument might run, they are no longer at risk of significant harm from him. They are therefore not in need of a remedy unless their housing situation or other such matters demand it.[60]

This places an abused woman in a difficult position. In order to fall within s. 33(7) she has to prove that any harm she is likely to suffer stems from the respondent. However, if she has managed to remove herself, even if only temporarily, from the family home, the court may consider that no harm exists, even if the accommodation is not suitable, as was the case in *B v B*. In this situation, the previous violence and harm suffered at the hands of the respondent is rendered irrelevant.

In addition to such difficulties, the courts have stressed on numerous occasions that an occupation order is 'draconian' and should only be used as a matter of last resort.[61] In *Chalmers v Johns*, Lord Justice Thorpe stated: 'The order remains Draconian, particularly in the perception of the respondent. It remains an order that overrides proprietary rights and it seems to me that it is an order that is only justified in exceptional circumstances'.[62] Given the difficulties that women face after leaving abusive relationships, which frequently concern lack of funds and appropriate alternative accommodation, conceptualising an occupation order in such a restrictive manner is problematic. This approach appears to place property rights over and

56 F. Kaganas, 'B v B (Occupation Order) and Chalmers v Johns: Occupation Orders Under The Family Law Act 1996', *Child and Family Law Quarterly* 11(2), 1999, 193–204, pp. 194–195.
57 Ibid.
58 *B v B* [1999] 1 FLR 715.
59 *Chalmers v Johns* [1999] 1 FLR 392, 397.
60 Kaganas, 'B v B (Occupation Order) and Chalmers v Johns', above n. 56, p. 201.
61 *Chalmers v Johns* [1999] 1 FLR 392, 397.
62 Ibid.

above an abused woman's right to protection, and perpetuates conceptions that a 'man's home is his castle'.

In addition to non-molestation and occupation orders, civil remedies are also available under the Protection from Harassment Act 1997 ('PHA') and are not restricted to 'associated persons'. Section 3 creates a statutory tort of harassment and, upon application, a court may grant an injunction, as well as award damages. The remedies go beyond those available under the FLA 1996, although it should be remembered that in order to fall within the ambit of PHA, s. 3 the applicant is required to establish an actual or apprehended harassment. The court also has the power to issue a restraining order under PHA, s. 4. Initially this was restricted to cases in which the respondent was found guilty of either harassment or putting the victim in fear of violence, and thus had limited scope. This was amended, however, by the DVCVA,[63] and a court can now issue a restraining order in cases where the defendant is acquitted of a criminal charge[64] but an order is considered appropriate 'to protect a person from harassment by the defendant'.[65] While this extension has generally been welcomed,[66] it is nevertheless dependent upon a case proceeding to trial, and attrition remains an issue in domestic violence cases.

Applying for and obtaining an order

In England and Wales, as will be discussed further at p. 101, civil protection orders now take on further importance as they are a gateway for public funds for other family law remedies.[67] However, there has been a significant reduction in the numbers of applications for, and the granting of, such orders,[68] which commenced prior to the enactment of the FLA 1996.[69] While an increase might have been expected in the wake of the 1996 reforms, due to the Act's 'victim-focused criteria',[70] this did not transpire and the biggest decline has been in relation to occupation orders.[71] Various theories have been advanced for this decline, including a judicial

63 Home Office, *Safety and Justice: The Government's Proposals on Domestic Violence*, 2003, p. 36.
64 DVCVA, s. 12.
65 PHA, s. 5A, inserted by DVCVA s. 12.
66 M. Hester et al., *Early Evaluation of the Domestic Violence, Crime and Victims Act 2004*, London: Home Office, 2008, pp. 30–31.
67 Legal Aid, Sentencing and Punishment of Offenders Act 2012, Sch. 1, s. 12.
68 Ministry of Justice, *Judicial and Court Statistics*, 2011, pp. 29–30. See also M. Burton, 'Civil Law Remedies for Domestic Violence Remedies: Why Are Applications For Non-Molestation Orders Declining?', *Journal of Social Welfare and Family Law* 31(2), 2009, 109–120, p. 109; M. Burton, *Domestic Abuse Literature Review*, London: Legal Services Commission, 2008, p. 7.
69 Burton, *Domestic Abuse Literature Review*, above n. 68, p. 3; S. Edwards, 'Domestic Violence and Harassment: As Assessment of the Civil Remedies', in J. Taylor-Browne (ed.), *What Works in Reducing Domestic Violence? A Comprehensive Guide for Professionals*, London: Whiting Birch, 2001, 187–210.
70 Burton, *Domestic Abuse Literature Review*, above n. 68, p. 3. See also M. Burton, *Legal Responses to Domestic Violence*, London: Routledge-Cavendish, 2008, p. 37.
71 Ministry of Justice, *Judicial and Court Statistics*, above n. 68, pp. 29–30.

reluctance prior to the DVCVA reforms to make an order because of the presumption of attaching a power of arrest,[72] an increased use of criminal, as opposed to civil, remedies because of developments in the criminal justice system,[73] and a reluctance on the part of victims because of a perceived inadequacy of penalties upon breach.[74] In relation to this last point, it may be presupposed that applications would increase following the enactment of the DVCVA, which criminalises breach of a non-molestation order and expands the scope of 'associated persons'.[75] Some commentators have suggested, conversely, that the move towards increased criminalisation may operate as a deterrent, as victims may not wish to criminalise their partners and may feel disempowered as the Crown Prosecution Service takes over the process.[76] However, as noted by Burton, '[n]o single factor appears to account for the decline in applications. . . . It is most likely to be a combination of legal and other developments'.[77] Whatever the cause, it is disconcerting that fewer victims are accessing justice.

In Australia, most family violence orders are issued by courts of summary jurisdiction. The civil standard of proof (the balance of probabilities test) is applied.[78] In South Australia, Victoria, Western Australia, ACT and pilots in Rockhampton Queensland and Wagga Wagga and Campbelltown in NSW, applications for orders are heard in a specialist list or stream in the magistrates' courts, which take a variety of approaches to the issue of family violence.[79]

Rosemary Hunter has identified problems with the court process for victims despite the usually positive outcome for most applicants.[80] For example, there may be lengthy waits, lack of protection and brevity of the proceedings. Further, a respondent is open to consent to an order without admissions, meaning that there are few findings that women's stories are true and a lack of tailoring of order provisions to the specific facts of the matter: 'those outcomes were compromised by inattentive, routinized practices in relation to the terms of orders, making the orders less effective and more difficult to enforce'.[81]

72 Edwards, 'Domestic Violence and Harassment', above n. 69.

73 J. Platt, 'The Domestic Violence, Crime and Victims Act 2004 Part 1: Is It Working?', *Family Law* 38, 2008, 642–647, p. 643.

74 Ibid., p. 642.

75 Burton, *Domestic Abuse Literature Review*, above n. 68, p. 7.

76 Platt, above n. 73, p. 642.

77 Burton, *Domestic Abuse Literature Review*, above n. 68, p. 4.

78 See, e.g., Domestic Violence and Protection Orders Act 2008 (ACT), s. 16.

79 See E. Schneller, *Family Violence Courts*, Sydney: NSW Parliamentary Research Service, 2012 for an overview of Domestic Violence Courts in Australia, Canada, New Zealand and the United States; J. Stewart, *Specialist Domestic/Family Violence Courts Within the Australian Context*, Australian Domestic and Family Violence Clearinghouse, Issues Paper No. 10, 2005.

80 R. Hunter, *Domestic Violence Law Reform and Women's Experience in Court: The Implementation of Feminist Reforms in Civil Proceedings*, New York: Cambria Press, 2008.

81 Ibid., p. 100.

However, consent without admission does mean that matters can be dealt with quickly.

If the order is contested (most are not), or if the applicant wants the respondent removed from the premises, the process can prove to be even more problematic.[82] For instance, in the ACT, if consent is not obtained, the matter will proceed to a hearing.[83] As discussed in Chapter 4, if the order is made ex parte, as with many interim orders, there is no protection until the respondent has been served.[84] The partner may also seek to minimise responsibility by deferring blame on to the victim and/or instigating proceedings against her in retaliation.[85]

In addition, there may be problems associated with legal representation. Women who have experienced domestic violence may not be their own best advocates, as one of the results of violence is a diminution in sense of self and self-confidence;[86] as such, women may need legal representation and support. Yet, even if access to a lawyer is not limited by financial constraints and women are offered free advice, there are other potential issues:

> Firstly, there is the possibility that lawyers will share non-feminist understandings of domestic violence as part of their 'internal' legal culture, and hence will have only a limited understanding of their client's position. Secondly, there is the possibility that women's voices will be silenced by the fact that court proceedings are dominated by the voices of lawyers. Thirdly, there is the possibility that lawyers will disempower their clients by transforming their stories into standardized legal narratives that misrepresent the client's actual experience and/or fail to respond to their actual needs.[87]

The significance of supportive and specialist lawyers cannot be underestimated as they play a very important role in a woman's ability to access civil justice.[88] However, in England and Wales concerns have been expressed that lawyers sometimes discourage clients from applying (including a case in which a pregnant woman was

82 In Hunter's sample only 14 of 100 applications were contested: ibid., p. 62.

83 Domestic Violence and Protection Orders Act 2008 (ACT), s. 43.

84 Alexander, 'Women and Domestic Violence', above n. 8.

85 H. Douglas, 'The Criminal Law's Response to Domestic Violence: What's Going On?', *Sydney Law Review* 30(3), 2008, 439–469, pp. 439–440.

86 R. J. Aguilar and N. Nunez Nightingale, 'The Impact of Specific Battering Experiences on the Self-Esteem of Abused Women', *Journal of Family Violence* 9(1), 1994, 35–45.

87 Hunter, *Domestic Violence Law Reform and Women's Experience in Court*, above n. 80, p. 64. See J. Barron, *Not Worth the Paper. . .? The Effectiveness of Legal Protection for Women and Children Experiencing Domestic Violence*, Bristol: Women's Aid, 1990, commenting on the situation in England and Wales.

88 M. Burton, A. McCrory and T. Buck, *The Civil Remedies for Domestic Violence Under the Family Law Act 1996: Is Section 60 the Way Forward?*, Lord Chancellor's Department, unpublished report, 2002; discussed in Burton, *Domestic Abuse Literature Review*, above n. 68, p. 19. See also Rights of Women, *Women's Access to Justice: A Research Report*, 2011, p. 2.

advised to return to her abusive partner[89]) and may be unsympathetic, believing that the victim has precipitated the violence.[90] Additionally, some practitioners have expressed views not only that the courts require evidence of physical violence before an order is granted, but also that they are reluctant to use public funds in the absence of such abuse.[91] Considering the importance of obtaining an order for the purposes of accessing legal aid, not to mention the issue of providing protection to those who suffer psychological or emotional abuse, such perspectives are disconcerting.

Colour it grey: police

In a number of Australian jurisdictions police can issue an order. For example, in Tasmania, since 2004 police officers who hold the rank of sergeant or above can make a police family violence order, which may apply for up to 12 months. These orders may be issued if the officer is 'satisfied that the person has committed, or is likely to commit, a family violence offence'.[92]

Alternatively, police officers may apply for a court order. However, an officer may be disinclined to do so for a number of reasons; for instance if he/she believes that a magistrate is erratic in handling order applications.[93] In addition, a view is held by at least some in the (policing) community that violence in the home includes mutuality and provocation. As one officer summonsed to a domestic violence call in the ACT told the victim, '[t]he reason men hit women is that you've got the gift of gab and you overpower men in an argument'.[94] With or even without this police response, '[i]t is often too difficult for victims to take matters into their own hands at this stage'.[95] It is therefore especially important that when police intervene in domestic violence situations the blame is not transferred verbally to the victim.

Within such ambivalent beliefs, the main influence on police behaviour appears to be how the jurisdiction's legislation and/or departmental internal policy define the role for officers.[96] For instance, an example of policy direction is the Code of

89 Women's National Commission, *Unlocking the Secret: Women Open the Door on Domestic Violence*, 2003, p. 14. See also Burton, *Domestic Abuse Literature Review*, above n. 68, p. 19.

90 Burton, *Domestic Abuse Literature Review*, above n. 68, p. 19.

91 Burton, *Legal Responses to Domestic Violence*, above n. 70, p. 40.

92 Family Violence Act 2004 (Tas), s. 14. These changes were part of the Tasmania Government's response to family violence: *Safe at Home*. Available online at www.safeathome.tas.gov.au.

93 NSW Ombudsman, *Domestic Violence: Improving Police Practice: A Special Report to Parliament Under s 31 of the Ombudsman Act 1974*, 2006.

94 P. Easteal, 'Violence Against Women in the Home: Kaleidoscopes on a Collision Course?', *Queensland University of Technology Law and Justice Journal* 3(2), 2003, 250–273.

95 Victorian Law Reform Commission, *Review of Family Violence Laws*, above n. 17, p. 122. As discussed throughout this book, the effects of violence may leave victims feeling shame, powerless, fearful and ineffective.

96 Alexander, 'Women and Domestic Violence', above n. 8, p. 165 notes 'that according to figures on various interstate websites, the number of police-initiated applications for protection orders

Practice for the Investigation of Family Violence, which took effect in 2004 and requires officers 'at a minimum ... [to] refer a family to an appropriate service'.[97] This appears to have increased the number and proportion of criminal charges being laid.[98] The legislative articulation of the police officers' role varies across jurisdictions, as described at p. 84. Section 49 of the Crimes (Domestic and Personal Violence) Act 2007 (NSW) prescribes that an application for an apprehended domestic violence order *must* be made if the police officer investigating an alleged family violence incident suspects or believes that domestic violence has been committed or is imminent or that abuse against a child or young person has occurred or is imminent. If the police officer has a good reason not to make an application, a written record of that reason must be made.[99]

As a result of the Victorian Law Reform Commission Review,[100] which was completed in 2006, police officers in the state of Victoria were given more powers under the Family Violence Protection Act 2008 (VIC), allowing them to issue safety notices, and to remove abusive spouses and parents for up to three days. These powers are taken to be equivalent to an application for a final order.[101] The definition of family violence was expanded to include economic and emotional abuse, as well as other types of threatening and controlling behaviour, for the purpose of seeking intervention orders.[102]

However, even legislative and policy direction may not result in police applications. Recent Queensland research revealed that in that state more than half of the applications for orders were made by the 'aggrieved spouse' – private applications as opposed to police applications.[103] This is despite the fact that Queensland places a mandatory obligation upon police to investigate complaints when the officer *reasonably* suspects that a person is aggrieved.[104] The officer may then 'apply for a protection order to

varies enormously – 75% in NSW, 49% in Victoria, [the] vast majority in South Australia and Tasmania and almost none in Western Australia'.

97 W. Steendham, *Better Policing, Better Outcomes: Changing Police Culture to Prevent Domestic Violence and Homicide*, Australian Domestic and Family Violence Clearinghouse, Issues Paper No. 19, 2009, p. 10. See Victoria Police, *Code of Practice for the Investigation of Family Violence*, 2010. Available online at www.police.vic.gov.au/content.asp?Document_ID=288.

98 K. Rollings and N. Taylor, 'Measuring Police Performance in Domestic and Family Violence', *Trends and Issues in Crime and Criminal Justice* No. 367, Canberra: Australian Institute of Criminology, 2008, p. 2.

99 Crimes (Domestic and Personal Violence) Act 2007 (NSW), s. 49(5).

100 Victorian Law Reform Commission, *Review of Family Violence Laws*, above n. 17.

101 In the Northern Territory, under the Domestic and Family Violence Act 2007 (NT), s. 44 the defendant must 'show cause as to why the DVO should not be confirmed by the court'.

102 See Family Violence Protection Act 2008 (Vic), ss 5–7.

103 Douglas and Godden, above n. 6, p. 36.

104 Part 6 of the Domestic and Family Violence Protection Act 1989 (Qld) lists police functions and powers and *requires* police to apply for an order *if* taking a person into custody and then lists conditions when the police *may* make an application.

protect the aggrieved'.[105] Similarly, in Western Australia[106] Alexander reports that almost no restraining orders were applied for by police.[107] Officers in that state may issue a police order (of either 24 or 72 hours' duration), but the victim must obtain a restraining order herself, except where 'under certain circumstances a police officer will apply for the order'.[108]

Even if police officers in any of the jurisdictions do initiate the order process, there are potential drawbacks. Research has shown that slow execution of service has resulted in expensive delays and postponements, applications being withdrawn, and, as a further result, a lack of protection for victims.[109]

In England and Wales, domestic violence protection notices and orders ('DVPNs' and 'DVPOs', respectively) have recently been piloted, and will be implemented nationally during 2014.[110] Under the Crime and Security Act 2010, s. 24 a senior officer may issue a DVPN if he/she reasonably believes that the perpetrator 'has been violent towards or has threatened violence towards, an associated person' and the DVPN 'is necessary to protect that person from violence or a threat of violence'. While the officer must consider, among other things, the victim's opinion regarding the DVPN, the notice can be issued without her consent. Once issued, the officer must apply to the magistrates' court within 48 hours for a DVPO. In addition to prohibiting molestation (which is mandatory), both the notice and order may prohibit the perpetrator from entering any relevant premises if he cohabits with the victim. A breach is a contempt of court.

Drawing upon similar provisions in Austria, Germany and Switzerland, these orders were considered necessary due to a 'dangerous "gap" in the criminal and civil justice systems'.[111] Their aim is to provide 'police led immediate protection, where, currently, immediate protection does not exist to enable victims of domestic violence to have the time and support needed to consider their future options, including longer-term civil injunctions'.[112] Without a doubt, such measures are to be welcomed, and the pilot indicated that the orders 'were associated with reduced

105 Domestic and Family Violence Protection Act 1989 (Qld), s. 67(2)(c).

106 Restraining Orders Act 1997 (WA), ss 62A–62C.

107 Alexander, 'Women and Domestic Violence', above n. 8, p. 165.

108 Western Australia Police, *Family and Domestic Violence*. Available online at www.police.wa.gov.au/Yoursafety/Familyviolence/tabid/895/Default.aspx. The site does not list these 'certain circumstances' and the legislation only enunciates the police role in issuing police orders.

109 Findings of the NSW Ombudsman, *Domestic Violence: Improving Police Practice*, above n. 93, condemned the lack of vigilance shown by police in the administration of the whole process, from application through to service.

110 Home Office, *Evaluation of the Pilot of Domestic Violence Protection Orders*, Research Report 76, 2013.

111 House of Commons Library, *Crime and Security Bill: Bill No 3 2009/10*, Research Paper 09/97, 2009, p. 28. See also Association of Chief Police Officers, *Tackling Perpetrators of Violence Against Women and Girls*, 2009.

112 Home Office, *Impact Assessment of Domestic Violence Protection Orders (DVPO) – A Pilot Scheme*, 2009, p. 1.

rates of re-victimisation (measured by police call-outs), compared to similar cases dealt with by arrest followed by "no further action"'.[113]

However, some difficulties remain. Both Refuge and the Fawcett Society cautioned that in Austria, Germany and Switzerland the equivalent measures are 'linked to wider systems of intervention';[114] hence, their effect may not be the same in England and Wales. During the pilot 'no perpetrator had engaged, via a DVPO, in interventions designed to end their abusive behaviour',[115] although it is noted that 'this may have been due to a lack of available programmes'.[116] Furthermore, their application relies on police involvement, which, as can be seen in Australia and as discussed in Chapter 4, is at times lacking. Indeed, the pilot evaluation indicated varying levels of police officer support,[117] with a minority of officers considering the order to be disproportionate, particularly in cases involving what was perceived to be '"low-level" violence'.[118] Such perspectives carry 'the potential for cases to be minimised where there was no serious physical assault, and coercive control exercised by perpetrators over victim-survivors to be ignored'.[119] Further difficulties relate to the role of the court, with some 'expecting higher levels of evidence that were more in keeping with criminal charge than a protection order'.[120] It was also reported that 'some victim-survivors had been compelled to attend court in favour of the defence – going against the aim of DVPOs not needing to involve victim-survivors'.[121]

The maximum length of an order is 28 days; thereafter the victim must apply for a civil protection to cover a longer period of time. An alternative solution, in England and Wales, might be to bring into force FLA 1996, s. 60, under which a third party is allowed to apply on behalf of a victim for a civil protection order – an approach that does appear to have the support of practitioners.[122] Despite acknowledging that 'this option could prove most helpful where the victim is particularly vulnerable, or unable to pursue an application

113 Home Office, *Evaluation of the Pilot of Domestic Violence Protection Orders*, above n. 110, p. 6.

114 Refuge, *Together We Can End Violence Against Women And Girls: A Consultation Paper*, 2009, cited in House of Commons Library, *Crime and Security Bill*, above n. 111, p. 32. See also Fawcett Society, *Consultation Response from the Fawcett Society to HM Government Together We Can End Violence Against Women and Girls*, 2009, cited in House of Commons Library, *Crime and Security Bill*, above n. 111, p. 32.

115 Home Office, *Evaluation of the Pilot of Domestic Violence Protection Orders*, above n. 110, p. 5.

116 Ibid.

117 Ibid.

118 Ibid., p. 20.

119 Ibid.

120 Ibid., p. 21.

121 Ibid., p. 22.

122 M. Burton, 'Third Party Applications for Protection Orders in England and Wales: Service Provider's Views on Implementing Section 60 of the Family Law Act 1996', *Journal of Social Welfare and Family Law* 25(2), 2003, 137–150.

themselves',[123] the government has yet to make a decision regarding the implementation of s. 60.[124]

Colour it grey: magistrates

Even dedicated domestic violence courts do not necessarily equate with specialised training. However, in Victoria, which is the 'closest example of a "one-stop shop" model for victims of family violence in Australia',[125] all judicial officers receive ongoing training.[126] Not surprisingly, then, given diverse understanding about domestic violence plus magisterial independence, variation in practice among judicial officers is reportedly widespread, with the NSW Ombudsman finding that police complained about inconsistent practices between courts and individual magistrates.[127] One senior officer commented that:

> Magistrates are the crux of it. We have two magistrates that are at opposite ends of the spectrum. One is completely supportive of implementing practices that support victims and police efforts; the other won't even meet with us. The success of local initiatives comes back to the court, and in the middle is a prosecutor – police need support from both to do their job well.[128]

Thus, very similar domestic violence allegations might be approached differently by different magistrates with a range of attitudes extending from sympathy to disbelief.[129] Hunter, in her study of Victorian magistrates' courts, found that in 55 per cent of applications, magistrates dealt with the matter in an 'impersonal' and 'bureaucratic' manner.[130] Women's stories were 'heard, filtered and interpreted' through narratives that are discordant with women's reality of domestic violence.[131] By focusing on incidents that were seen as one-off, judicial officers might not see the victim's reality of 'intimidation, a pattern of coercive behaviour, or behaviour producing fear or emotional distress'.[132] Accordingly, some magistrates did not

123 Her Majesty's Government, *Call to End Violence Against Women and Girls: Action Plan*, 2011, p. 30. See also P. Strickland and J. Beard, *Third Party Action on Behalf of Victims of Domestic Violence*, London: House of Commons Library, 2012, p. 6.

124 Strickland and Beard, above n. 123.

125 Australian Law Reform Commission, *Family Violence: A National Legal Response*, above n. 4, p. 1499.

126 Schneller, *Family Violence Courts*, above n. 79.

127 NSW Ombudsman, *Domestic Violence: Improving Police Practice*, above n. 93, p 34.

128 Ibid., p. 35.

129 Victorian Law Reform Commission, *Review of Family Violence Laws: Consultation Paper*, 2004, p. 177.

130 R. Hunter, 'Border Protection in Law's Empire: Feminist Explorations of Access to Justice', *Griffith Law Review* 11(2), 2002, 263–285, p. 272.

131 R. Hunter, 'Narratives of Domestic Violence', *Sydney Law Review* 28(4), 2006, 733–776, p. 733.

132 Hunter, *Domestic Violence Law Reform and Women's Experience in Court*, above n. 80, p. 54.

consider that a victim might be reluctant to make a statement, and were therefore critical of police who brought applications before the court without a statement from the victim.[133]

Some magistrates seem to prefer evidence of physical injury since they 'can't see fear'.[134] Researchers have identified such proclivity by magistrates in NSW[135] and Queensland.[136]

In the Northern Territory, magistrates who did not give women orders tended to frame the violence as a family problem or as something requiring counselling and as in part the responsibility of the victim, who needed to handle her partner better.[137] In these ways, violence may be seen as a response to mutual provocation[138] involving 'dysfunctional couples'.[139] The woman can/should leave the violent relationship;[140] therefore, those who stay are somehow culpable. This victim-blaming, or view that provocation is involved, can be discerned from the 54 per cent of magistrates in NSW[141] and 42 per cent of Queensland magistrates[142] who agreed with the statement that 'It takes two to tango in any relationship': 'I think that in some cases this is true. Some perpetrators are simply using victims as punching bags. Others, however, finally snap when outmatched verbally in an argument'.[143]

Some respondents in the Queensland sample also believed that domestic violence could be addressed appropriately through counselling and mediation and/or that women use proceedings for orders as a tactic in family law matters.[144] Indeed, despite claims of extreme violence, it is not unknown for magistrates to mandate

133 NSW Ombudsman, *Domestic Violence: Improving Police Practice*, above n. 93.

134 R. Wearing, 'A Search for Legal Protection from Family Violence', *Domestic Violence and Incest Resource Centre Newsletter*, 2001, 8–14, p. 13.

135 J. Hickey and S. Cumines, *Apprehended Violence Orders: A Survey of Magistrates*, Sydney: Judicial Commission of New South Wales, 1999. Discussed also by R. Simpson, *Incidence and Regulation of Domestic Violence in NSW*, Briefing Paper 4/2000, Sydney: NSW Parliamentary Library, 2000.

136 B. Carpenter, S. Currie and R. Field, 'Domestic Violence: Views of Queensland Magistrates', *Nuance* 3, 2001, 13–16, 15.

137 In their study of magistrates in the Northern Territory: H. Spowart and R. Neil, 'Stop in the Name of Love', *Alternative Law Journal* 22, 1997, 81–85, p. 82.

138 Hunter, 'Narratives of Domestic Violence', above n. 131, pp. 751, 758.

139 Hunter, *Domestic Violence Law Reform and Women's Experience in Court*, above n. 80, p. 117.

140 Hunter, 'Narratives of Domestic Violence', above n. 131, p. 758.

141 Hickey and Cumines, *Apprehended Violence Orders*, above n. 135, p. 59.

142 B. Carpenter and R. Field, 'What the Magistrates Say About Domestic Violence – Issues Relating to Queensland Magistrates Understandings of Domestic Violence' (paper presented at Domestic Violence Court Assistance Network 4th State Wide Conference, Brisbane, June 2003), p. 20.

143 Quote from an anonymous magistrate as cited in Hickey and Cumines, *Apprehended Violence Orders*, above n. 135, p. 6.

144 Carpenter and Field, above n. 142, p. 2.

mediation before granting a family violence order[145] or to encourage reconciliation and give praise for revocation of interim orders.[146]

Conclusion

Some see protection orders as a limited remedy since the family violence legislation confirms the 'view that the violence done to women by men at home is not "criminal" but "civil" only . . . [t]he man is not penalised for assaulting his wife; he is penalised, if at all, for breaking an order of the court'.[147] The efficacy of the plethora of provisions is also limited by their indeterminacy and the discretion of police, prosecutors, magistrates and judges. At the state level, law reform committee recommendations for reform such as those advocated in Victoria[148] were motivated by what has been described as legislation that was 'doctrinally weak, not providing clear statement of either the rationale or the goals', leaving both police and magistrates 'unconstrained in invoking their own beliefs and assumptions about domestic violence'.[149] As a consequence, despite numerous reforms, the onus frequently remains upon the victim to go through the application process. An example is portability of protection orders in Australia. Although all the jurisdictions' legislation allows for registration of interstate orders, the responsibility for registering is on the victim. A new national register of protection orders – one of the recommendations of the *Time for Action* report – is intended to provide the infrastructure 'to ensure ongoing protection for victims on relocation'.[150] However, it has not yet been implemented. The intention is therefore the same as the multitude of other changes made in civil family violence legislation examined in this chapter – remedying the inadequacies that have been apparent over the past three decades and improving the protection of women and children. However, as long as the laws retain a grey colour and those implementing the law view violence through the non-victim lens described in Chapter 4, then, despite law reform, added infrastructure and policy, inadequacies will remain. Any conclusion of domestic violence legislations' efficacy:

> must be tempered by a recognition of both the general limitations of law in addressing domestic violence as a coercive manifestation of power (particularly gender power), and the limited scope for change enabled through written law, as opposed to legal practice.[151]

145 Alexander, 'Women and Domestic Violence', above n. 8, p. 165.
146 Hunter, 'Narratives of Domestic Violence', above n. 131, pp. 759–761.
147 J. A. Scutt, *Women and the Law*, Sydney: The Law Book Company, 1990, pp. 458–459.
148 Victorian Law Reform Commission, *Review of Family Violence Laws*, above n. 17.
149 Hunter, *Domestic Violence Law Reform and Women's Experience in Court*, above n. 80, p. 54.
150 The National Council to Reduce Violence Against Women and their Children, *Time for Action*, above n. 18, p. 101.
151 Wilcox, *Recent Innovations in Australian Protection Order Law*, above n. 1, p. 22.

Yet, despite the problems of declining applications for orders, implementation and efficacy, the importance of obtaining a civil protection order in England and Wales has been heightened following the changes to legal aid. Under the Legal Aid, Sentencing and Punishments of Offenders Act 2012 ('LASPO'), public funding for family law remedies (such as a child arrangements order) will only be available in exceptional cases, for example domestic violence. The violence must be supported by a prescribed form of evidence, for example the existence of a protective injunction in favour of the applicant.[152] These reforms have been heavily criticised by feminist campaign groups and commentators.[153] As noted by a professional working with domestic violence victims: 'Asking for proof in this way colludes with and reinforces the idea that a) if there's no physical violence then it's not actually abusive and b) that a large number of women who allege abuse are lying'.[154]

Furthermore, research conducted by Rights of Women and Women's Aid demonstrates that the reforms are significantly restricting women's access to justice, as 'half of all women [surveyed] who had experienced or were experiencing domestic violence did not have the prescribed forms of evidence to access family law legal aid'.[155] Accordingly, access to justice has now become much more difficult for victims of domestic violence in an environment in which women are being hit the hardest by other budgetary cuts and pay freezes.

152 Civil Legal Aid (Procedure) Regulations 2012, reg. 33(2)(d). The other prescribed forms of evidence are: an unspent conviction for a domestic violence offence (reg. 33(2)(a)); a police caution (reg. 33(2)(b)); ongoing criminal proceedings (reg. 33(2)(c)); an undertaking (reg. 33(2)(e)); a multi-agency risk assessment conference (reg. 33(2)(f)); a finding of fact of domestic violence (reg. 33(2)(g)); a letter from a health professional (reg. 33(2)(h)); a Social Services letter (reg. 33(2)(i)); and a domestic violence support organisation letter (reg. 33(2)(j)). Further details and guidance are provided in Legal Aid Agency, *The Legal Aid, Sentencing and Punishment of Offenders Act (LASPO) 2012 – Evidence Requirements for Private Family Law Matters*, Legal Aid Agency, 2013.

153 See R. Hunter, 'Doing Violence to Family Law', *Journal of Social Welfare & Family Law* 33(4), 2011, 343–359; Rights of Women, *Women's Access to Justice*, above n. 88; Rights of Women and Women's Aid, *Evidencing Domestic Violence: The Facts. Legal Aid, Sentencing and Punishment of Offenders Bill*, 2012.

154 Rights of Women, *Women's Access to Justice*, above n. 88, p. 30.

155 Rights of Women and Women's Aid, *Evidencing Domestic Violence: A Barrier to Family Law Legal Aid*, 2013, p. 1

Chapter 6

Domestic violence and family law

Introduction

It is evident that violence and family law intersect frequently. Women whose former partners engage in controlling violence may find that the family law system is used as another tool to control and abuse them.[1] In extreme cases this may involve multiple applications to court on the most trivial of matters.[2] In fact, over half of the matters heard in Australian Family Court jurisdictions involve allegations of adult violence and child abuse,[3] and in England and Wales, while only 10 per cent of parental separation cases go to court, domestic violence is the most frequent welfare issue raised.[4] One Australian study found that 65 per cent of mothers and 53 per cent of fathers stated that they had either been emotionally abused or physically hurt by their spouses prior to or during separation.[5] Post-separation, 49 per cent of parents reported being subjected to controlling behaviour by the other parent, while 32 per cent indicated that they had been physically hurt.[6]

In this chapter we provide an overview of how the relevant legislation has been amended to define and address violence.[7] We also look at dispute-settlement processes and outcomes. Through case law and secondary materials, we identify differences in how the family law systems in England and Wales and Australia

1 L. Anderson, *Contact Between Children and Violent Fathers: In Whose Best Interests?*, London: Rights of Women, 1997; M. Coy et al., *Picking up the Pieces: Domestic Violence and Child Contact*, London: Rights of Women and Child and Woman Abuse Studies Unit, 2012.

2 B. Paxton, 'Domestic Violence and Abuse of Process', *Australian Family Lawyer* 17(1), 2003, 7–13.

3 T. Altobelli, 'Family Violence and Parenting: Future Directions in Practice', *Australian Journal of Family Law* 23(3), 2009, 194–221, p. 195.

4 J. Hunt and A. Macleod, *Outcomes of Applications to Court for Contact Orders After Parental Separation or Divorce*, London: Ministry of Justice, 2008.

5 R. Kaspiew et al., *Evaluation of the 2006 Family Law Reforms*, Melbourne: Australian Institute of Family Studies, 2009, p. 26. See also R. Chisholm, *Family Courts Violence Review*, Canberra: Attorney General's Department, 2009.

6 Kaspiew et al., *Evaluation of the 2006 Family Law Reforms*, above n. 5, p. 27.

7 Thanks to Dimian Grey for his invaluable research assistance with Australian case law and literature.

practise and implement protection of women and children from violence. Through the comparative analysis, we highlight the indeterminacy of the legislation and how that has the potential, for example, to translate into extensive variation in judicial determinations of a child's best interests.

It should be noted that we are not concerned with divorce law per se. In the early twentieth century, laws governing divorce in some jurisdictions moved from a fault-based system towards the concept of irretrievable breakdown of marriage.[8] In Australia, the Family Law Act 1975 (Cth) ('FLA')[9] introduced a single no-fault ground for divorce following 12 months of separation[10] – purportedly a 'god send' for women trapped in violent relationships.[11] In contrast, however, a mixed model approach is adopted in England and Wales.[12] A victim of abuse may petition for divorce after 12 months on the basis of what is commonly referred to as the 'unreasonable behaviour' fault-based fact.[13] With regards to the no-fault 'facts', a decree can be granted if the couple have been separated for two years; however, consent is required for this.[14] In the absence of the respondent's consent, an applicant must wait five years.[15]

Although in England and Wales moves were taken in 1996 to bring in a single no-fault ground for divorce,[16] this reform was eventually abandoned. Arguably, the approach adopted in Australia is to be recommended, and from 1975 to the present, there is no difficulty from a legal perspective in a woman getting a divorce from her violent husband. Nevertheless, if Family Court proceedings are initiated, domestic violence (which has taken place in the past or is current) and associated legislative provisions and processes can be very relevant in ancillary proceedings – particularly in children's matters. Before turning to that area, we first examine how violence is defined under the different jurisdictions.

Changing legislative definitions

In Australia, family violence was first defined in the 1995 amendments to the FLA. Violence was considered from the subjective view of the victim and was defined as 'conduct, being actual or threatened, towards the person, another family member or property, that *caused that person, or another family member, to fear or be apprehensive about their well being or safety*'.[17] In 2006, the government (purportedly to

8 L. Young et al., *Family Law in Australia*, Sydney: LexisNexis, 8th edn, 2013, p. 13.
9 With the exception of Western Australia the FLA became a national legislative framework.
10 FLA, ss 48–49.
11 H. Rhoades, C. Frew and S. Swain, 'Recognition of Violence in the Australian Family Law System: A Long Journey', *Australian Journal of Family Law* 24(3), 2010, 296–312.
12 See Matrimonial Causes Act 1973, s. 1.
13 Ibid., s. 1(2)(b).
14 Ibid., s. 1(2)(d).
15 Ibid., s. 1(2)(e).
16 See Family Law Act 1996, Pts I–III.
17 FLA, s. 60D (emphasis added), as amended by the Family Law Reform Act 1995 (Cth).

enable courts to better deal with 'far-fetched or fanciful' allegations of violence) added an 'objective' element of 'reasonableness' to the definition.[18] Accordingly, in one post-2006 case, for example, it was held that if the average person in the circumstances would not be fearful, then the behaviour was not to be regarded as family violence.[19]

In 2012 the definition was expanded and once again based on subjective fear. Defined as conduct that coerces or controls a family member, or causes her/him to be fearful, the definition of abuse includes assaults, sexual activity, stalking, repeated derogatory taunts, economic violence, or preventing the family member from making or keeping connections with his or her family, friends or culture.[20] A child is *exposed* to family violence 'if the child sees or hears family violence or otherwise experiences the effects of family violence'.[21]

Changing legislation and children's matters

In the early 1990s, academics criticised the Australian Family Court's failure to recognise the harm suffered to children due to family violence.[22] A 1976 matter had become notorious in the literature:

> there is no suggestion that Mr H has ever mistreated his children with the violence with which he has treated his wife. . . . Mr H's affection for his children is evident, and in assessing his potential as a custodial parent I have largely disregarded his behaviour as a husband . . .[23]

Drawing such distinctions has been labelled as 'childcare on different planets'.[24] Whereas in relation to domestic violence the safety of women and children is (ostensibly) a priority, the main concern in relation to child contact is with 'good enough fathering' and a corresponding pressure on women to facilitate an ongoing relationship.[25] In the mid-1990s, however, there seemed to be some change in

18 Family Law Amendment (Shared Parental Responsibility) Bill 2005 (Cth), Explanatory Memorandum, p. 20. In 2006 the definition was moved from FLA, s. 60D to s. 4(1).

19 *Nawaqaliva v Marshall* (2006) FLC 93-296, [118].

20 FLA, s. 4AB(2)(a)–(j).

21 Ibid., s 4AB(3).

22 J. Behrens, 'Domestic Violence and Property Adjustment: A Critique of "No Fault" Disclosure', *Australian Journal of Family Law* 7(1), 1993, 9–28; R. Graycar, 'The Relevance of Violence in Family Law Decision Making', *Australian Journal of Family Law* 9(1), 1995, 58–69.

23 *Marriage of Heidt* (1976) 1 Fam LR 11, 576.

24 M. Erkisson and M. Hester, 'Violent Men as Good-Enough Fathers? A Look at England and Sweden', *Violence Against Women* 7(7), 2001, 779–798, cited in Coy et al., *Picking up the Pieces*', above n. 1, p. 11.

25 M. Erkisson, 'Girls and Boys as Victims: Social Workers' Approaches to Children Exposed to Violence', *Child Abuse Review* 18(6), 2009, 428–455; M. Hester, 'Future Trends and Developments: Violence Against Women in Europe and East Asia, *Violence Against Women* 10(12),

judicial attitude. *JG v BG* was a major turning point, as violence was deemed to be a relevant consideration in determining the best interests of the child, 'whether or not they were the direct recipient of abuse'.[26] The same year, the Full Court (Appeals) of the Family Court of Australia demonstrated a similar increased awareness of the negative impact of violence on children in considering whether parents were appropriate role models.[27] Similarly, in England and Wales, Dame Butler-Sloss, in *Re L (A Child) (Contact: Domestic Violence)*,[28] noted that domestic violence tended to be narrowly constructed as only affecting the parents and not the child. Consequently, she stressed the importance of acknowledging that children suffer harm by witnessing domestic violence, a fact that is now recognised in statute.[29] Furthermore, Dame Butler-Sloss added 'that violence to a partner involves a significant failure in parenting – failure to protect the child's carer and failure to protect the child emotionally'.[30] These enlightened decisions took place shortly before the legislation 'caught up', with significant reforms pertinent to violence enacted in Australia first in 1995, then in 2006 and, most recently, in 2012. In England and Wales key developments include the 2001 decision in *Re L* and Practice Directions in 2008 and 2009.[31]

Before examining such developments, however, it is important to place law reform relating to child contact within the context of the Fathers' Rights Movement, which developed due to a perception that family law is biased in favour of mothers and discriminates against fathers. Key assertions of these Fathers' Rights members include that upon separation the courts overwhelmingly place children with their mothers, that some mothers are unreasonably hostile regarding paternal involvement, and that the family law system is ill-equipped to deal with such refusals.[32] The impact of this movement upon policy will be explored further

2004, 1431–1448; M. Hester, 'The Three Planet Model: Towards an Understanding of the Contradictions in Approaches to Women and Children's Safety in Contexts of Domestic Violence', *British Journal of Social Work* 41(5), 2011, 837–853; Coy et al., *Picking up the Pieces*', above n. 1, p. 11.

26 Rhoades, Frew and Swain, 'Recognition of Violence in the Australian Family Law System', above n. 11, p. 308, discussing Chisolm J's comments in *In the Marriage of JG and BG* (1994) 18 Fam LR 255.

27 *In the Marriage of Patsalou* (1994) 18 Fam LR 426.

28 [2001] Fam 260.

29 Adoption and Children Act 2002, s. 120 reformed the definition of harm as contained in Children Act 1989, s. 31(9) to include 'impairment suffered from seeing or hearing the ill-treatment of another'.

30 *Re L (A Child) (Contact: Domestic Violence)* [2001] Fam 260, 273.

31 *Practice Direction (Family Division: Residence and Contact Orders: Domestic Violence) (No. 1)* [2008] 1 WLR 1062; *Practice Direction (Family Division: Residence and Contact Orders: Domestic Violence and Harm) (No. 2)* [2009] 1 WLR 251.

32 See: R. Collier, 'Rethinking Fathers' Rights', *Family Law* 39, 2009, 45–49; R. Collier and S. Sheldon (eds), *Fathers' Rights Activism and Law Reform in Comparative Perspective*, Oxford: Hart Publishing, 2006; B. Gedolf, 'The Real Love That Dare Not Speak Its Name', in A. Bainham et al. (eds), *Children and their Families: Contact, Rights, and Welfare*, Oxford: Hart

at p. 110, with various reforms aiming to support an ongoing relationship between father and child, which in turn impacts upon cases involving domestic violence.

More broadly, this movement and attendant policy responses relate to a social panic regarding fatherless families and involve a reimagining of the notions of fatherhood and parenting, along with an erasure of motherhood. The demands of the Fathers' Rights Movement, however, can be seen to conflict with the day-to-day reality of parenting, which remains emphatically gendered. Mothers carry the overwhelming burden of childcare responsibilities, within both intact and separated families. However, as mentioned in Chapter 2, this domestic labour is frequently rendered invisible.

The reasons why mothers may resist contact by fathers are far more complex than tends to be acknowledged in official discourses; and, in order to understand maternal resistance to the involvement of fathers post-separation, Smart draws upon Tronto's theory of 'caring for' and 'caring about'.[33] Whereas 'caring for' involves 'the physical work of caring', 'caring about' is an 'intellectual concern' and is more abstract than the practical reality of undertaking daily childcare duties.[34] As 'caring for' is what mothers are considered to do naturally, it is taken for granted, and therefore rendered invisible. In contrast, fathers argue that as they also 'care about', they should be involved in their children's lives. However, a mother's resistance may be based on the father's lack of parenting skills.[35] Additionally, some fathers are unreliable with regards to maintaining contact and/or fail to spend quality time with the child during contact.[36] Nevertheless, '[w]omen who willfully resist paternal contact are constructed as renouncing the "normal" feminine traits of tenderness, softness and frailty'.[37] Consequently, a mother's hostility to contact is frequently constructed as 'implacable', even in cases in which the father has been violent towards her.[38]

Publishing, 2003, 171–200; A. Jordan, '"Dads Aren't Demons. Mums Aren't Madonnas". Constructions of Fatherhood and Masculinities in the (Real) Fathers 4 Justice Campaign', *Journal of Social Welfare and Family Law* 31(4), 2009, 419–433.

33 C. Smart, 'The Legal and Moral Ordering of Child Custody', *Journal of Law and Society* 18(4), 1991, 485–500; J. Tronto, 'Women and Caring: What Can Feminists Learn About Morality from Caring?', in A. Jaggar and S. Bordo (eds), *Gender/Body/Knowledge: Feminist Reconstructions of Being and Knowing*, New Brunswick: Rutgers University Press, 1989, 172–187.

34 Smart, 'The Legal and Moral Ordering of Child Custody', above n. 33, p. 488.

35 Anderson, *Contact Between Children and Violent Fathers*, above n. 1. See also H. Reece, 'UK Women's Groups' Child Contact Campaign: "So Long as it is Safe"', *Child and Family Law Quarterly* 18(4), 2006, 538–561.

36 H. Rhoades, 'The "No Contact Mother": Reconstructions of Motherhood in the Era of the "New Father"', *International Journal of Law, Policy and the Family* 16(1), 2002, 71–94.

37 J. Millbank, 'Castigating Mothers: The Judicial Response to "Wilful" Women in Disputes Over Paternal Contact in English Law', *Journal of Social Welfare and Family Law* 20(4), 1998, 357–376, p. 361. See also S. Day Sclater and F. Kaganas, 'Contact: Mothers, Welfare and Rights', in A. Bainham et al. (eds), *Children and Their Families*, Oxford: Hart Publishing, 2003, 155–170, for a discussion of the discourses mothers and fathers use in order to construct themselves as good parents.

38 *Re P (A Minor) (Contact)* [1994] 2 FLR 374; *Re O (Contact: Impositions of Conditions)* [1995] 2 FLR 124; *Re P (Contact) (Supervision)* [1996] 2 FLR 314. For a detailed analysis, see Millbank, 'Castigating Mothers', above n. 37.

In England and Wales in particular, it has been argued that the Fathers' Rights Movement utilises a tripartite discourse to advance its claims for post-separation involvement.[39] This involves 'rights talk', 'welfare talk' and 'care talk', with fathers arguing that as they care about their children, they have a corresponding right to contact and also that their involvement is in the child's welfare. Mothers are expected to take on the extra work in order to facilitate contact, which extends the nuclear family beyond separation. Hence, Smart argues that father's claims are not made to 'reconfigur[e] parenthood as a whole in order that both parents can share the responsibilities and disadvantages – as well as benefits: rather it is a campaign against mothers and a reassertion of paternal privilege which can be exercised at will'.[40]

Shared parenting versus protecting the children

Australia

In Australia in 1995, objects were added to Part VII of the FLA to ensure that children received adequate parenting and that parents fulfilled their parental duties,[41] while underlying principles included the right to know and be cared for by both parents.[42] The emphasis on protecting children's rights reflected Australia's signing of the Convention on the Rights of the Child[43] in 1990.

However, parenting orders could not expose children to an unacceptable risk of family violence.[44] Section 68F(g), in the newly drafted best interest list of 1995, clearly articulated the need to protect children from physical or psychological harm due to being abused or exposed to violence directed towards another person. What was not outlined, however, was *how* violence should be taken into account. The assessment of the 'best interests' checklist was (and is) an indeterminate process: 'it leaves a fairly broad discretion. The checklist does not, for example, exclude particular outcomes. Nor is any priority of factors indicated. The normative content of the list consists largely of hints – nothing stronger . . .'.[45]

39 C. Smart, 'The Ethic of Justice Strikes Back: Changing Narratives of Fatherhood', in A. Diduck and K. O'Donovan (eds), *Feminist Perspectives on Family Law*, London: Routledge, 2006, 123–138.

40 C. Smart, 'Preface', in R. Collier and S. Sheldon (eds), *Fathers' Rights Activism and Law Reform in Comparative Perspective*, Oxford: Hart Publishing, 2006, vii–xii.

41 FLA, s. 60B(1).

42 FLA, s. 60B(2).

43 Convention on the Rights of the Child, opened for signature 20 November 1989, 1577 UNTS 3 (entered into force 2 September 1990).

44 FLA, s. 69K.

45 J. Behrens, 'The Form and Substance of Australian Legislation on Parenting Orders: A Case for the Principles of Care and Diversity and Presumptions Based on Them', *Journal of Social Welfare and Family Law* 24(4), 2002, 401–421, p. 404.

The 2006 amendments had similar aims to the 1995 reforms: to maintain involvement of both parents in the lives of their children and to protect children from violence. A (now formal) presumption of shared parenting (responsibility) was introduced unless rebutted by violence.[46] If a shared parenting order is made, and if it is reasonably practical to do so, and meets the child's best interests, a court must consider making an order for equal or substantial parenting time.[47]

The pillars of protection and meaningful relationship with both parents are further evident in the best interest factors. Prior to 2006, there was a single list[48] to which the court could refer in determining the 'best interests' of the child. In 2006, these were separated into primary considerations and additional considerations. The former are: 'the benefit to the child of having a meaningful relationship with both parents', and 'the need to protect the child from physical and psychological harm from being subject to, or exposed to, abuse, neglect or family violence'.[49] Since neither primary factor was accorded more weight under the 2006 law, comparative weighting was left to the discretion of the judicial officer. Additionally, the legislative amendments did not include any further statutory guidance indicating how to apply the primary considerations in light of the additional considerations. This is particularly significant because the additional considerations included whether there had been family violence or a final domestic violence order issued.[50]

The harm pillar is narrowly worded and excludes the need to protect parents from harm;[51] consequently, parental safety was not a primary consideration until 2012. Also, given the relative heavy weighting of shared parental responsibility, consistency between family violence orders and family court contact orders continued, along with the 2006 amendments, to be a potential issue, despite s. 68K, which required that the court ensure that an order be consistent with a family violence order and not expose a person to an unacceptable risk of family violence.[52] As mentioned earlier (p. 87) if there is inconsistency, the order made under the FLA prevails.[53] Thus, judicial determinations directing contact conditions can make enforcement of a civil protection order difficult.[54]

Other changes introduced in 2006 may have contributed to victims' difficulty in alleging violence. Parents who were trying to protect children from exposure to

46 FLA, s. 61DA(4).

47 *Goode v Goode* (2006) 36 Fam LR 422; FLA, s. 65DAA(5).

48 The list appeared as subsections of FLA, s. 68F.

49 FLA, s. 60CC(2)(a)–(b).

50 FLA, s. 60CC(3)(j)–(k). The 2006 amendments excluded interim orders in the best interests list.

51 FLA, s. 60CC(2)(a).

52 However, FLA, s. 68P(1)(b) implies that the Family Court can in fact make a parenting order 'that is inconsistent with an existing family violence order.'

53 FLA, s. 68S.

54 H. Katzen, 'A Family Matter, Not a Police Matter: The Enforcement of Protection Orders', *Australian Journal of Family Law* 14(2), 2000, 119–141.

family violence or abuse could be seen as unfriendly, and the more they tried to protect children the less likely they were to succeed in doing so.[55] Under s. 117AB(1)(b) one party could be ordered to pay the costs of the other party if 'the court is satisfied that a party to the proceedings knowingly made a false allegation or statement in the proceedings'.

To address concerns raised by these particular provisions, the Family Law Legislation Amendment (Family Violence and Other Measures) Act 2011 (Cth) was passed in 2011 and came into force on 7 June 2012. Aside from amending the definition and the return of the subjective element to the definition of violence discussed at p. 103–4, other relevant changes included that the primary best interest considerations were now further qualified by s. 60CC(2A) requiring courts to give greater weight to the need to protect children from physical or psychological harm.

In addition, the word 'person', not 'child', has been used in the new legislation, so judges are directed not to make orders that expose *people* to an unacceptable risk of family violence or make orders inconsistent with a family violence order.[56] The false allegations and 'friendly parent' provisions were repealed.[57] Further, interim orders returned to the best interests list. However, the shared parenting presumption remains and the issue concerning dominance of a Family Court order over a family violence order persists.[58]

England and Wales

The developments in Australia have significant relevance for England and Wales due to the recent Family Justice Review and resulting reforms.[59] Key to these reforms is the insertion of a presumption into the Children Act 1989 that parental involvement 'will further the child's welfare'.[60] The Act continues to state that this presumption will apply unless 'there is some evidence before the court. . .to suggest that involvement of that parent in the child's life would put the child at risk of suffering harm whatever the form of the involvement'.[61] Arguably, these reforms are premised upon the anxiety around the involvement of fathers post-separation. The extent, however, to which the insertion of such a presumption is necessary,

55 FLA, s. 60CC(3)(c), (4), (4A) considered the willingness and ability of each of the child's parents to facilitate, and encourage, a close and continuing relationship between the child and the other parent. See, e.g., Chisholm, *Family Courts Violence Review*, above n. 5.
56 FLA, s. 60CG(1)(b) '. . . does not expose a person to an unacceptable risk of family violence'.
57 Family Law Legislation Amendment (Family Violence and Other Measures) Act 2011 (Cth), s. 18.
58 FLA, s. 68Q. Note that FLA, s. 68P enunciates the obligations of a court making an order or granting an injunction under this Act that is inconsistent with an existing family violence order.
59 Ministry of Justice, *Family Justice Review: Final Report*, 2011; Ministry of Justice and Department of Education, *The Government Response to the Family Justice Review: A System with Children and Families at its Heart*, 2012. See Children and Families Act 2014.
60 Children and Families Act 2014, s. 11.
61 Ibid., s. 11(3)(b).

can be queried. Moreover, it may be speculated that such a provision may cause mothers significant difficulties, not least in cases involving domestic violence. It is noteworthy that, in contrast to the recent reforms in Australia, the risk of harm is limited to the child.

When deciding issues of post-separation parenting, courts will consider what is in the best interests of the child.[62] Prior to 22 April 2014, the courts could make a residence order, which determined with whom the child should live, and a contact order, which stated that the non-resident parent should be allowed to have contact with the child. These orders have now been replaced with child arrangement orders, which will set out a child's living and contact arrangements.[63] As noted at p. 105, fathers' groups have argued that mothers were overwhelmingly granted residence and that many fathers struggled to be granted contact. However, over the years it can be seen that the perception that paternal contact is nearly always in the best interests of the child 'has passed into the realms of an incontestable "truth"'.[64] For example, in *Re O (Contact: Imposition of Conditions)*, Sir Thomas Bingham stated: 'contact is almost always in the interests of the child'.[65] What has developed is a de facto presumption in favour of contact: 'judges, magistrates and legal advisors all report[ed] that, whilst there is no statutory presumption, the courts operate on a *de facto* presumption that unless there were good reasons to the contrary there should be contact'.[66] Evidence does not suggest that the family law system discriminates against the non-resident parent, as the fathers' groups tend to maintain. On the contrary, research suggests that 'even if it's a domestic violence case, it's still the case that the courts just bend over backwards to try and assist and accommodate the father'.[67]

The approach to be adopted in domestic violence cases was initially set down by the Court of Appeal in *Re L (A Child) (Contact: Domestic Violence)*.[68] In *Re L*, Dame Butler-Sloss cautioned that in the past the assumption in favour of contact may have led courts to pay insufficient attention to allegations of domestic violence. Nevertheless, she stated that domestic violence would not be a bar to contact, but was instead a factor that would offset the assumption in favour of contact. In the course of her judgment, her Ladyship states that in domestic violence cases a court: 'should consider the conduct of both parties towards each other and towards the

62 Children Act 1989, s. 1.

63 Children and Families Act 2014, s. 12 (3): 'child arrangements order' means any order relating to any of the following: (a) with whom a child is to live, spend time or otherwise have contact, and (b) when a child is to live, spend time or otherwise have contact with any person.

64 F. Kaganas and S. Day Sclater, 'Contact Disputes: Narrative Constructions of "Good" Parents', *Feminist Legal Studies* 12(1), 2004, 1–27, p. 5. See also R. Bailey-Harris, J. Barron and J. Pearce, 'From Utility to Rights? The Presumption of Contact in Practice', *International Journal of Law Policy and the Family* 13(2), 1999, 111–131.

65 [1995] 2 FLR 124, 128.

66 Hunt and Macleod, *Outcomes of Applications to Court*, above n. 4, p. 189.

67 Ibid., p. 190.

68 [2001] Fam 260.

children, the effect on the children and on the residential parent and the motivation of the parent seeking contact'.[69] This statement recognises the possibility that some violent men seek out contact in order to carry on the abuse.[70] The preceding Practice Direction also emphasises issues of safeguarding the child *and* the resident parent from future violence.[71] Following the Practice Direction, courts are required to investigate any allegations of domestic violence – however raised – at the earliest opportunity, and consider whether a fact-finding hearing is necessary. Significantly, an allegation of domestic violence does not lead to an automatic hearing, and the direction on split hearings stipulates that a fact-finding hearing should only be ordered if the court 'takes the view that the case cannot properly be decided without such a hearing';[72] thus, the discretion resides with the judge.

Both the Practice Direction and the judgment in *Re L* have, however, been subject to criticism. In particular, it has been argued that the court places too much emphasis on the assumption that contact is good for children.[73] The extent to which contact is always in the child's best interests can be disputed.[74] Empirical research indicates that many factors can influence the extent to which contact with a non-resident parent is positive for a child. As discussed by Gilmore, what appears to be more important is the *quality* of the contact, as opposed to the *quantity* of contact.[75] Moreover, it can also be argued that the psychiatric report by Sturge and Glaser, which was made available to the Court of Appeal, does not support the contention that domestic violence should only displace the assumption in favour of contact.[76] Arguably it should lead to an assumption against contact.

With regards to the Practice Direction, Hunter and Barnett outline four conceptual difficulties. First, the adversarial approach adopted in the fact-finding hearing 'is unique to the UK'[77] and 'may appear as an unwelcome intrusion in a system with a

69 Ibid., p. 275.

70 In making her judgment, Dame Butler-Sloss draws upon Children Act Sub-Committee of the Advisory Board on Family Law, *A Report to the Lord Chancellor on the Question of Parental Contact in Cases where there is Domestic Violence*, Lord Chancellor's Department, 2000, and C. Sturge and D. Glaser, 'Contact and Domestic Violence: The Experts' Court Report', *Family Law* 30, 2000, 615–628.

71 *Practice Direction (Family Division: Residence and Contact Orders: Domestic Violence and Harm) (No. 2)* [2009] 1 WLR 251, [27].

72 *President's Guidance in Relation to Split Hearings* [2010] 2 FLR 1897, [6].

73 S. Gilmore, 'The Assumption that Contact is Beneficial: Challenging the "Secure Foundation"', *Family Law* 38, 2008, 1226–1229.

74 Ibid.

75 S. Gilmore, 'Contact/Shared Residence and Child Well-Being: Research Evidence and Its Implications for Legal Decision Making', *International Journal of Law, Policy and the Family* 20(3), 2006, 344–365.

76 Sturge and Glaser, 'Contact and Domestic Violence', above n. 70.

77 R. Hunter and A. Barnett, *Fact-Finding Hearings and the Implementation of the President's Practice Direction: Residence and Contact Orders: Domestic Violence and Harm: A Report to the Family Justice Council*, Family Justice Centre Domestic Abuse Committee, 2013, p. 16.

strong inquisitorial and conciliatory ethos'.[78] Second, the definition of domestic violence adopted therein resonates with social science perspectives, and focuses on patterns of abusive and coercive controlling behaviour.[79] This, however, conflicts with the process of fact finding, which tends to be incident based. Consequently, this 'results in underestimates of both the extent and severity of domestic violence and of its impacts'.[80] Third, a further conflict arises as the Practice Direction indicates that a causal link must exist between incidents of violence and the harm caused to the child and/or other party. This supports a decontextualised approach, which may in turn misconstrue incidents of 'mutual violence' and render irrelevant '"old" or "historic" allegations'.[81] The fourth difficulty relates to the relevance and consequence of a hearing, as a temporal dissonance exists between a contact/residence hearing – which is fundamentally forward looking, being concerned as it is with the child's future welfare – and the more 'backward-looking, criminal and public law-type' process of a fact-finding hearing.[82] Consequently, the latter may be construed 'as tangential to the main issue, and possibly a waste of time'.[83]

Furthermore, uncertainty exists regarding the relevance of a finding of violence. As Hunter and Barnett note, the Practice Direction 'does not specify any particular consequence of a finding that domestic violence has occurred'.[84] Rather, abuse is just another factor for the judge to take into account when applying the welfare test. This level of indeterminacy and discretion enables a 'spectrum of views' on the relevancy of domestic violence to a decision regarding contact and residence. These can range from domestic violence always being regarded as relevant and consequently impacting upon the court's orders, to those who consider that contact between child and parent is 'of such overriding importance that past violence should have very little effect on the court's ultimate orders'.[85] Subsequently, variations exist with regards (a) to judicial decisions to hold fact-finding hearings and (b) to the impact of domestic violence on orders.

Another significant development, prior to the 2014 reforms, was the increased judicial acceptance of shared residence orders. Traditionally, such orders were considered to be 'prima facie wrong'.[86] Over time, however, perceptions evolved, from a shared order being 'exceptionally rare' and 'only appropriate in very unusual

78 Ibid.

79 The Practice Direction defines domestic violence as 'physical violence, threatening or intimidating behaviour and any other form of abuse which, directly or indirectly, may have caused harm to the other party or to the child or which may give rise to the risk of harm': *Practice Direction (Family Division: Residence and Contact Orders: Domestic Violence and Harm) (No. 2)* [2009] 1 WLR 251, [2].

80 Hunter and Barnett, *Fact-Finding Hearings and the Implementation of the President's Practice* Direction, above n. 77, p. 16.

81 Ibid., p. 17.

82 Ibid.

83 Ibid.

84 Ibid.

85 Ibid.

86 *Riley v Riley* [1986] 2 FLR 429, 431.

circumstances',[87] to no longer being unusual.[88] Moreover, while initially orders were restricted to cases in which children could be said realistically to share their time between parental homes (i.e. 50/50 or, at the least, a 75/25 split), they were increasingly used in a symbolic manner, to send the message that 'the parents are equal in the eyes of the law, and have equal duties and responsibilities to their children'.[89] Consequently, the requirement of a link between the reality of shared time and the granting of a shared order diminished, and in one case a shared order was granted when the child's time was split approximately 85/15 between mother and father.[90] Arguably, in this situation a residence and a contact order would more accurately reflect the reality of parenting.[91] As noted by Harris-Short, 'residence and contact orders were originally intended not to deal with questions of "parental status" but to deal with practical questions of the children's living arrangement'.[92] In contrast, the appropriate vehicle for sending symbolic messages is parental responsibility, which is concerned with affording and affirming parents' equal rights and responsibilities in relation to their children.

While Fathers 4 Justice once argued that 'it is quite clear that without a statutory presumption in favour of shared parenting, the judiciary will continue to prevent fathers from enriching the lives of their children',[93] this can be questioned. There is little to suggest that a bias against fathers operates within the law. The Family Justice Review, after examining evidence from Australia, explicitly rejected any proposal to insert either a presumption of shared/equal parenting or a 'meaningful relationship' provision into legislation.[94] Drawing upon the Australian experience, concerns were expressed that such reforms not only increase litigation but also compromise the safety of children.[95] In addition, any such presumption will increase the pressure on the main care-giving parent when he/she is opposed to contact, especially in cases involving allegations of domestic violence.[96] Accordingly, the decision of the government to press ahead with its reforms is bewildering and suggests a misplaced anxiety regarding the legal position and involvement of fathers.

87 *Re H (A Minor)* (Unreported, Court of Appeal, 4 December 1997, Thorpe LJ), cited in S. Gilmore, 'Court Decision-Making in Shared Residence Order Cases: A Critical Examination', *Child and Family Law Quarterly* 18(4), 2011, 478–498, p. 486.

88 *Re A (A Child: Joint Residence/Parental Responsibility)* [2008] EWCA Civ 867, [66] (Sir Mark Potter).

89 *A v A* [2004] EWHC 142 (Fam), [2004] 1 FLR 1195.

90 *Re O (A Child)* [2009] EWCA Civ 1266.

91 S. Harris-Short, 'Resisting the March Towards 50/50 Shared Residence: Rights, Welfare and Equality in Post-Separation Families', *Journal of Social Welfare and Family Law* 32(3), 2010, 257–274, p. 261.

92 Ibid., p. 259.

93 Cited in HM Government, *Parental Separation: Children's Needs and Parents' Responsibilities: Next Steps*, 2005, p. 16.

94 Ministry of Justice, *Family Justice Review: Final Report*, above n. 59, p. 139.

95 Ibid., pp. 139–141.

96 F. Kaganas, 'Shared Parenting – a 70% Solution?', *Child and Family Law Quarterly* 14(4), 2002, 365–380.

Courts

The Family Court of Australia has been described in one study as a place where people spoke for and about the women, and that many 'felt silenced and frustrated' during their proceeding, with one woman stating that 'she was never allowed to speak about the violence she had experienced, and never felt heard'.[97] Other research has found the same silencing: '[women] felt that their experiences of family violence had been ignored, minimized or suppressed by lawyers and judges within the legal system'.[98]

This is despite many victim-based initiatives such as the Family Court of Australia's family violence strategy[99] and Family Law Council and the Family Law Section of the Law Council of Australia having best practice guidelines for lawyers to better screen for violence and to advise women about practical steps in relation to leaving home in cases of violence.[100]

Proving violence

In Australia, *M v M* established the 'unacceptable risk of harm' test, to be applied when considering allegations of child sexual abuse.[101] The risk of the allegation being true and the magnitude of the potential harm are to be considered when determining a child's best interests.[102] Courts are not required to find that past violence occurred to show that there is an 'unacceptable risk' of harm.[103] Primarily this is due to the significant difficulties in establishing that child abuse has occurred and a need for corroborative evidence.[104] This may also be the case for women:

> To the extent that it is submitted that the mother's allegations of 'horrific domestic violence' could only be accepted if objectively corroborated, we do not find that any such requirement exists. Where domestic violence occurs in

97 A respondent, cited in R. Hunter, *Domestic Violence Law Reform and Women's Experience in Court: The Implementation of Feminist Reforms in Civil Proceedings*, New York: Cambria Press, pp. 186–187.

98 D. Bagshaw et al., *Family Violence and Family Law in Australia*, Canberra: Attorney General's Department, 2010, p. 135.

99 See Family Court of Australia, *Family Violence Best Practice Principles*, 2013. An integrated family violence strategy was launched by the Family Court of Australia in 2004.

100 Family Law Council and Family Law Section of the Law Council of Australia, *Best Practice Guidelines for Lawyers Doing Family Law Work*, 2nd edn, 2010.

101 [1988] 166 CLR 69.

102 Ibid., [24]; *W v W (Abuse Allegation: Unacceptable Risk)* [2005] FamCA 892.

103 *Amador v Amador* (2009) 43 Fam LR 268, [96]. See R. Chisholm, 'Recent Cases: How to Treat Allegations of Violence and Abuse: *Amador v Amador*', *Australian Journal of Family Law* 24(2), 2010, 276–282.

104 P. Easteal and D. Grey, 'Risk of Harm to Children from Exposure to Family Violence: Looking at how it is Understood and Considered by the Judiciary', *Australian Journal of Family Law* 27(1), 2013, 59–77, p. 72.

> a family it frequently occurs in circumstances where there are no witnesses other than the parties to the marriage, and possibly their children. We cannot accept that a court could never make a positive finding that such violence occurred without there being corroborative evidence from a third party or a document or an admission.[105]

However, the Full Court, reflecting on *M and M* in *Amador*, also emphasised that:

> The best interests of a child the subject of an application for a parenting order must require that the court determine relevant allegations of violence where that can be done.... The more serious the allegation of violence the more important it will be to the child to investigate and determine the allegation. As stated earlier we regard an allegation of rape by the father or the mother to be a very serious allegation which should, if possible, be determined.[106]

How does black letter law and case authority translate into decision-making? In England and Wales, any harm a child has suffered or 'is at risk of suffering' is a relevant factor when applying the welfare test.[107] Additionally, as discussed at p. 111, courts are required to investigate any allegations of domestic violence at the earliest opportunity, and if necessary hold a fact-finding hearing. In 2010 Sir Nicholas Wall stated: 'unfortunately, it has transpired that judges have been holding unnecessary fact finding hearings, sometimes lasting several days, as a result of which they find facts which are not relevant to the ultimate issue'.[108] However, more recent research has demonstrated inconsistent implementation of the Practice Direction and some practitioners,[109] in particular the Children and Family Court Advisory and Support Service,[110] have expressed concerns that hearings are not ordered in cases in which they should be. Of particular note is the construction of domestic violence as not relevant to decisions regarding contact,[111] a failure to recognise psychological abuse as domestic violence,[112] unjustifiably restricted hearings to cases involving extreme violence and/or violence to the children,[113] disregarding disputed allegations of violence,[114] and the perpetuation of ideal victim

105 *Amador v Amador* (2009) 43 Fam LR 268, [79].
106 Ibid., [95].
107 Children Act 1989, s. 1(3)(e).
108 Sir N. Wall, 'Seeking Safety – The Whole Picture' (paper presented at the Nation Resolution Domestic Abuse Conference, London, 15 October 2010), [5].Available online at www.resolution.org.uk/news-list.asp?page_id=228&n_id=132.
109 Coy et al., *Picking up the Pieces*', above n. 1, p. 48.
110 Hunter and Barnett, *Fact-Finding Hearings and the Implementation of the President's Practice Direction*, above n. 77, p. 24.
111 Coy et al., *Picking up the Pieces*', above n. 1, p. 60.
112 Ibid., p. 51.
113 Ibid., pp. 51–52.
114 Hunter and Barnett, *Fact-Finding Hearings and the Implementation of the President's Practice Direction*, above n. 77, p. 22.

types.[115] One victim/survivor noted that the fact that she 'wasn't a weak small-voiced person' in court went against her: 'they said you don't seem like somebody who could be how I was describing I was in the relationship'.[116] Accordingly, it has been argued that in some courts 'the scope of the practice direction may be excessively curtailed'.[117]

In the final analysis, the determination of what is best for the child is the judge's responsibility, and judges may reasonably differ on what is best for children in a given case.[118] This will differ depending on whether they believe that violence has taken place and, if so, on their perception of its seriousness. Stereotypes about domestic violence, gender roles and personal prejudices may become more influential than legislation and guide judicial reasoning.[119] Stereotypes persist among some judicial officers, as evidenced in comments about violence: 'situation specific. That is, it was related to the relationship between the husband and the wife';[120] 'Somehow a product of the relationship between the parties rather than of the husband's personality';[121] an exaggeration of a histrionic woman;[122] or describing pushing or hitting with an open hand which sometimes resulted in bruising to the victim's face and body as 'of a relatively minor nature and do not appear to be part of any long term strategy on the part of the husband to cause harm to the wife or to the children'.[123]

A 2000 study of Australian relocation cases found that:

> Part of the reason that violence does not necessarily produce a decision in the favour of the 'mover' may be the fairly low frequency of judges' 'finding' that violence had taken place: less than half of those who had alleged past violence had it officially affirmed by the judge; less than a third with post-separation violence; and none of the alleged child abuse by the non-mover.[124]

The Australian Institute of Family Studies, looking at the time period before the 2006 reforms, confirmed that, unless there was strong corroborative evidence,

115 Coy et al., *Picking up the Pieces*', above n. 1, p. 51.
116 Ibid.
117 Hunter and Barnett, *Fact-Finding Hearings and the Implementation of the President's Practice Direction*, above n. 77, p. 32.
118 P. Parkinson, 'The Values of Parliament and the Best Interests of Children – A Response to Professor Chisholm', *Australian Journal of Family Law* 21(3), 2007, 213–228.
119 Katzen, 'A Family Matter, Not a Police Matter', above n. 54.
120 *Palmer v Palmer* (2010) 244 FLR 121, 123.
121 *In the Marriage of Blanch* (1998) 148 FLR 156.
122 In *T v S* (2001) 28 Fam LR 342, the full court upheld the woman's appeal and ordered a new trial.
123 Stated by Baker J in first instance hearing, as reported in the appellate judgment, *In the Marriage of A* (1998) 22 Fam LR 756, 759.
124 P. Easteal, J. Behrens and L. Young, 'Relocation Decisions in Canberra and Perth: A Blurry Snapshot', *Australian Journal of Family Law* 14(3), 2000, 234–258, p. 246.

outcomes for children were generally unaffected.[125] Overnight contact was most commonly ordered by the courts, 'irrespective of the apparent severity of the allegation and the apparent weight of evidence that supported these allegations'.[126] Other studies confirmed that, following 1995, unsupervised contact became far more common for fathers, despite allegations of family violence; supervised contact took place for increasingly serious levels of violent and abusive conduct.[127]

Even when courts have found that the mother's claims were factually sound, the father's behaviour was ignored, with ongoing father/child contact being ordered:[128] 'This outcome pattern underlines the prevalent reluctance in the family law system to sever relationships between fathers and children, even against backgrounds of severe violence and ongoing manipulation and control'.[129]

It is not surprising, then, that in the lead-up to the 2006 reforms in Australia, with its legislated presumption, concern was expressed that judicial officers would emphasise shared parenting more than the violence-related provisions in assessing the best interests of the child(ren).[130] Such concerns appear to have been well-founded, since three evaluative reports commissioned by the Commonwealth Attorney General concluded that the family law system still has a way to go in responding effectively to family violence:[131] 'An important message of these reports is that shared parenting is being agreed to, or ordered judicially, in circumstances that are harmful to children in a significant minority of cases'.[132]

These findings hold a stark warning for England and Wales, and a 2012 Rights of Women report indicates that direct unsupervised contact is frequently ordered in cases involving domestic violence.[133] In contrast, a more recent study found that

125 L. Moloney et al., *Allegations of Family Violence and Child Abuse in Family Law Children's Proceedings: A Pre-Reform Exploratory Study*, Australian Institute of Family Studies, Research Report No. 15, 2007, p. 102.

126 Ibid.

127 H. Rhoades, R. Graycar and M. Harrision, *The Family Law Reform Act 1995: The First Three Years*, University of Sydney and Family Court of Australia, 2000, p. 3.

128 R. Kaspiew, 'Empirical Insights into Parental Attitudes and Children's Interests in Family Court Litigation', *Sydney Law Review* 29(1), 2007, 131–162, p. 148.

129 R. Kaspiew. 'Violence in Contested Children's Cases: An Empirical Exploration', *Australian Journal of Family Law* 19(2), 2005, 112–143, p. 138.

130 Z. Rathus, 'Shifting the Gaze: Will Past Violence be Silenced by a Further Shift of the Gaze to the Future Under the New Family Law System?', *Australian Journal of Family Law* 21(1), 2007, 87–112.

131 Kaspiew et al., *Evaluation of the 2006 Family Law Reforms*, above n. 5; Chisholm, *Family Courts Violence Review*, above n. 5; Family Law Council, *Improving Responses to Family Violence in the Family Law System: An Advice on the Intersection of Family Violence and Family Law Issues*, 2009.

132 J. Dewar, 'Can the Centre Hold?: Reflections on Two Decades of Family Law Reform in Australia', *Australian Journal of Family Law* 24(2), 2010, 139–149, p. 142.

133 Coy et al., *Picking up the Pieces*', above n. 1.

'findings of domestic violence are taken relatively seriously',[134] with courts ordering supported, supervised or indirect contact. Nevertheless, concern was expressed regarding the 'practicability and sustainability' of such contact arrangements: 'What remains unknown is for how long supervised and supported contact arrangements remain in place, on what basis they are "progressed", and how this relates to ongoing levels of risk of harm to children and resident parents'.[135]

Changing process: emphasis on private settlement

The 1995 Australian reforms included an emphasis on private agreement. In 2006, this was further emphasised in two ways. First, 65 family relationship centres around Australia were funded by the federal government providing three free hours of mediation, information and other support.[136] Second, the legislation mandates dispute-resolution unless the court is satisfied that there are *reasonable* grounds to believe that there has been family violence or child abuse by one of the parties to the proceedings or that there is a risk of family violence.[137] Similar developments have occurred in England and Wales. Unfortunately, however, the dynamics and effects of violence may make screening problematic. In fact, one Australian survey found that 40 per cent of those who had experienced past or current family violence and who had gone to a family relationship centre did not disclose the violence,[138] and in England and Wales mediation has been required 'despite domestic violence having been raised as an issue'.[139] While the move towards mediation seems set to continue, concerns have been expressed that 'ensuring the safety of children and adults receives insufficient attention'.[140]

The vast majority of family law matters in Australia and England and Wales settle without a hearing; some end with a consent order. Interestingly, in Australia, the court is not obliged to consider the primary or secondary considerations in the case of a consent order.[141] In England and Wales, courts, following the Practice Direction, are required to ensure that a consent order accords with the welfare principle under

134 Hunter and Barnett, *Fact-Finding Hearings and the Implementation of the President's Practice Direction:* above n. 77, p. 57.

135 Ibid.

136 See Family Relationships Online, 'Family Relationship Centres – Helping Families Build Better Relationships'. Available online at www.familyrelationships.gov.au/Brochuresand-Publications/Pages/FRC_Brochure_May_2008.aspx.

137 FLA, s. 60I(9)(b).

138 Bagshaw et al., *Family Violence and Family Law in Australia*, above n. 98, p. 21.

139 Coy et al., *Picking up the Pieces*', above n. 1, p. 36.

140 Her Majesty's Inspectorate of Court Administration, *Domestic Violence, Safety and Family Proceedings: Thematic Review of the Handling of Domestic Violence Issues by the Children and Family Court Advisory and Support Service and the Administration of Family Courts in her Majesty's Courts Service*, 2005, p. iv. See Coy et al., *Picking up the Pieces*', above n. 1, p. 35.

141 FLA, s. 60CC(5). If the court is considering whether to make an order with the consent of all the parties to the proceedings, it may, but is not required to, have regard to all or any of the matters set out in subs. (2) or (3).

s. 1(1) of the Children Act 1989.[142] However, concern has been expressed that such orders may be inadequately judicially scrutinised, due to time constraints and lack of information.[143] Generally it is considered that parental consensus and agreement is preferable to, and more successful than, judicially imposed arrangements.[144] Accordingly, in England and Wales a study of 308 parental separation cases found that only 11 per cent went to a final contested hearing.[145] In the vast majority of cases the parents managed to reach an agreement that was not imposed upon them by the court. A significant aspect of this 'settlement culture' has been the availability of in-court conciliation schemes, which 'typically consist of a brief meeting at court where parents are encouraged to negotiate arrangements with the assistance of family justice system professionals'.[146] However, research suggests that the fact that the parents have come to an agreement does not necessarily indicate parental satisfaction, especially if the parties felt under pressure. Furthermore, many parents find the process distressing.[147] Moreover, conciliation is not successful at resolving 'embedded conflict' between the parents, such as anger, hurt and distrust, and thus parental conflict may remain.[148]

American research has shown that 'women in custody and divorce mediation have reported that mediation enabled them to have a voice and express their views, and they perceived that they had equal influence over the terms of the agreements'.[149] However, the 'equal' influence may be an issue if there is a history of violence:[150]

> Women who have been the targets of family violence and abuse are at a disadvantage in a specifically legal context when it comes to exercising personal agency and asserting their views. This is because violence has been used to create and maintain an imbalance of power between the perpetrator and the

142 *Practice Direction 12J – Child Arrangements and Contact Order: Domestic Violence and Harm*, 22 April 2014, [7].

143 Hunter and Barnett, *Fact-Finding Hearings and the Implementation of the President's Practice Direction*, above n. 77, pp. 58–59.

144 R. Bailey-Harris, J. Barron and J. Pearce, 'Settlement Culture and the Use of the "No-Order" Principle', *Child and Family Law Quarterly* 11(1), 1999, 53–62; Hunt and Macleod, *Outcomes of Applications to Court*, above n. 4.

145 Hunt and Macleod, *Outcomes of Applications to Court*, above n. 4, p. 167.

146 L. Trinder and J. Kellett, *The Longer-Term Outcomes of In-Court Conciliation*, Ministry of Justice Research Series 15/07, 2007. See also L. Trinder and J. Kellett, 'Fairness, Efficiency and Effectiveness in Court-Based Dispute Resolution Schemes in England', *International Journal of Law Policy and the Family* 21(3), 2007, 322–340.

147 Trinder and Kellett, 'Fairness, Efficiency and Effectiveness', above n. 146, p. 329.

148 L. Trinder, 'Conciliation, the Private Law Programmes and Children's Wellbeing: Two Steps Forward, One Step Back?', *Family Law* 38, 2008, 338–342.

149 J. Kelly, 'Power Imbalance in Divorce and Interpersonal Mediation: Assessment and Intervention', *Mediation Quarterly* 13(2), 1995, 85–98.

150 H. Astor, *Guidelines for Use if Mediating in Cases Involving Violence Against Women*, Canberra: Australian Government Publishing Service, 1992.

> target, a dynamic that may remain entrenched even after separation ... The philosophy of mediation requires the parties to be able to negotiate on an equal footing ... but in relationships where there has been violence, 'habits of coercion and compliance' make this ideal difficult to achieve.[151]

Shuttle mediation – having the two parties in separate rooms or on a conference phone call – has been suggested as a means of leveling the playing field. However, even with this arrangement the abuser may control the dynamics and the agenda.[152]

Although there might be disadvantages to mediation for victims of violence, Juliet Behrens concludes that family dispute resolution ('FDR') may be better than judicial hearings at providing protection:

> However the possibility that it will be preferable for a woman to use FDR rather than going to court should not be ignored. Practitioners may develop working relationships with particular FDR practitioners with specialist understanding of how such violence affects women and children. Outside of Family Relationship Centres legal practitioners can be present during FDR with such a practitioner ...[153]

Property division and violence

Arguments against violence being relevant to property division include 'a reluctance to return to a fault-based approach' and 'a fear of "opening the floodgates"'.[154] Those who disagree and believe that violence should be considered in property settlement have argued that the impacts of violence will 'often make a victim's role, whether as child-carer, homemaker or in maintaining a position in the paid workplace, more onerous'.[155] Moreover, it could be argued that financial redistribution may be a 'socially acceptable' means by which to hold 'parties responsible for their culpable behaviour'.[156] This may consequently operate as a deterrence as well as ensuring that a victim has the financial means to escape the abuse.[157]

151 B. Fehlberg and J. Behrens with R. Kaspiew, *Australian Family Law: The Contemporary Context*, Melbourne: Oxford University Press, 2008, pp. 189–90, as cited in J. Behrens, 'Women and Family Law', in P. Easteal (ed.), *Women and the Law in Australia*, Sydney: LexisNexis, 2010, 192–212, p. 197.

152 This dynamic was witnessed when one of the authors was a support person in a telephone shuttle.

153 Behrens, 'Women and Family Law', above n. 151, p. 197.

154 NSW Law Reform Commission, *Relationships*, Report No. 113, 2006, p. 219. The report thoroughly critiques arguments for and against both positive and negative contributions.

155 Ibid., p. 221.

156 C.J. Lee, 'Escaping the Lion's Den and Going Back for Your Hat – Why Domestic Violence Should be Considered in the Distribution of Marital Property Upon Dissolution of Marriage', *Pace Law Review* 23(1), 2002, 273–312, pp. 279–280.

157 Ibid., p. 295.

Women who have experienced violence tend to get a lower percentage of the property pool either with a court determination or private ordering.[158] A range of factors may explain this, including the impacts of continuing dominance, control and fear on the decision-making process. Women may want to settle quickly in order to secure safety for themselves and their children. This also needs to be placed in the context of the unequal financial impact of divorce. As noted by Lee:

> there is no longer any doubt that women experience the heaviest financial losses in the divorce equation. Battered women suffer doubly from this inequity, because economic control is often a facet of the coercive relationship between them and their abusers.[159]

Financial redistribution upon divorce is one means by which the law can effectively readdress concerns regarding the invisibility of reproductive labour and the devastating impact that domestic violence can have upon the life of victims. However, as Lee has commented in relation to the regime in New York, it can be seen in some jurisdictions that personal prejudices of judges 'as well as societal biases against battered women are working to deny these victims financial remedies against their partners'.[160]

In Australia, how has the Family Court dealt with this situation? In 1997, although rejecting the idea of domestic violence as a negative contribution, the Full Court provided clear authority that family violence is a relevant factor in determining a party's contribution under FLA, s. 79(4). A party must prove, on the balance of probabilities:

> a course of violent conduct by one party towards the other during the marriage *which is demonstrated* to have had a *significant adverse impact* upon that party's contributions to the marriage, or, put the other way, to have made his or her contributions significantly more arduous than they ought to have been, that is a fact which a trial judge is entitled to take into account in assessing the parties' respective contributions . . .[161]

Referred to as the *Kennon* 'principle', 'adjustment' or 'factor', subsequent Full Court decisions have further discussed its meaning. The term 'which is demonstrated'

158 G. Sheehan and J. Hughes, *Division of Matrimonial Property in Australia*, Australian Institute of Family Studies, Research Paper 25, 2001; G. Sheehan and B. Smyth, 'Spousal Violence and Post-Separation Financial Outcomes', *Australian Journal of Family Law* 14(3), 2000, 102–118.

159 Lee, 'Escaping the Lion's Den and Going Back for Your Hat', above n. 156, p. 275.

160 Ibid., p. 281.

161 *In the Marriage of Kennon* (1997) 22 Fam LR 1, 24 (Fogarty and Lindenmayer JJ) (emphasis added). In addition, in considering FLA, s. 75(2) factors the court can look at any disability resulting from the violence.

has been interpreted as that a trial judge may infer from the evidence that the result of the violence would be an *effect* on the party's contributions. The test of that *effect* would be whether there was evidence of a significant adverse impact and/or a discernible impact upon the person's ability to make contributions.[162]

Other phrases in *Kennon* have been the object of Full Court scrutiny. In dismissing the appeal of a federal magistrate's adjustment of five per cent, the Full Court held that the term 'course of conduct' is a broad one; it need not be frequent to constitute a course of conduct, although a degree of repetition is required. The conduct alleged against the husband apparently comprised 'arguments or incidents' occurring about twice yearly. The court also affirmed that a five per cent adjustment in favour of the wife, taking account of the husband's violence towards her, was not beyond a reasonable exercise of the trial magistrate's discretion.[163]

Application of *Kennon* is indeed, like so much in family law, discretionary. Brewster FM (as he then was) has refused to apply the *Kennon* principle:[164]

> I am not bound by the dicta of the Court in *Kennon* and for the reasons I have given I decline to follow it. I believe that contributions are to be measured in absolute terms and not weighted by considerations of arduousness, whether caused by domestic violence or otherwise.[165]

Further, he explicitly refers to a prior matter in which he 'declined to extend the principle to apply to only verbal violence'.[166]

The effect of *Kennon* has been limited:

> The *Kennon* factor, which has attracted little superior reconsideration, is a complex combination of vague phrases and it is not surprising then that, like some legal practitioners, there are judicial officers who appear to be unclear about the test in general and whether it fits the facts in a particular case. When combined with the Full Court's exhortation that this is a principle of exceptional application, this may well contribute to the fact that there are so few successful claimants.[167]

162 *Spagnardi v Spagnardi* [2003] FamCA 905.

163 *Stevens v Stevens* (2005) FLC 93-246.

164 Brewster FM outlined his reasons in detail in *Palmer v Palmer* (2010) 244 FLR 121, 131–136 and as an addendum in *Brandow v Brandow* [2010] FMCAfam 1026, [27]. In *Palmer v Palmer* (2010) 244 FLR 121, 134–135, his Honour suggested that, if violence is to be relevant to contributions, perhaps a more appropriate consideration would be to reduce the contributions of the perpetrator to the welfare of the family, rather than to increase the weight of the victim's contributions.

165 *Palmer v Palmer* (2010) 244 FLR 121, 135.

166 Ibid., p. 130.

167 P. Easteal, C. Wynter Warden and L. Young, 'The *Kennon* "Factor": Issues of Indeterminacy and Floodgates', *Australian Journal of Family Law* 28, 2014, 1–28.

An analysis of cases in the years immediately following *Kennon* found that in 17 of 27 unreported first instance matters in which the wife argued for an increased contribution because of violence, adjustments were made in her favour.[168] However, a 2013 study of *Kennon* adjustment applications between 2006 and 2012 found a downward trend in the number of claims in that time period (57 first instance hearings), in success (only 42 per cent) and in percent of adjustment (a mean of 7.3 per cent.)[169]

Those who succeeded were able to show that long-standing violence had been perpetrated (usually physical) and that it had impacted on women's contribution:

> cases that have taken domestic violence into account (both prior to and subsequent to the decision in *Kennon*) have referred variously to the victim's contributions as having been made more 'arduous', 'onerous' or 'difficult' by virtue of the violence.[170]

An important variable correlating with an adjustment that was found in the 2013 study was whether or not the allegations of violence were corroborated by evidence in addition to that of the alleged victim and perpetrator.[171]

Exactly how much adjustment is again discretionary and may depend upon a range of variables. For instance, in one matter the adjustment was reduced by the judge's view that the violence was in part the effect of the husband's 'war related psychological condition'.[172] In another case, although the federal magistrate made a 10 per cent contribution-based adjustment in favour of the wife, he was critical of the concept of the adjustment as 'compensatory', stating that the judges in *Kennon* must have intended it as a 'perhaps symbolic recognition of the extraordinary efforts of one's spouse in persisting with contributions in the face of enormous and unjustified adversity'.[173]

Such ambivalence is not uncommon. Some regard *Kennon* as too limited and advocate for a statutory incorporation of violence:

> The provisions of the *Family Law Act 1975* (Cth) dealing with the distribution of property should refer expressly to the impact of violence on past contributions and on future needs, as recommended by the ALRC in *Equality Before the Law* (ALRC 69).[174]

168 S. Middleton, 'Domestic Violence, Contributions, and s 75(2) Considerations: An Analysis of Unreported Property Judgments', *Australian Journal of Family Law* 15(3), 2001, 230–260.
169 Easteal, Wynter Warden and Young, 'The *Kennon* "Factor"', above n. 167, p. 10–1.
170 Middleton, 'Domestic Violence, Contributions, and s. 75(2) Considerations', above n. 168, p. 233.
171 Easteal, Wynter Warden and Young, above n. 167, 'The *Kennon* "Factor"', p. 19.
172 *Cuneo v Cuneo* [2006] FamCA 158, [90].
173 *Kozovski v Kozovski* [2009] FMCAfam 1014, [99].
174 Australian Law Reform Commission, *Family Violence – Improving Legal Frameworks*, Consultation Summary Paper 1, 2010, p. 32.

The Family Law Council also has advocated for violence as a negative contribution under s. 79 apart from any effect it had on the assessment of victim's contribution.[175] There have also been recommendations that 'relevant financial losses might include – for the victim – lost earnings and medical expenses and – for the perpetrator – the costs of defending criminal or civil proceedings or a damages liability'.[176]

Arguably, a similar approach is adopted in England and Wales. As with other jurisdictions, the courts are granted a wide discretion with regards to financial orders. The key criteria are set down in Matrimonial Causes Act 1973, s. 25, which includes eight non-hierarchal factors a court must take into account. Additionally, guiding principles are found in the key cases of *White v White*[177] and *Miller v Miller; McFarlane v McFarlane.*[178] In the former case Lord Nicholls stated that, implicitly, the objective of the court 'must be to achieve a fair outcome',[179] and further that in 'seeking to achieve a fair outcome, there is no place for discrimination between husband and wife and their respective roles',[180] which significantly acknowledges the contribution and value of reproductive labour. A further key element to ensuring fairness is ensuring that, as far as possible, the needs of both parties are met.

Domestic violence may become relevant by virtue of s. 25(2)(g), which states that the court shall have regard to 'the conduct of the parties, if that conduct is such that it would in the opinion of the court be inequitable to disregard it'.[181] Thus, the question becomes whether it was inequitable to disregard the violence. If so, 'the proper way to have regard to conduct is as a potentially magnifying factor when

175 Ibid.

176 S. Middleton, 'Matrimonial Property Reform: Legislating for the "Financial Consequences" of Domestic Violence', *Australian Journal of Family Law* 19(1), 2005, 9–28, p. 11.

177 [2000] UKHL 54, [2001] 1 AC 596, 604.

178 [2006] UKHL 24, [2006] 2 AC 618.

179 [2000] UKHL 54, [2001] 1 AC 596, 604.

180 Ibid., p. 605. For a detailed analysis of the law and issues relating to ancillary relief, see, e.g.: A. Diduck, 'Ancillary Relief: Complicating the Search for Principle', *Journal of Law and Society* 18(2), 2011, 272–300; J. Eekelaar, 'Property and Financial Settlement on Divorce – Sharing and Compensating', *Family Law* 36, 2006, 754–758; B. Hale, 'Equality and Autonomy in Family Law', *Journal of Social Welfare and Family Law* 33(1), 2011, 3–14; J. Herring, 'Why Financial Orders on Divorce Should be Unfair', *International Journal of Law, Policy and the Family* 19(2), 2005, 218–228; J. Miles, 'Principle or Pragmatism in Ancillary Relief: The Virtues of Flirting with Academic Theories and Other Jurisdictions', *International Journal of Law, Policy and the Family* 19(2), 2005, 242–156; J. Miles and R. Probert (eds), *Sharing Lives, Dividing Assets: An Interdisciplinary Study*, Oxford: Hart Publishing, 2009.

181 For an overview of some of the key cases, principles and issues relating to the specific issue of conduct and ancillary relief, see, e.g.: A. Bainham, 'Men and Women Behaving Badly: Is Fault Dead in English Family Law?', *Oxford Journal of Legal Studies* 21(2), 2001, 219–238, pp. 226–231; C. Burton, 'Affairs, Acrimony and Accusations: What is a Judge to Do', *Family Law* 42, 2012, 447–451; A. Commins, 'Ancillary Relief and Sexual (Mis)conduct: Negating Need: K v L', *Family Law* 40, 2010, 642–646; N. Howell, 'Super Injunctions: Gasp or Gulp at Conduct', *Family Law* 41, 2011, 832–834; L. Tyler, 'Obvious and Gross', *Family Law* 96, 2010, 5–8.

considering the wife's position under the other subsections and criteria'.[182] Consequently, 'it places her needs ... as a much higher priority to those of the husband';[183] nevertheless, the court should not aim to be 'punitive or confiscatory for its own sake'.[184] Significantly, however, only exceptionally severe forms of domestic abuse will amount to conduct 'inequitable to disregard'. Such cases have included attempted murder, wounding and attempted rape.[185] It is, however, disconcerting that 'lesser' forms of violence will be disregarded. For example, in *S v S (Non-Matrimonial Property: Conduct)*,[186] despite convictions for assault occasioning actual bodily harm, such conduct was not construed as being sufficiently grave to be inequitable to disregard. Thus, 'it is only in the gravest of cases – generally those in which the life of one party has been placed in jeopardy – that the courts have accepted that such conduct should influence the outcome of an application'.[187] This, consequently and problematically, limits the application of the 'conduct' factor in cases involving domestic violence, and in doing so, as Inglis notes, the courts 'have failed to reflect society's increasing condemnation of such behaviour'.[188] Indeed, arguably it normalises a certain amount of violence in a relationship.

The other key issue is the extent to which the violence that has been inflicted should be required to correlate with a financial impact on the victim in order for it to be considered relevant. Significantly, in *H v H (Financial Relief: Attempted Murder as Conduct)* the court spoke at length regarding how the conduct had had a detrimental financial impact on the victim and, in noting that the wife's needs should take priority to those of the husband, commented that this was because 'the situation the wife now finds herself in is, in a very real way, his fault'.[189] While this was undoubtedly the situation in this case, should this be necessary? In the United Kingdom, Inglis has concluded that there need not be a link between the violence and the financial impact.[190] In contrast, in the United States, Lee notes that in cases where a victim has been awarded a larger share, judges frequently point 'to the

182 *H v H (Financial Relief: Attempted Murder as Conduct)* [2005] EWHC 2911 (Fam), [2006] 1 FLR 990, 999.

183 Ibid. The Law Commission is currently involved in a consultation regarding the concept of need, along with the issues of matrimonial property and agreements: see Law Commission, *Matrimonial Property, Needs and Agreements Supplementary Consultation*, Consultation Paper No. 208, 2012. However, neither the issues of conduct nor domestic violence are being considered as part of this evaluation.

184 *H v H (Financial Relief: Attempted Murder as Conduct)* [2005] EWHC 2911 (Fam), [2006] 1 FLR 990, 999.

185 Ibid.; *H v H (Financial Provision: Conduct)* [1994] 2 FLR 801.

186 [2007] EWHC 2793 (Fam), [2007] 1 FLR 1496.

187 A. Inglis '"The Ordinary Run of Fighting"? – Domestic Violence and Financial Provision', *Family Law* 33, 2003, 181–185, p. 185.

188 Ibid.

189 *H v H (Financial Relief: Attempted Murder as Conduct)* [2005] EWHC 2911 (Fam), [2006] 1 FLR 990, 999.

190 Inglis, '"The Ordinary Run of Fighting"?', above n. 187.

diminished earning capacity of the domestic violence victim'.[191] As Lee notes, however, '[i]t would be incongruous to minimize the harm caused by the husband merely because the abuse did not have the result of destroying the woman's earning capacity'.[192]

Conclusion

Much of family law is primarily conducted 'in the shadow' of the law, with most matters settling outside of the court. There are numerous variables that mitigate against disclosure of violence: denial, minimising, rationalising and shame. Screening for family dispute resolution is at best uncertain, which is of great concern as so many of the amendments are underpinned with the apparent misunderstanding that cases of violence will in fact be effectively filtered out at different stages of the Family Court processes. Unless effectively screened, women who have experienced violence may be forced to continue to be exposed to situations that increase their vulnerability to the perpetrator's abusive behaviours, since a number of the amendments to the FLA are focused on the father having a meaningful relationship with his child(ren) and sharing in decision-making. As we have seen, similar reforms have recently been implemented in England and Wales.

In addition, much of family law is painted grey. As noted in these pages, the best interests test is the quintessential indeterminate provision. When judicial officers make decisions, including those on violence, they consider the evidence and arguments in court in light of the legislation at the time, their beliefs about violence and their 'own understanding of what is and is not good for children':[193]

> The ultimate creation of the picture of a child's best interest involves the compilation of all of the variables into a collage. What parts are emphasized in the story varies both between the judges and by an individual in different cases.[194]

There is little case authority in Australia for working through the different provisions of Part VII, and the few authorities differ on order and emphasis.[195] It is difficult to see how judicial decision-making can be altered by legislative amendment because decisions are based on 'considerations that are not to be found in the legislation at

191 Lee, 'Escaping the Lion's Den and Going Back for Your Hat', above n. 156, p. 290.

192 Ibid.

193 Parkinson, 'The Values of Parliament and the Best Interests of Children', above n. 118, p. 213.

194 Easteal, Behrens and Young, 'Relocation Decisions in Canberra and Perth, above n. 124, p. 257.

195 This results in a lack of uniformity in judicial approach. See, e.g., relocation research such as P. Easteal and K. Harkins, 'Are We There Yet? An Analysis of Relocation Judgments in Light of Changes to the Family Law Act', *Australian Journal of Family Law* 22(3), 2008, 259–278.

all'.[196] 'Unacceptable risk', 'apprehension' or 'fear', 'adverse impact', 'arduousness', 'reasonable grounds' and 'inequitable to disregard' are all indeterminate terms open to interpretation by mediators, lawyers and judicial officers. Physical battery continues to be emphasised; for instance, one reason that alleged violence was not accepted by the court as an issue meriting weighting in relocation decision-making was that the abuse was verbal.[197]

Although some improvements have been made – such as the recognition in Australian Law that domestic violence against mothers is also harmful to children – practices and recent reforms may only restrict their effectiveness. This is particularly the case with regards to legislative amendments aimed at facilitating parental involvement. While the rights-based arguments developed by fathers' groups seem to have influenced the reforms, we call upon judges and practitioners in their practices and interpretations to respond to their ethical responsibility to acknowledge the suffering of domestic violence victims.

196 Parkinson, 'The Values of Parliament and the Best Interests of Children', above n. 118.
197 Easteal and Harkins, 'Are We There Yet?', above n. 195.

Chapter 7

Battered women who kill[1]

Homicide is emphatically gendered. Statistics illustrate that men kill more than women, and are more likely to be victims of homicide.[2] Significantly, however, women are far more likely to be killed by a former or current partner. In England and Wales in 2010/11 only five per cent of the 435 male victims over 16 were killed by an (ex)partner, compared with 47 per cent of the 201 female victims.[3] In addition, research into marital murder in Australia identified that in the vast majority of the homicides in which the female partner was the killer, there was a history of domestic violence perpetrated against her.[4] The killing is often preceded by an incident of violence that is outside the usual repertoire of the abuser. For example, the batterer may have started to sexually abuse the children. This exceptional occurrence has been coined 'the turning point'; it goes beyond what the woman has already learned to live with, or is prepared to continue living with.[5] This was the case with Queensland woman, Susan Falls, who in 2010 poisoned her violent partner and then shot him in the head.[6] After 20 years of domestic violence, the 'turning point' for her was when her husband threatened to kill their youngest child.[7] She was acquitted of both murder and manslaughter. Was that a typical outcome though? A key concern is that women who kill their partners have

1 Australian material in this chapter is drawn in part from P. Easteal and A. Hopkins, 'Women and Criminal Law: Defences to Homicide', in P. Easteal (ed.), *Women and the Law in Australia*, Sydney: LexisNexis, 2010, 109–130; and P. Easteal, *Less Than Equal: Women and the Australian Legal System*, Sydney: Butterworths, Ch. 3.

2 K. Smith (ed.), S. Osborne, L. Lau and A. Britton, *Homicides, Firearm Offences and Intimate Violence 2010/11: Supplementary Volume 2 to Crime in England and Wales*, London: Home Office, 2012.

3 Ibid., p. 20.

4 For example, research found that in 10 of the 11 cases involving a female offender, where presence or absence of violence was known, there had been a history of physical battering of the woman: P. Easteal, *Killing the Beloved: Homicide Between Adult Sexual Intimates*, Canberra: Australian Institute of Criminology, 1993, p. 74.

5 See J. Blackman, *Intimate Violence*, New York: Columbia University Press, 1989.

6 *R v Falls* (Unreported, Supreme Court of Queensland, 2–3 June 2010, Applegarth J).

7 As reported in numerous media outlets. See, e.g., I. Woods, 'Abused Wife Cleared of Murdering Husband', *Sky News*, 4 June 2010. Available online at http://news.sky.com/home/world-news/article/15643281.

historically been treated harshly in comparison to their male counterparts. Writing in the 1990s, McColgan noted:

> for every example of a woman who kills in circumstances where she fears for her life at the hands of her abuser and receives a significant custodial sentence, examples may be found of men who kill 'nagging', unfaithful or departing wives or girlfriends, and who escape comparatively lightly.[8]

In this chapter we look at how defences to homicide may be gendered and hence a problematic 'fit' (or plea) for women like Susan Falls.

Defences to homicide

In theory the battered woman who kills can claim to have acted in self-defence.[9] If so, the burden then falls upon the prosecution to disprove either that there was a belief that the killing was necessary or that it was reasonable, beyond reasonable doubt.[10] If the prosecution fails to do this, the defendant is entitled to a complete acquittal. For the offence of murder, the prosecution must establish beyond reasonable doubt that the defendant had the specific intent to kill.[11] Failing this, the prosecution can only expect a manslaughter verdict.

There is evidence to suggest that, in Australia, cases in which battered women kill are most often resolved by way of either a plea of guilty to manslaughter on the basis of lack of intent[12] or provocation, or by the jury finding the woman guilty of manslaughter but not guilty of murder. Stubbs and Tolmie found that of 25 cases before Australian courts between 2000 and 2007, almost two-thirds (64 per cent) ended in a guilty plea.[13] Pleading guilty to manslaughter appears to be the default

8 A. McColgan, 'General Defences', in L. Bibbings and D. Nicholson (eds), *Feminist Perspectives on Criminal Law*, London: Cavendish, 2000, 137–158, p. 148.

9 Criminal Code Act 1995 (Cth), Sch. 1, s. 10.4; Criminal Code 2002 (ACT), s. 42; Crimes Act 1900 (NSW), s. 418; Criminal Code Act (NT), Sch. 1, s. 43BD; Criminal Code 1899 (Qld), ss 271–272; Criminal Law Consolidation Act 1935 (SA), s. 15; Criminal Code Act 1924 (Tas), Sch. 1, s. 46; Crimes Act 1958 (Vic), ss 9AC, 9AE; Criminal Code Compilation Act 1913 (WA), App B, s. 248.

10 'The question to be asked . . . is whether the accused believed upon reasonable grounds that it was necessary in self-defence to do what he did': *Zecevic v DPP (Vic)* (1987) 162 CLR 645, 657 ('*Zecevic*').

11 The requisite mental state that must be proved to establish a murder charge varies from jurisdiction to jurisdiction, ranging from intent to kill, at the top end of the scale, down to reckless indifference to the probability that one's actions will cause grievous bodily harm, at the bottom.

12 R. Bradfield, *The Treatment of Women Who Kill Their Violent Male Partners Within the Australian Criminal Justice System* (PhD Thesis, University of Tasmania, 2002), cited in J. Stubbs and J Tolmie, 'Battered Women Charged With Homicide: Advancing the Interests of Indigenous Women', *Australian and New Zealand Journal of Criminology* 41(1), 2008, 138–161, p. 149.

13 Ibid., p. 148.

option: an action that women may choose to avoid the risk of a murder conviction[14] but which has the potential for a significantly lengthy sentence or even a mandatory life sentence to be imposed.[15]

The lack of acquittals is not surprising if it is remembered that legal defences for murder have evolved through a history of male-perpetrated homicides within a male-dominated court system.[16] Next we look at these gendered common law legacies, and law reform attempts to remove such biases from self-defence.

Self-defence

Killing in self-defence is said to be an act that is rational or reasonable to the ordinary person in the face of serious threat.[17] The common law requirements are that the person believed that his/her actions were both necessary in self-defence (an honest belief) and that there were 'reasonable grounds' for that belief. In all Australian jurisdictions,[18] apart from Queensland, legislation explicitly states that the 'reasonableness' of the response must be considered from the point of view of the defendant,[19] taking into account how *he/she perceives*[20] or *believes his/her circumstances*[21] to be, and not just those of the 'reasonable man'.[22] However, the tests

14 Robyn Kina (discussed in Ch. 2), for instance, was found guilty of murder and was sentenced to life imprisonment in 1988. The verdict was set aside on 29 November 1993 by the Queensland Appellate Court. See www.boewilliams.com.au/documents/001.Kina.21.11.93.pdf for the judgment.

15 They may be persuaded to so plead by the fact that sentences for women convicted of manslaughter are lower on average than for men. See F. Stewart and A. Frieberg, *Provocation in Sentencing Research Paper*, Melbourne: Sentencing Advisory Council, 2nd edn, 2009, p. 76.

16 Easteal found that of the 150 marital murders in Australia between 1989 and 1991, 121 were committed by men (81 per cent): Easteal, *Killing the Beloved*, above n. 4, p. 138. This gender breakdown does not seem to have changed with time. Of 80 such homicides in Australia from 2007–2008, 62 involved male offenders (78 per cent): M. Virueda and J. Payne, *Homicide in Australia 2007–08*, Canberra: Australian Institute of Criminology, 2010, p. 19.

17 Easteal and Hopkins, 'Women and Criminal Law', above n. 1.

18 Criminal Code 2002 (ACT), s. 42; Crimes Act 1900 (NSW), s. 418; Criminal Code 1983 (NT), Sch. 1, s. 29; Criminal Law Consolidation Act 1935 (SA), s. 15; Criminal Code 1924 (Tas), Sch. 1, s. 46. Victoria has retained the *Zecevic* formulation in the sense that the second limb of the test directs attention to whether there were 'reasonable grounds' for the belief. However, Crimes Act 1958 (Vic), ss 9AE and 9AH, as amended in 2006, require that the question of 'reasonable grounds' be addressed within the social context of family violence where appropriate.

19 Criminal Code 1899 (Qld), ss 271–272. Australian Law Reform Commission, *Family Violence – A National Legal Response*, 2010, p. 628 states: 'The Queensland formulation of self-defence is distinct from that of other jurisdictions in that it does not expressly recognize the contextual nature of reasonableness, and requires acts of self-defence to be undertaken in response to an unlawful assault'.

20 Criminal Code Act 1995 (Cth), Sch. 1, s. 10.4; Criminal Code 2002 (ACT), s. 42; Crimes Act 1900 (NSW), s. 418.

21 Criminal Law Consolidation Act 1935 (SA), s. 15; Criminal Code 1924 (Tas), s. 46.

22 *R v Conlon* (1993) 69 A Crim R 92, 98 (Hunt CJ); *R v Hawes* (1994) 35 NSWLR 294.

'are not intended to be so context dependent as to become fully subjective' and a woman may not be acquitted even if the jury accepts that she 'genuinely believed her actions were necessary' but not *reasonable*,[23] perhaps having killed while her partner was asleep,[24] with a weapon[25] or after enlisting the support of others.[26]

Part of the source of differing views of *reasonable* belief that one's life is in danger comes from how the events preceding the homicide are viewed. If the antecedent violence is minimised, it becomes difficult, or even impossible, to equate it with criminal offences of the same calibre as assaults outside the home. In *R v Osland*, for example, Victorian Supreme Court Justice Hedigan, in sentencing, went over the prolonged history of domestic violence, which included violent beatings, punching, poking, prodding, very violent threats with guns and promises of beatings and death. However, he used the trivialising description of 'difficult relationships' as a cover term for these acts:

> There was some debate in the course of the plea as to whether [general deterrence] involved the imposition of a sentence sufficient to deter battered women from taking the law into their own hands in respect of battering males, or to deter pre-meditated crimes of this kind or simply to deter homicide between spouses in difficult relationships.[27]

Despite the wording in the various pieces of legislation, it appears that courts will resort to assessing the *reasonableness* of the offender's actions against the jurors' and judges' personal values and experiences, which, for the most part, are unlikely to accord with those of the woman under judgment.[28] For instance, it is not uncommon in Australian case law (see *Russell*[29] and *Yeoman*[30] as examples), for judges to refer to Chief Justice Hunt's stricture in *Roberts*:

> It has been made very clear by the courts that the taking of a human life, even within the context of domestic violence, will not be reviewed with leniency.

23 Easteal and Hopkins, 'Women and Criminal Law', above n. 1, pp. 117–118.
24 *DPP v Secretary* (1995) 129 FLR 39; *Secretary v DPP* (1996) 5 NTLR 96.
25 *R v Whalen* (Unreported, Supreme Court of New South Wales, 12 October 1990, Wood J). The defendant received a five-year non-parole period: *R v Russell* [2006] NSWSC 722; *R v Yeoman* [2003] NSWSC 194.
26 *R v Morabito* (1992) 62 A Crim R 82. The court took a harsh view of the planning involved in this case and sentenced Morabito to ten-and-a-half years' minimum. See also Victorian Law Reform Commission, *Defences to Homicide: Final Report*, 2005, pp. 61–62.
27 *R v Osland* (Unreported, Supreme Court of Victoria, 12 November 1996, Hedigan J). Osland and her son were tried for murder: he was acquitted at retrial; she was convicted and spent the full bottom sentence of nine years incarcerated.
28 *R v Malott* [1998] 1 SCR 123, [43] (L'Heureux-Dubé and McLachlin JJ), where the judges recognised 'that a battered woman's experiences are generally outside the common understanding of the average judge and juror'.
29 *R v Russell* [2006] NSWSC 722, [87] (Newman AJ).
30 *R v Yeoman* [2003] NSWSC 194, [44] (Buddin J).

> Not even extreme domestic discord can ever be an excuse for the victim to take the law into her own hands or to extinguish the life of the aggressor.[31]

In contrast, in England and Wales, the common law defence of self-defence states that a belief in serious harm does not need to be reasonable, but only genuine, thus applying a subjective test.[32] A mistaken and unreasonable belief in serious harm will not by law exclude the defence, provided the jury believes that it was genuinely held. However, while the belief in harm is viewed from a subjective point of view, the level of defensive force used is judged from an objective standard, and the objective notion of reasonableness once again enters the equation. The test can be expressed as: 'a person may use such force as is [objectively] reasonable in the circumstances as he [subjectively] believes them to be'.[33] Concerns may be expressed, however, at the ease with which the courts appear to classify a battered woman's belief in serious harm as mistaken. In *R v Oatridge*[34] the Court of Appeal acquitted the defendant after she had stabbed and killed her partner, on the basis that the trial judge had failed to direct the jury with regards to the issue of mistaken belief. However, the stabbing occurred in the context of a violent relationship, during an altercation in which the victim was intoxicated, uttered threats to kill the defendant and squeezed the defendant's throat. In such circumstances it is, arguably, difficult to understand why her belief in serious harm was considered to be mistaken.

Expert evidence may prove invaluable in assisting the judge and/or the jury to comprehend 'what it must really be like to live in a situation of ongoing violence'[35] and why the battered woman's ultimate response could be seen as 'truly' reasonable.[36] Experts, with or without reference to battered woman syndrome ('BWS'), can not only help judges and jurors to learn more about the violent antecedents in specific cases, but also address the relationship of common law legacies of proportionality,

31 *R v Roberts* (Unreported, Supreme Court of New South Wales, 31 August 1989, Hunt J), p. 5.

32 *R v Williams* (1984) 78 Cr App R 276.

33 *R v Owino* [1996] 2 Cr App R 128, 134, as cited in Law Commission, *Partial Defences to Murder: Final Report*, Report No. 290, 2004, p. 74.

34 (1991) Cr App R 367.

35 Victorian Law Reform Commission, *Defences to Homicide: Final Report*, above n. 26, p. 134, advocated that judges and jurors need to learn 'what it must really be like to live in a situation of ongoing violence'. R. Schuller, B. McKimmmie and T. Janz, 'The Impact of Expert Testimony in Trials of Battered Women Who Kill', *Psychiatry, Psychology and Law* 11(1), 2004, 1–12, found that respondents in Australia and Canada were more likely to support a woman's claim of self-defence if they had been provided with either battered woman syndrome ('BWS') or situational expert testimony.

36 BWS, recognised as a sub-category of post traumatic stress disorder, is a term that refers to both a certain pattern of violence and the psychological and emotional consequences for its recipient. The concept of 'learned helplessness' is used to describe battered women's loss of ability to see options out of the situation, or to predict whether their natural responses will protect them when the pattern of violence is random and variable. It was first successfully used in Australia in proving self-defence in *R v Kontinnen* (Unreported, Supreme Court of South Australia, 30 March 1992, Legoe J).

immediacy and necessity (no other recourse) to battered women.[37] Professional qualifications in psychiatry or forensic psychology, and the language of 'syndromes' and diagnostic criteria, may make it easier to have expert evidence admitted.[38] According to Freckton, however, the forensic status of BWS is 'under a grave cloud'.[39]

Evidence of BWS was admitted in Helen Secretary's second trial. She had killed her de facto partner while he was asleep.[40] Similarly, BWS has been used successfully to acquit others in Australia (where homicide did not conform to traditional common law legacies), such as in *R v Falls*[41] and *R v MacDonald*.[42] These homicides involved premeditation. For example, in 2006 in Victoria, Clare McDonald, nicknamed 'Sniper Woman' by the press, had dressed herself in camouflage and had shot her husband with a rifle.[43] Both Falls and MacDonald were acquitted of murder. In both cases evidence was provided explaining the severe abuse these women had suffered at the hands of their victims and the resultant psychological effects of that abuse.

Consultant psychiatrist Danny Sullivan gave evidence that MacDonald's position in her marriage fitted the psychological state of 'learned helplessness'.[44] In this case, domestic violence evidence was adduced to prove both the subjective and objective limbs of the self-defence test – i.e. the existence of the belief and whether there were reasonable grounds for it.[45] Under the 2005 Victorian reforms, such evidence may include: the history of and violence within the relationship; the cumulative effect, including the psychological effect, of the violence on the person; the social, cultural and economic factors that impact upon the person; the general

37 Discussed in Easteal, *Less Than Equal*, above n. 1, pp. 53–54.

38 L. Walker, *Terrifying Love: Why Battered Women Kill and How Society Responds*, New York: Harper & Row, 1989, p. 39. Walker's theory has been the subject of much criticism in the literature with attacks upon both her methodology and her essentialising of battered women's experiences.

39 I. Freckleton, 'Psychiatrists as Expert Witnesses and Report Writers', in W. Brookbanks and A. Simpson (eds), *Psychiatry and the Law*, New Zealand: LexisNexis, 2007, 229–263, p. 257. See *Osland v The Queen* (1998) 197 CLR 316, 370–378 (Kirby J). Justice Kirby discusses the legitimacy, issues and application of BWS as expert evidence.

40 The details of the homicide and Secretary's trials are discussed further at p. 136.

41 Unreported, Supreme Court of Queensland, 4 June 2010, Applegarth J.

42 Unreported, Supreme Court ofVictoria, 4 March 2006, Nettle J.

43 Media coverage is particularly common when the facts include premeditation and/or accomplices, and women are not infrequently sensationalised, labelled with terms such as 'The Black Widow' or 'Sniper Woman'. Other cases, such as Tasha Wright's acquittal in 2002 in New South Wales ('NSW'), do not seem to be as controversial – no doubt because Tasha stabbed her de facto in the chest during a physical altercation. In another acquittal, Dagmar Stephenson stabbed her husband during a struggle. After 32 hours of deliberation, the jury acquitted her after deciding that she had perceived herself at risk of sustaining grievous bodily harm or being killed.

44 See n. 36.

45 Although Victorian legislation does not explicitly state that the reasonableness of the defendant's actions must be judged in response to *her* circumstances.

nature and dynamics of relationships affected by family violence, including the possible consequences of separation; the psychological effect of violence on people in such relationships; and social or economic factors that impact on people in such relationships.[46]

In England and Wales, the relevance of such expert testimony is, however, less certain. In *R v Martin*[47] the Court of Appeal made it clear that as a standard rule expert/psychiatric evidence would not be admissible when assessing whether the level of force used was reasonable in the circumstances the defendant believed himself to be in. Lord Woolf noted that 'the jury are entitled to take into account the physical characteristics of the defendant',[48] which clearly renders gender a relevant consideration. However, his Lordship continued:

> we would not agree that it is appropriate, except in exceptional circumstances which would make the evidence especially probative, in deciding whether excessive force has been used to take into account whether the defendant is suffering from some psychiatric condition.[49]

Indeed, the court doubted the overall relevancy of such evidence:

> the only other issue, as to which the medical evidence could possibly be relevant . . . is as to what Mr Martin believed the situation to be when he fired the shots. However, he himself gave evidence as to this and it was for the jury to decide the extent to which they could act on his evidence.[50]

While the *Martin* case concerned a male defendant who shot a burglar, and whose depression and anxiety was caused in no small part by the frequency with which his property was burgled, by analogy it seems that BWS is unlikely to be relevant in cases involving abused women who kill.

Indeed, self-defence has not proved a successful defence for women in England and Wales and it is interesting to note that during the recent reform process, self-defence was not seriously considered as a defence for women who kill their abusive partners. This is particularly significant given the political, media and public sympathy expressed towards householders who maim or kill burglars,[51] including a recent reform to permit householders to use disproportionate force to defend

46 Crimes Act 1958 (Vic), s. 9AH(3). A number of other relevant evidence types are also stated in this section.

47 [2001] EWCA Crim 2245.

48 Ibid., [67].

49 Ibid.

50 Ibid., [68].

51 See House of Commons, *Legal Aid, Sentencing and Punishment of Offenders Bill*, Hansard Debates, 31 October 2011, cols 620–626 (Kenneth Clarke).

themselves from burglars, provided it is not grossly disproportionate.[52] Gender dimensions with regards to property, belongings and domestic violence can be seen to permeate the perspective that 'a man's house is his castle',[53] and thus he should be permitted to defend his property and belongings to the highest degree, whereas women who are subjected to abuse are expected to flee. It is interesting that victims of burglary are not confronted with comments such as 'why did he/she just not leave?', while such is expected of abused women. These perspectives fail to acknowledge the overall dynamic and power structures of abusive relationships and the general failure of society and law adequately to protect victims of domestic violence.

Moreover, in Australia, Falls' and McDonald's acquittals for killings that lacked immediacy and were seemingly disproportionate to the antecedent violence, are the exception to the norm. In looking through media reports and judgments, one gets the distinct impression that the objective component of the test means that self-defence continues to fit most comfortably (and most often) with the situation where a person has reacted spontaneously and proportionally to an immediate threat.[54] This is despite both case law and legislative change to the contrary. For example, within the common law, starting with the High Court case of *Zecevic*,[55] there has been a subtle and small shift from the perception that 'reasonable' must include a threat of immediate harm. Two jurisdictions in Australia have also sought to dispel this shadow of the common law through amendments to the law.[56] The amended legislation in Western Australia makes no reference to an assault, and goes further to make clear that a person may act in self-defence even where he/she is defending him/herself, or another, against 'a harmful act that is not imminent'.[57] The definitions in the other Australian jurisdictions' provisions do not specifically require that the accused be responding to an imminent threat.[58]

52 Crime and Courts Act 2013, s. 43. See also S. Lipscombe, *Householders and the Criminal Law of Self Defence*, House of Commons Library Standard Note, 2013.

53 E. Coke, *The Third Part of the Institutes of the Laws of England*, first published 1681, 2012 edn, London: The Lawbook Exchange, p. 162.

54 This reasoning was evident when an NSW Aboriginal woman charged with murder was released on bail. The magistrate accepted that the defence would rely on evidence that she was a "battered wife" acting in selfdefence' and noted that there were 'references to [the victim] going towards her with arms stretched out as if to grab her throat': C. Mardon, 'Murder Accused Acted in Self-Defence: Court', *Illawarra Mercury*, 28 March 2013. Available online at www.illawarramercury.com.au/story/1394545/murder-accused-acted-in-self-defence-court/.

55 162 CLR 645 (Wilson, Dawson and Toohey JJ).

56 Crimes Act 1958 (Vic), s. 9AH(1)(c) and Criminal Code Compilation Act 1913 (WA), App. B, s. 248(4)(a).

57 Criminal Code Compilation Act 1913 (WA), App. B, s. 248(4)(a).

58 Criminal Code Act 2002 (ACT), s. 42; Crimes Act 1900 (NSW), s. 418; Criminal Code (NT), Sch. 1, s. 43BD(2); Criminal Code Act 1899 (Qld), s. 271(2); Criminal Law Consolidation Act 1935 (SA), s. 15; Criminal Code Act 1924 (Tas), Sch. 1, s. 46.

In contrast, in England and Wales the requirement of imminence remains a strict test and little legal or political will appears to exist to widen its scope. Indeed, during the recent reform process the Law Commission dismissed the application of the 'hostage analogy', which was adopted by the Canadian Supreme Court in *R v Lavallee*[59] and also considered by McColgan.[60] This analogy highlights that the law would be unlikely to require a person held hostage, who knows or fears that he/she will be killed or seriously injured in the next few days, to wait until the threat is carried out. Rather, the law would permit him/her to use a pre-emptive strike against his/her captors. While in *Lavallee* it was maintained that the situation of an abused woman is similar to that of a hostage,[61] the Law Commission disagreed, maintaining that, unlike a battered woman, a hostage is held captive against their will, 'without access to outside help'.[62] The Commission further stated: 'it would be wrong in principle for the law to permit the use of pre-emptive force in protection of oneself or another against a perceived threat if there are other means of protection available to the person concerned'.[63]

Such a statement, however, draws upon problematic assumptions regarding not only the emotional, physical and financial ability of an abused person to ask for help, but also the efficacy of any available protection. Moreover, it is difficult to reconcile this perspective with the more lenient and sympathetic attitude shown towards victims of burglary, as discussed at p. 135.

Furthermore, in Australia, there is no doubt that immediacy continues to have a bearing on prosecutors, jurors and judges when it comes to evaluating the honesty and reasonableness of a claim of self-defence. In *R v Vandersee*, for instance, James J highlighted the period of time that 'elapsed between the last provocative conduct on the part of the deceased before he went to bed and the killing of the deceased'.[64] Evidently James J was not considering that 'the danger that women who are habitually and seriously abused face is not so much embodied in a single attack as in the day to day experience of living under continuous threat'.[65] He, like many others, perhaps could not understand how unreasonable an 'immediate' response could be for someone who is, in all likelihood, not as strong, aggressive or as skilled in assault, and particularly a person who has been beaten down (externally and internally), usually for an extended period of time.

Helen Secretary, who shot her violent partner Darren Nelson while he slept, is a case in point.[66] For eight years, she and her six children had lived in conditions of

59 [1990] 1 SCR 852, 889.

60 A. McColgan, 'In Defence of Battered Women Who Kill', *Oxford Journal of Legal Studies* 13(4), 1993, 508–529, p. 518.

61 [1990] 1 SCR 852.

62 Law Commission, *Partial Defences to Murder*, 2003, p. 205.

63 Ibid.

64 *R v Vandersee* [2000] NSWSC 916, [145] (James J).

65 J. Stubbs and J. Tolmie, 'Battered Woman Syndrome in Australia', in J. Stubbs (ed.), *Women, Male Violence and the Law*, Sydney: Federation Press, 1994, 192–225, p. 196.

66 *DPP v Secretary* (1995) 129 FLR 39 (Kearney J); J. Tolmie, 'Case and Comment: Secretary', *Criminal Law Journal* 20(4), 1996, 223–230.

horrific abuse. Police had been called, weapons confiscated, refuge sought at a shelter and a restraining order taken out but never enforced. On several occasions she was raped and beaten and Nelson began to tell people that he intended to kill her and had dug her grave. Events on the day preceding the homicide were typical. After a 'terror [road] trip' with assault and death threats, Darren Nelson punched Helen in the mouth, attempted to suffocate her and then went off to sleep, threatening that when he woke up 'I'm fucking (inaudible) haven't fuckin' started'.[67] While he slept, Helen got a rifle from the back of the utility and shot him. The trial judge held that self-defence was unavailable under the Northern Territory's Criminal Code Act, which required the defensive action to be in response to an imminent danger.[68] Because the aggressor was asleep, rather than in the act of attacking her, the judge held that he had no 'actual or apparent present ability to effect his purpose'.[69] Consequently, at what turned out to be her first trial, Helen Secretary was convicted of manslaughter on the basis of provocation.

There are other common law factors aside from imminence that appear to remain informal considerations when assessing the reasonableness of the accused's belief and the necessity of her actions. These include proportionality and whether the woman had attempted to retreat from the situation. In relation to the first criterion, one judge commented:

> In addition, it must not be forgotten that the appellant acted upon that belief by viciously bludgeoning the deceased to the head and body, and stabbing him to the upper abdomen. This was grossly disproportionate, as well as being objectively unnecessary in order to defend herself.[70]

This disapproval of the apparent disproportionality between the threat and the way in which the women killed their partners is clearly based on masculine assumptions about one-on-one conflict situations. Again, however, in Victoria self-defence may be claimed when 'responding to a harm that is not immediate' and the 'response involves the use of force in excess of the force involved in the harm or threatened harm'.[71]

67 S. Gray, 'Aboriginal Women and the "Battered Woman" Syndrome: Secretary v The Queen', *Indigenous Law Bulletin* 4(13), 1998, 18–19.

68 In fact, the Criminal Code Act 1983 (NT), Sch. 1, s. 28(f) stated that 'necessary' deadly force was justified 'in the case of any person acting in self-defence . . . where the nature of the assault being defended is such as to cause the person using the force reasonable apprehension that death or grievous bodily harm will result'. This was repealed and replaced by s. 29(2)(a), which states that the act is self-defence if it is necessary and if it is a reasonable response (s. 29(2)(b)) in the circumstances as the person perceives. The changes to self-defence were recommended by the Law Reform Committee of the Northern Territory, *Self Defence and Provocation*, 2000.

69 *DPP v Secretary* (1995) 129 FLR 39, 71 (Kearney J)

70 *Creamer v The Queen* [2012] VSCA 182, [51] (Weinberg J).

71 Crimes Act 1958 (Vic), ss 9AH(1)(c)–(d).

Without an understanding about the dynamics of violence and its effects (discussed in Chapter 4), the court and jurors may ask how the act of killing could be reasonable when, from their perspective, the battered woman could have left the violent relationship. For example, in *R v McIntyre,* McInerney J stated, '[s]he was free to leave at any time'.[72]

Due to these common law artefacts and a lack of acceptance or understanding of the battered woman's subjective reality, a broader interpretation of reasonably believing one's life is in danger is not the norm, despite legislative reform. Thus, between 1980 and 2000 across Australia, of 65 cases in which a battered woman killed, self-defence was raised by less than one-third (21) and only nine were successful.[73] Helen Secretary, mentioned earlier, was one of those found guilty (of manslaughter). The Court of Appeal in the Northern Territory overturned her conviction in 1996[74] and she was acquitted at her retrial in 1998. However, only those threats uttered by her violent partner before he went to sleep were constructed as the threat, and not the background of domestic violence in general.

Manslaughter

We have shown that in order to use self-defence the court must believe that the defendant's actions were a reasonable response to the threat from the victim. But what happens if the prosecutor, judge and/or jury do not believe that the woman's actions were reasonably proportionate to the threat? She is then likely to be charged with, plead guilty to, or be convicted of manslaughter.[75] As mentioned in the opening of this chapter, the norm in Australia is for the battered woman to plea bargain. This occurs most frequently with indigenous women – 80 per cent of these accused plea-bargained.[76]

The most common basis for a manslaughter plea is lack of intent or unintentionality.[77] A study by Rebecca Bradfield on intimate homicide cases in

72 *R v McIntyre* (Unreported, Supreme Court of New South Wales, 15 March 1996, McInerney J), 22.

73 See Bradfield, *The Treatment of Women Who Kill Their Violent Male Partners*, above n. 12, p. 194, cited in Victorian Law Reform Commission, *Defences to Homicide: Options Paper*, 2003, p. 110.

74 *R v Secretary* (1996) 5 NTLR 96 (Martin CJ, Angel and Mildren JJ); Tolmie, Case and Comment: Secretary', above n. 66.

75 *R v Bradley* (Unreported, Supreme Court of Victoria, 14 December 1994, Coldrey J). In a case with one of the most horrific litanies of antecedent violence, the judge would not allow self-defence stating, at pp. 150–151: 'There is no right to take the life of a person because their conduct is outrageous and despicable. Courts must be careful not to appear to condone vigilante actions or to suggest that self-help in eliminating the problem of the battering males is legally acceptable'. Bradley was convicted of manslaughter and received a suspended prison sentence.

76 Stubbs and Tolmie, 'Battered Women Charged With Homicide', above n. 12, p. 148.

77 See, e.g.: *R v Duncan* [2010] NSWSC 1241; *R v Kulla Kulla* [2010] VSC 60; *R v Doolan* [2010] NSWSC 615; *R v Yeoman* [2003] NSWSC 194; *R v Coldbeck* [2005] VSC 187; *Western Australia v Walley* [2008] WASCA 12.

New South Wales ('NSW') over the period 1985 to 2000 found that there were 16 cases where women who had killed their spouses successfully relied on a lack of intent for murder (i.e. lack of intent to kill or inflict grievous bodily harm) and, as a result, were convicted of manslaughter instead of murder. She writes: 'My reading of the cases suggests that lack of intent was being used as a de facto defence of "domestic violence"'.[78]

Within this sub-set of cases, the killing usually took place in the context of intoxication and during a struggle,[79] with the judge reaffirming lack of intent: 'Yours is an unintended offence'.[80] For instance in *R v Kennedy*,[81] *R v Melrose*[82] and *R v Yeoman*,[83] each offender was a battered indigenous woman who had stabbed to death her respective violent partner. Each had pleaded guilty to manslaughter by reason of an unlawful and dangerous act. All three were placed on good behaviour bonds.

However, other defendants with similar long-term antecedents, aboriginality and intoxication have been sentenced to prison. In *R v Hudson*[84] although King J stated that '[f]rom the material, it appears that all the family members of both families, yours and Edward's, expected that you would be the one who died as a result of this relationship',[85] the defendant was sentenced to a three-year non-parole prison term.

What of those cases where an intention to kill or inflict grievous bodily harm appears to be evident from the facts? There are a number of possible bases for arguing manslaughter: diminished responsibility, excessive self-defence, provocation and, in Queensland, battered person's defence. Their availability and actual wording vary depending upon the jurisdiction. In England and Wales, battered women are limited to two partial defences: diminished responsibility and loss of control (which replaced provocation in 2010).[86]

78 R. Bradfield, 'Women Who Kill: Lack of Intent and Diminished Responsibility as the Other "Defences" to Spousal Homicide', *Current Issues in Criminal Justice* 13(2), 2001, 143–167, p. 151.
79 See, e.g.: *R v Kulla Kulla* [2010] VSC 60, in which an Aboriginal woman was given three years non-parole; *R v Coldbeck* [2005] VSC 187, in which the defendant received a non-parole period of four years and six months.
80 *R v Doolan* [2010] NSWSC 615, [14] (Grove J): sentenced to non-parole period of three years and nine months.
81 [2000] NSWSC 109.
82 [2001] NSWSC 847
83 [2003] NSWSC 194.
84 [2013] VSC 184.
85 Ibid., [23].
86 See Coroners and Justice Act 2009, ss 52–56, which came into force in October 2010.

Diminished responsibility or substantial impairment by abnormality of mind

The defence of diminished responsibility or substantial impairment of the mind is available in the Australian Capital Territory ('ACT'), NSW, Queensland and the Northern Territory.[87] It is not used very often by battered women: one case out of ten in an early 1990s sample[88] and eight cases in Rebecca Bradfield's NSW sample.[89] In at least four of these, the killing followed a prolonged history of domestic violence. In three of the four, the female offender also successfully claimed provocation and was sentenced on the basis of both partial defences.

In contrast, in England and Wales the defence of diminished responsibility has historically proved more successful for women who kill their abusers. McColgan's survey of cases in 1996 and 1997 highlighted that: 'women indicted for homicide were about twice as likely as men to be convicted of section 2 manslaughter [diminished responsibility]'.[90] The concern with this approach, however, is that while an abused woman avoids a murder conviction and the attendant life sentence, the focus and excusatory factors relate to the woman's mental state, as opposed to the violence she suffered. Hence, she is partially excused because she was suffering from an 'abnormality of mental functioning', as opposed to recognising that she killed because of the violence she suffered and the fear she felt. Rather than looking at the actions of the deceased, '[h]er personality, characteristics, and problems are on trial'.[91] Frequently, evidence of mental abnormality has been provided by the admission of expert testimony claiming that the accused, at the time of the killing, suffered from post-traumatic stress disorder or BWS.[92]

Consequently, both the defence and the expert testimony constructs battered women as crazy and incapable,[93] which maintains and perpetuates stereotypical constructions of female offenders as either mad or bad. This mad/bad binary can be seen to be based on the construction of deviant women as masculine, unfeminine women, or as suffering from disturbed hormones, which subsequently impacts upon their treatment within the criminal justice system.[94] A woman who is constructed as bad may receive an unduly harsh sentence, as she is doubly

87 Crimes Act 1900 (ACT), s. 14; Crimes Act 1900 (NSW), s. 23; Criminal Code 1899 (Qld), s. 304A; Criminal Code Act (NT), Sch. 1, s. 159.

88 Easteal, *Killing the Beloved*, above n. 4, p. 132, from her in-depth sample of cases from NSW and Victoria.

89 Bradfield, *The Treatment of Women Who Kill Their Violent Male Partners*, above n. 12.

90 McColgan, 'General Defences', above n. 8, p. 140.

91 K. O'Donovan, 'Defences for Battered Women Who Kill', *Journal of Law and Society* 18(2), 1991, 219–240, p. 230. See also McColgan, 'In Defence of Battered Women Who Kill', above n. 59.

92 See p. 132 for an overview of BWS. See also K. O'Donovan, 'Law's Knowledge: The Judge, The Expert, and The Battered Woman, and Her Syndrome', *Journal of Law and Society* 20(4), 1993, 427–437.

93 O'Donovan, 'Defences for Battered Women Who Kill', above n. 91, pp. 229–230.

94 F. Heidensohn, *Women and Crime*, London: McMillan Press, 2nd edn, 1996.

deviant or, if considered to be mad, may be compelled to undergo (in)appropriate medical treatment.[95]

This over reliance on the defence of diminished responsibility and expert testimony in England and Wales has led to the production of certain 'intelligible gendered scripts' against which the behaviour of a battered woman charged with murder is judged.[96] In order to avoid a murder conviction, women must conform to standards of 'appropriate femininity',[97] which consists of the following: domesticity, which 'requires women to be good and caring mothers, loyal and supportive wives, competent housewives'; sexuality – 'neither promiscuous nor frigid. The single woman is chaste and demure. On marriage her sexuality is unlocked by her husband upon whom her sexual fulfilment depends';[98] and pathology – women are 'emotional, irrational, compulsive, unstable, fickle and contrary . . . weak, neurotic and prone to illness'.[99] Women who contravene such scripts are constructed to be socially and legally 'unintelligible'.[100]

Moreover, these scripts are not only constructed via gender norms, but also with regards to race and ethnicity, as amply demonstrated by the cases of Zoora Shah[101] and Kiranjit Ahluwalia.[102] Both women were convicted for murder when they killed their abusive partners. During their appeals, notions of 'Asian honour' and the existence of appropriate expressions of shame permeated the judgments. Zoora's appeal was rejected and she was considered to be insufficiently shameful. Indeed, she was described as an 'unusual woman' whose way of life, in the opinion of the court, was such that 'there might not have been much left of her honour to salvage'.[103] In contrast, Kiranjit's appeal was upheld. The court considered that she had demonstrated that she experienced a high level of shame, not only for killing her husband, but also for the abuse suffered,[104] and on retrial she was convicted for manslaughter on the grounds of diminished responsibility. Zoora, on the other hand, fell within the 'bad' side of the mad/bad dichotomy and her conviction for murder was upheld.[105]

95 Ibid., p. 95.
96 See, e.g.: A. Carline, 'Women Who Kill Their Abusive Partners: From Sameness to Gender Construction', *Liverpool Law Review* 26(1), 2005, 13–44; A. Carline, 'Zoora Shah "An Unusual Woman"', *Social and Legal Studies* 14(2), 2005, 215–238; D. Nicolson, 'Telling Tales: Gender Discrimination, Gender Construction and Battered Women Who Kill', *Feminist Legal Studies* 3(2), 1995, 185–206.
97 Nicolson, above n. 96, pp. 185–188.
98 Ibid., pp. 188–189.
99 Ibid.
100 Carline, 'Women Who Kill Their Abusive Partners', above n. 96.
101 *R v Shah* [1998] EWCA Crim 1441.
102 *R v Ahluwalia* (1993) 96 Cr App R 133. See also *R v Sangha* [1997] 1 Cr App R (S) 202.
103 *R v Shah* [1998] EWCA Crim 1441, [67].
104 See Carline, 'Zoora Shah', above n. 96; A. Phillips, 'When Culture Means Gender: Issues of Cultural Defence in the English Courts', *Modern Law Review* 66(4), 2003, 510–531.
105 See further Carline, 'Zoora Shah', above n. 96.

Excessive self-defence

In Australia, excessive self-defence was abolished at common law in *Zecevic*[106] in 1987, but was subsequently reintroduced by statute in NSW,[107] South Australia,[108] Western Australia[109] and in Victoria,[110] where it is also an offence – defensive homicide. In jurisdictions where excessive self-defence is not laid down in statute, the belief that the defendant's actions were necessary will be a matter taken into account as a mitigating factor during sentencing when mandatory life sentences do not apply. In England and Wales the introduction of a new partial defence of excessive self-defence was rejected by the Law Commission on the basis that it considered that reforming the defence of provocation would 'be the simplest and most effective way of ameliorating the deficiencies' of the law.[111]

In Australian states where excessive self-defence is permitted, a genuine belief is sufficient in and of itself to warrant a verdict of manslaughter despite what is seen as an objectively unreasonable over-reaction to the threat. As with self-defence, however, it may be difficult for a jury to understand, in the context of masculine entrenched values and beliefs, why the defendant genuinely believed that to kill her partner was the only option. Her reactions may just be seen as excessive,[112] particularly if she used a weapon and the victim was unarmed.[113] In recent Australian cases where women argued excessive self-defence successfully or were found guilty of defensive homicide, each defendant was being attacked at the time of the killing.[114] The sentence appears usually to involve some imprisonment. In 2012, Edwards pleaded guilty to defensive homicide and received a sentence of a non-parole period of almost five years. Justice Weinberg identified a history of domestic violence:

> You suffered domestic violence at the hands of the deceased on a number of occasions over the years. Indeed, as at the time of the fatal incident, an

106 162 CLR 645.

107 Crimes Act 1900 (NSW), ss 418, 421, as reintroduced under the Crimes Amendment (Self-Defence) Act 2001 (NSW). The reasons for the reintroduction are outlined in New South Wales, *Parliamentary Debates*, Legislative Assembly, 28 November 2001, p. 19093 (Bob Debus): [If a person] 'honestly believes he is acting in self-defence but who uses more force than is reasonable in the circumstances, [he] should not be liable for murder but be liable for the lessor offence of manslaughter'.

108 Criminal Law Consolidation Act 1935 (SA), s. 15(2).

109 Criminal Code Compilation Act 1913 (WA), App B, s. 248(3).

110 Crimes Act 1958 (Vic), s. 9AD, reintroduced in 2005.

111 Law Commission, *Partial Defences to Murder: Final Report*, above n. 33, p. 80.

112 South Australia explicitly states that the conduct of the defendant can still be considered reasonably proportionate, even if it exceeds the force used by the victim against the defendant. See Criminal Law Consolidation Act 1935 (SA), s. 15B.

113 *R v Creamer* [2011] VSC 196, in which the defendant received a sentence of seven years' non-parole.

114 *R v Scott* [2003] NSWSC 627; *R v Trevenna* [2003] NSWSC 463; *R v Creamer* [2011] VSC 196; *R v Black* [2011] VSC 152.

> intervention order was in place protecting you from your late husband. That order was taken out in June 2010.

Potential issues with defensive homicide have been identified by Toole in her examination of Victorian case law post enactment of this offence and partial defence.[115] Toole's primary concern is that stereotypes of women and domestic violence may be perpetuated and result both 'in convictions for defensive homicide where complete acquittals would seem to be more appropriate' and guilty verdicts of defensive homicide 'where conviction for murder might be more in line with community expectations and standards'.[116]

It should be noted, then, that given the criticism that, in Australia, the expert focus has been on subjective exaggeration of a threat and the medically explicable 'irrationality' of battered women's actions, rather than on the objective context of the killing and the reasonableness of the women's actions in response to the violence,[117] expert BWS evidence might better support a defence of excessive self-defence by explaining the killing as an overreaction to a threat. By establishing the subjective, perceived gravity of the provocation, it might also assist with a defence of provocation (discussed next).

Provocation/loss of self-control[118]

Over the years, provocation became a significant cause of concern for feminist legal academics. It has been argued that this partial defence has embodied and excused masculine outbursts of anger and mitigated killings motivated by male honour, jealousy and possessiveness,[119] but has failed to respond adequately to the grievous situation of battered women. Writing in the 1990s, Bandalli noted how blame was frequently placed upon the woman, whether she is the victim or offender:

> Whatever the formal structure of the law, ultimately the success or failure of a provocation defence depends upon ingrained cultural judgement

115 K. Toole, 'Self-Defence and the Reasonable Woman: Equality Before the New Victorian Law', *Melbourne University Law Review* 36(1), 2012, 250–286.

116 Ibid, p. 286. Note that, at the time of writing, largely due to misuse by men as a defence against murder charges, the defensive homicide law was set to be repealed in Victoria – see State of Victoria, Department of Justice, *Defensive Homicide: Proposals for Legislative Reform*, Consultation Paper, 2013.

117 J. Stubbs and J. Tolmie, 'Falling Short of the Challenge? A Comparative Assessment of the Australian Use of Expert Evidence on the Battered Woman Syndrome', *Melbourne University Law Review* 23(3), 1995, 709–748.

118 For an in-depth comparative analysis of provocation and intimate homicide in Australia and the United States, see C. Ramsey, 'Provoking Change: Comparative Insights on Feminist Homicide Law Reform', *Journal of Criminal Law & Criminology* 100(1), 2010, 33–108.

119 See J. Horder, *Provocation and Responsibility*, Oxford: Clarendon Press, 1992.

> and the hidden agenda of this partial defence, as it operates in practice in spousal homicide, is one of *female responsibility*, whether as victim or offender.[120]

In England and Wales provocation was abolished by the Coroners and Justice Act 2009 and replaced with a new partial defence of 'loss of control'. In Australia, provocation was also abolished as a defence in Tasmania in 2003, Victoria in 2005 and Western Australia in 2008, leaving the circumstances of any provocation to be taken into account by the sentencing judge. Nevertheless, provocation continues to exist as a partial defence to murder in the other Australian jurisdictions.[121] In NSW, as a consequence of a 2013 parliamentary inquiry,[122] the government may rename it as the partial defence of gross provocation,[123] which could no longer be used by those in a domestic relationship other than by victims of long-term domestic violence as their situation constitutes 'circumstances of a most extreme and exceptional character'.[124]

In contrast to self-defence, killing due to provocation is not seen as a justified response. The reaction may, however, be seen as understandable in light of the circumstances, and therefore result in a charge of manslaughter instead of murder. Within the law, killing due to provocation is considered to have occurred because of a partial absence of rationality. In the case of the battered person it would mean that because of the constant abuse she has endured, she lost self-control, or 'mastery of her mind',[125] to such an extent that she formed an intention to commit murder.[126] In saying this, the actions that occurred as a result of this 'loss of mastery' must still have fallen within the range of behaviours considered 'ordinary' for their circumstance.[127] Once the defence has been sufficiently raised in terms of the evidence, a

120 S. Bandalli, 'Provocation – A Cautionary Note', *Journal of Law and Society* 22(3), 1995, 398–409, p. 398 (emphasis in original). See also M. Burton, 'Sentencing Domestic Homicide Upon Provocation: Still Getting Away With Murder', *Feminist Legal Studies* 11(3), 2003, 279–289.

121 Crimes Act 1900 (ACT), s. 13; Crimes Act 1900 (NSW), s. 23; Criminal Code Act (NT), Sch. 1, s. 158; Criminal Code 1899 (Qld), s. 304. In South Australia the defence continues to be defined at common law.

122 Select Committee on the Partial Defence of Provocation, *The Partial Defence of Provocation*, 2013. The Inquiry was precipitated by the outcome of *R v Singh* [2012] NSWSC 637, which caused some controversy. Singh's defence was that he had lost self-control after his wife told him that she had never loved him and was in love with someone else, and threatened to have him removed from the country.

123 As recommended by the Select Committee on the Partial Defence of Provocation, above n. 122, p. 125.

124 Ibid, p. 197.

125 *R v R* (1981) 28 SASR 321, 321–322 (King CJ).

126 Crimes Act 1900 (ACT), s. 13; Crimes Act 1900 (NSW), s. 23; Criminal Code Act (NT), Sch. 1, s. 158; Criminal Code 1899 (Qld), s. 304.

127 *Stingel v The Queen* (1990) 171 CLR 312, 325–327.

burden falls upon the prosecution to prove beyond reasonable doubt that provocation did not occur.[128]

The general contention is that the subjective requirement of a loss of self-control embodies the masculine reaction to violence. The judiciary has, over the years, tended to construe the subjective requirement strictly, requiring a 'sudden and temporary loss of self-control',[129] which occurs at the same time, or very shortly after, the provocation. Any time lapse between the provocative conduct and the loss of self-control was considered to amount to evidence of premeditation – that the accused had actually regained his/her self-control and that the attack was an act of revenge, as opposed to a provoked killing.[130] Commentators have argued that the subjective test is biased in favour of male defendants as men tend to respond immediately and angrily to provocative conduct.[131] Moreover, the difficulties caused by the different modes of reaction are further exacerbated because a situation in which a battered woman finds herself does not fall into the circumstances presupposed by the partial defence. The defence is more concerned with a one-off angry encounter as opposed to an ongoing abusive relationship, and hence fails adequately to acknowledge battered women's experiences of a '"slow-burn" of fear, despair and anger which eventually erupts into the killing of her batterer, usually when he is asleep, drunk, or otherwise indisposed'.[132]

Provocation has tended to be used by those who could show that they acted in 'the heat of passion'[133] immediately following an event caused by the deceased. However, as with self-defence, there are jurisdictional differences in terms of the requirement for immediacy. Historically, in England and Wales, under the requirement of a sudden and temporary loss of self-control the judiciary disregarded any abuse which had occurred over a long period of time. The only relevant provocative conduct would be that which immediately preceded the killing.

128 In recommending that the partial defence of provocation be retained in Queensland, where a mandatory life sentence for murder applies, the Queensland Law Reform Commission suggested that Criminal Code 1899 (Qld), s. 304 should be amended to place an onus on the defendant to prove the defence on the balance of probabilities: Queensland Law Reform Commission, *A Review of the Excuse of Accident and the Defence of Provocation*, Report No. 64, 2008, p. 501. The provision was accordingly amended – s. 304(7). Other amendments included s. 304(2) – sudden provocation could not be based on words alone and s. 304(3) – provocation can only be argued under exceptional circumstances if there was a domestic relationship.

129 *R v Duffy* [1949] 1 All ER 932 (Devlin J, cited by Lord Goddard at p. 932).

130 See *R v Ahluawlia* (1993) 96 Cr App R 133.

131 See, e.g.: D. Nicolson and R. Sanghvi, 'Battered Women and Provocation: The Implications of R v Ahluwalia', *Criminal Law Review*, 1993 (October), 728–738, p. 730; A. Young, 'Conjugal Homicide and Legal Violence: A Comparative Analysis', *Osgoode Hall Law Journal* 31(4), 1991, 761–808, p. 771.

132 Nicolson and Sanghvi, above n. 131, p. 730, quoted with approval by Gleeson CJ in *R v Chhay* (1994) 72 A Crim R 1.

133 For discussion of provocation and 'heat of passion', see NSW Legislative Council Select Committee on the Partial Defence of Provocation, *Defences and Partial Defences to Homicide*, 2012, pp. 4–6.

Moreover, a long-standing history of abuse was also held to connote circumstances of revenge killing.[134] For example, in *R v Ahluwalia*,[135] Lord Taylor stated:

> Time for reflection may show that after the provocative conduct makes its impact on the mind of the defendant, he or she kept or regained self-control. The passage of time following the provocation may also show that the subsequent attack was planned or based on motives, such as revenge or punishment, inconsistent with the loss of self control and therefore with the defence of provocation.[136]

However, following the case of *R v Humphreys*,[137] the judiciary eventually recognised the relevance of 'cumulative provocation' and conceded that the entire history of an abusive relationship was relevant to the issue of the loss of self-control.

In Australia, among the four jurisdictions which have a statutory provision for provocation, the ACT, NSW and Northern Territory explicitly state that provocation does not need to be immediate,[138] with recognition in case law that for a battered women 'a loss of self-control can develop even after a lengthy period of abuse, and without the necessity for a specific triggering event',[139] and may be associated with emotions other than anger.[140] Queensland, however, requires the defendant's actions to have occurred 'before there is time for the person's passion to cool';[141] this can, of course, be a very subjectively defined time period.

As noted at p. 144, in England and Wales the provocation defence has been replaced with a new partial defence of 'loss of control',[142] amid concerns that provocation 'elevate[d] the emotion of sudden anger above emotions of fear, despair, compassion and empathy'.[143] This new defence mitigates killings which are carried out when a defendant suffers and kills due to a loss of self-control which has a legally recognised trigger – either a fear of serious violence from the victim against the defendant or another identified person[144] – and/or that thing(s) done and/or

134 In *R v Ibrams* (1982) 74 Cr App R 154 the Court of Appeal concurred with the trial judge in holding that a homicide committed five days after the provocative act was not a case of provocation, despite the years of abuse the accused had suffered. On the contrary, it was held that the circumstances denoted a revenge killing.

135 (1993) 96 Cr App R 133.

136 Ibid, p. 138.

137 [1995] 4 All ER 1008.

138 Crimes Act 1900 (ACT), s. 13(2)(b)(ii); Crimes Act 1900 (NSW), s. 23(2)(b), (3)(b); Criminal Code Act (NT), Sch. 1, s. 158(4).

139 *R v Chhay* (1994) 72 A Crim R 1, 13–14 (Gleeson CJ).

140 *Van Den Hoek v The Queen* (1986) 161 CLR 158, 166–167 (Mason J).

141 Criminal Code 1899 (Qld), s. 304.

142 See Coroners and Justice Act 2009, ss 54–56. For a commentary on the underlying philosophy of the new defence, see A. Norrie, 'The Coroners and Justice Act 2009 – Partial Defences to Murder: Loss of Control', *Criminal Law Review* 4, 2010, 275–289.

143 Law Commission, *Partial Defences to Murder*, above n. 62, p. 82.

144 Coroners and Justice Act 2009, s. 55(3).

said by the victim 'constituted circumstances of an extremely grave character' and caused the defendant 'to have a justifiable sense of being seriously wronged'.[145] While some disquiet remains with regards to the retention of the requirement of a loss of self-control (which will be considered in further detail at p. 148), the loss no longer needs to be 'sudden'. However, the defence will not apply if the defendant 'acted in a considered desire for revenge'.[146]

Furthermore, and in what has been considered to be a controversial move, Coroners and Justice Act 2009, s. 55(6)(c) states that 'the fact that a thing said or done constituted sexual infidelity is to be disregarded' when 'determining whether a loss of self-control had a qualifying trigger'. This is without doubt a radical change, and one which was subject to intense parliamentary debate. Arguably, this reform sends out a normative message that killing in response to sexual infidelity will not be tolerated in today's society, a position which reflects the opinion of Lord Hoffmann in *R v Smith*, who stated: 'male possessiveness and jealously should not today be an acceptable reason for loss of self-control leading to homicide, whether inflicted upon the woman herself or her new lover'.[147]

However, in the first appeal case dealing with the new partial defence, the Court of Appeal significantly, and problematically, held that 'sexual infidelity is not subject to a blanket exclusion when the loss of control defence is under consideration'.[148] Concerns were expressed that in many cases it would be impossible to 'isolate' and 'compartmentalise' an act of sexual infidelity,[149] particularly as it may exist in the context of other factors which are not expressly excluded as a qualifying trigger, such as threats to terminate the relationship or taunts regarding the sexual indiscretion. Indeed, in relation to the latter, Lord Chief Justice Henriques stated: 'The idea that, in the search for a qualifying trigger, the context in which such words are used should be ignored represents an artificiality which the administration of criminal justice should do without'.[150] Accordingly, sexual infidelity will not be excluded if it forms part of a wider set of circumstances which legitimately fall within the scope of the defence. While space does not permit a detailed analysis of this decision,[151] it can be argued that the approach adopted by the Court of Appeal

145 Ibid., s. 55(4).
146 Ibid., s. 54(4).
147 *R v Smith* [2000] 3 WLR 654, 674.
148 *R v Clinton* [2012] EWCA Crim 2, [37]. See also the criticisms of legal practitioners in England and Wales regarding the exclusion of sexual infidelity in K. Fitz-Gibbon, 'Replacing Provocation in England and Wales: Examining the Partial Defence of Loss of Control', *Journal of Law and Society* 40(2), 2013, 280–305, pp. 292–296.
149 *R v Clinton* [2012] EWCA Crim 2, [39].
150 Ibid., [23].
151 See, e.g.: A. Clough, 'Sexual Infidelity: The Exclusion That Never Was?', *Journal of Criminal Law* 76(5), 2012, 382–388; D. Baker and L.X. Zhao, 'Contributory Qualifying and Non-Qualifying Triggers in the Loss of Control Defence: A Wrong Turn on Sexual Infidelity', *Journal of Criminal Law* 76(3), 2012, 254–275.

is due, in a large part, to the poor phrasing and bad drafting of the sexual infidelity exclusion. Furthermore, it is disconcerting that the approach adopted indicates that threats to leave the relationship and taunts regarding an affair are considered to be sufficiently and justifiably grave to support the defence. Arguably, these should also be excluded from the defence, particularly as the exclusion explicitly refers to things *said* as constituting sexual infidelity. But more so, this judgment represents a failure of the judges to act ethically and heed Cornell's call to 'remember the future' when engaging in interpretation, as discussed in Chapter 3. Rather than acknowledging the historical suffering of women due to legal constructs which have maintained and supported male violence against women, the interpretation reinvigorates the male possessiveness aspect of the provocation defence which the government was so keen to avoid. Edwards' concern that 'habituated gendered thinking will continue to impress on the construction' of the defence was not misplaced.[152]

The 'fear of serious violence' trigger was brought in specifically to deal with cases involving battered women, a move which garnered 'widespread support',[153] and there is no strict requirement that the violence which is feared be 'immediately imminent'.[154] Imminence is a factor which the jury may take into account when deciding whether an 'ordinary person' would have reacted in a similar manner.[155] Moreover, the government rejected a key recommendation put forward by the Law Commission – that of abolishing the loss of self-control requirement. To a significant extent, the Commission's recommendation to reform the defence in this manner was premised upon its consideration of domestic violence cases. The Commission felt that it was wrong to exclude the defence in a case in which a battered woman kills her abuser while he is asleep, after suffering 'a grave attack or threat of a grave attack',[156] on the basis that her actions are motivated by fear and despair, and believing that such action is the only way in which she can escape the abuse. In such a situation, it was considered to 'be wrong to rule out her plea simply because there was no evidence of a loss of self control'.[157] Indeed, it was noted that 'women's reactions are less likely to involve a "loss of self control", but more likely to comprise

152 S. Edwards, 'Loss of Self-Control: When His Anger is Worth More than Her Fear', in A. Reed and M. Bohlander (eds), *Loss of Control and Diminished Responsibility: Domestic, Comparative and International Perspectives*, Farnham: Ashgate Publishing, 2011, 79–96, p. 79.

153 Ministry of Justice, *Murder, Manslaughter and Infanticide: Proposals for Reform of the Law*, 2008, p. 10. But see Herring's argument that a battered woman may also fall under the 'justifiable sense of being seriously wronged' trigger: J. Herring, 'The Serious Wrong of Domestic Abuse and the Loss of Control Defence', in A. Reed and M. Bohlander (eds), *Loss of Control and Diminished Responsibility: Domestic, Comparative and International Perspectives*, Farnham: Ashgate Publishing, 2011, 65–78.

154 Ministry of Justice, *Murder, Manslaughter and Infanticide*, above n. 153, p. 10.

155 Ministry of Justice, *Murder, Manslaughter and Infanticide: Proposals for Reform of the Law: Summary of Responses and Government Position*, 2009, p. 11.

156 Law Commission, *Partial Defences to Murder: Final Report*, above n. 33, p. 52.

157 Law Commission, *Murder, Manslaughter and Infanticide*, Report No. 304, 2006, p. 83.

a combination of anger, fear, frustration and a sense of desperation'.[158] Furthermore, expressing anger via a loss of self-control tends to be the preserve of those in a dominant position:

> those who give vent to anger by 'losing self-control' to the point of killing another person generally do so in circumstances in which they can afford to do so. An angry strong man can afford to lose his self-control with someone who provokes him, if that person is physically smaller and weaker. An angry person is much less likely to 'lose self control' and attack another person in circumstances in which he or she is likely to come off worse by doing so.[159]

By requiring a battered woman to lose self-control when she is in fear of serious violence the government has maintained and perpetuated the gender inequalities deep within the law. It is unlikely that a victim of domestic violence would feel that she could lose self-control without placing herself in a significantly more vulnerable position. Despite such arguments, the government retained the loss of self-control requirement due to fears that in its absence cases involving 'honour killings' may fall within the scope of the defence.[160] It is submitted, however, that such concerns are easily dealt with. First, as already noted, the new defence explicitly excludes cases in which the defendant 'acted in a considered desire for revenge'.[161] This section would encompass many cases of 'honour killings', particularly if there has been significant planning. Second, the loss of self-control requirement could be limited to cases which fall within Coroners and Justice Act 2009, s. 55(4), i.e. where a defendant has a 'justifiable sense of being seriously wronged', particularly as such situations are more likely to be concerned with angry outbursts, as opposed to a killing due to a state of fear. As Edwards notes:

> Instead of an eruptive moment, as is anger, fear is an enduring underlying state. For the abused woman living with and in domestic violence, the state of fear is in the continuous present. . . . they suffer from an extreme and continuous fear or state of continuous terror. Fear, therefore does not sit comfortably with loss of self-control as an eruptive moment. Fear is a breakdown in control; it is an inability to control circumstances because of an outside force rather than an inner eruptive response.[162]

158 Ibid., p. 81.

159 Law Commission, *Partial Defences to Murder: Final Report*, above n. 33, p. 36.

160 Ministry of Justice, *Murder, Manslaughter and Infanticide*, above n. 153, p. 12. Honour killings can be defined as murders that take place to protect/restore the honour of a family.

161 Coroners and Justice Act 2009, s. 54(4).

162 S. Edwards, 'Anger and Fear as Justifiable Preludes for Loss of Self Control', *Journal of Criminal Law* 74(3), 2010, 223–241, p. 228. See also the critique of B. Mitchell, 'Loss of Control Under the Coroners and Justice Act 2009: Oh No!', in A. Reed and M. Bohlander (eds), *Loss of Control and Diminished Responsibility: Domestic, Comparative and International Perspectives*, Farnham: Ashgate Publishing, 2011, 39–50. Concerns regarding the retention of the

If the law is adequately to recognise the plight of battered women, it should not require abused women to act out of fear and suffer a loss of self-control.

In relation to both the defences of provocation and loss of self-control, once a subjective loss of self-control has been established, a jury must then be satisfied that an 'ordinary/reasonable person' would react in a similar manner. In England and Wales, the adoption of the new defence of loss of self-control provided the opportunity to revisit the objective test, which had frequently caused the courts significant difficulties, and had been subject to rigorous academic critique.[163] The new test moves away from previous problematic notions of 'reasonableness' and 'characteristics', and refers to 'a person of [the defendant's] sex and age, with a normal degree of tolerance and self-restraint and in the circumstances of [the defendant]'.[164] Of particular note is the change of language – from characteristics to circumstances – which brings about a welcomed shift in focus from the individual defendant's psychology to the abusive relationship.[165]

This 'ordinary/reasonable person test' continues to be interpreted through common law.[166] As in self-defence, we see a test that includes subjective and objective elements. In Australia, the High Court in *Stingel v The Queen*[167] established a two-tier test, which first requires a consideration of the gravity of the provocation 'from the viewpoint of the particular accused'.[168] This requires the court to consider all the relevant characteristics of the accused, such as his age, gender, personal relationships and past history. The second tier of the test involves the court assessing whether the gravity of the provocation felt by the defendant would make an 'ordinary person', with the same characteristics, respond in the same way as the defendant,[169] if the ordinary person had the lowest level of self-control that could be considered 'ordinary'.[170] The requirement to consider the ordinary person with the *lowest level of self-control* should at least in theory remove the power of the court to consider how well the battered woman has coped in the past, or appears to be

requirement of a loss of control, particularly in relation to the fear of violence trigger, have been expressed by legal practitioners in England and Wales. See Fitz-Gibbon, 'Replacing Provocation in England and Wales', above n. 148, pp. 289–292, 296–299.

163 See, e.g., the discussion and references in Law Commission, *Partial Defences to Murder*, above n. 62, pp. 47–82.

164 Coroners and Justice Act 2009, s. 54(1)(C).

165 A. Clough, 'Loss of Self-Control as a Defence: The Key to Replacing Provocation', *Journal of Criminal Law* 74(2), 2010, 118–126; Edwards, 'Anger and Fear', above n. 162. For a further analysis, see N. Cobb and A. Gaudsen, 'Feminism, "Typical" Women, and Losing Control', in A. Reed and M. Bohlander (eds), *Loss of Control and Diminished Responsibility: Domestic, Comparative and International Perspectives*, Farnham: Ashgate Publishing, 2011, 97–114.

166 *Masciantonio v The Queen* (1995) 183 CLR 58, 66. In relation to the previous law of provocation in England and Wales, see *R v Camplin* [1978] 2 All ER 168.

167 (1990) 171 CLR 312.

168 Ibid., pp. 325–326.

169 Ibid., pp. 326–327. This is similar to the approach adopted in England and Wales under *R v Camplin* [1978] 2 All ER 168.

170 *Stingel v The Queen* (1990) 171 CLR 312, 312, 329.

coping at present. It means that because a defendant has previously dealt with horrific incidents where she did not lose self-control, the court should not simply assume that her self-control is any better than the 'ordinary person' in *her* circumstances. At this point, the court is also likely to need the help of expert witnesses to understand the gravity of the provocation/trigger as experienced by the battered woman and her loss of self-control.

In weighting the gravity of the provocation in one Australian battered woman case, and whether it would cause an ordinary person to lose control, the judge stated that the degree of provocation 'should be assessed as medium, rather than great' and sentenced the defendant to a minimum term of five years' imprisonment.[171] He reiterated that the dead man:

> had sought to control and dominate the defendant and used cruel and abusive language to the prisoner . . . made cruel comments about her alleged lack of intelligence and about her physical appearance . . . smacking her legs and buttocks with a ruler, pinching her, lightly punching her in the stomach or arm, twisting her nipples and requiring her to have sexual intercourse with him, when she was unwilling, indicating that he was using the prisoner for his own sexual relief.[172]

Although the judge went on to acknowledge that these actions were 'humiliating and distressing' for the defendant, he seems to be unaware of how, with domestic violence, the bizarre may become normalised and minimised and emphasises how the defendant had told the police that the violence was primarily psychological abuse, rather than as physical violence.[173]

The 'reality' of the battered woman and that of the court may collide, as discussed at p. 130 in relation to self-defence. There is a possibility of unconscious biases affecting how court players construct 'ordinary'. Provocation is, after all, a defence that developed as a concession to 'male frailty',[174] and excused hot-tempered immediate responses to breaches of honour and marital infidelity in circumstances where the murderous passions of an 'ordinary man' might be understood.[175]

171 As one might expect in comparing sentences when provocation has been argued with those found guilty of lack of intent, sentences appear to be higher for the former. See, e.g.: *R v Cavanough* [2007] NSWSC 561 – where the judge handed down a non-parole period of five years; *R v Russell* [2006] NSWSC 722 – three years; and *R v Quealey* [2011] NSWSC 42 – three years, six months.

172 *R v Vandersee* [2000] NSWSC 916, [137], [139] (James J).

173 Ibid., [140] (James J).

174 *R v Chlay* (1994) 72 A Crim R 1, 11 (Gleeson CJ).

175 P. Papathanasiou and P. Easteal, 'The "Ordinary Person" in Provocation Law: Is the "Objective" Standard Objective?', *Current Issues in Criminal Justice* 11(1), 1999, 53–70, p. 54.

Battered person's defence

In England and Wales there is no specific battered person's defence, and it was not consulted upon during the reform process leading up to the Coroners and Justice Act 2009. The idea of a 'battered woman syndrome' defence was notionally raised, but was quickly dismissed during the homicide law reform consultation. The Law Commission argued that the syndrome could not 'satisfactorily form the basis of a specific defence', and that 'defences to murder ought to be based on principles of general application'.[176] Arguably, this was a lost opportunity. There is no explanation as to why the Commission limited its consideration to a gender-specific 'battered woman syndrome' defence as opposed to examining the possibility of a general and gender-neutral defence. Furthermore, given the gender-specific nature in which the defences of provocation and self-defence have developed over the years, the introduction of a defence which acknowledges the unique situation of abused persons is long overdue.

Such developments have taken place in Australia where, until 2010, there was no separate defence. On 10 February 2010, Criminal Code 1899 (Qld), s. 304B was enacted. It states that a person who kills another is guilty of manslaughter if the deceased had committed serious acts of domestic violence against the offender.[177] Section 304B remains in line with common law by also requiring that the defendant believed that her actions were reasonably necessary to preserve her own life or safety,[178] and those reasonable beliefs are taken in regard to the circumstances of the abusive domestic relationship.[179] The legislative definition of 'abusive domestic relationship' correlates to a great extent with the victims' reality of violence since it acknowledges that '[a] history of acts of serious domestic violence may include acts that appear minor or trivial when considered in isolation'.[180]

Some commentators are concerned that 'there is a real risk that the enactment of s 304B will hinder efforts in that State to have judges and jurors engage with the 'reality' of battered women in assessing their claims to justified self-defence'.[181]

However, Susan Falls, as discussed earlier in the chapter, was acquitted of both murder and manslaughter in that state some four months after s. 304B was enacted.

Pathways to better justice?

As we have seen in previous chapters, society and its laws fail all too often to protect women from the violence they have long endured at the hands of their abusers. This chapter has shown that, around the globe, communities and criminal justice

176 Law Commission, *Partial Defences to Murder*, above n. 62, p. 204.
177 Criminal Code 1899 (Qld), s. 304B(1)(a).
178 Ibid., s. 304B(1)(b).
179 Ibid., s. 304B(1)(c).
180 Ibid., s. 304B(4).
181 A. Hopkins and P. Easteal, 'Walking in her Shoes: Battered Women Who Kill in Victoria, Western Australia and Queensland', *Alternative Law Journal* 35(3), 2010, 132–137, p. 137.

systems may also fail to protect these women when they exercise their only true option of self-preservation.

Part of the problem, as we have seen, comes from the collision of the victim's reality of violence with a non-victim's view. Both legislators and the courts need to recognise this and, at the very least, increase the courts' understanding of the dynamics, manifestations and effects of domestic violence and to increase jurors' and judges' ability to understand how the woman's act of killing can be seen as the rational and reasonable behaviour of an ordinary battered woman. Given that domestic violence has been persuasively argued to be, in its own right, an area of specialised knowledge,[182] there is a need for experts. An understanding of the battered woman's situational and psychological predicaments is critically relevant to the assessment of the reasonableness of her actions.[183] It is only with a full appreciation of the 'extraordinary circumstances' she faced that the reasonableness or otherwise of her actions becomes intelligible.[184] As discussed in this chapter, in most jurisdictions evidence is more likely to be admitted by a psychologist or psychiatrist who can discuss BWS. However, one change that could assist the defences of these women is a broader definition of expertise; for instance, those with extensive experience at the 'coalface' are in a position to give expert evidence. This has been done to a limited extent in Australia.[185] By linking and contextualising what might otherwise appear to be a history of discrete incidents of violence, such a witness provides a holistic rather than an 'atomized' account of what it is really like to live under the constant shadow of abuse:[186] how the unpredictable dynamics of domestic violence create an atmosphere with threat permeating, how leaving the relationship may be prohibitively difficult, and that for those who do leave, the violence might not stop – and in fact sometimes gets worse.[187]

Further legislative reforms are needed to better safeguard these women. In most Australian States and Territories, in contrast to England and Wales, it appears that

182 R. Bradfield, 'Understanding the Battered Woman Who Kills her Violent Partner – the Admissibility of Expert Evidence of Domestic Violence in Australia', *Psychiatry, Psychology and the Law* 9(2), 2002, 177–199, p. 190.

183 As stated by the judges in *R v Lavallee* [1990] 1 SCR 852, 871–872, 882–883 (Wilson J); *R v Malott* (1998) 155 DLR (4th) 513, 521–522 (Major J); *Osland v The Queen* (1998) 197 CLR 316, 375–378 (Kirby J).

184 *Osland v The Queen* (1998) 197 CLR 316, 375 (Kirby J).

185 For example, Patricia Easteal, an academic, testified in a 2005 NSW Supreme Court case heard in Bathurst (*R v Morgan*) in which the defendant was acquitted; Danielle Castles, who was working in social welfare, provided a report in *R v Yeoman* [2003] NSWSC 194. Easteal also testified in the 2014 Victoria murder trial of Angela Williams. She had buried the body of her husband and waited four years before going to the police. She was found guilty of defensive homicide: *DPP v Angela Williams*, Vic Sup ct. 2014.

186 Bradfield, 'Understanding the Battered Woman', above n. 182, p. 180. For more detail about the role of a situational expert, see Easteal, *Less Than Equal*, above n. 1.

187 T. Hotton, 'Spousal Violence After Separation', *Juristat* 21(7), 2001, 1–18; H. Johnson and T. Hotton, 'Losing Control: Homicide Risk in Estranged and Intact Intimate Relationships', *Homicide Studies* 7(1), 2003, 58–84.

reforms to self-defence have been attempting to better encompass the reality of battered women. Whether these reforms will make any kind of real difference remains to be seen. The recent insertion of s. 304B into Queensland's Criminal Code does seem to recognise the gendered limitations of the previous defences;[188] however, as this simply results in a reduction of the charge from murder to manslaughter it is questionable whether the judicial system is truly understanding the reality of the 'abusive domestic relationship and all the circumstances of the case'.[189] Similarly, while in England and Wales the reforms to provocation appear to be premised on the need to provide a suitable defence for abused women, the retention of the loss of self-control requirement is at odds with the recognition that such killings are committed due to fear, as opposed to anger. Moreover, if there was a complete understanding of the woman's reality and how she was acting in self-defence, surely the defence would result in an acquittal. Ideally, other jurisdictions, including England and Wales, will follow in Queensland's footsteps and create a distinct defence for battered women;[190] however, they need to take one step further and have this result in complete acquittal.

188 Easteal and Hopkins, 'Women and Criminal Law', above n. 1.

189 Criminal Code 1899 (Qld), s. 304B(1)(c).

190 This was recommended in reports in South Australia in 1987 and in Western Australia in 1994. See L. Roth, *Provocation and Self-Defence in Intimate Partner and Homophobic Homicides*, Briefing Paper No. 3/07, NSW Parliamentary Library Research Service, 2007.

Chapter 8

Consent, corroboration and recent complaint in rape and sexual assault

The law of rape and sexual assault has been subject to continuous scrutiny and significant reforms over the years. Changes to the law relating to corroboration and recent complaint, along with introducing and/or amending definitions of consent, *mens rea* and rules pertaining to the vitiation of consent, have all taken place in order to update the law and challenge mistaken assumptions and myths regarding rape and sexual assault. Despite such reforms, however, the number of cases reported to the police remains very low and the overall attrition rate for rape is exceedingly high. Moreover, concerns remain with regards to the extent to which notions of 'real rape' and false allegations continue to pervade the public and legal imagination, impacting upon all of those who are involved in or come into contact with the law – from legislators and judges, to complainants and jurors.

Definitional shades of grey

The ongoing law reform and the ensuing legislative heterogeneity, especially among the different states and territories in Australia, make generalising about rape law challenging, but possible. The definition of rape has evolved considerably over the years. For example, in England and Wales, the Sexual Offences Act 1956, s. 1(1) simply stated: 'It is an offence for a man to rape a woman'. Today, the physical acts that form the basis of the rape offence have been expanded to include non-consensual penile penetration of the mouth and anus, as well as the vagina.[1] Most jurisdictions now also have provisions ensuring that people who have undergone genital surgeries are included within the law,[2] and non-consensual

1 Sexual Offences Act 2003, s. 1. For Australia, see: Crimes Act 1900 (ACT), s. 50; Crimes Act 1900 (NSW), s. 61H(1); Criminal Code Act 1983 (NT), Sch. 1, s. 1; Criminal Code Act 1899 (Qld), s. 349(2); Criminal Law Consolidation Act 1935 (SA), s. 5; Criminal Code Act 1924 (Tas), Sch. 1, s. 1; Crimes Act 1958 (Vic), s. 35; Criminal Code Compilation Act 1913 (WA), App B, s. 319(1).

2 Australia: Crimes Act 1900 (ACT), s. 50(2); Crimes Act 1900 (NSW), s. 61H(1)(a); Criminal Code Act 1983 (NT), Sch. 1, s. 1; Criminal Code Act 1899 (Qld), s. 1; Criminal Law Consolidation Act 1935 (SA), s. 5(3); Criminal Code Act 1924 (Tas), Sch. 1, s. 1; Crimes Act 1958 (Vic), s. 35. England and Wales: Sexual Offences Act 2003, s. 79(3).

continuation of intercourse is also generally recognised as amounting to rape, except in Queensland.[3]

Interestingly, however, shades of grey permeate throughout the definition of rape, particularly with regards to whether rape should be restricted to penile penetration, and also whether the term 'rape' should be used at all.

In England and Wales, the offence of *rape* is restricted to penile penetration, whereas other non-penile penetrations are labelled 'sexual assault by penetration'.[4] Consequently, the principal offender for the offence of rape can only be a man, thus retaining the gendered nature of the offence. Such an approach is in distinction to the overall gender-neutral stance adopted in the Sexual Offences Act 2003, which governs the law in England and Wales. During the reform process, retaining the gendered nature of the offence was justified on the basis that penile penetration is 'of a particularly personal kind, [which] carrie[s] risks of pregnancy and disease transmission and should properly be treated separately from other penetrative assaults'.[5]

In most Australian jurisdictions, penetration with any body part or with an object is included in the legislative definition of sexual intercourse,[6] on the basis that such conduct is just 'as frightening, humiliating, invasive and injurious'.[7] Heath comments: 'Feminists have argued for an understanding of sexual assault that de-centres the penis and thus challenges traditional understandings of "the sex that counts" and therefore "the sexual assault that counts"'.[8] Some jurisdictions, such as New South Wales ('NSW'), along with Canada and Michigan, have completely abandoned the term 'rape', preferring instead the label of 'sexual assault'.[9] In such legal systems, the law sets down different degrees or grades of severity of sexual

3 Australia: Crimes Act 1900 (ACT), s. 50(1)(f); Crimes Act 1900 (NSW), s. 61H(1)(d); Criminal Code Act 1983 (NT), s. 1; Criminal Law Consolidation Act 1935 (SA), s. 5; Criminal Code Act 1924 (Tas), s. 1; Crimes Act 1958 (Vic), s. 38(2)(b); Criminal Code Compilation Act 1913 (WA), s. 319(1). While continuation is not specifically addressed in Queensland legislation, the 'weight of authority supports treating the continuation of sexual intercourse as satisfying the physical act required for a charge of rape': Thomson Reuters, *The Laws of Australia*, Vol. 10, *Criminal Offences*, 10.3, [190], as cited in Australian Law Reform Commission, *Family Violence – A National Legal Response*, Report No. 114, 2010, p. 1148. England and Wales: Sexual Offences Act 2003, s. 79(2).

4 Non-penile penetration of the vagina and the anus (but notably not the mouth) amount to 'sexual assault by penetration' under Sexual Offences Act 2003, s. 2.

5 Home Office, *Setting the Boundaries: Reforming the Law on Sex Offences*, 2000, p. 15.

6 For Australia, see: Crimes Act 1900 (ACT), s. 50(1)(b); Crimes Act 1900 (NSW), s. 61H(1)(a)(ii); Criminal Code Act 1983 (NT), Sch. 1, s. 1; Criminal Code Act 1899 (Qld), Sch. 1, s. 349(2)(b); Criminal Law Consolidation Act 1935 (SA), s. 5; Crimes Act 1958 (Vic), s. 35(1); Criminal Code Compilation Act 1913 (WA), s. 319(1). In Tasmania, penetration with an object is classified as aggravated sexual assault: Criminal Code Act 1924 (Tas), Sch. 1, s. 127A.

7 M. Heath, 'Disputed Truths: Australian Reform of the Sexual Conduct Elements of Common Law Rape', in P. Easteal (ed.), *Balancing the Scales: Rape, Law Reform and Australian Culture*, Sydney: Federation Press, 1998, 13–25, p. 18.

8 Heath, 'Disputed Truths', above n. 7, p. 20.

9 For a detailed discussion of these provisions, see J. Temkin, *Rape and the Legal Process*, Oxford: Oxford University Press, 2002, Ch. 2.

assault. The advantages of such an approach are not, however, universally accepted. Those in favour argue that the term 'rape' is too emotive and steeped in cultural and social stereotypes regarding 'real rape'.[10] Subsequently, moving away from the term may help to improve the conviction rate, as jurors may be less reluctant to convict. It is also argued that the phrase 'sexual assault' duly emphasises that the conduct in question is conceptualised 'as a crime of violence, rather than as a crime of sex'.[11] Those who argue against such reforms, however, maintain that they lead to a devaluation of the offence and fail to acknowledge its unique nature.[12] While space does not permit a detailed analysis of the range of different definitions of 'rape' and 'sexual assault', it is important to note that around the globe variants exist. What 'rape' is, is far from settled.

Myths, stereotypes and consent

Overwhelmingly, although not universally,[13] the pivotal element of the rape/sexual assault definition is the complainant's lack of consent. Establishing that sexual intercourse occurred without the complainant's consent is a major hurdle for the prosecution, particularly in non-stranger rape cases, which represent the majority of cases. The burden of proof means that the complainant is effectively treated as consenting unless the prosecution can prove otherwise beyond reasonable doubt, producing a significant focus on the complainant's mental state.[14] The prosecution must prove two elements: the physical – that the woman did not consent; and the mental – that the accused was aware that the complainant was not consenting, or might not be consenting, did not care about consent or had no reasonable grounds to believe that the complainant was consenting (depending on the jurisdiction). The focus of the trial, then, is on the physical element of consent, together with complicated judicial directions.[15] It is not surprising that an Australian mock jury study found that jurors had trouble understanding the concept of consent, debating

10 J. Scutt, 'Sexual Assault and the Australian Criminal Justice System', in D. Chappell and P. Wilson (eds), *The Australian Criminal Justice System – The Mid 1980s*, Sydney: Butterworths, 3rd edn, 1986, 57–83, p. 64, cited in Heath, 'Disputed Truths', above n. 7, p. 22. See also Temkin, *Rape and the Legal Process*, above n. 9, p. 178.

11 L. Gottel, 'Canadian Sexual Assault Law: Neoliberalism and the Erosion of Feminist-Inspired Law Reforms', in C. McGlynn and V. Munro (eds), *Rethinking Rape Law: International and Comparative Perspectives*, Abingdon: Routledge, 2010, 209–223, p. 210.

12 Temkin, *Rape and the Legal Process*, above n. 9, p. 178. See also D. Warburton, 'The Rape of a Label – Why it Would be Wrong to Follow Canada in Having a Single Offence of Unlawful Sexual Assault', *Journal of Criminal Law* 68(6), 2004, 533–543.

13 See, in particular, the variety of approaches adopted among US States, explored in J.F. Decker and P.G. Baroni, 'Criminal Law: "No" Still Means "Yes": The Failure of the "Non-Consent" Reform Movement in American Rape and Sexual Offence Assault Law', *Journal of Criminal Law and Criminology* 101(4), 2011, 1081–1169.

14 Home Office, *Setting the Boundaries: Reforming the Law of Sexual Offences*, 2000, p. 23.

15 P. Easteal and C. Feerick, 'Sexual Assault by Male Partners: Is the License Still Valid?', *Flinders Journal of Law Reform* 8(2), 2005, 185–207.

how consent is defined and when it should be assessed.[16] This is no doubt also in part a consequence of the beliefs that people continue to have about male and female sexuality and about what constitutes a *genuine* rape – a *true* negation of consent.

There is a view of female sexuality that women enjoy being 'coerced' or persuaded to engage in sexual intercourse. Therefore, the art of 'seduction' allows for any reservations on the part of the woman to be rightfully overcome by the persistence of the man. Women have been (and continue to be) expected to say 'no', and resist, struggle and incur other injuries as a consequence: 'because of the pervasiveness of [these] assumptions about "normal" heterosexual intercourse, it is little wonder that the law has traditionally presumed that a woman consents to sexual penetration unless she in some way strongly resists her assailant'.[17] Accordingly, in law, physical inaction was traditionally viewed by the courts as signalling consent; and, conversely, 'the easiest way to show lack of consent is through signs of physical resistance'.[18] This has now changed in the substantive law, if not in actual practice.

In England and Wales, the Sexual Offences Act 2003 introduced a statutory definition of consent. Section 74 states: 'a person consents if he agrees by choice, and has the freedom and capacity to make that choice'. Significantly, a complainant is under no legal obligation to expressly signal her *non*-consent.[19] The Home Office at the time surmised that this definition was 'clear and unambiguous' and a significant improvement on the previous common law.[20] However, research with mock jurors clearly demonstrates that the definition is not readily comprehended.[21] As noted by Temkin and Ashworth, the words 'freedom' and 'capacity' 'raise philosophical issues of such complexity as to be ill-suited to the needs of criminal justice',[22] and barristers working in the field of rape commented that while the definition was perfectly explicable from a lawyer's perspective, they doubted the extent to which it was comprehensible to jury members.[23]

16 N. Taylor and J. Joudo, *The Impact of Pre-recorded Video and Closed-circuit Television Testimony on Jury Decision-Making*, Research and Public Policy Series No. 68, Canberra: Australian Institute of Criminology, 2005.

17 B. McSherry, 'Constructing Lack of Consent', in P. Easteal (ed.), *Balancing the Scales: Rape, Law Reform and Australian Culture*, Sydney: Federation Press, 1998, 26–40, p. 30.

18 Ibid., pp. 29, 35.

19 *R v H* [2007] EWCA Crim 2056.

20 Home Office, *Protecting the Public: Strengthening Protection Against Sex Offenders and Reforming the Law on Sexual Offences*, 2002, p. 16.

21 E. Finch and V. Munro, 'Breaking Boundaries? Sexual Consent in the Jury Room', *Legal Studies* 26(3), 2006, 303–320.

22 J. Temkin and A. Ashworth, 'The Sexual Offences Act 2003: (1) Rape, Sexual Assaults and the Problems of Consent', *Criminal Law Review*, 2004 (May), 328–346, p. 336.

23 A. Carline and C. Gunby, 'Barristers' Perspectives on Rape and the Sexual Offences Act 2003', *Criminal Law and Justice Weekly* 174(31), 2010, 472–474; C. Gunby, A. Carline and C. Beynon, 'Alcohol-related Rape Cases: Barristers' Perspectives on the Sexual Offences Act 2003 and its Impact on Practice', *Journal of Criminal Law* 74(6), 2010, 579–600; A. Carline and C. Gunby, '"How an Ordinary Jury Makes Sense of it is a Mystery". Barristers'

In contrast, it was suggested that the main advantage of a statutory definition was that it reduced the likelihood of unnecessary appeals due to judicial 'ad libbing and anecdotal comparisons'.[24] Barristers also noted that a definition of consent was of little use in a case in which the complainant and the accused gave 'completely different versions about what happened in the privacy of a room somewhere',[25] a factor which tends to be pivotal in 'acquaintance rape' cases. While this opinion may appear unsurprising, the need to develop a definition of consent was premised, partially, on the increased reporting of acquaintance rape cases. It therefore seems problematic that in such cases the statutory definition is considered minimally useful. Moreover, in a review of the handling of rape cases, it was noted that the rationale behind the legal changes to the definition of consent (and also the *mens rea* of rape, discussed at p. 168) was:

> to move from the underlying presumption that victims are likely to be lying or were somehow negligent in letting rape happen towards a standpoint that sex without consent is rape and all other factors about a person making a complaint of rape are irrelevant to that central fact.[26]

However, studies of mock juries in England and Wales demonstrate that the reforms to the wording of the offence have not had this impact, and stereotypes remain influential.[27] Women are frequently judged and considered to be blameworthy due to their behaviour, including the perception that they are responsible for being raped if they voluntarily get into bed with a man.[28] Moreover, 'some complain of the tendency to lecture women on what they should and should not do rather than making it clear to men that sex without consent is rape'.[29] This approach can be seen to maintain and perpetuate a victim-blaming culture.

The ongoing concern regarding the seemingly entrenched nature of stereotypical opinions and their impact upon rape cases has led to the recent development, in

Perspectives on Rape, Consent and the Sexual Offences Act 2003', *Liverpool Law Review* 32(3), 2011, 237–250.

24 'Barrister 11', as cited in Carline and Gunby, 'How an Ordinary Jury Makes Sense of it is a Mystery', above n. 23, p. 241.

25 Ibid.

26 Baroness Stern, *The Stern Review: A Report by Baroness Vivien Stern CBE of an Independent Review into How Rape Complaints are Handled by Public Authorities in England and Wales*, London: Government Equalities Office and the Home Office, 2010, pp. 13–14.

27 E. Finch and V. Munro, 'Juror Stereotypes and Blame Attribution in Rape Cases Involving Intoxicants: The Finding of A Pilot Study', *British Journal of Criminology* 45(1), 2005, 25–38; L. Ellison and V. Munro, 'Reacting to Rape: Exploring Mock Jurors' Assessments of Complainant Credibility', *British Journal of Criminology* 49(2), 2009, 202–219; E. Ellison and V. Munro, 'Of "Normal Sex" and "Real Rape": Exploring the Use of Socio-Sexual Scripts in (Mock) Jury Deliberations', *Social and Legal Studies* 18(3), 2009, 1–22.

28 Opinion Matters, *Wake Up To Rape Research Summary Report*, Prepared for the Havens (Sexual Assault Referral Centres), 2010, p. 9.

29 Stern, *The Stern Review*, above n. 26, p. 33.

England and Wales, of detailed model jury directions. These directions cover a range of 'mistaken assumptions' relating to factors such as the complainant's dress, the lack of violence, the ability to recall the events consistently and the victim's demeanour in the courtroom.[30] The need to introduce such directions gives weight to the concerns that the substantive changes to the law of rape have failed to ensure justice. The extent to which such directions will, however, be influential in challenging stereotypes remains to be seen. Moreover, the opinion of counsel is that additional directions will only serve to further confuse a jury.[31]

Vitiating consent

In most jurisdictions the law now explicitly sets out circumstances in which consent will be deemed to be absent.[32] With regards to Australia, Heath notes that reform has:

> expanded and clarified circumstances which vitiate consent through non-exhaustive lists of contexts in which consent is *not* legally recognised. . . . Every state and territory includes the use of force and threats of violence or force as vitiating consent. Some also include threats against third parties; intimidation, threats against property, threats of public humiliation, disgrace, or harassment; non-violent but 'intimidatory or coercive threats'; or 'threats of any kind'. Fear, intimidation or helplessness are included in every jurisdiction except Western Australia. Various forms of fraud or mistake as well as abuse of authority or trust are recognised as vitiating consent in most jurisdictions. Unlawful detention vitiates consent in all jurisdictions except Queensland and Western Australia. Conditions which affect consciousness – ranging from being asleep, unconscious or intoxicated – are recognised as vitiating factors in all jurisdictions.[33]

In England and Wales, the Sexual Offences Act 2003 brought the law more or less in line with Australia (and also Canada), by introducing a range of 'presumptions' regarding the absence of consent and the defendant's belief in consent. Section 75 details six circumstances under which it will be presumed that (a) the complainant did not consent and (b) the accused did not reasonably believe in consent. The list of circumstances include situations in which violence or threats of violence had

30 Judicial Studies Board, *The Crown Court Bench Book: Directing the Jury*, 2010, pp. 353–362.

31 Carline and Gunby, 'Barristers' Perspectives', above n. 23; Carline and Gunby, 'How an Ordinary Jury Makes Sense of it is a Mystery', above n. 23.

32 In Australia: Crimes Act 1900 (ACT), s. 67; Crimes Act 1900 (NSW), s. 61HA(6); Criminal Code Act (NT), Sch. 1, s. 192(2); Criminal Code (Qld), s. 348(2); Criminal Law Consolidation Act 1935 (SA), s. 46(3); Criminal Code Act 1924 (Tas), Sch. 1, s. 2A; Crimes Act 1958 (Vic), s. 36; Criminal Code (WA), s. 319(2).

33 M. Heath, 'Women and Criminal Law: Rape', in P. Easteal (ed.), *Women and the Law in Australia*, Sydney: LexisNexis, 2010, 88–108, p. 97 (emphasis in original).

been used; the complainant was unlawfully detained, asleep or unconscious; and cases involving surreptitious intoxication, whether via drinks or drugs. As originally drafted, the provision placed a persuasive burden on the defendant, thus requiring him to convince the jury on the balance of probabilities that the complainant did consent and/or that the defendant's belief that consent had been given was reasonable. However, such a provision was met with opposition during the reform process and fears were expressed that it would potentially contravene the presumption of innocence, as secured under the European Convention on Human Rights, Art. 6.[34] Consequently, the provision places an evidential burden on the defendant; and the trial judge will decide not only whether a presumption has been triggered, but also whether the defendant has raised sufficient evidence in rebuttal. Commentators have surmised that little evidence would be necessary in order for a defendant to convince the judge that the presumption had been rebutted;[35] and interviews with barristers support this contention.[36] Nevertheless, the Court of Appeal in *R v Cirrarelli* made it clear that evidence beyond 'fanciful or speculative' is required to discharge the burden.[37] Research, however, suggests that the presumptions are not being utilised to their full extent and that significant confusion exists among practitioners as to their operation.[38] Consequently, the impact that s. 75 will have upon a trial may be significantly reduced compared to that which was originally proposed.

Section 76 of the Sexual Offences Act 2003 introduced conclusive presumptions; thus, if the prosecution proves that the relevant circumstances existed, consent will be presumed to be absent and the jury will be directed to convict. Due to the severity of the section, the circumstances encompassed are very narrow. Under s. 76 a presumption will only be trigged in two situations: (a) the defendant intentionally deceived the complainant as to the nature and purpose of the act; or (b) the defendant intentionally induced the complainant to consent to the relevant act by impersonating someone personally known to the complainant. To a large extent, this reflects the previous common law approach to deception and consent, although historically impersonation was limited to pretending to be the complainant's husband or a fiancé. The restricted definition of 'nature and purpose' was confirmed by the Court of Appeal in *R v Jheeta*,[39] in which the court held that a

34 Convention for the Protection of Human Rights and Fundamental Freedoms, opened for signature 4 November 1950, 213 UNTS 221 (entered into force 3 September 1953). See Temkin and Ashworth, 'The Sexual Offences Act 2003', above n. 22, pp. 334–335.

35 E. Finch and V. Munro, 'The Sexual Offences Act 2003: Intoxicated Consent and Drug Assisted Rape Revisited', *Criminal Law Review*, 2004 (October), 789–802.

36 Carline and Gunby, 'How an Ordinary Jury Makes Sense of it is a Mystery', above n. 23; Gunby, Carline and Beynon, 'Alcohol-related Rape Cases', above n. 23.

37 [2011] EWCA Crim 2665, [18].

38 Carline and Gunby, 'How an Ordinary Jury Makes Sense of it is a Mystery', above n. 23; Gunby, Carline and Beynon, 'Alcohol-related Rape Cases', above n. 23.

39 [2007] EWCA Crim 1699. For a heated debated regarding the scope of s. 76 and whether other forms of deception should be able to negate consent, see J. Herring, 'Mistaken

deception was limited to misconceptions regarding the physical act that was taking place, thus following older cases such as *R v Flattery*[40] and *R v Williams*,[41] as opposed to the use of 'common garden lies' to persuade the complainant to agree to engage in sexual intercourse.

However, significant differences between Australia and England and Wales remain. In Australia the circumstances are listed as non-exhaustive, and lack of consent is conclusively determined if certain grounds are established, such as if the defendant used violent threats or terror, or unlawfully detained the complainant.[42] The Australian approach is stricter and also potentially wider ranging, and arguably this is the better approach. In England and Wales the law seems to have taken a step backwards. Previously, if the complainant was unconscious at the time of the sexual intercourse, her lack of consent was established.[43] In such a case, under s. 75 a defendant could technically argue that consent was present, although it appears clear that being unconscious will fall foul of s. 74, as the complainant will lack the freedom and capacity to consent.[44] Despite these differences, however, a defendant in Australia is entitled to argue that he held a reasonable belief in consent (as discussed later in the chapter). Hence, the Australian vitiation provisions fall somewhere in between the evidential presumptions in s. 75 and the conclusive presumptions contained in Sexual Offences Act 2003, s. 76.

Intoxication and consent

One issue which has caused significant consternation involves cases in which the complainant was extremely, but voluntarily, intoxicated and therefore potentially no longer had the capacity to consent. As Heath has commented:

> intoxication has historically represented a particularly contentious limit on capacity to consent. In the past, case law suggested a complainant had to be 'insensible' through intoxication to be incapable of consent. The language of the reformed law suggests a different standard. Standards of free agreement and free and voluntary consent raise the implication that something short of unconsciousness may render the complainant incapable of consent. Some jurisdictions suggest that consent will not be present if the intoxicated person is incapable of freely and voluntarily agreeing to sex or unable to form a rational opinion about consent because of alcohol or drug use.[45]

Sex', *Criminal Law Review*, 2005 (July), 511–524; H. Gross, 'Rape, Moralism and Human Rights', *Criminal Law Review*, 2007 (March), 220–227; J. Herring, 'Human Rights and Rape: a Reply to Hyam Gross', *Criminal Law Review*, 2007 (March), 228–231.

40 [1877] 2 QBD 410.

41 [1923] 1 KB 340.

42 For further detail see Heath, 'Women and Criminal Law', above n. 33; and see n. 32 for the relevant consent provisions.

43 *R v Larter* [1995] Crim LR 78; *R v Maloney* [1998] Crim LR 834.

44 *R v Kamki* [2013] EWCA Crim 2335.

45 Heath, 'Women and Criminal Law', above n. 33, p. 97.

In NSW, amendments introduced in 2007 made clear that 'substantial intoxication' of the complainant is a ground 'on which it may be established that a person does not consent'.[46]

In England and Wales, the Court of Appeal considered the issue in *R v Bree*.[47] The appellant was initially convicted of rape after engaging in sexual intercourse with a complainant who was voluntarily intoxicated. His conviction was quashed, however, due to the trial judge's inadequate directions to the jury, on the basis that 'the jury should have been given some assistance with the meaning of capacity'.[48] The court stated that 'a drunken consent is still a consent', and that under s. 74 the issue is whether the complainant 'has temporarily lost her capacity to choose whether to have intercourse'.[49] If this is so, she is not consenting. The court further commented that 'capacity to consent may evaporate well before a complainant becomes unconscious',[50] but emphasised that such an issue is 'fact-specific' and noted that people react differently to alcohol and an individual's tolerance is by no means consistent.[51]

In 2006 the Office of Criminal Justice Reform led a consultation to consider, among other matters, whether or not the s. 75 presumptions should also encompass cases in which the complainant was voluntarily intoxicated. One-third of the respondents agreed that s. 75(2)(d) should be reformed to read: 'Where a person was asleep, unconscious or too affected by alcohol or drugs to give free agreement'. However, the Home Office decided against this approach due to the fear of 'mischievous accusations'.[52] The myth of false allegations being commonplace has become a 'truth', with research indicating that people believe women are more likely to lie about being raped when they have been drinking.[53] Significantly, however, such beliefs are not substantiated by statistics.[54]

It is for the jury to decide whether the complainant, due to her voluntary intoxication, was incapable of consenting. However, research indicates that jurors

46 Crimes Amendment (Consent – Sexual Assault Offences) Act 2007 (NSW), s. 3, reflected in Crimes Act 1900 (NSW), s. 61HA(6)(a). This legislative reform is discussed fully in T. Dwyer, P. Easteal and A. Hopkins, 'Did She Consent? Law and the Media in New South Wales', *Alternative Law Journal* 17(4), 2012, 249–253.

47 [2007] 2 Cr App R 13, [39].

48 Ibid.

49 Ibid., [32].

50 Ibid., [34].

51 Ibid., [35].

52 Office for Criminal Justice Reform, *Convicting Rapists and Protecting Victims – Justice for Victims of Rape: Responses to Consultation*, 2007, p. 12.

53 Opinion Matters, *Wake Up To Rape Research Summary Report*, above n. 28; E. Finch and V. Munro, 'Juror Stereotypes and Blame Attribution in Rape Cases Involving Intoxicants: The Finding of A Pilot Study', *British Journal of Criminology* 45(1), 2005, 25–38; E. Finch and V. Munro, 'The Demon Drink and the Demonised Woman: Socio-Sexual Stereotypes and Responsibility Attribution in Rape Trials Involving Intoxicants', *Social and Legal Studies* 16(4), 2007, 591–614.

54 See the discussion in P. Rumney, 'False Allegations of Rape', *Cambridge Law Journal* 65(1), 2004, 128–158.

tend to draw upon problematic stereotypes regarding appropriate female behaviour, especially in cases involving voluntary intoxication.[55] People tend to hold a woman responsible if the rape/sexual assault occurred when she was voluntarily intoxicated. Therefore, jurors may be reluctant to find a defendant guilty, even if the facts seem to indicate that the complainant had lost the capacity to consent.[56]

Passivity versus activity: the move towards a positive consent standard

While the letter of the law no longer requires complainants actively to demonstrate their *lack* of consent, some Australian jurisdictions, like Victoria and Tasmania, have gone a step further and have moved toward a positive consent standard with a definition of 'free agreement' that makes it clear that if 'a person did not say or do anything to indicate free agreement . . . [it] is enough to show that the act took place without that person's free agreement'.[57] Such reform was intended to protect sexual autonomy by countering the community (and jury) beliefs that passivity could constitute consent.[58] According to Heath, however, free agreement definitions 'do little to explain consent and do not explain what might make agreement "free"'.[59]

A study of the implementation of the 1991 Victorian amendments identified six trials out of 27 in which there was a failure to direct juries that 'saying and doing nothing' ought not to be construed as an indication of consent in circumstances where such a direction may have been relevant.[60] More recent research also found that some judges were not advising jurors about the factors that could vitiate or negate consent and/or were adding commentary to their directions, which was sometimes not in synch with the aims of the legislation.[61] An example would be a judge advocating blanket consent or implied consent by advising jurors that consent can be given at a time prior to the act. Therefore, in its 2004 report, the Victorian Law Reform Commission recommended additional changes to the legislation, such as deleting the word 'normally' from what was then s. 37(1)(a) of the Crimes Act 1958 (Vic). Accordingly, in 2007, that Act was amended to further

55 Finch and Munro, 'The Demon Drink and the Demonised Woman', above n. 53.

56 Ibid. See also Opinion Matters, *Wake Up To Rape Research Summary Report*, above n. 28, p. 9.

57 Crimes Act 1958 (Vic), s. 37AAA(d). See also Criminal Code Act 1924 (Tas), Sch. 1, s. 2A(2)(a). Note that those participating in sexual activity are required to exercise a reasonable standard of care to ensure that consent is obtained: Crimes Act 1900 (NSW), ss 61HA(3)(c)–(d). This implies that consent be actively communicated, although there is no requirement that this be verbal.

58 Model Criminal Code Officers Committee, *Model Criminal Code: Sexual Offences Against the Person*, 1999, p. 265.

59 Heath, 'Women and Criminal Law', above n. 33, p 96.

60 M. Heenan and H. McKelvie, *Rape Law Reform Evaluation Project*, Report No 2: *The Crimes (Rape) Act 1991: An Evaluation Project*, Melbourne: Department of Justice, 1998, p. 298.

61 Victorian Law Reform Commission, *The Sexual Offences: Final Report*, 2004.

define consent. This round of changes established a mandatory direction to the jury that 'the fact that a person did not say or do anything to indicate free agreement to a sexual act ... is enough to show that the act took place without their free agreement'.[62]

Similarly, in Canada, consent is defined as 'voluntary agreement',[63] and the move towards an affirmative consent standard was advanced in *R v Ewanchuk*,[64] with the Supreme Court's rejection of the defence of implied consent.[65] Nevertheless, as discussed by Gotell,[66] this move towards a 'yes means yes' model does not necessarily promote feminist arguments relating to sexual autonomy and the harmful nature of coerced sex. Rather, judgments indicate the influence of a neoliberal governmentality, which is concerned with risk management and responsibilisation. While this may involve a reformulation of the good/bad victim dichotomy, which places less emphasis upon 'chastity and sexual propriety',[67] it nevertheless leads to the judgment and rejection of complainants who are perceived as having engaged in 'risky behaviour'. Consequently, 'the new "ideal" and valorized victim is a responsible, security conscious, crime-preventing, subject who acts to minimize her own risk'.[68] Hence, although an affirmative consent model may be 'capable of providing enhanced legal recognition of women's sexual autonomy',[69] judgments of appropriate female behaviour may still endure.

Consent-plus model

An alternative approach, as developed by Munro,[70] is to adopt a 'consent-plus' model, under which 'something more than "consensual minimalism" – that is a mere token of acquiescence or affirmation in the absence of force or deception – is required to render sexual contact permissible'.[71] Accordingly, 'a token of consent must be accompanied ... by a critical endorsement of a reciprocal benefit (be it

62 Crimes Act 1958 (Vic), s. 37AAA(d).

63 Criminal Code, RSC 1985, c C–46, s. 273.1(1)–(2).

64 [1991] 1 SCR 330.

65 See further R. Ruparelia, 'Does No "No" Mean Reasonable Doubt? Assessing the Impact of Ewanchuk on Determination of Consent', *Canadian Woman Studies* 25(1/2), 2006, 167–172.

66 L. Gotell, 'Rethinking Affirmative Consent in Canadian Sexual Assault Law: Neoliberal Sexual Subjects and Risky Women', *Akron Law Review* 41(4), 2008, 865–898.

67 Ibid., p. 868

68 Ibid., p. 879.

69 Ibid., p. 872.

70 See V. Munro, 'Concerning Consent: Standards of Permissibility in Sexual Relations', *Oxford Journal of Legal Studies* 25(2), 2005, 335–352; V. Munro, 'Constructing Consent: Legislating Freedom and Legitimating Constraint in the Expression of Sexual Autonomy', *Akron Law Review* 41(4), 2008, 923–956; V. Munro, 'From Consent to Coercion: Evaluating International and Domestic Frameworks for the Criminalization or Rape', in C. McGlynn and V. Munro (eds), *Rethinking Rape Law: International and Comparative Perspectives*, Abingdon: Routledge, 2010, 17–29.

71 Munro, 'From Consent to Coercion', above n. 70, p. 22.

emotional, relational, physical, or even material), which accrues as a result of engaging in sexual intercourse'.[72] As such, consent-plus recognises 'the influence of external pressures on personal self-determination',[73] without at the same time constructing female consent to (hetero)sexual activity as a product of 'false consciousness'.[74] Consequently, under a consent-plus model, a 'yes' is not taken at face value, but is instead contextualised and scrutinised, and may potentially go further than affirmative consent approaches in protecting and promoting women's sexual autonomy.

Interestingly, as Munro notes, the definition of consent in England and Wales, with its references to choice, freedom and capacity, does lend itself to the application of a more expansive consent-plus model. However, Munro identifies that there has been a 'judicial reluctance . . . to flesh out the contours' of Sexual Offences Act 2003, s. 74 in a manner which would 'require jurors to abandon their typically minimalist baseline'.[75] Herein we can perhaps see a call for judges to 'remember the future' – an ethical approach which recognises the suffering of women and that the (ongoing) legitimation of sexual abuse requires judges to abandon their reticence and move towards engaging more productively with the legislative terms.

Two recent cases suggest, perhaps, a willingness within the High Court to further analyse the terms. Both decisions involved cases dealing with the procedural side of the system, as opposed to appeals against conviction. In *Assange v Swedish Prosecution Authority*,[76] the appellant unsuccessfully challenged a European arrest warrant. One of the grounds for his appeal was that the conduct alleged – that he had proceeded to have sexual intercourse with a woman without the use of a condom after she had made it clear that use of a condom was a prerequisite to her consent – would not amount to an offence in England and Wales. While the High Court agreed that his conduct did not amount to a s. 76 deception, limited as that section is to the 'nature and the purpose of the act', it was nevertheless held to be relevant in relation to s. 74. Drawing upon *Smith and Hogan*, the court commented that 'the deception in relation to the use of a condom would "be very likely to be held to remove any purported agreement by the complainant under s.74"'.[77] Similarly, in *R v Director of Public Prosecutions*,[78] a woman initiated a judicial review against the refusal of the Director of Public Prosecutions ('DPP') to prosecute her ex-partner for rape. Of particular note was an incident in which, against the explicit request of the applicant, her ex-partner declined to withdraw from the act of intercourse prior to ejaculation. The High Court stated that 'What *Assange* underlines is that "choice" is crucial to the issue of "consent"', and that, due to her ex-partner's actions, the applicant 'was

72 Ibid.
73 Munro, 'Constructing Consent', above n. 70, p. 947.
74 Ibid, p. 955.
75 Ibid, p. 954.
76 [2011] EWHC 2849 (Admin).
77 Ibid., [89].
78 [2013] EWHC 945 (Admin).

deprived of choice relating to the crucial feature on which her original consent to sexual intercourse was based'.[79]

Rogers criticises the approach adopted in *Assange* on the basis that the only deceptions that should be relevant are those that fall within s. 76.[80] It is not, however, clear why this should be the case. While it may be understandable that s. 76 is narrowly construed, given that it is a conclusive presumption, why should the same apply to the general definition of consent in s. 74? How can it be a matter of no relevance if a man engages in intercourse without a condom or ejaculates, in express contravention of a woman's wishes? Although Rogers argues that such issues are not relevant to sexual autonomy, but relate instead to concerns about sexual health and/or pregnancy, it is difficult to see how they can be so easily separated. If we are to take seriously a woman's sexual autonomy and her right to refuse to engage in sexual encounters which fail to offer a reciprocal benefit, these two decisions are a step in the right direction.

From objective recklessness to strict liability: shades of grey in the mens rea of rape/sexual assault

The *mens rea* of rape is another area which has caused feminists consternation over the years. This was due in particular to the House of Lords decision in *Director of Public Prosecutions v Morgan*,[81] which adopted a subjective test regarding the defendant's belief in consent. To this end, the prosecution had to prove beyond reasonable doubt that the defendant did not have an *honest* belief in consent. However, even if this *honest* belief was objectively unreasonable, the defendant could still avoid a conviction. Thus, under the *Morgan* test, the principle question for the jury in relation to this element was, 'What was in the mind of the accused?'. As the law of rape has been reformed over the years, a steady move away from this subjective test has emerged. In NSW, for example, it was argued that 'the law should ensure that a reasonable standard of care is taken to ascertain whether a person is consenting before embarking on what could be potentially damaging behaviour'.[82] Accordingly, if the prosecution proves there was no consent (physical element), even if the accused holds a belief in consent, the accused may still be convicted if this belief is *unreasonable* under Crimes Act 1900 (NSW), s. 61HA(3)(c). This is an 'objective fault test'. Therefore, a defendant who has an intellectual disability (not sufficient to give the person a mental illness defence) and who engages in intercourse believing that consent has been given, could be found guilty if no reasonable person could have held that belief.

79 Ibid., [26].

80 J. Rogers, 'The Effect of "Deception" in the Sexual Offences Act 2003', *Archbold Review* 4, 2013, 7–9.

81 [1976] AC 182.

82 New South Wales Attorney General, Criminal Law Review Division, *The Law of Consent and Sexual Assault*, 2007, p. 25.

Similarly, during the reform process in England and Wales, a move away from the subjective test was promoted, among fears that 'proving that some defendants did not truly have an "honest belief" in consent contributes in some part to the low rate of convictions'.[83] Under Sexual Offences Act 2003, s. 1(3), any belief in consent must now be reasonable. Moreover, the law places a level of responsibility on the defendant to ensure that the complainant was consenting, as the jury is entitled to take into account 'any steps A has taken to ascertain whether B consents'.[84]

When questioned with regards to the reformulated *mens rea* in England and Wales, barristers expressed opinions decisively in favour of the move away from the subjective test, echoing the perception that the honest belief approach fostered injustice. Likewise, the move towards examining the behaviour of the defendant and requiring him to take appropriate steps was supported by counsel:

> I think it requires positive actions by a defendant and it's effectively saying, well, were you really paying attention to what this other person was doing? . . . I think that is quite important because what it is doing is saying that sex is to do with two individuals. And you can't focus on one, the person who is making the complaint; you've got to focus on the other as well.[85]

Nevertheless, the definition has been criticised on the basis that it requires a jury to take into account 'all the circumstances' when determining whether the belief was reasonable.[86] One concern is that this contextualisation may permit a jury to take into account stereotypical and sexist views regarding appropriate female behaviour when determining whether a defendant's belief was reasonable.[87] In *R v B*[88] the Court of Appeal held that a delusional psychotic illness was not of relevance when assessing whether a belief in consent was reasonable, which was to be judged against objective standards.[89] The court commented that this was not to say that the 'personalities or abilities or the defendant' would never be taken into account,[90] for example a case in which a person of 'less than ordinary intelligence' is unable to read 'subtle social signals' or 'behavioural cues'.[91] In such a situation, beliefs 'might be judged by a jury not to be unreasonable on their particular facts'.[92]

83 Home Office, *Protecting the Public*, above n. 20, p. 17.
84 Sexual Offences Act 2003, s. 1(2).
85 Barrister 12, as cited in Carline and Gunby, 'How an Ordinary Jury Makes Sense of it is a Mystery', above n. 23, p. 247.
86 Temkin and Ashworth, 'The Sexual Offences Act 2003', above n. 22.
87 Ibid., p. 342.
88 [2013] EWCA Crim 3.
89 Ibid., [40].
90 Ibid., [41].
91 Ibid.
92 Ibid.

Hence, a level of discretion to direct the jury to take into account a defendant's characteristics remains. Furthermore, this contextualisation contained in Sexual Offences Act 2003, s. 1(3) appears to enable jurors to place undue emphasis upon the complainant's activity in the time frame prior to the sexual encounter. This has included drawing problematic inferences from behaviour such as flirting or inviting a person back for coffee after drinks.[93] The complainant's behaviour, therefore, remains the key focus during the trial, as opposed to a more detailed analysis of whether the defendant adequately ensured that the complainant was consenting.

It is noteworthy, however, that the *Morgan* subjective test has not been universally rejected; for example, it is still in force in Victoria. This is perhaps surprising given the adoption of the 'free agreement' definition of consent and the correlating recognition in that state that silence cannot be taken to indicate consent. It was recognised during the 2004 review of the law that the application of a subjective test was incompatible with the 'free agreement' definition, as it 'does nothing to discourage the *assumption* of consent in ambiguous situations'.[94]

At the other end of the spectrum, however, many of the code states (the Commonwealth, ACT, Northern Territory, Queensland, Tasmania and Western Australia) appear to go beyond the imposition of an objective reasonableness test as they do not per se require the prosecution to prove that the defendant did not believe that consent had been given: rape is an offence of strict liability as the prosecution only has to prove sexual intercourse without consent.[95] In these jurisdictions it is not the case that rape is an *absolute* liability offence as the defendant is still permitted to raise a defence that he made an honest and reasonable mistake as to consent: reasonableness in this context would require that the accused had turned his mind to the issue, usually by taking steps to ascertain consent, and had some basis for his belief. Moreover, he does not have a persuasive burden placed upon him. Rather, there only needs to be some evidence that he held a mistaken belief in consent. In such a situation the burden is in fact placed on the prosecution to prove beyond reasonable doubt that the defendant did not hold a reasonable belief in consent. Although, prima facie, this approach appears to be radical, especially in contrast to the *Morgan* test, the prosecution in many cases will still be required to prove legal fault.

Even though the *mens rea* for rape has been the subject of heated debate both in Australia and England and Wales, the extent to which it is a decisive factor in rape cases is debateable. Most defence lawyers argue that there was consent, as it is a dangerous strategy to argue mistaken belief. As a consequence, the key issue,

93 Ellison and Munro, 'Reacting to Rape', above n. 27. See also the discussion in Munro, 'Constructing Consent', above n. 70, pp. 945–946.

94 Victorian Law Reform Commission, *The Sexual Offences*, above n. 61, p. 412 (emphasis in original).

95 See, e.g., Criminal Code Compilation Act 1913 (WA), App. B, s. 325, where neither recklessness nor intent is included in the definition of sexual assault without consent.

especially in acquaintance rape cases, is that the sexual intercourse was consensual, and defences of mistaken belief are therefore relatively rare.

More effects of myths and beliefs: corroboration and delay in reporting

Myths regarding the credibility of complainants in sexual assault and rape cases have had a significant impact on procedural elements of trials. Nowhere is this more explicit than with regards to corroboration warnings and recent complaint testimony. Until relatively recently, judges in Australia and England and Wales were required to warn a jury that it was dangerous to convict on the uncorroborated evidence of complainants. Significantly, this requirement was premised upon the contention that rape complainants were especially unreliable as a class of witness. Such warnings often drew upon the perception that false allegations were common in rape cases, for example '[t]his is a sex case. Experience has shown that women can and do tell lies for some reason, sometimes for no reason at all'.[96]

Reform has now abolished any *requirement* to warn juries about the dangers of convicting an accused of a sexual offence on the uncorroborated testimony of the victim. However, divergences exist with regards to the extent to which judges may still give a warning. In England and Wales, under Criminal Justice and Public Order Act 1994, s. 32, judges retain a discretion to issue a corroboration warning. Notably, the Court of Appeal in *Makanjuola*[97] held that a warning should only be given in cases in which there was 'an evidential basis for suggesting that the evidence of the witness may be unreliable', and that 'mere suggestions by cross examining counsel' would not suffice.[98] Research conducted with judges and barristers, however, indicates that this discretion is being utilised in a less restrictive manner than determined by the Court of Appeal, with judges frequently directing the jury to look for independent evidence in addition to the complainant's testimony. As noted by Temkin and Krahe, such an approach goes 'some way towards the institution of a corroboration requirement'.[99]

Legislative reform in some Australian jurisdictions provides no direction as to what courts should or should not say. Some jurisdictions' provisions state that warnings are not to be given, or not to be given unless justified in the circumstances of the particular case, or that the courts must/shall not suggest that the law regards complainants in sexual assault cases as unreliable. Other jurisdictions retain judicial power to warn or comment on uncorroborated evidence, if

96 B. Toner, *The Fact of Rape*, London: Arrow Books, 1982, p. 218, cited in J. Temkin and B. Krahe, *Sexual Assault and the Justice Gap: A Question of Attitude*, Oxford: Hart Publishing, 2008, p. 25.

97 [1995] 3 All ER 730.

98 Ibid., p. 1352.

99 Temkin and Krahe, *Sexual Assault and the Justice Gap*, above n. 96, p. 144.

appropriate or necessary in the interests of justice – a real mixed bag of law reform across jurisdictions.[100]

The question arises whether these reformulated laws and directions were effective. In practice, two High Court cases certainly diluted the effectiveness of the reforms. In *Longman v The Queen*[101] ('*Longman*') the High Court unanimously reversed a conviction on the basis that the trial judge had failed to warn that it was unsafe to convict on the uncorroborated testimony of the complainant. A year earlier, legislation had been enacted which stated that the judge 'shall not give a warning unless *satisfied that such a warning is justified in all the circumstances*'.[102]

Following *Longman*, judges generally now give a '*Longman* warning' in order to avoid appeals.[103] For instance, despite legislative changes in NSW, with the Crimes Act 1900 (NSW), s. 405C(2) being repealed and replaced by Evidence Act 1995 (NSW), ss 164–165, judges in that state gave corroboration warnings in 78 of 92 trials.[104] They issued an old style warning (dangerous to convict on her evidence alone) in 40 per cent of the cases and a new style warning (evidence of complainant must be scrutinised with great care) in 59 per cent of the cases.[105]

Judges have continued to exercise their discretion to comment on the evidence because of 'social and judicial attitudes, which accept and endorse the myths which were used to justify the older practices of denigrating the credibility of those who testify about sexual assault'.[106] One justification for judges needing to warn jurors about the credibility of rape victims has been victims' delay in reporting sexual assaults. The majority in the High Court case of *Crofts v The Queen*[107] held that the reforms were intended only to abolish the rules that presumed that women *as a class of witness* were untrustworthy; they were not intended to create a presumption of reliability for all women who allege rape. Trial judges in individual cases may continue to warn the jury that, in fairness to the accused, complainants who do not report their sexual abuse at the first *reasonable* opportunity lack credibility as witnesses – the effect of which is to impugn the credibility of alleged

100 See, e.g.: Evidence Act 1995 (Cth), ss 164–165; Evidence Act 1995 (NSW), ss 164–165; Sexual Offences (Evidence and Procedure) Act 1983 (NT), s. 4(5)–(6); Evidence (National Uniform Legislation) Act (NT), ss 164–165; Evidence Act 1929 (SA), s. 34L(5); Evidence Act 2001 (Tas), ss 164–165; Evidence Act 2008 (Vic), ss 164–165; Crimes Act 1958 (Vic), s. 61.

101 (1989) 168 CLR 79.

102 Evidence Act 1906 (WA), s. 36BE(1) (emphasis added), replaced by s. 50 in 1988.

103 A. Grey, 'Not-So-Uniform Evidence Law: Reforming Longman Warnings', *Current Issues in Criminal Justice* 19(2), 2007, 172–182.

104 Department for Women [NSW], *Heroines of Fortitude: The Experiences of Women in Court As Victims of Sexual Assault*, 1997, pp. 118–190.

105 Ibid., p. 188.

106 K. Mack, '"You Should Scrutinise Her Evidence With Great Care": Corroboration of Women's Testimony About Sexual Assault', in P. Easteal (ed.), *Balancing the Scales: Rape, Law Reform and Australian Culture*, Sydney: Federation Press, 1998, 59–75, p. 65.

107 (1996) 186 CLR 427.

victims of rape.[108] Accordingly, delay in bringing a complaint continues to be used by defence lawyers.

Commencing in 1997, under Crimes Act 1900 (NSW), s. 405B judges in NSW were required to warn the jury that delay in reporting sexual abuse did not *necessarily* mean a false allegation. Research in that jurisdiction, however, indicated that the warning was given in only 51 per cent of trials in which delay in complaint was raised by the defence.[109] This section was repealed and replaced in 2006 with Criminal Procedure Act 1986 (NSW), s. 294(2), under which the judge now:

> (a) must warn the jury that absence of complaint or delay in complaining does not necessarily indicate that the allegation that the offence was committed is false, and (b) must inform the jury that there may be good reasons why a victim of a sexual assault may hesitate in making, or may refrain from making, a complaint about the assault.

Section 294(2)(c) states that judges 'must not warn the jury that delay in complaining is relevant to the victim's credibility unless there is sufficient evidence to justify such a warning'. 'Sufficient evidence' remains open to judicial interpretation since each case is to be decided on its own facts and circumstances.[110]

In the ACT, as in NSW and Western Australia, there are mandatory judicial directions that highlight to the jury that there may be 'good reasons' for delay in making a complaint of sexual assault.[111]

In Victoria the judiciary seems to have complied to a greater extent in giving the direction as prescribed in the legislation.[112] Analysis of court proceedings has shown, however, that the impact of mandatory directions may be neutralised by general

108 S. Bronitt, 'The Rules of Recent Complaint: Rape Myths and the Legal Construction of the "Reasonable" Rape Victim', in P. Easteal (ed.), *Balancing the Scales: Rape, Law Reform and Australian Culture*, Sydney: Federation Press, 1998, 41–58. Hum discusses the same emphasis upon recent complaint in s. 66 of the Uniform Evidence Acts 2008: F. Hum, 'The Evidential Process and the Complainant', in P. Easteal (ed.), *Women and the Law in Australia*, Sydney: LexisNexis, 2010, 174–191, pp. 179–180. Evidence of relevant prior statements made by a witness may be admitted, but '[a]lthough the reforms now provide that the Crown can lead the complaint for the purposes of credit and truth, the requirement of it being "fresh in the memory" mirrors the common law requirement of reporting the rape at the "first opportunity"'.

109 Department for Women [NSW], *Heroines of Fortitude*, above n. 104, p. 211.

110 H. Donnelly, 'Delay and the Credibility of Complainants in Sexual Assault Proceedings', in *Sexual Assault Trials Handbook*, Sydney: Judicial Commission of NSW, 2007. Available online at www.judcom.nsw.gov.au/publications/benchbks/sexual_assault/donnelly-delay_and_credibility_of_complainants.html.

111 Evidence (Miscellaneous Provisions) Act 1991 (ACT), s. 71(2)(b); Criminal Procedure Act 1986 (NSW), s. 294(2)(b); Evidence Act 1906 (WA), s. 36BD.

112 Crimes Act 1958 (Vic), s. 61(1)(b).

comments about the significance of prompt, as compared to delayed, complaints.[113] Crimes Act 1958 (Vic), s. 61(1)(b) was amended to delete the word 'necessarily' and states that there may be good reasons why a victim of a sexual assault may delay or hesitate in making a complaint. However, research of cases that were heard after amendment of the section revealed that, in 12 of 14 cases, judges gave the old warning – using the word 'necessarily'.[114]

The impact of delayed reporting directions can also be negated by the fact that they contradict each other:

> On the one hand, juries are told that there may be good reason for the delay and delay does not necessarily mean that the allegation is false. On the other hand, juries are also told that they can take the delay into account when determining whether to believe the complainant. The two directions together can be nonsensical.[115]

The law relating to recent complaints has also seen significant changes in England and Wales. As in Australia, the exception to the rule against hearsay evidence regarding recent complaint was, historically, based upon a stereotypical assumption that a genuine rape victim would 'raise the hue and cry' immediately after being attacked.[116] Significantly, a complainant could be cross-examined on the issue if she delayed or declined to confide in another person. The exception to permit hearsay in the form of recent complaint evidence was just as likely to hinder, as opposed to assist, a prosecution, especially due to the fact that many victims are frequently very reluctant to speak to others about their ordeal.

Gradually, however, the law moved away from imposing a strict requirement with regards to the timing of the complaint. The Court of Appeal in *R v Valentine*[117] held that a statement would be admissible provided it was made 'within a reasonable time of the alleged offence and on the first occasion that reasonably offers itself'.[118] The court further commented that what was 'reasonable' would be assessed according to the complainant's characteristics and the circumstances of the case. In 2003, by virtue of Criminal Justice Act, s. 120, this requirement was further reformed to permit a complaint which had 'been made as soon as could be reasonably expected after the alleged offence'.[119] Moreover, the recent complaint exception was extended to all offences, and not just limited to sex crimes.

113 M. Heenan and H. McKelvie, *The Crimes (Rape) Act 1991: An Evaluation Project*, Report No. 2, Rape Reform Evaluation Project, Melbourne: Department of Justice, 1998, pp. 70–71.
114 Victorian Law Reform Commission, *The Sexual Offences*, above n. 61, p. 362.
115 D. Boniface, 'The Common Sense of Jurors vs the Wisdom of the Law', *University of New South Wales Law Journal* 28(1), 2005, 261–271, p. 268.
116 Temkin, *Rape and the Legal Process*, above n. 9, p. 187.
117 [1996] 2 Cr App R 213.
118 Ibid., p. 225.
119 Criminal Justice Act, s. 120(4)(d).

In *R v O*, the Court of Appeal confirmed the application of this newly worded requirement to rape cases and also, significantly, noted that a previous statement was now 'admissible to prove the truth of the matter stated and not merely to prove consistency of the complainant's account, as was the case under the old law'.[120] The relevancy of a previous complaint is therefore no longer limited to the witness's credibility, provided the prosecution does not introduce evidence of 'complaint upon complaint which may merely be self-serving'.[121]

Despite such changes, concern remained regarding the requirement that the complaint had to be made as soon as could be reasonably expected. Notions of 'reasonableness' have long been assessed from a male perspective and permit stereotypes with regards to how rape victims should respond. Furthermore, as argued by Temkin:

> A requirement of reasonableness even if it takes into account individual circumstances and what could be expected of this particular person misses the point. The idea should not be to penalise the complainant for not acting reasonably. Those who have been abused or raped may not act in a way that might be regarded as reasonable for them in the particular circumstances.[122]

Consequently, Coroners Justice and Crime Act 2009, s. 112 reformed Criminal Justice Act 2003, s. 120 and there is no longer any requirement that the complaint was made 'as soon as could reasonably be expected'. This represents an important and significant change in the law, which recognises that delays are not unusual, and prevents victims from being punished if they are reluctant to speak about their ordeal. Nevertheless, while the law relating to recent complaint has reformed to recognise that delays are not unusual, it appears that jurors are still persuaded by stereotypes that real victims are quick to report the offence and assume that any delay indicates that the allegation was fabricated.[123]

Complexity of Directions

Aside from myths and lack of corroborating evidence, there are ongoing concerns about the overall complexity of the law, with rape trials generally involving 'a multitude of directions', as enunciated by Wood CJ in the 2002 NSW case of *R v BWT*.[124] These directions may serve as the source of appeals: 55.5 per cent of conviction appeals concerned alleged defects in a trial judge's warnings and directions in sexual assault trials.[125] Indeed, research in one Australian jurisdiction

120 *R v* O [2006] 2 Cr App R 27, [23].
121 Ibid.
122 Office for Criminal Justice, *Convicting Rapists and Protecting Victims*, above n. 52, pp. 24–25.
123 Ellison and Munro, 'Reacting to Rape', above n. 27.
124 (2002) 54 NSWLR 241, 250, as cited in Boniface, 'The Common Sense of Jurors', above n. 115, pp. 263–264.
125 Boniface, 'The Common Sense of Jurors', above n. 115, p. 263.

found that the judge's summing-up of evidence in sexual assault hearings was less helpful than in other trials: jurors in trials concerning adult/child sexual offences were 1.4 times more likely than jurors in trials dealing with non-sexual offences to report that this judicial discourse did not help them 'at all' in reaching a verdict, or only helped 'a little bit'.[126] In fact, 'a direction instructing jurors that a particular use of evidence is forbidden is likely to fail to the extent that it conflicts with the jury's common sense reasoning'.[127]

How mythology may ripple into reporting

The crimes of rape and sexual assault are notoriously under reported. The most current Australian personal crime victim survey conducted in 2005 found that only 19 per cent of women who experienced sexual assault by a male perpetrator reported it to the police.[128]

Those who fall at the 'genuine rape' end of the covert but omnipresent rape continuum are more likely to report: for instance in Queensland, only five to ten per cent of victims go to the police when the rapist is a current partner, in contrast to 35 per cent of those assaulted by a stranger.[129] Aboriginal and non-English speaking women may also be less likely to report.[130]

In their study of rape cases in England and Wales, Kelly et al. noted that a range of factors were relevant to a woman's decision not to report, including fear of disbelief, blame and judgement, and a lack of trust in the police, courts and legal process.[131] The report also noted with concern the high number of cases which fell out of the system due either to withdrawal of complaints by victims at an early stage or to the assaults being classified as not a crime by the police.[132] A victim's initial contact and experiences with the police were particularly influential in her decision to continue or withdraw the case. Many lamented the lack of female personnel among the police and forensic examiners, and criticised the behaviour and attitudes of police officers.[133] Among the minority who do go to the police, some do not do so immediately. Delayed reporting can lead to the disappearance of evidence and, as described at p. 172, can be used in trial to discredit the witness.

126 L. Trimboli, 'Juror Understanding of Judicial Instructions in Criminal Trials', *Crime and Justice Bulletin* 119, Sydney: NSW Bureau of Crime Statistics and Research, 2008, 1–16.
127 Boniface, 'The Common Sense of Jurors', above n. 115, p. 267.
128 Australia Bureau of Statistics, *Personal Safety Survey, Australia, 2005*, Cat. No. 4906.0, 2006, p. 8.
129 S. Kift, 'A Legal Process or a Justice System? Sex offences in Queensland: Still Seeking Justice', *Alternative Law Journal* 28(6), 2003, 292–296, p. 294.
130 P. Easteal, 'Reaching Out to Survivors in the ACT: Culturally or Linguistically Diverse, Disabled, and Older', *Women Against Violence: An Australian Feminist Journal* 6, 1999, 56–59; J. Atkinson, 'Violence Against Aboriginal Women: Reconstitution of Community Law – The Way Forward', *Indigenous Law Bulletin* 5(11), 2001, 4–6.
131 L. Kelly, J. Lovett and L. Regan, *A Gap or a Chasm? Attrition in Reported Rape Cases*, Home Office Research Study 293, London: Home Office Research, Development and Statistics Directorate, 2005, pp. 25, 31–32.
132 Ibid., pp. 36–37.
133 Ibid., pp. 59–63.

Of particular note is the existence of a 'culture of scepticism' among the police and prosecutors, due to a misconceived assumption that false allegations are commonplace in rape cases.[134] Significantly, however, Kelly et al. estimated that, applying Home Office counting rules, only three per cent of the cases in their sample which had been reported to the police were false allegations, and there was a 'tendency to conflate false allegations with retractions and withdrawals', as opposed to understanding the difficulties faced by rape victims.[135] Disconcertingly, any evidence of inconsistency within a victim's testimony tends to be construed as evidence that the complaint was false, as opposed to appreciating not only how the trauma of being raped impacts upon a victim, but also the extent to which the discourse of 'real rape' and a culture of scepticism may influence the victim's recollection and narrative of events.[136]

Numerous developments in practice and policy have taken place over the years in order to support rape complainants and improve investigations.[137] In England and Wales, the first sexual assault referral centre ('SARC') was opened in Manchester in 1986, with such centres becoming more widespread in the early-to-mid-2000s. Many police forces now have trained rape specialists and there is an increased use of independent sexual violence advisors ('ISVAs') to support rape complainants through the ordeal of proceeding with a case.[138] Similarly, most Australian jurisdictions have specialist police units for investigating sexual assault complaints and providing support for complainants. In the ACT, for example, the Sexual Assault and Child Abuse Team has medical examination rooms, bedrooms and interview rooms. The Adult Sexual Assault Team is made up of eight specialist investigators who are required to complete the Sexual Offences Investigation Program conducted by the Australian Federal Police Training College. They are trained to treat complainants sensitively as well as learning how to build a strong case for the prosecution. However, this is not the initial response team, and those officers first at the call are likely not to have had such training.

134 Ibid., p. 83. See also Stern, *The Stern Review*, above n. 26, pp. 33–34, 56–57.

135 Kelly, Lovett and Regan, *A Gap or a Chasm?*, above n. 131, p. 51.

136 Ibid., pp. 49–50. See also the discussions in M. Burton, 'How Different are "False" Allegations of Rape from False Complaints of GBH?', *Criminal Law Review* 3, 2013, 203–213; C. Saunders, 'The Truth, The Half-Truth, and Nothing Like the Truth: Reconceptualizing False Allegations of Rape', *British Journal of Criminology* 52(6), 2012, 1152–1171.

137 See, e.g.: Association of Chief Police Officers and the Crown Prosecution Service, *Guidance on Investigating and Prosecuting Rape*, 2009; Association of Chief Police Officers and the Crown Prosecution Service, *A Protocol Between the Police and the Crown Prosecution Service in the Investigation and Prosecution of Allegations of Rape*, ND. Available online at www.cps.gov.uk/publications/agencies/rape_protocol.html#_02.

138 For more information on SARCs and ISVAs, see: J. Lovett, L. Regan and L. Kelly, *Sexual Assault Referral Centres: Developing Good Practice and Maximising Potentials*, Home Office Research Study 285, London: Home Office, 2004; A. Robinson, *Independent Sexual Violence Advisors: A Process Evaluation*, London: Home Office, 2009.

Despite these developments, policy and good practice have not necessarily been implemented. Due to confusion about guidelines, some police officers do not refer all rape complaints to the prosecution.[139] Perhaps because those who are specially trained do not conduct interviews with rape victims, most of the women in one study who turned to the police did not feel wholly supported.[140] Similarly, in Victoria, focus group research with several centres against sexual assault and police identified room for improvement of police attitudes and understanding about sexual assault.[141]

Insensitivity may be evidenced by police minimising what had occurred through their choice of words in questions they ask. For example, in an interview with one woman, whose ex-boyfriend was charged with 'unlawfully confining a person', 'sexual intercourse without consent' and 'intentional threat to kill', the officer asked: 'How did he come to rape you?'. After the complainant responded that he had forced her legs open, the officer asked: 'How long did he lay on top of you in that position making love to you, fucking you, whatever words you want to use . . . raping you?'.[142] Such treatment by the police may have an effect on a victim's decision about whether to continue legal proceedings.[143]

Another common complaint about police is their lack of relaying information and keeping the complainant informed of progress with the investigation. This includes the lack, or inadequacy, of explanations given for why charges were not laid.[144]

One infamous case in England and Wales, which has recently reached the High Court, is that of John Worboys, a taxi driver, who was convicted for numerous sexual offences and linked to 81 offences in total. Worboys drugged his victims by offering them a spiked drink under the pretence of celebrating a lottery win. The Independent Police Complaints Commission ('IPCC') upheld complaints against five Metropolitan police officers after two of his victims made formal complaints. The IPCC unveiled a litany of errors, including insensitive behaviour on behalf of the police officers and a failure to conduct a thorough investigation. The police chose to believe Worboys' contention that the victim was drunk; they also failed to search his cab or home for corroborating evidence and stated that 'it would seem unlikely that a cab driver would have alcohol in his vehicle let alone

139 Office of the Director of Public Prosecutions (ACT) and the Australian Federal Police, *Responding to Sexual Assault: The Challenge of Change*, Sexual Assault Response Program Report, 2005.

140 Easteal and Feerick, 'Sexual Assault by Male Partners', above n. 15, p 190.

141 Victorian Law Reform Commission, *The Sexual Offences*, above n. 61, p. xxii.

142 Easteal and Feerick, 'Sexual Assault by Male Partners', above n 15, p. 190.

143 Ibid.

144 NSW Violence Against Women Specialist Unit, *Improving Service and Criminal Justice Responses to Victims of Sexual Assault: A Report of a State-Based Consultation With Adult Victims of Sexual Assault, Services and Agencies*, 2006; P. Easteal and L. McOrmond-Plummer, *Real Rape, Real Pain*, Melbourne: Hybrid Publishers, 2006.

drug substances'.[145] Significantly, the High Court has held that the failure of the police to investigate amounted to a breach of the victims' human rights under the European Convention on Human Rights, Art. 3,[146] which prohibits torture, inhuman or degrading treatment.[147]

How mythology may ripple into prosecuting[148]

Attrition remains high at the stage of police investigation. Concerns continue with regards to the pervasive nature of a 'culture of disbelief' among police forces, with data in England and Wales for 2012/13 demonstrating alarming high levels of 'no criming' – up to 33 per cent.[149] In 2012, Australian data show that 30 days after the initial complaint of sexual assault, an offender had been proceeded against in only 21 per cent of cases, as compared to 20.8 per cent in 2011 and 18.6 per cent in 2010:[150] '[a] 2000–03 Victorian study found that police did not proceed with more than 60% of sexual assault investigations. Offenders were charged in only 15% of cases'.[151] The Australian Institute of Criminology has estimated that less than 20 per cent of sexual offence incidents which are reported to the police result in charges being laid and criminal proceedings being investigated.[152]

When cases do proceed, prosecutors review the case to determine whether there are reasonable prospects of a conviction in accordance with prosecution policy. As cases reflecting the 'real' rape stereotype are most likely to result in a conviction, it

145 Independent Police Complaints Commission, *IPCC Independent Investigation into the Metropolitan Police Service's Inquiry into Allegations Against John Worboys*, Commissioner's Report, 2010, p. 10. See also the discussion in Stern, *The Stern Review*, above n. 26, pp. 46–47.

146 Convention for the Protection of Human Rights and Fundamental Freedoms, opened for signature 4 November 1950, 213 UNTS 221 (entered into force 3 September 1953); Human Rights Act 1998.

147 *DSD v The Commissioner of Police for the Metropolis* [2014] EWHC 436 (QB).

148 Calculating the attrition rate in sexual assault prosecution is problematic. There is limited availability of statistics due to under reporting and 'inconsistencies in definitions of sexual assault as well as limitations associated with current methods of data collection and evaluation': Australian Law Reform Commission, *Family Violence – A National Legal Response*, above n. 3, p. 1187.

149 Her Majesty's Inspectorate of Constabulary, *Rape Monitoring Group: Adult and Child Rape Data 2012–13*, 2014. Available online at www.hmic.gov.uk/publication/rape-monitoring-group-digests-data-and-methodology-2014/.

150 Australia Bureau of Statistics, *Recorded Crime – Victims, Australia, 2012*, Cat No. 4510.0, 2013.

151 Statewide Steering Committee to Reduce Sexual Assault (Vic), *Study of Reported Rapes in Victoria 2000–03*, Summary Research Report, 2006, p. 5, cited in Australian Law Reform Commission, *Family Violence – A National Legal Response*, above n. 3, p. 1188.

152 Australian Institute of Criminology, *Guilty Outcomes in Reported Sexual Assault and Related Offence Incidents*, 2007, cited in Australian Law Reform Commission, *Family Violence – A National Legal Response*, above n. 3, p. 1189.

is these cases that are most likely to proceed to trial at the prosecutor's discretion.[153] Additionally, if there are any differences between what the victim said to police between different interviews and/or at committal, the prosecutor may pre-empt the defence raising these discrepancies at trial by labelling the victim as unreliable and dropping the case.[154] Indeed, prosecutors assess a complainant's credibility, paying attention to such 'inconsistency'[155] and evaluating the victim's degree and manifestation of distress, as well as her ability to recall and communicate.[156]

Criminal matters require a high standard of proof and, in the absence of corroborating evidence such as forensics, there is little chance of conviction. Therefore, a reluctance to prosecute results also from a lack of such evidence and an absence of physical injuries.[157] In England and Wales, some police officers have lamented the decisions taken by prosecutors:

> I feel there's different standards within CPS [Crown Prosecution Service] depending on who's assessing the papers . . . I had a case where . . . the decision file went into CPS, that came back, discontinued, before even the toxicology reports had come back from the lab. I was really quite disheartened . . . I feel like whenever you have one that comes down to [an] issue of consent, unless you have areas of bruising, tearing, damage or whatever, from the medical examination as supporting evidence, it is going to be one word against another, and very, very few of those cases ever get to court whereby that IP [injured party] is given the opportunity to put his or her side across. I just feel that the CPS give up too easy, too soon.[158]

There is therefore significant attrition at this point. In 2011–2012, 18.9 per cent of cases where sexual assault or related offences were the principle offence were withdrawn by the prosecution in the higher criminal courts in Australia, compared to 20 per cent in 2010–2011.[159] Looking at five jurisdictions in Australia, Lievore found that those more likely to proceed involved 'force *and* the victims actively expressed non-consent'.[160] Reforms on consent are seemingly limited in their

153 K. Cripps and C. Taylor, 'White Man's Law, Traditional Law, Bullshit Law: Customary Marriage Revisited', *Balayi: Culture, Law and Colonialism* 10, 2009, 59–72.
154 Easteal and Feerick, 'Sexual Assault by Male Partners', above n. 15, p 193.
155 Office of the Director of Public Prosecutions (ACT) and the Australian Federal Police, *Responding to Sexual Assault*, above n. 139, p 89.
156 D. Lievore, 'Victim Credibility in Adult Sexual Assault Cases', *Trends and Issues in Crime and Criminal Justice* 288, Canberra: Australian Institute of Criminology, 2004, p. 4.
157 Ibid.
158 REACH, Police Officer CID/Sexual Offence Liaison Officer (SOLO), F1, May 2003, cited in Kelly, Lovett and Regan, *A Gap or a Chasm?*, above n. 131, p. 57.
159 Australian Bureau of Statistics, *Criminal Courts, Australia, 2011–2012*, Cat. No. 4513.0, 2013.
160 D. Lievore, 'Prosecutorial Decisions in Adult Sexual Assault Cases', *Trends and Issues in Crime and Criminal Justice* 291, Canberra: Australian Institute of Criminology, 2005 (emphasis in original).

ability to overcome the stereotypes to which prosecutors believe potential jurors subscribe – in other words, prosecutors discontinue the matters that they believe have little chance of conviction. In the same vein, the complainant may ask for the matter to be discontinued because the prosecution has dissuaded her (sometimes subtly and sometimes directly) that there is little hope of a guilty verdict, or because her cross-examination at the committal hearing was prohibitively traumatic.[161] Thus, not surprisingly, one study found that victims show more willingness to pursue prosecution if there is evidence that increases the likelihood of conviction.[162]

Kelly et al.'s 2005 study of rape cases in England and Wales demonstrated similar concerns about the level of attrition, with only 14 per cent of cases reported to the police proceeding to trial.[163] Victim withdrawal was a significant factor. Many victims cited as their reasons for retreating the fear of giving evidence, and a belief that they would be 'torn to pieces' during the cross-examination, an issue which will be discussed further in Chapter 9.[164] In order to improve the prosecution of rape cases, the CPS in England and Wales has introduced specialist rape prosecutors and all districts now have a rape co-ordinator. As with the police, a review into rape cases noted that there was little criticism with regards to the CPS *policy* for prosecuting rape cases; however, concerns existed with regards to its *implementation.* Not all districts have specialist prosecutors in place and in some trials the prosecutor was not fully prepared. Concern was also expressed with regards to the lack of additional resources to handle rape cases,[165] which will only increase due to the ongoing budgetary cuts faced by the Ministry of Justice.[166]

Shades of grey and the impact of law reform

This chapter has highlighted the shades of grey which exist with regards to the law relating to the definition of rape/sexual assault, consent and corroboration, in addition to the factors which impact upon a victim's decision to report and the criminal justice system's decision to prosecute a rape/sexual assault case. Various myths and misconceptions, particularly those relating to 'real rape' and false allegations, have circulated and shaped the law and legal responses in various ways. While historically such myths were embedded within the law, recent reforms have witnessed a concerted effort to challenge such perspectives. Across the globe this has led to a diverse plethora of law reform.

161 Easteal and Feerick, 'Sexual Assault by Male Partners', above n. 15.

162 W. Kerstetter, 'Gateway to Justice: Police and Prosecutorial Response to Sexual Assaults Against Women', *Criminology* 81(2), 1990, 267–313.

163 Kelly, Lovett and Regan, *A Gap or a Chasm?*, above n. 131, p. 40.

164 Ibid., pp. 65–68.

165 Stern, *The Stern Review*, above n. 26, p. 86.

166 See, e.g., J. Hyde, 'Osborne Imposes Further £142m of Cuts on MoJ', *The Law Society Gazette*, 18 March 2013. Available online at www.lawgazette.co.uk/70016.article.

Significantly, however, victim-blaming attitudes and perspectives regarding what amounts to rape are proving difficult to displace, and research indicates that the reforms have done little to assist juries in understanding the notion of consent. It remains a nebulous concept. Reforms aimed at dramatically reforming the offence so to render consent less pivotal have not been entirely successful. Consent still seems to retain its 'moral magic'.[167] In addition, and disappointingly, the number of cases reported to police remains very low and the overall attrition rate for rape is still too high. Something more needs to be done to engender justice for rape victims. Some suggestions are included in Chapter 12.

167 H.M. Hurd, 'The Moral Magic of Consent', *Legal Theory* 2(2), 1996, 121–146.

Chapter 9

More on myths and indeterminacy in sexual assault law

Given some community beliefs that involve victim blaming and provocation in rape,[1] the differentiation between 'real' rape and 'not so real' rape, discussed in Chapter 8, and a common (mis)perception that rape allegations are 'very easy to fabricate but extremely difficult to refute',[2] it is easy to see why the evidence of many victims of sexual assault in courtrooms across the world is assumed to be intrinsically unreliable. Apart from resulting in cross-examinations that are gruelling and permeated by such myths, these beliefs may be contributing to a high attrition rate through the criminal justice system. In fact, the fear of the courtroom experience, particularly cross-examination, may be a substantial barrier for rape victims.[3] A sexual assault referral centre counsellor expressed this fear in no uncertain terms:

> [They are] absolutely terrified of going to court, and what they always say is, 'His defence is going to tear me apart, how am I going to deal with that?' Terrified. Terrified of the brief, terrified of the culture of gowns and wigs and the judge, terrified of being able to see the offender, but most of all what they seem terrified of is bringing up all their past history and him getting off.[4]

1 N. Taylor and J. Mouzos, *Community Attitudes to Violence Against Women Survey: A Full Technical Report*, Canberra: Australian Institute of Criminology, 2006, p. xii.

2 Victorian Law Reform Commission, *Sexual Offences: Law and Procedure*, Discussion Paper, 2001, p. 155. For example, Clark found that 98 per cent of participants considered the victim's dress, behaviour, chastity, alcohol consumption and prior acquaintance with the assailant in determining the seriousness of the alleged sexual offence: H. Clark, 'Judging Rape: Public Attitudes and Sentencing', *Australian Centre for the Study of Sexual Assault Newsletter* 14, 2007, 17–25.

3 L. Kelly, J. Lovett and L. Regan, *A Gap or a Chasm? Attrition in Reported Rape Cases*, Home Office Research Study 293, London: Home Office Research, Development and Statistics Directorate, 2005, p. 65.

4 St Mary's Sexual Assault Referral Centre counsellor, cited in ibid., p. 74.

Mythology and movement through the criminal justice system

In Chapter 8 we looked at how the myths about 'real' rape affect both the reporting of the offence and decisions to prosecute. Not surprisingly, then, the conviction rate for rape trials that actually make it to the courtroom is very low, with even fewer defendants convicted for assaults that are not conceptualised as 'real' rape.[5] In Australia, for example, acquittals occur more often than guilty verdicts and more often than in other serious offences.[6] In 2011–12, 17.7 per cent of defendants who were facing a charge of sexual assault in higher courts were acquitted,[7] a slight decrease from 19 per cent in 2010–11.[8] In 2011–12, 48.6 per cent of defendants pleaded guilty, 12.3 per cent pleaded not guilty and were convicted, and 18.9 per cent of cases were withdrawn by the prosecution.[9]

In England and Wales, concerns regarding the conviction rate prompted many of the substantive and procedural reforms to the law of rape. In Kelly et al.'s study, *A Gap or a Chasm*, it was noted that the conviction rate for rape had fallen from 32 per cent in 1977 to 5.6 per cent in 2002.[10] Consequently, in 2009 Baroness Stern was invited to undertake an independent review into the handling of rape complaints. One key issue discussed was the widely cited conviction rate of six per cent.[11] It was noted that there was little appreciation as to what this figure represented and that its ongoing circulation may unduly dissuade many rape victims from reporting an offence.[12] The review, in contrast, emphasised that the conviction rate of cases which actually reach court is 58 per cent,[13] whereas the six per cent rate pertains to cases which are reported to the police and result in a conviction. This leads to the finding that the key problem is attrition prior to the trial, and that a conviction for rape is no more or less likely than it is for any other crime of violence. Further analysis conducted by the Home Office, Ministry of Justice and the Office for National Statistics has established that in 2011 the conviction rate for rape cases prosecuted was 51.8 per cent.[14] However, the report

5 M. Heath, 'Women and Criminal Law: Rape', in P. Easteal (ed.), *Women and the Law in Australia*, Sydney: LexisNexis, 2010.
6 N. Taylor, 'Juror Attitudes and Biases in Sexual Assault Cases', *Trends and Issues in Crime and Criminal Justice* 344, Canberra: Australian Institute of Criminology, 2007.
7 Australian Bureau of Statistics, *Criminal Courts, Australia, 2011–2012*, Cat. No. 4513.0, 2013.
8 Australian Bureau of Statistics, *Criminal Courts, Australia, 2010–2011*, Cat. No. 4513.0, 2012, p. 17.
9 Australian Bureau of Statistics, *Criminal Courts Australia, 2011–2012*, above n. 7.
10 Kelly, Lovett and Regan, *A Gap or a Chasm?*, above n. 3, p. 25.
11 Baroness Stern, *The Stern Review: A Report by Baroness Vivien Stern CBE of an Independent Review Into How Rape Complaints are Handled by Public Authorities in England and Wales*, London: Government Equalities Office and the Home Office, 2010, p. 9.
12 Ibid., pp. 9, 42–46.
13 Ibid., p. 92.
14 Ministry of Justice, Home Office and the Office of National Statistics, *An Overview of Sexual Offender in England and Wales*, 2013.

also notes that among sexual offences, rape of a female had the lowest conviction *ratio* – this being the 'number of convictions as a proportion of the number of proceedings' – at 39.7 per cent.[15] One reason for this is that many rape cases are downgraded to sexual assault.

The Stern Review concludes: 'When the policies described in this report are adopted everywhere more rape cases will proceed to court and more will end in a conviction'.[16] Notably, however, elsewhere in the report it is stated that the Crown Prosecution Service ('CPS') could not be faulted for its decision-making processes and that more cases should not be prosecuted, especially if the evidence base is deemed to be weak.[17] It is, with respect, difficult to reconcile these two assertions. Moreover, Alison Saunders, Chief Crown Prosecutor for London, has lamented the ongoing impact of rape myths and misconceptions upon criminal justice practitioners.[18] Saunders further suggests a move away from a 'bookmakers' approach to determining the 'realistic prospect of conviction test',[19] to a more merit-based approach. Thus, 'instead of asking what is the likelihood of conviction we should ask ourselves, what would be the merits of a prosecution', and consequently 'prejudices against complainants' (i.e. the fact that she had been drinking and/or had delayed reporting the offence) should be ignored.[20]

In *A Gap or a Chasm?*, the 'real rape' template featured strongly in cases in which a conviction was achieved. Indeed: 'cases involving use of a weapon and external injuries were twice as likely to result in conviction'.[21] Research with mock juries likewise supports the contention that the existence of violence is critical to the outcome of a trial, with participants 'routinely [emphasising] the significance of [the] lack of bruising to their not guilty verdicts'.[22] Further, Ellison and Munro note that for many, '[t]heir commitment to the belief that a "normal" response to sexual attack would be to struggle physically was . . . unshakeable'.[23] Not only did some participants hypothesise alternative causes for the injury, numerous members 'also intimated that the possibility could, and should, not be ruled out that the complainant's bruises were deliberately self-inflicted in order to support her fabricated allegation of rape'.[24] A culture of scepticism continues to haunt the jury room.

15 Ibid., p. 35.
16 Stern, *The Stern Review*, above n. 11, p. 10.
17 Ibid., p. 94.
18 A. Saunders, 'Speech on the Prosecution of Rape and Serious Sexual Offences' (speech delivered at City Hall, London, 30 January 2012). Available online at www.cps.gov.uk/news/articles/speech_on_the_prosecution_of_rape_and_serious_sexual_offences_by_alison_saunders_chief_crown_prosecutor_for_london/.
19 Ibid.
20 Ibid.
21 Kelly, Lovett and Regan, *A Gap or a Chasm?*, above n. 3, p. 73.
22 L. Ellison and V. Munro, 'Reacting to Rape: Exploring Mock Juror's Assessments of Complainant Credibility', *British Journal of Criminology* 49(2), 2009, 202–219, p. 206.
23 Ibid.
24 Ibid., p. 208.

Another striking feature, which undoubtedly entrenches the perceived necessity of evidence of violence, was the high burden of proof that mock jurors were prone to apply. During deliberations, numerous mock jurors expressed the opinion that 'beyond reasonable doubt' required participants to be 100 per cent certain that the defendant had committed the crime, before they could find him guilty.[25] Participants had a propensity to adopt a significantly stricter test than is legally required. Ellison and Munro noted a lack of engagement with the law, with many reaching 'a verdict without any discursive reference to, or examination of, the law to be applied'.[26] More attention tended to be paid to notions of real rape and 'normal sex'. When the law was discussed, 'there was ample evidence of misunderstanding'.[27] The extent to which the letter of the law and judicial directions impact upon juries can, therefore, be disputed. Similar perspectives have also been expressed by rape/sexual assault barristers.[28]

Interestingly, in light of the reforms discussed at p. 185, another study also using mock juries found that how the victim witness gave her evidence (via closed-circuit television ('CCTV'), pre-recorded) did not appear to affect jurors' decision-making. Of more importance were 'the pre-existing attitudes, biases and expectations that jurors bring with them into the courtroom'.[29]

Upon a finding of guilt, the sentencing guidelines in England and Wales indicate that the offender should be sentenced for a minimum of four years.[30] This move to ensure that the punishment reflects the severity of the crime may have had a negative impact upon the conviction rate. Mock jury members frequently referred to the likely sentence a defendant would receive during their assertions that they had to be 100 per cent certain of guilt.[31] Barristers have also commented that juries may often be deterred by the fact that the offender would be placed on the sex

25 L. Ellison and V. Munro, 'Getting to (Not) Guilty: Examining Juror's Deliberative Processes in, and Beyond, the Context of a Mock Rape Trial', *Legal Studies* 30(1), 2010, 74–97, p. 84.

26 Ibid., p. 94.

27 Ibid. See also the findings of C. Thomas, *Are Juries Fair?*, London: Ministry of Justice, 2010, who highlights the difficulties juries face in understanding judicial directions.

28 A. Carline and C. Gunby, '"How an Ordinary Jury Makes Sense of it is a Mystery". Barristers' Perspectives on Rape, Consent and the Sexual Offences Act 2003', *Liverpool Law Review* 32(3), 2011, 237–250.

29 N. Taylor and J. Joudo, *The Impact of Pre-Recorded Video and Closed Circuit Television Testimony by Adult Sexual Assault Complainants on Jury Decision-Making: an Experimental Study*, Canberra: Australian Institute of Criminology, 2005, p. 66. Similar findings regarding the impact, or lack thereof, of special measures on decision-making processes has been reported in England and Wales. See L. Ellison and V. Munro, 'Do Special Measures Affect Jurors' Verdicts in Rape', *Criminal Law and Justice Weekly* 177(7), 2013, 103–104; L. Ellison and V. Munro, *Special Measures in Rape Trials: Exploring the Impact of Screens, Live Links and Video-Recorded Evidence on Mock Juror Deliberation*, Leeds: Economic and Social Research Council, Briefing Report, 2013.

30 Sentencing Council, *Sexual Offences Definitive Guidelines*, 2013, p. 9.

31 Ellison and Munro, 'Getting to (Not) Guilty', above n. 25, p. 84.

offenders register.[32] One particular assertion is that a guilty verdict would 'ruin the defendant's life'.[33] In such a scenario, the trauma caused to the complainant by the accused's violation is diminished. Failing to convict due to the concern that the defendant's life would be ruined normalises rape and constructs it as something that women should endure and men should not be punished for.

The sentencing process appears to be further tainted by rape mythology.[34] As a consequence of issues canvassed in cross-examination, some Australian judges, for instance, are apt to draw negatively on the victim's supposed character or sexual history.[35] It is possible that myths about 'real' rape, including the relationship between the rapist and the victim, affect judicial weighting of harm. We will look at this issue more in Chapter 10, which focuses on partner rape.

Mythology and cross-examination

The myths affecting conviction and sentencing are reflective of scepticism toward complainants. These remain embedded in legal doctrines and procedures that may negatively affect victim witnesses' experiences on the stand and the perception of their credibility, which in turn reduces the quality of their evidence – no doubt contributing to a low conviction rate.

Research in one Australian jurisdiction, New South Wales ('NSW'), found that judges remain reluctant to intervene in the conduct of cross-examination despite legislative changes and judicial education.[36] Another example from England and Wales is where, strictly speaking, witnesses are protected from ongoing attacks against their credibility under the 'finality rule'. This rule dictates that once a witness has answered a question which relates to his/her credibility, as opposed to an issue in the case, that answer is to be taken as final. The defence is not permitted to question and re-question the complainant with regards to credibility. The application of this rule to cases involving sexual offences has, however, been

32 Comments made to one of the authors during an empirical project into rape and the Sexual Offences Act 2003. For further detail on the study, see: Carline and Gunby, 'How an Ordinary Jury Makes Sense of it is a Mystery', above n. 28; C. Gunby, A. Carline and C. Beynon, 'Alcohol-Related Rape Cases: Barristers' Perspectives on the Sexual Offences Act 2003 and its Impact on Practice', *Journal of Criminal Law* 74(6), 2010, 579–600.

33 Ellison and Munro, 'Getting to (Not) Guilty', above n. 25, p. 84.

34 P. Easteal and M. Gani, 'Sexual Assault by Male Partners: A Study of Sentencing Variables', *Southern Cross University Law Review* 9, 2005, 39–72.

35 S.C. Taylor, 'A Name By Any Other Word Does Not Necessarily Make It Merely Another Rose', in A. Mills and J. Smith (eds), *Utter Silence: Voicing the Unspeakable*, New York: Peter Lang, 2001, 211–223.

36 A. Cossins, 'Prosecuting Child Sexual Assault Cases: Are Vulnerable Witness Protections Enough?', *Current Issues in Criminal Justice* 18(2), 2006, 299–317; A. Cossins, 'A Cross-Examination in Child Sexual Assault Trials: Evidentiary Safeguard or an Opportunity to Confuse?', *Melbourne University Law Review* 33(1), 2009, 68–104.

questioned in numerous cases,[37] and by various commentators. Tapper has challenged the distinction between credibility and issue in sex offence cases:

> Evidence is often effectively limited to that of the parties, and much is likely to depend on the balance of credibility between them. This has important effects for the law of evidence since it is capable of reducing the difference between questions going to credit and questions going to issue to vanishing point. If the only issue is consent and the only evidence is the testimony of the complainant, the conclusion that she is unworthy of credit must be decisive of the issue.[38]

The perspective that the credibility of the complainant is of unique and particular importance is troubling. In order to be believed, she must fall into a very narrow categorisation of a 'true rape victim', an approach which places unrealistic and unjustified expectations upon women.[39] A phallocentric perspective regarding rape is maintained and perpetuated in the courtroom through the body of the rape victim.[40]

Therefore, as mentioned in Chapter 8, the victim's credibility is often attacked through cross-examination and judicial warnings to the jury.[41] Barristers may be even more ruthless in their cross-examination of certain types of victims (e.g. incest survivors, partner rape).[42] Witnesses may be asked questions to which they can only answer 'yes' or 'no', but which are impossible to answer in that way. Questions may be asked in a non-chronological way with the objective to confuse and make the victim appear unreliable. Complainants may be cross-examined about a variety of issues that are designed to make them lose credibility. In one Australian study, for example, over half (53.7 per cent) the victims were queried about whether they had a motive for false reporting. A median of victims were asked five questions on this issue, while 84.3 per cent were asked an average of seven questions focused on lying and '58% were asked if they had flirted or engaged in "sexually provocative" behaviour towards or in the presence of the accused'.[43] Sue Lees' study of rape cases in the Old Bailey in the 1990s highlighted how, in these ways, women frequently suffered a second rape, or a 'judicial rape', in the courtroom. During the proceedings the woman's 'reputation [was] put on trial' and the experience was considered by

37 *R v Funderburk* [1990] 1 WLR 587; *R v Nagrecha* [1997] 2 Cr App R 401.

38 C. Tapper, *Cross & Tapper on Evidence*, Oxford: Oxford University Press, 2007, p. 358.

39 See J. Temkin, 'Prosecuting and Defending Rape: Perspectives from the Bar', *Journal of Law and Society* 27(2), 2000, 219–248.

40 C. Smart, *Feminism and the Power of Law*, London: Routledge, 1995, pp. 26–49.

41 D. Lievore, *Intimate Partner Sexual Assault: The Impact of Competing Demands on Victims' Decisions to Seek Criminal Justice Solutions*, Canberra: Australian Institute of Criminology, 2003.

42 Taylor, 'Juror Attitudes and Biases in Sexual Assault Cases', above n. 6.

43 P. Van de Zandt, 'Heroines of Fortitude', in P. Easteal (ed.), *Balancing the Scales: Rape, Law Reform and Australian Culture*, Sydney: Federation Press, 1998, 124–142.

many victims to be just as 'humiliating as the actual rape'.[44] The 'culture of scepticism' travels with the complainant into the courtroom where she is accused of falsifying her story. Any inconsistencies within her testimony are used to bolster the notion that the accusation is false,[45] an approach which fails to appreciate the impact caused by the trauma of being raped.

Following a sexual assault, victims often feel scared, anxious, sad, angry, shameful, responsible and unconfident. They may experience rape trauma syndrome[46] or post traumatic stress disorder.[47] Given their psychological fragility, there is an enormous potential for re-traumatisation of sexual assault victims through their involvement with the criminal justice system and its processes. Of particular concern is when victims testify and are cross-examined. For victims of sexual assault, the traumatic effects of the trial can trigger similar feelings of powerlessness to those experienced as a result of the original abuse:[48] 'there is no difference between being raped and giving evidence as a key witness at the trial of your alleged rapist, except that this time it happens in front of a crowd'.[49] The NSW *Heroines of Fortitude* study found that 65 per cent of the trials studied had two or more interruptions to evidence because of the distress of the victim.[50]

Some of the factors that compound the trauma of a trial for sexual assault victim witnesses, and which have resulted in much law reform, include: being able to see the accused in the courtroom; being cross-examined by a self-represented accused; the use of traumatising questions by the defence; having to give evidence multiple times; giving evidence in a court open to the public; and the length of the process. We now look at a few examples of legislation enacted in Australia and England and Wales to better protect vulnerable witnesses from such ordeals, and how these grey-shaded laws have been susceptible to interpretation by judges and counsel. Some commentators have suggested that the ensuing discretion has limited the efficacy of such legislation, and in some cases has undermined Parliament's intent.

44 S. Lees, *Carnal Knowledge: Rape on Trial*, London: Women's Press, 2002, p. 36. Similar concerns were expressed in 1975 by the Heilbron Committee, *Report of the Advisory Group on the Law of Rape*, Cmnd 6352, London: Her Majesty's Stationery Office, 1975.

45 J. Temkin, *Rape and the Legal Process*, Oxford: Oxford University Press, 2005, p. 235.

46 Described by A.W. Burgess and L.L. Holmstrom, 'Rape Trauma Syndrome', *American Journal of Psychiatry* 131(9), 1974, 981–986.

47 P. Easteal and L. McOrmond-Plummer, *Real Rape, Real Pain*, Melbourne: Hybrid Publishers, 2006, pp. 221–234.

48 Ibid. See also: C. Eastwood, 'The Experiences of Child Complainants of Sexual Abuse in the Criminal Justice System', *Trends and Issues in Crime and Criminal Justice* 250, Canberra: Australian Institute of Criminology, 2003.

49 D. Stuart, 'No Real Harm Done: Sexual Assault and the Criminal Justice System', in P. Easteal (ed.), *Without Consent: Confronting Adult Sexual Violence*, Canberra: Australian Institute of Criminology, 1993, 95–106.

50 Van de Zandt, 'Heroines of Fortitude', above n. 43, p. 126.

Legislation: less invasive and traumatic questions

Traditionally, one of the limits on the evidence the defence may adduce has been its relevance. This has enabled extensive interrogation into many contentious issues including previous consensual sex between the victim and the defendant. Prior to reforms in England and Wales, for example, questions regarding the complainant's sexual activity with third persons were only permitted if the judge granted leave; however, similar constraints did not exist with regards to previous activity involving the defendant.[51] Such questioning was used to imply that there was consent or that, because of past consensual sex, the defendant mistakenly believed that the victim was consenting. Moreover, judges had significant discretion to permit questioning regarding third parties, and research highlighted that defence barristers frequently asked irrelevant questions in order to discredit the complainant.[52]

As a result of ongoing concerns regarding the extensive and problematic manner in which complainants were interrogated, legislation was amended to limit and structure judicial discretion. In England and Wales, the Youth Justice and Criminal Evidence Act 1999, ss 41–43 ('YJCEA') restricted the introduction of sexual history evidence and aimed to: encourage rape victims to report; improve the attrition rate;[53] prevent undue distress to complainants; and 'cut through the myths and stereotypes in order to produce fair outcomes in trials for sexual offences'.[54] Section 41 stipulates that defence counsel is not permitted to adduce any evidence relating to the complainant's sexual experience or behaviour unless leave is granted. Significantly, this exclusion is wider than that under the previous law (Sexual Offences (Amendment) Act 1976, s. 2), as it is not restricted to evidence involving third parties but also encompasses, ostensibly, any previous sexual activity with the defendant. Leave is only to be granted if the evidence falls into one of four 'gateways' *and* its exclusion 'might have the result of rendering unsafe a conclusion of the jury'.[55]

Section 41(3)(a) states that evidence may be permitted if it is relevant to an issue in the case other than the issue of consent. This includes: the defendant's belief in consent; evidence relating to identity; sexual offences where consent is not the issue; and motive to lie.[56] With regards to the defendant's belief in consent, it can be argued

51 Sexual Offences (Amendment) Act 1976, s. 2.

52 See, e.g.: Z. Adler, *Rape on Trial*, London: Routledge & Kegan Paul, 1985; L. Ellison, 'Cross-Examination in Rape Trials', *Criminal Law Review*, 1998 (September), 605–615; Lees, *Carnal Knowledge*, above n. 44; L. Kelly, J. Temkin and S. Griffiths, *Section 41: An Evaluation of New Legislation Limiting Sexual History Evidence in Rape Trials*, London: Home Office, 2006, p. 12; J. Temkin, 'Sexual History Evidence – The Ravishment of Section 2', *Criminal Law Review*, 1993 (January), 3–20.

53 Kelly, Temkin and Griffiths, *Section 41*, above n. 52, p. 61.

54 Ibid., p. 4.

55 YJCEA, s. 41(2)(a)–(b).

56 *R v A* [2001] UKHL 25, [2002] 1 AC 45, 78 (Lord Hope). See also Kelly, Temkin and Griffiths, *Section 41*, above n. 52, pp. 14–16.

that this is now out of line with the changes to the *mens rea* requirement of the offence of rape, as discussed in Chapter 8. Significantly, during the parliamentary debates relating to the Sexual Offences Act 2003 it was argued that the new *mens rea* 'should focus the court's attention on what is happening at the time of the offence' and 'should make the previous sexual history of the complainant far less relevant'.[57] Notably, however, research demonstrates that this is the most popular application ground.[58] It is also disconcerting that evidence of sexual behaviour may be adduced in trials in which consent is not an issue. These cases tend to involve very vulnerable complainants, including those under the age of consent, and matters involving historical sexual abuse. The use of such evidence leads to a perception of such children as being 'sexually active' as opposed to 'sexually vulnerable'.[59]

If the evidence does relate to the issue of consent, leave may be granted if the sexual behaviour is alleged to have taken part at or about the same time as the alleged rape,[60] or is so similar to the sexual behaviour which either: (a) took place as part of the event in question; or (b) took place at or about the same time that the similarity cannot reasonably be explained as a coincidence.[61] This latter gateway was introduced during the parliamentary debates and relates to cases in which it was perceived that the complainant's 'behaviour cannot reasonably be explained otherwise than she consented on this occasion as well'.[62] This fails to acknowledge that 'consent is given to a person not to a circumstance'.[63] A woman always retains the right to withhold or withdraw consent. As demonstrated by Tuerkheimer in her analysis of US cases,[64] such 'sexual pattern' exceptions to the rape shield protection are not only conceptually flawed, but are also a mechanism through which courts pass normative judgments about and aim to control female sexuality. In her close reading of notable cases, such as *Gagne v Booker*[65] and *Chew v State*,[66] Tuerkheimer illustrates how the 'sexual pattern' exception tends to be applied in cases involving non-conformist or what is considered to be 'deviant' expressions of female sexuality, such as group and/or public sex. Consequently, 'deviancy is quietly functioning as a justification for diminished legal protection of unapproved sexual behaviours'.[67] This leads to a 'presumption of unrapeability' along with the construction of 'aconsensual sex', in which 'consent is implied from prior sexual acts of a like

57 Sexual Offences Bill [Lords], House of Commons Standing Committee B, 9 September 2003, col. 21, cited in Kelly, Temkin and Griffiths, *Section 41*, above n 52, p. 15.

58 Kelly, Temkin and Griffiths, *Section 41*, above n 52, p. 43.

59 Ibid., p. 37.

60 YJCEA, s. 41(3)(b)

61 YJCEA, s. 41(3)(c)(i)–(ii).

62 Temkin, *Rape and the Legal Process*, above n. 45, p. 214.

63 Ibid., p. 215.

64 D. Tuerkheimer, 'Judging Sex', *Cornell Law Review* 97(6), 2012, 1461–1504.

65 680 F.3d 493 (6th Cir. 2012).

66 804 S.W.2d 633 (Tex. Ct. App. 1991).

67 Tuerkheimer, 'Judging Sex', above n. 64, p. 1474.

nature'.[68] The admission of such evidence is, however, inconsistent with the 'contingent view of consent, which is essentially codified in the rape shield rule'.[69]

Returning to England and Wales, one further restriction operates in relation to the three gateways set down:[70] leave will be denied if the court reasonably assumes that its purpose, or main purpose, is to 'impugn the credibility of the complainant'.[71] This issue will be addressed in further detail at p. 195.

The fourth gateway concerns evidence introduced by the prosecution. Section 41 only applies to the defence; hence, the prosecution is in no way barred from introducing sexual history evidence. As such, the defence may be granted leave to introduce evidence which 'goes no further than is necessary in order to enable' it to rebut or explain the prosecution's evidence.[72]

In Australia, every jurisdiction also now limits the admissibility of evidence of sexual history or sexual experience, requiring court permission based on stated criteria. For example, the Criminal Procedure Act 1986 (NSW) states that evidence that discloses or implies sexual experience, or the complainant's involvement in any sexual activity, is inadmissible,[73] subject to six exceptions.[74] These exceptions are fairly broad: that the evidence relates to activities that occurred at or about the time of the commission of the alleged offence and the events are connected to the circumstances of the alleged offence; that the evidence relates to an existing or recent relationship between the accused and the complainant; that the accused denies having had sexual intercourse with the complainant, and the evidence is relevant to whether the presence of semen, pregnancy, disease or injury is attributable to the alleged sexual intercourse; that the evidence relates to a disease that was present in either the accused or the complainant at the time of the offence and was absent in the other party; that the evidence is relevant to whether the allegation was made by the complainant following the realisation of pregnancy or disease; or that the evidence has been given by the complainant in cross-examination by or on behalf of the accused person. These exceptions apply where the 'probative value of the evidence outweighs any distress, humiliation or embarrassment the complainant might suffer as a result of its admission'.[75]

Reform has also prohibited the admission of evidence relating to 'sexual reputation' in all jurisdictions except the Northern Territory, which treats evidence of sexual experience and history the same, allowing for such evidence with the leave of the court.[76] However, even in jurisdictions that differentiate

68 Ibid., p. 1493.
69 Ibid., p. 1461.
70 See YJCEA, s. 41(3).
71 Ibid., s 41(4).
72 Ibid., s 41(5).
73 Criminal Procedure Act 1986 (NSW), s. 293(3).
74 Ibid., s. 293(4)(a)–(f).
75 Ibid, s. 293(4).
76 Sexual Offences (Evidence and Procedure) Act 1983 (NT), s. 4(1). Jurisdictions where it is non-admissible: Evidence (Miscellaneous Provisions) Act 1991 (ACT), s. 50; Criminal

between the two, the legislation offers no guidance on distinguishing between 'sexual reputation' (inadmissible) and 'sexual experience/history' (admissible with judicial permission), which leaves considerable room for discretion. This is discussed further at p. 196.

In addition, in Australia, the uniform evidence legislation makes it mandatory rather than discretionary for judges to intervene in improper questioning.[77] It was enacted because legislatures and law reform bodies took the view that vulnerable witnesses continued to be exposed to such questions. Prior to the 1 January 2009 changes, courts merely had the discretion to disallow improper questions, and the exercise of that discretion was found to be 'patchy and inconsistent' and 'seldom invoked by judges'.[78]

Indeterminacy in 'questions' reforms

The most significant case in relation to the interpretation of YJCEA, s. 41 in England and Wales is *R v A*.[79] The accused had sought to introduce evidence of a previous consensual sexual relationship between himself and the complainant, with the most recent encounter taking place a week prior to the alleged rape. The House of Lords, in a controversial yet unanimous decision, held that the evidence could be admissible under s. 41(3)(c). Lord Slynn commented that 'good sense suggests that it may be relevant to the issue of consent whether the accused and the complainant were ongoing lovers or strangers',[80] a perspective which clearly draws upon the distinction between 'real rapes' and 'acquaintance rapes'. His Lordship continued:

> [with] due regard always being paid to the importance of seeking to protect the complainant from indignity and from humiliating questions, the test of admissibility is whether the evidence (and questioning in relation

Procedure Act 1986 (NSW), s. 293(2); Criminal Law (Sexual Offences) Act 1978 (Qld), s. 4(1); Evidence Act 1929 (SA), s. 34L(1)(a); Evidence Act 2001 (Tas), s. 194M(1)(a); Criminal Procedure Act 2009 (Vic), s. 341; Evidence Act 1906 (WA), s. 36B.

77 See: Evidence Act 1995 (Cth), s. 41; Evidence Act 2011 (ACT), s. 41; Evidence Act 1995 (NSW), s. 41; Evidence (National Uniform Legislation) Act 2011 (NT), s. 41; Evidence Act 2001 (Tas), s. 41; Evidence Act 2008 (Vic), s. 41. In Victoria and the Northern Territory the court must disallow improper questions only if witnesses are deemed as vulnerable. However, both jurisdictions also deal with improper questioning defined in Evidence (National Uniform Legislation) Act 2011 (NT), s. 43(3), Evidence Act 2008 (Vic), s. 41(3) as 'a sequence of questions'. South Australia also has a mandatory provision: Evidence Act 1929 (SA), s. 25. This is still only an option in the other Australian jurisdictions: Evidence Act 1977 (Qld), s. 21; Evidence Act 1906 (WA), s. 26.

78 Australian Law Reform Commission, *Final Report Uniform Evidence Law*, Report No. 102, 2005, 148–151.

79 [2001] UKHL 25, [2002] 1 AC 45.

80 Ibid., p. 62.

> to it) is nevertheless so relevant to the issue of consent that to exclude it would endanger the fairness of the trial under article 6 of the Convention.[81]
>
> The result of such a reading would be that sometimes logically relevant sexual experiences between a complainant and an accused may be admitted under section 41(3)(c).[82]

Hence, an 'implied provision' was read into s. 41(3)(c) in order for the subsection to be compatible with the defendant's right to a fair trial. Some commentators have criticised this decision, noting that it 'reinstated most of the judicial discretion which the new Act sought to remove'.[83] Others have argued that *R v A* in no way permits 'open-ended discretion',[84] and ostensibly does not apply to incidents with third parties.[85] Nevertheless, the opinion of trial judges suggests otherwise, with many indicating that the House of Lords established a 'broad residual discretion' to admit sexual history evidence.[86] This arguably amounts to a judicial failure to 'remember the future', as discussed in Chapter 3. Given that the aim of s. 41 was to protect victims from an unnecessary and traumatic scrutiny of their sexual history evidence, and to restrict judicial discretion, the decision is disconcerting. As with the judgment of the Court of Appeal in *R v Clinton*[87] regarding sexual infidelity (see Chapter 7), we can see the courts interpreting statutes in a manner which subverts Parliament's intention and fails to appreciate the suffering of women. We will return to *R v A* in Chapter 10, and consider the extent to which the Canadian regime may provide a better approach, as suggested by McGlynn in her feminist rewriting of the judgment.[88]

81 Ibid., p. 69.
82 Ibid., p. 68.
83 F. Klug, 'Judicial Deference Under the Human Rights Act 1998', *European Human Rights Law Review* 2, 2003, 125–133, p. 128.
84 A. Kavanagh, 'Unlocking the Human Rights Act: The "Radical" Approach to Section 3(1) Revisited', *European Human Rights Law Review* 3, 2005, 259–275, p. 267.
85 *R v White* [2004] EWCA Crim 946. In this case the Court of Appeal recognised that incidents with third parties would only be admissible via the implied provision in 'very special cases'. See Kelly, Temkin and Griffiths, *Section 41*, above n. 52, p. 19.
86 Kelly, Temkin and Griffiths, *Section 41*, above n. 52. See also: D. Birch, 'Rethinking Sexual History Evidence: Proposals for Fairer Trials', *Criminal Law Review*, 2002 (July), 531–553; J. Temkin, 'Sexual History Evidence: Beware the Backlash', *Criminal Law Review*, 2003 (April), 217–242; D. Birch, 'Untangling Sexual History Evidence: A Rejoinder to Professor Temkin', *Criminal Law Review*, 2003 (June), 370–383; N. Kibble, 'Judicial Perspectives on the Operation of s.41 and the Relevance and Admissibility of Prior Sexual History Evidence: Four Scenarios: Part 1', *Criminal Law Review*, 2005 (March), 190–205; N. Kibble, 'Judicial Discretion and the Admissibility of Prior Sexual History Evidence Under Section 41 of the Youth Justice and Criminal Evidence Act 1999: Sometimes Sticking to Your Guns Means Shooting Yourself in the Foot: Part 2', *Criminal Law Review*, 2005 (April), 263–274.
87 [2012] EWCA Crim 2.
88 C. McGlynn, 'R v A (No 2)', in R. Hunter, C McGlynn and E Rackley (eds), *Feminist Judgments: From Theory to Practice*, Oxford: Hart Publishing, 2010, 211–227.

Further concerns regarding s. 41 have been highlighted in an evaluation conducted by Kelly et al., who found that applications to admit sexual history evidence were made in around one-quarter of cases, with an approximate two-thirds success rate. Disconcertingly, the evaluation found that practices adopted in trials did not always conform to the spirit of the legislation. First, as opposed to adopting the pre-trial procedure, defence counsel frequently made verbal applications during the trial, sometimes immediately prior to cross-examining the complainant.[89] Such practice severely restricts the ability of prosecuting counsel thoroughly to investigate and formulate arguments against the application. Second, numerous defence counsel evaded the section by questioning the complainant without making an application and also by 'deliberately flouting the judge's ruling on the limits of the questions to be asked'.[90] Third, in many cases there was a 'trial by agreement' in which prosecution and defence counsel would agree on the applicability of the sexual history evidence. Evidence would then be introduced by the prosecution, or the defence's application would not be contested.[91] Consternation was also expressed with regards to the terms 'sexual experience' and 'sexual behaviour', with some judges adopting narrow definitions. For example, questioning a complainant as to whether she had had a relationship (as opposed to a *sexual* relationship) with the defendant and/or a third party was not considered to fall within s. 41.

Of further note is the extent to which previous unproven or 'false' complaints have been held to fall outside s. 41. During the parliamentary debates, the then Minister of State asserted that these complaints amounted to evidence of untruthful conduct, as opposed to sexual history evidence, and therefore would be admissible as 'it goes to credibility'.[92] The extent to which unproven complaints should, however, be considered relevant to the issue of credibility needs to be challenged. Attrition is far from unusual in rape cases. Many cases are unproven and it is disconcerting that this may be used by the defence to discredit the complainant and may also prevent a case from proceeding to trial.[93]

The Court of Appeal has held that questions relating to a prior unproven allegation will only be deemed to fall outside s. 41 if there is a 'proper evidential basis' that the complaint was false.[94] However, the case of *R v M*[95] indicates that this

89 Kelly, Temkin and Griffiths, *Section 41*, above n. 52, p. 43. For a further discussion of the findings of Kelly et al.'s study, see I. Dennis, 'Sexual History Evidence: Evaluating Section 41', *Criminal Law Review*, 2006 (October), 869–870.

90 Kelly, Temkin and Griffiths, *Section 41*, above n. 52, p. 41.

91 Ibid., p. 55.

92 House of Lords, Youth Justice and Criminal Evidence Bill, Hansard Debates, 8 March 1999, col. 34 (Lord Williams of Mostyn). Cited in Kelly, Temkin and Griffiths, *Section 41*, above n. 52, p. 13.

93 Kelly, Lovett and Regan, *A Gap or a Chasm?*, above n. 3, p. 56.

94 *R v T* [2001] EWCA Crim 1877, [2002] 1 WLR 632.

95 [2009] EWCA Crim 618.

test is easily satisfied.[96] The evidence in question referred to an alleged rape which the complainant delayed reporting for four months, and only did so after being informed by a housing officer that in the absence of an official complaint her application to be rehoused would be declined. Upon reporting the incident to the police, the complainant made it clear that she did not want the allegation to be investigated and was only reporting due to her wish to be rehoused, which stemmed from the attack. The police report noted that she held concerns for her personal safety and welfare. Furthermore, medical evidence established that she had visited her doctor three days after the alleged assault in a distressed state, complained that she had been raped, and was suffering from bleeding and abdominal pain.

Despite the existence of such evidence, and also the fact that her reason for not wishing to report the crime remained consistent, the Court of Appeal held that a 'proper evidential basis' existed. This opinion appears to demonstrate a complete lack of understanding of the trauma suffered by rape victims and the myriad and complex reasons why they would wish not to proceed with a case. The ease with which the court determined that a 'proper evidential basis' existed may demonstrate the extent to which misogynistic myths regarding women's propensity to 'cry rape' continue to pervade the judicial imagination.

The tenacity of the 'false allegation' myth can also be seen in the categorisation of 'a motive to lie' falling within gateway YJCEA, s. 41(3)(a). This in particular has caused difficulties with respect to s. 41(4), which prescribes that leave will not be granted if it appears to the court that the purpose, or main purpose, of the evidence/questioning is to impugn the credibility of the complainant. In *R v Martin*[97] the defence applied for leave to question the complainant regarding an alleged previous sexual act with the defendant, which she denied, as it was argued that this went to her motive to lie. The trial judge rejected this application, and the defendant appealed. While his appeal against conviction was rejected, the Court of Appeal nevertheless found that the trial judge had erred in his decision to exclude the evidence. In particular, it was stated that, while one 'purpose of the proposed questions clearly was to impugn ... the credibility of the complainant', it should have been permitted as it was not 'the purpose' or 'the main purpose',[98] but was instead relevant to strengthen the defendant's case that the complainant had a motive to fabricate the incident. It is interesting to note that in Michigan, evidence regarding a motive to lie would not be admissible as, prima facie, sexual history evidence can only be admitted if it falls into one of two categories: (a) evidence of the victim's past sexual conduct with the actor; and (b) evidence of specific instances

96 See also *R v C* [2007] EWCA Crim 2551; *R v V* [2006] EWCA Crim 1901; and D.A. Thomas and N. Kibble, 'Sexual History Evidence: Whether Defendant Charged with Sexual Assault Should be able to Cross-Examine About Previous False Complaint', *Criminal Law Review* 10, 2010, 792–796.

97 [2004] EWCA Crim 916.

98 Ibid., [37]. See also the opinions of judges that support this approach in N. Kibble, 'Judicial Perspectives in the Operation of s.41', above n. 86.

of sexual activity showing the source of origin of semen, pregnancy or disease.[99] However, in a move similar to the House of Lords in *R v A*, it can be seen that a wider discretion has been read into the cases by Michigan courts.[100]

Turning to Australia, some states have legislated that in determining admissibility, the judge must weigh the potential for 'unnecessary distress, humiliation, or embarrassment' to the complainant against the probative value of evidence and its capacity to materially impair the victim's credibility.[101] However, Heath asserts that in practice: 'Any relevance to the complainant's credibility, no matter how slight, may be seen as requiring admission of the evidence to ensure a fair trial'.[102]

Indeed, research has shown that the indeterminacy inherent in the various reforms results in the admission of evidence about sexual reputation.[103] Where applications for the admission of sexual history evidence *are* made, this process does not always provide 'genuine scrutiny of evidence in the prescribed terms'.[104] Evaluation in several Australian jurisdictions shows that such questions are still being admitted, often without reference to relevant legislation.[105] For instance, in examining the effectiveness of relevant reform in its state, the Victorian Law Reform Commission found that cross-examination on sexual history was still taking place without a written application in about half of all cases.[106]

There appears to be enough grey-shading in the relevant statutes to provide the defence with extensive opportunities to adduce sexual experience evidence. For example, the Evidence (Miscellaneous Provisions) Act 1991 (ACT) allows evidence of sexual activities of the complainant which is deemed to have 'substantial relevance to the facts in issue' or to 'be a proper matter for cross-examination about credit'.[107] In Victoria, some barristers manage to get sexual history evidence admitted by arguing that the complainant's evidence may be unreliable because of prior sexual assaults.[108] This is facilitated by a lack of clarity in some of the laws on 'whether evidence of *non-consensual* prior sexual activity falls within the scope of sexual history provisions'.[109]

99 Mich Comp Laws, § 750.520(j) (1974).

100 *People v Hackett* (1984) 421 Mich 338. See further: H. Galvin, 'Shielding Rape Victims in the State and Federal Courts; a Proposal for the Second Decade', *Minnesota Law Review* 70(4), 1986, 763–916; N. Kibble, 'Judicial Discretion and the Admissibility of Prior Sexual History Evidence', above n. 86.

101 See, e.g., Evidence Act 1929 (SA), ss 34L(1)–(2), 25.

102 Heath, 'Women and Criminal Law: Rape', above n. 5, p. 102.

103 T. Henning and S. Bronitt, 'Rape Victims on Trial: Regulating the Use and Abuse of Sexual History Evidence', in P. Easteal (ed.), *Balancing the Scales: Rape, Law Reform and Australian Culture*, Sydney: Federation Press, 1998; New South Wales Law Reform Commission, *Review of Section 409B of the Crimes Act 1900 (NSW)*, Report No. 87, 1998.

104 Henning and Bronitt, 'Rape Victims on Trial', above n. 103, p. 90.

105 Heath, 'Women and Criminal Law: Rape', above n. 5.

106 Victorian Law Reform Commission, *Sexual Offences: Final Report*, 2004, p. 203.

107 Evidence (Miscellaneous Provisions) Act 1991 (ACT), ss 51, 53.

108 M. Heenan, 'Reconstituting the "Relevance" of Women's Sexual Histories in Rape Trials', *Women Against Violence* 13, 2002, 4–17.

109 Heath, 'Women and Criminal Law: Rape', above n. 5, p. 102 (emphasis added).

Unlike the sexual history laws, the new s. 41 of the uniform Evidence Acts includes a mandatory requirement for judges to intervene. However, the question may be asked, 'how mandatory is mandatory?'. Under s. 41, unless the judge or prosecutor perceives the question to be disallowable, the issue of 'mandatory' is moot. It is the perception of the judge, prosecutor and, to a lesser extent, the defence lawyer that is determinative. Their perceptions are informed by a long history of training in adversarial trial dispute-resolution and may remain steeped in rape mythology. Such perceptions will often not be the same as those of the complainant who is under cross-examination. Further, the definition of 'improper questions' is largely indeterminate, although the legislation does provide some additional guidance in s. 41 as to what is an improper question. In South Australia, for instance, the court may disallow a question if it 'is misleading or confusing', 'apparently based on a stereotype', 'unnecessarily repetitive, offensive or oppressive', or 'put in a humiliating, insulting or otherwise inappropriate manner or tone'.[110]

There has been little research so far on how this mandatory judicial intervention is working in practice. One study, in which a small sample of NSW prosecutors and defence barristers were interviewed, found that s. 275A, which mandated judicial intervention if a child sexual assault witness was being improperly or unfairly questioned, had not resulted in an increase in the number of times the section was invoked. Respondents believed that this was because improper questions were not generally being asked before the enactment of the new section.[111] The practitioners' responses also indicated that the section had not resulted in a change in the approach to questioning for the same reason: 'improper questions were not and are not generally being asked'.[112] A question asked in cross-examination may appear improper from the perspective of the victim, or a person who works with sexual assault victims, but the same question may be viewed as entirely proper by a legal practitioner or judicial officer who is looking at it solely from a legal perspective with the accused's right to a fair trial in mind. Not surprisingly, therefore, research on the application of the old s. 41 of the uniform Evidence Acts, which could be germane to the two jurisdictions in which judges continue to have the discretion to disallow improper questions,[113] suggests that the restrictions were rarely applied and failed to protect vulnerable witnesses.[114]

110 Evidence Act 1929 (SA), s. 25.

111 Section 275A was repealed and replaced by the new s. 41. See R. Boyd and A. Hopkins, 'Drawing the Line Between Acceptable and Unacceptable Cross-Examination of Child Sexual Assault Complainants: Concerns About the Application of s 41 of the Evidence Act', *Criminal Law Journal* 34(3), 2010, 149–166, p. 162.

112 Ibid., p. 163.

113 This includes Evidence Act 1977 (Qld), s. 21; Evidence Act 1906 (WA), s. 26.

114 See, e.g., Victorian Law Reform Commission, *Sexual Offences: Final Report*, above n. 106; New South Wales Adult Sexual Assault Interagency Committee, *A Fair Chance: Proposals for Sexual Assault Law Reform in NSW*, 2004, p. 37; T. Drabsch, 'Cross-Examination and Sexual Offence Complainants', Briefing Paper No. 18/03, NSW Parliamentary Library Research Service, 2003.

In another small study – this one in the ACT – three judges stated that the changes to the wording of s. 41 had not resulted in them disallowing more questions.[115] One judicial officer provided an interesting explanation for the lack of change on his behalf: 'I am always a little conscious that the Appeal Court is not necessarily composed of judges who understand the need to protect witnesses'.[116] The six prosecutors and defence barristers surveyed also confirmed the view that more questions were not being disallowed as a result of the changes.[117]

Looking at both Australia and England and Wales, it is easy to see how the fear of detailed questioning and humiliating scrutiny regarding their sexual history continues to impact upon many rape victims' decision to report a crime or proceed to trial. Despite the tightening of the law relating to sexual history evidence, the perception that the complainant is the one on trial remains:

> Women who actually have nothing to fear are still frightened of those questions. Even when a woman is believed and he is convicted she still feels victimised by the court process, questions etc. The woman is 'on trial' and always says she would never go through it again and advises others not to go forward with the trial.[118]

Legislation: special measures

Reforms have been enacted with the intention of making the experience of vulnerable witnesses less traumatic, reducing the rate of victim-initiated discontinuances and enabling the best testimony to be given. Arguments behind the reforms included the ideas that accuracy of testimony would be increased, that the fair trial principle also needs to apply to victim witnesses and that reporting rates might increase.[119] In all Australian jurisdictions, there has been a raft of law reform measures similar to those sections of the YJCEA which, in England and Wales, introduced a range of special measures for vulnerable and intimidated witnesses. The Sexual and Violent Offences Legislation Amendment Act 2008 (ACT), for instance, was 'designed to extract the "best" evidence possible from witnesses who may otherwise suffer a disadvantage'.[120]

115 J. Kennedy and P. Easteal, 'View From the Inside: The Sexual and Violent Offences Legislation Amendment Act 2008', in P. Easteal (ed.), *Justice Connections*, England: Cambridge Scholars Publishing, 2013, 10–36.

116 Ibid., p. 35.

117 Ibid.

118 Rape Crisis Centre 15 (support worker), cited in Kelly, Temkin and Griffiths, *Section 41*, above n. 52, p. 68.

119 Discussed in Drabsch, 'Cross-Examination and Sexual Offence Complainants', above n. 114, pp. 24–26.

120 Revised Explanatory Statement, Sexual and Violent Offences Legislation Amendment Bill 2008 (ACT), p. 2. The Sexual and Violent Offences Legislation Amendment Act 2008 (ACT) commenced 1 June 2009. This legislation is discussed in Chapter 3.

The traumatic ordeal feared and experienced by most rape complainants is undoubtedly intensified when cross-examination is conducted by the defendant himself. During the 1990s a handful of cases in England and Wales sparked a furore, after the complainants were subjected to a tortuous and interminable examination by the accused.[121] Consequently, under YJCEA, s. 34, a defendant is no longer permitted personally to cross-examine a complainant in a sex offence case. As in England and Wales, this is the case in all Australian jurisdictions, with the exception of Tasmania.[122] In Western Australia the self-represented accused can cross-examine but the judge can order that questions have to be repeated by another person and not directly asked by the defendant and that the witness be in another room or separated from the accused by a screen.[123]

Other special measures provided for in the YJCEA include:[124] the provision of screens to shield the witness from the accused; permitting the complainant to give evidence via a live link; permitting the complainant to give evidence in private (i.e away from members of the public); the removal of wigs and gowns of judicial personnel; permitting video-recorded evidence-in-chief; permitting video-recorded cross-examination or re-examination;[125] and permitting examination through an intermediary. It has been argued that these reforms, 'taken as a package, were the most radical rewriting of the orthodox rules for treatment of witnesses in the adversarial trial system in the common law world'.[126]

In Australia most jurisdictions have amended the number of times a victim witness can be cross-examined, by making the committal a matter of paper with no hearing.[127] A transcript or written statement of an audiovisual recording between

121 See, e.g., *R v Brown* [1998] 2 Cr App R 364 and the cases discussed in S. Tendler and R. Ford, 'Rape Victims to be Spared Extra Ordeal at Trial', *The Times* (London), 20 May 1998; Home Office, *Speaking Up for Justice: The Report of the Interdepartmental Working Group on the Treatment of Vulnerable or Intimidated Witnesses in the Criminal Justice System*, 1998, p. 64; Temkin, *Rape and the Legal Process*, above n. 45, pp. 320–321.

122 Evidence (Miscellaneous Provisions) Act 1991 (ACT), s. 38D. Criminal Procedure Act 1986 (NSW), s. 294A(2); Sexual Offences (Evidence and Procedure) Act 1983 (NT), s. 5; Evidence Act 1977 (Qld), s. 21N; Evidence Act 1929 (SA), s. 13B(1)(a). In Victoria if deemed a 'protected' witness: Criminal Procedure Act 2009 (Vic), s. 356.

123 Evidence Act 1906 (WA), s. 25A(1).

124 YJCEA, ss 23–29.

125 At the time of writing, s. 28, which pertains to pre-recorded cross-examination, is not yet in force.

126 L.C.H. Hoyano, 'Coroners and Justice Act 2009: Special Measures Directions Take Two: Entrenching Unequal Access to Justice?', *Criminal Law Review* 5, 2010, 354–367, p. 354.

127 All jurisdictions except the Northern Territory and Queensland provide adult sexual assault victims with paper committals: Magistrates Court Act 1930 (ACT), s. 90AB; Criminal Procedure Act 1986 (NSW), ss 91–93; Summary Procedure Act 1921 (SA), s. 106(3); Criminal Procedure Act 2009 (Vic), ss 123–124. 'Western Australia and Tasmania have effectively abolished committal hearings and committal to the higher court takes place administratively': Australian Law Reform Commission, *Family Violence – A National Legal Response*, Report No. 114, 2010, p. 1215.

police and a witness is now also potentially admissible at trial in the ACT.[128] As noted in Chapter 3, that jurisdiction provides for a pre-trial hearing for children and intellectually impaired victims, as well as other sexual assault victims who are likely to 'suffer severe emotional trauma' or be 'intimidated or distressed'.[129] In addition to the ACT, the Northern Territory,[130] Queensland,[131] South Australia[132] and Western Australia[133] offer the option for pre-recording of prosecution evidence to a category of vulnerable witnesses that includes adults (special pre-trial hearings); in other jurisdictions pre-recorded evidence is restricted to children and/or cognitively impaired witnesses.[134] In some jurisdictions, such as Victoria, the recording of victim witnesses' evidence given at trial, including cross-examination and re-examination, can be used as their testimony in any new trial, appeal or other proceeding.[135]

Sexual assault complainants in the ACT are entitled to have a person of their choice present for emotional support while giving their evidence.[136] In the Northern Territory, vulnerable witnesses (which include sexual assault victims, children and intellectually disabled witnesses) are entitled to be accompanied by a friend, relative or other support person.[137] This is also the case in South Australia if the witness is considered to be vulnerable,[138] and in Tasmania[139] and Western Australia[140] if the witness is deemed a 'special witness'.

In the ACT, as we saw in Chapter 3, victim witnesses no longer have to see the accused when giving evidence in the courtroom. Screens or other arrangements must be made available for this purpose[141] or the complainant may be given the option of testifying by audiovisual link.[142] Other jurisdictions, such as South Australia, also offer special arrangements, including the exclusion of the accused from the place where the complainant gives evidence,[143] permitting the presence

128 Evidence (Miscellaneous Provisions) Act 1991 (ACT), ss 40A–40M.
129 Ibid., ss 40P(1)(c), 40Q.
130 Evidence Act (NT), s. 21B(2).
131 Evidence Act 1977 (Qld), s. 21A(1)(b)(ii), (2)(e).
132 Evidence Act 1929 (SA), s. 13C(1)(b).
133 Evidence Act 1906 (WA), ss 106T(2a), 106RA.
134 Criminal Procedure Act 1986 (ACT), ss 306M(1), 306U; Criminal Procedure Act 1986 (NSW), ss 306M(1), 306U; Evidence (Children and Special Witnesses) Act 2001 (Tas), s. 5(1); Criminal Procedure Act 2009 (Vic), s. 370.
135 Criminal Procedure Act 2009 (Vic), s. 379.
136 Evidence (Miscellaneous Provisions) Act 1991 (ACT), s. 38E(3).
137 Evidence Act (NT), s. 21A(2)(c)
138 Evidence Act 1929 (SA), s. 13A(2)(e).
139 Evidence (Children and Special Witnesses) Act 2001 (Tas), s. 8.
140 Evidence Act 1906 (WA), s. 106R(4)(a).
141 Evidence (Miscellaneous Provisions) Act 1991 (ACT), s. 38C.
142 Ibid., s. 43.
143 Evidence Act 1929 (SA), s. 13A(2)(d).

of a support person,[144] CCTV or other audiovisual means,[145] or providing a screen.[146] Similar provisions are in place in NSW,[147] the Northern Territory (if the witness is deemed 'a vulnerable witness'),[148] Queensland (if the witness is deemed a 'special witness'),[149] Tasmania (again, if the witness is deemed a 'special witness'),[150] Victoria[151] and Western Australia.[152] There may be further statutory limits or guidance, such as provisions in South Australia that require the court to decide whether certain facilities are 'readily available' and to balance the complainant's interest in special arrangements against the prejudice this might cause to the accused in order to ensure that there will be 'no prejudice to any party' if such facilities are used.[153]

Issues with special measures

In England and Wales, under YJCEA, s. 17(4), rape/sexual assault complainants are automatically deemed 'eligible' as intimidated witnesses to apply for special measures, unless they inform the court that they do not wish to do so. An application may be made by any party to the proceedings and, in deciding whether to grant the application, a court will consider whether the measures might inhibit such evidence being effectively tested by a third party. Further reform was introduced by the Coroners and Justice Act 2009, and now a court *must* give a special measure direction with regards to s. 27 (video-recorded evidence-in-chief) unless it considers that the measure 'would not be likely to maximize the quality of the complainant's evidence'.[154] The (then) Labour Government justified this approach 'on the basis that it would enable complainants to have early certainty about the way their evidence would be given'.[155]

However, research into the use of special measures in England and Wales indicates that many applications are made late,[156] with some only being made on the first

144 Ibid., s. 13A(2)(e).
145 Ibid., s. 13A(2)(a)–(b).
146 Ibid., s. 13A(2)(c).
147 Criminal Procedure Act 1986 (NSW), ss 294B(3), 291(1)–(3).
148 Evidence Act (NT), s. 21A(2).
149 Evidence Act 1977 (Qld), s. 21A(2).
150 Evidence (Children and Special Witnesses) Act 2001 (Tas), s. 8(2); Justices Act 1959 (Tas), s. 61(7).
151 Criminal Procedure Act 2009 (Vic), s. 360; Magistrates' Court Act 1989 (Vic), s. 126(2)(a); Supreme Court Act 1986 (Vic), s. 18(1)(a).
152 Evidence Act 1906 (WA), s. 106R(4)(c).
153 Evidence Act 1929 (SA), s. 13A(1)(b).
154 YJECA, s. 22A, introduced by Coroners and Justice Act 2009, s. 101.
155 Hoyano, 'Coroners and Justice Act 2009', above n. 126, p. 365. See also Office for Criminal Justice Reform, *Convicting Rapists and Protecting Victims – Justice for Victims of Rape: A Consultation Paper*, 2006; Office for Criminal Justice Reform, *Convicting Rapists and Protecting Victims – Justice for Victims of Rape: Responses to Consultation*, 2007.
156 C. Charles, *Special Measures for Vulnerable and Intimidated Witnesses: Research Exploring the Decisions and Actions Taken by Prosecutors in a Sample of CPS Case Files*, London: Crown Prosecution Service, 2012.

day of the trial.[157] While a move towards reassuring complainants that they will be able to rely upon their video testimony is to be welcomed, arguably this is coming too late in the process. Other areas in which the CPS has stressed the need for improvement include the identification of, and communication with, vulnerable and/or intimidated witnesses.[158] In addition, this 'piecemeal reform' has the consequence of creating anomalies, for example that victims of domestic violence are not necessarily subject to the same provision.[159]

Concerns have also been expressed with regards to the quality of the videos that may be shown as evidence-in-chief. These include: the adoption of an overly rigid and counter-productive interview structure; amateurish recording; and excessively long interviews, with one lasting five hours and 38 minutes.[160] It has also been noted that the police at times have used inappropriate interviewing techniques, with some treating adult complainants as though they were children.[161] One judge commented that the 'interviewing technique was so poor that all it achieved was to emphasize discrepancies in the witnesses' accounts, giving defence counsel a field day'.[162]

Australian research has found, however, that having legislative provisions available does not necessarily result in the courtroom being closed, or CCTV or screens being used[163] or allowed:[164]

> Some of the primary reasons for such reluctance stemmed from the fact that given the very nature of the adversary system of giving evidence in person, absence of physical presence gave a stronger perception that it would reduce the impact of the complainant's evidence.[165]

Despite the mandatory language of Evidence Act 1929 (SA), s. 13A, the legislation allows objections on the basis that the witness 'is not in fact a vulnerable witness', which is to be determined by the court with consideration being given to a number of factors in deciding whether to grant such arrangements. Section 13D gives the court '*discretion* to admit'[166] an audiovisual recording as an 'official record of the evidence' of a vulnerable witness. The court '*may* [then] relieve the

157 M. Burton, R. Evans and A. Sanders, *Are Special Measures for Vulnerable and Intimidated Witnesses Working? Evidence from the Criminal Justice Agencies*, London: Home Office, 2006, p. vii.
158 Charles, *Special Measures for Vulnerable and Intimidated Witnesses*', above n. 156.
159 Hoyano, 'Coroners and Justice Act 2009', above n. 126, p. 365.
160 Stern, *The Stern Review*, above n. 11, p. 69.
161 Ibid.
162 Ibid.
163 NSW Law Reform Commission, *Questioning of Complainants by Unrepresented Accused in Sexual Offence Trials*, Report No. 101, 2003, pp. 89–90.
164 Eastwood, 'The Experiences of Child Complainants of Sexual Abuse', above n. 48, p. 3.
165 F. Hum, 'Women Complainants and the Evidential Process', in P. Easteal (ed.), *Women and the Law in Australia*, Sydney: LexisNexis, 2010, 174–191, p. 187.
166 Emphasis added.

witness ... from an obligation to give evidence in later proceedings'.[167] Further, s. 13A(11) allows the court to dispense with special arrangements for vulnerable witnesses where the witness is an adult, facilities are not readily available and it is not reasonably practicable to make them available given 'cost, inconvenience and delay' and 'the urgency of the proceedings'.

As discussed in Chapter 3, in at least some of the Australian protective provisions, there is an underlying question that can affect the use of these practices: Who is deemed eligible? The statutory definition of vulnerable or special varies across jurisdictions but there is one commonality – the ambiguity and indeterminacy of the language: 'these victims are required to demonstrate vulnerability or distress in order to be eligible for some of the protections. The prosecutor must perceive the victim as vulnerable before informing them and making an application ...'.[168]

This might prove to be yet another fertile ground for myths to flourish both in prosecutorial and judicial decision-making. While research indicates that the special measures in England and Wales have been effective in reducing anxiety and have enabled 44 per cent of sexual offence complainants to give evidence 'that they would not otherwise have been willing or able to give',[169] improvements can still be made. Indeed, only 54 per cent of complainants stated that they would repeat their experience of giving evidence.[170] Despite the presence of special measures, many still find the process too traumatic.

The power of mythology

What comes through most strongly in this chapter and in Chapter 8 is the pervasiveness of myths in both Australia and England and Wales that limit the efficacy of what could have been excellent reform. Helena Kennedy wrote this about the power of mythology:

> Myths are tent pegs which secure the status quo. In the law, mythology operates almost as powerfully as legal precedent in inhibiting change. And the law is full of mythology. Women are particularly at its mercy, although men do not escape its force, especially when issues of class and race emerge. . . . Mythology is a triumph of belief over reality, depending for its survival not on evidence but on constant reiteration. Myths are not the same as lies, in that they do not involve deliberate falsification. They endure because they serve social needs.

167 Emphasis added.

168 Kennedy and Easteal, 'View From the Inside', above n. 115, p 36.

169 B. Hamlyn et al., *Are Special Measures Working? Evidence from Surveys of Vulnerable and Intimidated Witnesses*, Home Office Research Study 283, London: Home Office, 2004, p. 78. See also Burton, Evans and Sanders, *Are Special Measures for Vulnerable and Intimidated Witnesses Working?*, above n. 157.

170 Hamlyn et al., *Are Special Measures Working?*, above n. 169, p. 97.

> The notion that judges are invariably impartial is also pervasive and unreal, but it is supposed to sustain our faith in the legal system.[171]

In the mid-1990s, Carol Smart discussed how myths about female sexuality and rape are reconstructed in the court, describing how the rape trial is 'the Original Story being re-enacted on a daily basis'.[172] Almost two decades later, in Australia, England and Wales we see the effects of such beliefs in low conviction rates for rape. We know that location, level of physical injury sustained by the victim, admissions of guilt by the accused, whether a medical examination was conducted, and *community attitudes towards sexual violence*, can influence jury decision-making and sexual assault trial outcomes.[173] Thus, although one of the main aims of the sexual history and special victim measures reforms was to increase the reporting and conviction rates for sexual assault, these have so far proved resistant to change.[174] A 2011 study in the Australian state of Victoria found that there has been a decline in the conviction rate for sexual offence matters in the County Court: the conviction rate was at its lowest since 2004[175] – 38 per cent.[176]

As we have seen in this chapter, the mindset as described by Smart contributes to a persistent focus on complainant credibility and victim provocation in cross-examination, despite rape shield laws and provisions intended to prevent improper questions. The power of these myths is evidenced by the most common application ground for allowing sexual history in English courts –its alleged relevance to the accused's belief in consent. This is despite changes to *mens rea* provisions discussed in Chapter 8 and the law reform overviewed in the current chapter. Here we see myths curtailing the effect of *two* legislative reforms concurrently. The mythology permeates through the lattice-like indeterminacy of the statutes, for example in how the terms 'vulnerable' and 'improper' are interpreted. In Australia, England and Wales, victim witnesses continue to be asked about their sexual history and other 'improper' questions, which they may find humiliating, inappropriate or confusing.

In Australia, amendments intended to better protect victim witnesses from

171 H. Kennedy, *Eve Was Framed: Women and British Justice*, London: Chatto and Windus, 1992, p. 32.

172 C. Smart, *Law, Crime and Sexuality*, London: Sage Publications, 1995, p. 84. At p. 80, she also describes how mythology: 'Constructs sexual encounters or relationships in terms of how men can gain control of, or access to, their pleasure which is inconveniently located in women's bodies.... It is within this dominant regime of meanings that law presides over contested accounts of rape and seduction'.

173 M. Heenan and H. McKelvie, *Evaluation of the Crimes (Rape) Act 1991*, Report No. 2, Rape Law Reform Evaluation Project, Melbourne: Department of Justice, 1997.

174 Victorian Department of Justice, *Success Works, Sexual Assault Reform Strategy: Final Evaluation Report*, 2011.

175 Ibid., p. 78.

176 Ibid., p. 80. Victoria's Chief Crown Prosecutor, Gavin Silbert SC, believes that the Office of Public Prosecution's practice of pursuing weak cases with little prospect of success has led to this drop in conviction rate.

trauma induced by confusing and humiliating interrogation are often only available if the victim is deemed a 'vulnerable' or 'special' witness.[177] Eligibility is based on prosecutorial screening of those considered most vulnerable to severe emotional trauma, intimidation or distress. It is possible that mythology or invisible assumptions are at play in this process, with prevailing notions of sexuality and sexual behaviour contributing to the 'definition of "real" or "legitimate" rape and stereotypical constructions of the "good" victim'.[178]

At the time of writing, the Ministry of Justice in England and Wales is piloting pre-recorded cross-examination, some 14 years after this special measure was introduced in the YJCEA.[179] However, the pilot is being restricted to children and victims who suffer from a mental or physical disorder. When/if the provision becomes widely available, the legislation states that a party to the proceedings may apply for this procedure or the court may simply make a direction. However, given the provision's indeterminacy, who knows if the prosecutors will bother? Preliminary research findings of similar reform in the ACT are indicative of a poor rate of prosecutorial application.[180] Too much paperwork? A failure to understand how traumatic the cross-examination can be for the victim? Perhaps the courts and their players in Australia, England and Wales need to better acknowledge that sexual assault victims' experiences with the criminal justice system can compound their trauma and victimisation, which contributes to low reporting and/or discontinuing with their case.[181]

Two recent reviews of victim witness provisions in Australia found improvement in this area. A Victorian report concluded that 'for many, but not all, victims of sexual assault their experience of the criminal justice system is vastly improved'.[182] Further, an evaluation of the ACT provisions (the legislation focused on in Chapter 3) found that 'stakeholders felt strongly that legislative changes have improved the criminal justice process for sexual offence victim/survivors . . .'.[183]

177 See: Evidence Act (NT), s. 21A(2)(a), (2)(d); Evidence Act 1977 (Qld), s. 21A(2)(b)–(c); Evidence (Children and Special Witnesses) Act 2001 (Tas), s. 6; Justices Act 1959 (Tas), s. 61(7).

178 Kennedy and Easteal, 'View From the Inside', above n. 115, p. 11.

179 C. Grayling, *Pre-Trial Cross-Examination Testing*, Written Ministerial Statement, London: Ministry of Justice, 2013.

180 Interviews of key criminal justice personnel and victim support staff indicate that in the first two years of the ACT amendments, there had been very few applications by the ACT Director of Public Prosecutions. This is discussed by J. Kennedy, P. Easteal and L. Bartels, 'How Protected is She? "Fairness" and the Rape Victim Witness in Australia', *Women's Studies International Forum* 35(5), 2012, 334–342.

181 Office of the Director of Public Prosecutions (ACT) and Australian Federal Police, *Responding to Sexual Assault: The Challenge of Change*, 2005.

182 Victorian Department of Justice, *Success Works, Sexual Assault Reform Strategy*, above n. 174.

183 J. Anderson, K. Richards and K. Willis, *Evaluation of the ACT Sexual Assault Reform Program (SARP): Final Report*, Canberra: Australian Institute of Criminology, 2012.

However, it is possible that the reforms may have led to different and subtler ways of harassment in cross-examination:

> Judges said they were seeing a reduction in the use of aggressive tones and overbearing and overly repetitive questions in cross examination. Judges felt that this change in behaviour by defence lawyers was significant and the direct result of the reforms. They noted, however, that the approach of some defence counsel was now more subtle and that intervention was still needed in relation to overly complex questioning and the speed at which questions were fired at the witness.[184]

Therefore, despite this reported improvement, one victim described the cross-examination process as feeling 'like I was on a cross. I just felt like someone was throwing stones at me'.[185] Although legislation does not expressly provide for it, the right of an accused to a fair trial must be balanced with the needs of the interests of the other parties involved, including the interests of the victim witness not to be exposed to such emotional harm: 'It is the clear duty of the trial judge to do everything he can, consistently with giving the defendant a fair trial, to minimise the trauma suffered by other participants'.[186]

However, as we note in this chapter and in Chapter 8, the '"balancing" approach . . . is structurally skewed in favour of the accused',[187] and questions of admissibility and victims' eligibility for special provisions must be seen in this context. Judges are forced to choose between 'conflicting moral imperatives' within a legal system in which the 'central, indeed overriding, importance attached to the fair trial principle' means that one of the moral imperatives is more heavily weighted.[188] Assumptions of impartiality and so-called objective evidentiary standards ignore the cultural backdrop, which is not a blank slate:[189] 'As a result, the value of reform is limited since the systemic gender partiality, which arises in a cultural maelstrom of intrinsic sexism, is not being confronted or challenged'.[190] This appears to be the same in Australia, England and Wales, and no doubt in other countries around the globe. Despite the recent plenitude of statutory reform enacted to assist sexual assault victims in their experiences as witnesses, we question whether these laws will in fact protect them from secondary wounding by the criminal justice system.

184 Victorian Department of Justice, *Success Works, Sexual Assault Reform Strategy*, above n. 174, p. 120.
185 Ibid., p. 117.
186 *R v Brown* [1998] 2 Cr App R 364, 371 (Bingham LCJ).
187 S. Bronitt, 'No Records, No Time, No Reason', *Current Issues in Criminal Justice* 8(2), 1996, 130–143, p. 130.
188 S. Bronitt and B. McSherry, 'The Use and Abuse of Counselling Records in Sexual Assault Trials: Reconstructing the "Rape Shield"', *Criminal Law Forum* 8(2), 1997, 259–291.
189 See, e.g.: Clark, 'Judging Rape', above n. 2, p. 17; Heath, 'Women and Criminal Law: Rape', above n. 5, p. 88.
190 P. Easteal, 'Beyond Balancing', in P. Easteal (ed.), *Balancing the Scales: Rape, Law Reform and Australian Culture*, Sydney: Federation Press, 1998, p. 209.

Chapter 10

Partner rape

Partner rape is sexual assault by a current or former intimate partner, and is usually perpetrated by an individual as part of a pattern of violence and control. However, while battered women are statistically more likely to experience rape and sexual assault,[1] rape may occur in relationships not characterised by other forms of violence or which appear to be otherwise egalitarian.[2] Some women are attacked when they first articulate their desire to leave the relationship or when they try to leave.[3] For example, in one US study of rural Ohio women, 74 per cent were sexually assaulted when they expressed a desire to leave the relationship; 49 per cent were sexually abused while they were trying to leave or while they were leaving, and 33 per cent were victimised after they left.[4] Partner rape may also be a sign of increasing overall violence in the relationship. Its occurrence has been observed more often in relationships where the abuse had been occurring over a longer period of time.[5] This type of rape is a significant predictor of intimate partner homicide and a risk factor in relation to the HIV virus.[6]

1 D. Russell, *Rape in Marriage*, Bloomington: Indiana University Press, 1990, p. 100.

2 M.C. Black et al., *The National Intimate Partner and Sexual Violence Survey: 2010 Summary Report*, Atlanta: National Center for Injury Prevention and Control, Centers for Disease Control and Prevention, 2011.

3 A. Sev'er, *Fleeing the House of Horrors: Women Who Have Left Abusive Partners*, Toronto: University of Toronto Press, 2002.

4 W. DeKeseredy and M.D. Schwartz, *Dangerous Exits: Escaping Abusive Relationships in Rural America*, New Brunswick: Rutgers University Press, 2009.

5 M.A. Dutton et al., 'Patterns of Intimate Partner Violence: Correlates and Outcomes', *Violence and Victims* 20(5), 2005, 483–497.

6 J. Anderson, J. Draughon and J. Campbell, 'Fatality and Health Risks Associated with Inter Partner Sexual Violence', in L. McOrmond-Plummer, P. Easteal and J. Levy-Peck (eds), *Intimate Partner Sexual Violence: A Multidisciplinary Approach to Survivor Support and System Change*, London: Jessica Kingsley Publishers, 2014, 54–64.

History? A licence to rape[7]

A licence to rape – the 'alleged' spousal exemption from sexual assault charges – evolved from at the least the days of William the Conqueror, when rules allowed victims to 'forgive' their 'seducer' by consenting to marriage.[8] This immunity went on to be officially sanctioned in medieval England with marriage rights and duties directed by Church law[9] and rape laws existing solely to protect virginity. As a consequence:

> The normal presumption of the courts [in the thirteenth century] being that any history or implication of consent on the part of the woman was a valid defence to an appeal of rape . . . previous or subsequent sexual intercourse with the same man was fatal to such an appeal.[10]

Given the dearth of rape adjudication or relevant material about the law itself over the following several hundred years, this medieval perspective was the legal backdrop to a pronouncement by Lord Hale in the seventeenth century that subsequently became the most cited authority in English marital rape cases, and in other countries like Australia and the United States where the English common law was the basis of legal codes and decisions. Hale asserted that once a woman agreed to marriage, she was agreeing to a marriage contract, with one provision of that contract being the legal right of the husband to have sexual intercourse with her.[11] This was the equivalent of a contractual promise of an implied and permanent consent, with the man as the right holder having the power to compel it. Hale offered 'no argument, case law, or legal basis to support his assertion and did not acknowledge the existence of somewhat contrary legal authority'.[12] Nevertheless, his *dictum* did, for the most part, prevail either as an explicit, or more often as an implicit, part of rape law until relatively recently.

7 The historical discussion is extracted from P. Easteal, 'Rape in Marriage: Has the Licence Lapsed?', in P. Easteal (ed.), *Balancing the Scales: Rape, Law Reform and Australian Culture*, Sydney: Federation Press, 1998, 107–123..

8 Discussed in R. de Glanville, *The Treatise on the Laws and Customs of the Realm of England Commonly Called Glanville*, G.D.G. Hall (ed.), London: Thomas Nelson Printers, 1965, p. 176. Glanville, writing the treatise from 1187–1189 in Latin, stated: 'But before judgment is given the woman and the accused can be reconciled to each other by marriage . . .'.

9 J.L. Barton, 'The Story of Marital Rape', *The Law Quarterly Review* 108(2), 1992, 260–271.

10 J. Temkin, *Rape and the Legal Process*, London: Sweet & Maxwell, 1987, p. 43.

11 Sir M. Hale, *Historia Placitorum Coronae*, S. Emlin (ed.), London: Professional Books, first published 1736, 1971 edn, Vol. 1, p. 629.

12 R. Augustine, 'Marriage: The Safe Haven for Rapists', *Journal of Family Law* 29(3), 1990–1991, 559–590, pp. 560–561 discusses Lord Hale and points to an earlier case that Hale could have used as an authority for the opposite view. In 1631 Lord Audley was convicted of raping his wife 'for holding her by force, while one of his minions forcibly, against her will, had carnal knowledge of her'.

The lack of legal authority was more than compensated for by the weight of sociocultural norms and legal mores, which liberal theorist John Stuart Mill critiqued as giving a wife less rights than a slave: 'to refuse to her master the last familiarity . . . [she can be] made the instrument of an animal function contrary to her inclinations'.[13] Under English common law the wife had to 'submit and defer to her husband's rule'.[14] Women were denied a freedom of choice, bodily integrity and physical safety in the realm of the law, conforming to the societal perspective of females as the possession of men. Since they were regarded as chattel, rape laws were designed to protect men's property: 'In the same way that a person cannot be charged with the offence of wilful damage to their own property, a man could not be charged with violating his own woman'.[15]

Hale's 'legal fiction'[16] was pointed out in some courts, and even before the immunity was legislatively abolished it was possible for a man to be tried for raping his wife. In 1888, conflicting views about Hale were given in *R v Clarence*.[17] This seems to be the first time that the doctrine inspired judicial commentary. The defendant had been convicted of fraud for not disclosing to his wife that he had gonorrhoea before having sex with her. Upon appeal, a majority of nine to four quashed the conviction; and all except one who commented on the issue of irrevocable consent 'expressed serious reservations as to the accuracy of Hale's pronouncement'.[18]

At what point wifely consent could be considered as abrogated was not considered by English courts for another 60 years. Separation orders containing non-cohabitation clauses (*Clarke* 1949), a decree nisi of divorce (*O'Brien* 1974) and an undertaking to the court not to molest his wife (*Steele* 1977) were each considered as acceptable grounds for revoking the wife's consent. A petition for divorce (*Miller* 1954) was not, with the court stating that a separation agreement was necessary.[19] A few Australian courts also handed down decisions which either established exceptions or repudiated Hale. For example, the Western Australian Supreme Court ruled that a man who raped his wife could not be immune from prosecution for indecent assault.[20] A case in Victoria saw the defendant lose his appeal

13 Cited in R. Graycar and J. Morgan, *The Hidden Gender of the Law*, Sydney: Federation Press, 1990, p. 116.

14 M. May, 'Violence in the Family: An Historical Perspective', in J.P. Martin (ed.), *Violence and the Family*, Chichester and New York: John Wiley and Sons, 1978, 135–167, p. 138.

15 Z. Rathus, *Rougher Than Usual Handling*, Brisbane: The Women's Legal Service, 1994, p. 14.

16 Both the presumption of consent in every case of marital sex and the lack of legal authority make it a 'legal fiction'.

17 (1888) 22 QBD 23.

18 J. Scutt, 'Judgements of Right Thinking Men', *Scarlet Woman* 21, 1986, 23–26, p. 24.

19 *R v Clarke* [1949] 2 All ER 448; *R v O'Brien* [1974] 3 All ER 633; *R v Steele* (1977) 65 Cr App R 22; and *R v Miller* [1954] 2 QB 282. These case are discussed by Temkin, *Rape and the Legal Process*, above n. 10, pp. 49–50.

20 *Caldwell v The Queen* [1976] WAR 204, described in Scutt, 'Judgements of Right Thinking Men', above n. 18, p. 24.

against a conviction of rape since his estranged wife had possessed a Family Court order that restrained him from molesting her.[21] The court held that the jury could find him guilty since the order eliminated the wife's consent.

In England and Australia it appears, therefore, that if the woman was seen by the court as having established her status as a separate woman (through legal decrees or orders), the husband was indictable and culpable. In the same vein, the New South Wales Supreme Court in 1981 held that a man could be charged with the rape of his wife since there was a court order in existence which revoked her implied consent and the accused was aware of the order and its effects.[22]

Using a justification other than nullification of consent, the Western Australian Court of Criminal Appeal held that the marital exemption did not apply in the case of *Beck*, who had forced his de facto wife at knife point to have sex first with him and then with his cousin. The court stated: 'section 325 ... makes it an offence for any person to have carnal knowledge of a woman not his wife without her consent ... In my view the word "wife" in s 325 clearly does not mean a de facto wife'.[23]

In other words, a woman with a marriage licence had less protection from the law than a woman without one.

No more immunity: messages from courts and legislators

Courts in the United States, beginning in the late 1970s, began to critically assess the suppositions underlying the exemption, with statements that described it as 'fatally anachronistic', 'bondage of a wife' and 'no law, common or otherwise' and that 'women do not consent to being raped merely by marrying'.[24]

In Hale's homeland, the House of Lords unanimously dismissed an appeal against a decision of the Court of Appeal in a case which involved the estranged partner breaking into the house of the victim's parent and raping her. It was submitted by the defendant's counsel that an immunity existed based on common law. The House of Lords ruled that such an exemption was not supported by any direct legal authority; moreover, it was 'an anachronistic and offensive common law fiction', which no longer represented the position of a wife in present day society.[25] This development was subsequently enshrined in the Criminal Justice and Public Order Act 1994 following the removal of the word 'unlawful' from the definition of rape.

21 *R v McGinn* (1982) VR 53. Although the appeal was in 1982, the offence took place before the 1980 Victorian marital rape reform.

22 *R v C* (1981) 3 A Crim R 146.

23 *Beck v The Queen* [1984] WAR 127, 136.

24 Review of US states appears in Augustine, 'Marriage: The Safe Haven for Rapists', above n. 12, pp. 564–570.

25 *R v R* [1991] 2 All ER 257.

Immunity from marital rape was formally abolished by the common law in Australia the same year. The High Court upheld the validity of the partial South Australian reform in *R v L*,[26] and questioned whether permanent consent to sex had ever been a part of common law. The majority stated that the court 'would be justified in refusing to accept a notion that is so out of keeping with the view society now takes of the relationship between the parties to a marriage'.[27]

Statutes have been enacted in all Australian jurisdictions to abolish the exemption.[28] In 1980, Victoria initially legislated that 'living separately and apart' was necessary to prosecute a rape in marriage. In South Australia there was only a limited abrogation requiring an assault or an act of gross indecency until 1992, when these qualifications were removed by Criminal Law Consolidation (Rape) Amendment Act 1992 (SA), s. 73(3). This relative tardiness may be attributed in part to active women's organisations such as the National Council of Women and the South Australian Women's Council of the Liberal Party, whose memberships objected to the lifting of the exclusion since it would 'undermine the family and contribute to the breakdown of marriages . . .'.[29]

The first state in the United States to eliminate its marital rape exemption did so in 1976; however, it was not until 2005 that the complete exemption was eliminated under all state, federal and military law. Several states (at the time of writing) still retain special qualifications for marital rape charges, such as short reporting periods and a requirement that the couple be living apart.[30]

The problems and pitfalls of reform: cultural and legal artifacts

In South Africa, one Member of Parliament, at the time of discussion about the exemption being dropped in that country, stated that the law should recognise

26 *R v L* (1991) 174 CLR 379.

27 Ibid., p. 390 (Mason CJ, Deane and Toohey JJ).

28 Express legislation provisions in Australia: Crimes Act 1900 (ACT), s. 69; Crimes Act 1900 (NSW), s. 61T; Criminal Law Consolidation Act 1935 (SA), s. 73(3); Crimes Act 1958 (Vic), s. 62(2). 'The remaining jurisdictions have removed the immunity by inference': Australian Law Reform Commission, *Family Violence – A National Legal Response*, Report No. 114, 2010, p. 1121.

29 P. Sallman and D. Chappell, *Rape Law Reform: A Study of the South Australian Experience*, Report to the Australian Criminology Research Council, 1980, p. 29. See also: J. Scutt, 'Consent in Rape: The Problem of the Marriage Contract', *Monash University Law Review* 3(4), 1977, 255–288; J. Scutt, 'To Love, Honour, and Rape with Impunity: Wife as Victim of Rape and the Criminal Law', in H.J. Schneider (ed.), *The Victim in International Perspective*, Berlin: Walter de Gruyter, 1982, 423–440.

30 National Judicial Education Program, *Intimate Partner Sexual Abuse: Adjudicating This Hidden Dimension of Domestic Violence Cases*, 2009. Free online course available at www.njep-ipsacourse.org.

'the human frailties and weaknesses of man'.[31] Such a comment is illustrative of the persistence of cultural beliefs that justify excluding partners from sexual assault charges.[32] Since the 1980s, studies of attitudes toward partner rape have found that some people simply do not believe that husbands ever use force to compel their wives to have sex; some believe that it is rare; some believe that wives have no right to say no; and many do not think that this type of sexual assault harms the victim because she is used to having consensual sex with her abuser.[33] Thus, it seems that (what we might have hoped to have been) outdated ideas of what is reasonable behaviour between partners continue to be a significant factor.[34] A mythology persists which constructs marital rape as less damaging or injurious than other types of rape.[35] Police, prosecutors and judges are not immune from these myths, as will become evident in the remaining sections of this chapter.

Artifact: misunderstandings about consent

As discussed in Chapter 8, the centrality of consent to both the physical and fault elements of the offence of sexual assault is problematic, and these problems seem to be magnified in the context of partner rape. Unsurprisingly in a partner context, proving that the woman did not consent (a physical element) or an absence of consent that the defendant knew of, but chose to ignore (the fault element) is difficult, because of the history of consensual intercourse. As one Australian judge stated:

> It would hardly be surprising in an allegation of sexual intercourse without consent in the context of a marriage, and particularly where there has been explicit evidence of a history of consensual sexual intercourse (and of the kind the subject of one of the charges), if the jury regarded the issue of the state of mind of the accused person as a primary one. That is more particularly so where, as is here the case, the evidence that the complainant did not consent is rather weak. Even weaker is the evidence that the complainant did anything to convey to the appellant that she was not consenting.[36]

31 Cited in F. Kaganas and C. Murray, 'Law Reform and the Family: The New South African Rape-in-Marriage Legislation', *Journal of Law and Society* 18(3), 1991, 287–299, p. 292.

32 Discussed in V. Garnier Barshis, 'The Question of Marital Rape', *Women's Studies International Forum* 6(4), 1983, 383–393.

33 K. Basile, 'Attitudes Toward Wife Rape: Effects of Social Background and Victim Status', *Violence and Victims* 17(3), 2002, 341–354; C. Ferro, J. Cermele and A. Saltzman, 'Current Perceptions of Marital Rape: Some Good and Some Not-So-Good News', *Journal of Interpersonal Violence* 23(6), 2008, 764–779.

34 Easteal, 'Rape in Marriage', above n. 7.

35 K. Edwards et al., 'Rape Myths: History, Individual and Institutional-Level Presence, and Implications for Change', *Sex Roles* 65(11–12), 2011, 761–773.

36 *TK v R* (2009) 74 NSWLR 299, 326 (Simpson J).

The judge indicated that defence counsel in the final address focused on the defendant's knowledge of lack of consent. The judge reminded the jury that the defendant's advocate had asked the jury to take into account the fact that the complainant and the appellant were married. The barrister had stated: 'you are entitled to take into account that they have been living together for fifteen years and *how married couples might relate to each other in a sexual environment* . . .'.[37] The barrister had also stated that such communication might be verbal or non-verbal.[38]

Therefore, it would seem that the potential for misunderstanding consent and its negation in rape cases in general, as discussed in Chapter 8, is magnified with partner rape. Negation of consent is further problematised by the victims' experience of at least four categories of coercion: social coercion; interpersonal coercion; threat of physical force; and physical force.[39] One woman, for example, learned not to say 'no' as she would then have to endure a beating. She decided that rape was preferable to being battered as it was quieter and did not wake up the children.[40] Other sources of duress include the woman trying to keep the peace, and the man's threats to leave, withdraw his love or to cut off money. Among one sample, the last was reported by 27 per cent of those assaulted by partners.[41] Survivors may experience multiple types of coercion both concurrently and over time, in the context of changing abuse patterns.[42] The legal interpretation of consent and its negation, however, focuses far more upon physical force. There are some who consider a degree of physical coercion as acceptable with marital sex. As one Australian judge infamously stated over two decades ago:

> There is, of course, nothing wrong with a husband faced with his wife's initial refusal to engage in intercourse, in attempting, in an acceptable way, to persuade her to change her mind, and that may involve a measure of *rougher than usual handling*. It may be, in the end, that handling and persuasion will persuade the wife to agree. Sometimes it is a fine line between not agreeing, then changing of the mind, and consenting.[43]

37 Ibid., p. 328 (emphasis added).

38 Ibid.

39 D. Finkelhor and K. Yllo, *Licence to Rape: Sexual Abuse of Wives*, New York: Holt, Rinehart & Winston, 1985.

40 D. Parkinson and S. Cowan, *Raped by a Partner: A Research Report*, Wangaratta: Women's Health Goulburn North East, 2008, p. 32.

41 NSW Sexual Assault Committee, *Sexual Assault Phone-In Report*, Sydney: Ministry for the Status and Advancement of Women, 1993, p. 22.

42 P. Mahoney and L. Williams, 'Sexual Assault in Marriage: Prevalence, Consequences, and Treatment of Wife Rape', in J.L. Jasinski and L.M. Williams (eds), *Partner Violence: A Comprehensive Review of 20 Years of Research*, Thousand Oaks, CA: Sage, 1998, 113–163.

43 *R v Johns* (Unreported, Supreme Court of South Australia, 26 August 1992, Bollen J), in summing up to jury (emphasis added), as mentioned in *Question of Law Reserved on Acquittal Pursuant to Section 350(1a) Criminal Law Consolidation Act (No. 1 of 1993)* 59 SASR 214, 219.

That judge's perspective unfortunately does not seem to be an aberration. Australian judicial use of phrases like 'little short of rape'[44] to describe violent marriages and sexual assault are indicative of how some judges perceive sexual assault by a partner to be at the less 'real' end of the rape continuum, as compared to rape by a stranger.[45] This type of perspective continues to appear in more recent judgments:

> Although fearful of the Appellant the Complainant at least knew him and no doubt was capable of making some assessment of the situation. . . . The case was not one where a victim walking through a lonely street or park at night is seized by a complete stranger about whom she knows nothing and who, for all the victim knows, may well kill her when the intercourse is over . . .[46]

Partner rape may also be seen as 'quite different from the characteristics of the more usual cases of non-consensual sexual intercourse which come before the Courts'.[47] In one case, the Full Court upheld an appeal against sentence and reduced it to a non-parole period of four years. In a sense, the judge was justifying or minimising the husband/rapist's violence, given the victim's infidelity:

> It does not seem to me to be difficult to understand that the appellant, when the truth of that infidelity dawned on him, reacted with affront; that the affront developed into rage; and that the rage caused him to lash out at the complainant in ways which were, as the learned sentencing Judge found and I agree, totally out of character. None of that excuses his having forced sexual intercourse upon the complainant. All of those considerations do, however, explain to some extent the appellant's offending behavior . . .[48]

Similarly in England and Wales, we continue to see a minimisation of the harm of partner rape and the culpability of the offender. In one matter, the advice provided by the sentencing panel suggested that in a case of relationship breakdown 'an offender may be subject to an unusual degree of provocation or stress'.[49]

In Canada, despite the abolition of the marital rape exemption in 1983, Lazar's analysis demonstrates how 'both Crown and defence counsel generally

44 *In the Marriage of Schwartzkopff* (1992) 15 FamLR 545, 555.

45 Easteal, 'Rape in Marriage', above n. 7; P. Easteal and M. Gani, 'Sexual Assault by Male Partners: A Study of Sentencing Factors', *Southern Cross University Law Review* 9, 2005, 39–72.

46 *Boney v The Queen* [2008] NSWCCA 165, [106], in which the victim had been in a consensual sexual relationship with the defendant.

47 *Turnell v The Queen* [2006] NSWCCA 399, [65].

48 Ibid.

49 Sentencing Advisory Panel, *Advice to the Court of Appeal – 9: Rape*, 2002, [25]. See P. Rumney, 'Progress at a Price: The Construction of Non-Stranger Rape in the *Millberry* Sentencing Guidelines', *Modern Law Review* 66(6), 2003, 870–884, p. 874.

translated wife/partner rape as "bad sex" or "unwanted sex" but not *really* as rape'.[50]

The underlying premise in many of these matters seems to be that if the victim has had consensual sex with her (ex)partner the day before, or even months before, any future act loses potential interpretation as rape.[51] This can lead to the imposition of informal 'presumed consent' or 'continuing consent' models, even in jurisdictions which appear to require affirmative consent (such as Canada), in cases involving marital/partner rape.[52] Consequently, a higher evidential bar may be set in marital rape cases and, as Sack notes, such differential treatment 'demonstrates ongoing toleration for the view that married women are not entitled to legal autonomy'.[53]

The outcome of such judicial attitudes can be unspeakably tragic:

> A prime example of what happens when judges do not understand IPSV [intimate partner sexual violence] is the case of Dr. Amy Castillo, a pediatrician in Baltimore, Maryland. In 2008 Amy was divorcing her increasingly violent, erratic, and suicidal husband, Mark, who told her the worst thing he could do to her would be to kill their three children and leave her alive. Amy obtained a Temporary Protective Order against Mark. At the hearing for the Final Protective Order the defense attorney brought out that Amy had sexual relations with Mark shortly before seeking the order. The judge was unable to grasp that this was not a romantic reconciliation but rather a terrified woman acquiescing in a violent man's sexual demand to protect her children and herself from further harm. The judge denied the Final Order and awarded Mark unsupervised visitation. Shortly after, Mark drowned the three children in a hotel room bathtub.[54]

Attrition through the system

Although the immunity of husbands from prosecution and a 'license to rape' have been abolished for decades in western industrial countries around the world,

50 R. Lazar, 'Negotiating Sex: The Legal Construct of Consent in Cases of Wife Rape in Ontaria, Canada', *Canadian Journal of Women and Law* 22, 2010, 329–363, p. 333 (emphasis in original).

51 P. Easteal and C. Feerick, 'Sexual Assault by Male Partners: Is the License Still Valid?', *Flinders Journal of Law Reform* 8(2), 2005, 185–207.

52 Lazar, 'Negotiating Sex', above n. 50, pp. 358–360.

53 E.J. Sack, 'Is Domestic Violence a Crime?: Intimate Partner Rape as Allegory', *St John's Journal of Legal Commentary* 24(3), 2009, 535–566, p. 557.

54 L. Hecht Schafran, 'Intimate Partner Sexual Violence and the Courts', in L. McOrmond-Plummer, P. Easteal and J. Levy-Peck (eds), *Intimate Partner Sexual Violence: A Multidisciplinary Approach to Survivor Support and System Change*, London: Jessica Kingsley Publishers, 2014, 221–233.

partner rape has particularly low reporting, prosecution and conviction rates.[55] As Darlington writes:

> This is the 'whispered' subject that women won't discuss. Child sexual abuse has come out of the closet in many ways, so has physical abuse in marriage and in general, but marital rape and sexual abuse in marriage is still seen by most women as a subject of extreme personal significance and therefore, very private.[56]

In one Australian study, only four of 21 partner rape survivors sought help from the police for rape at the time of the assault, five reported domestic violence only and two made enquiries years later about laying charges. The remaining ten women did not seek assistance from the police through lack of belief in themselves or in the system:[57] 'I don't think you'd get any help from police. I don't think they'd class it as rape. Even rape that happens by someone they don't know, I don't think they really see it as a big deal'.[58]

When reporting does take place, police may feel frustrated having committed significant resources to investigating the crime only to have the charges withdrawn. Police also believe that if the victim is reluctant to make a statement and to agree to a medical examination or forensic testing, the chance of a successful prosecution is greatly reduced by not having evidence.[59] Prosecutors are also influenced either consciously or unconsciously by the continuum of 'real' rape and will 'run' with the cases they believe will result in a conviction; the high rate of prosecutorial discontinuances that can be seen in all sexual assault cases is slightly higher in partner rape.[60]

55 Easteal and Feerick, 'Sexual Assault by Male Partners', above n. 51; Easteal and Gani, 'Sexual Assault by Male Partners', above n. 45; M. Heenan and S. Murray, *A Study of Reported Rapes in Victoria 2000–2003: Summary Research Report*, Victoria: Office of Women's Policy, Department for Victorian Communities, 2006; L. Kelly, J. Lovett and L. Regan, *A Gap or a Chasm? Attrition in Reported Rape Cases*, Home Office Research Study 293, London: Home Office Research, Development and Statistics Directorate, 2005.

56 B. Darlington, 'Marital Rape', in J. Milne-Horne (ed.), *Proceedings From the Psychology Conference 1992*, NSW: Kingswood, 1993.

57 Parkinson and Cowan, *Raped by a Partner*', above n. 40, p. 58.

58 'Jacqui', pseudonym for respondent, in ibid.

59 Ibid., p. 92.

60 M. Heenan, 'Just "Keeping the Peace": A Reluctance to Respond to Male Partner Sexual Violence', *Australian Centre for the Study of Sexual Assault Issues* 1, 2004; S. Lea, U. Lanvers and S. Shaw, 'Attrition in Rape Cases: Developing a Profile and Identifying Relevant Factors', *British Journal of Criminology* 43(3), 2003, 583–599.

The trial

Contributors to secondary wounding for victims[61] *and to a low conviction rate*

A trial may be particularly distressing for the victim of partner rape if the judge disallows certain evidence, such as a history of domestic violence. As discussed at p. 213, from the perspective of the victim, *fear* of physical force may be the source of coercion. If evidence of prior violence is not admitted and the incident is looked at in isolation from prior abuse, then the threat of force that vitiates or negates the victim's consent may not be comprehended. In *R v C* the appellate court upheld the decision of the trial judge to admit this type of evidence:

> The appellant said he wanted to 'make up' for hitting her, and asked to 'make love', and the complainant said 'no' but as she explained in her evidence, 'I had to say it very gently because from past experience . . . I thought he would have done it again' [that is, hit her].[62]

Another contributor to the low rate of convictions is the perceived *extra* unreliability of victims of partner rape.[63] Delayed reporting can lead to the disappearance of evidence and can be used against the woman in court to further discredit her as a witness. The rape myth operating here is that the 'good' victim reports immediately, as discussed in Chapter 9. With partner rape, prompt disclosure and reporting are not the norm. Therefore, as is so often the case in sexual assault trials, the complainant's words end up being on trial:

> Securing convictions in male partner rape cases remains difficult for prosecutors. Like most rape trials, the defence is likely to devote considerable attention to attacking the victim's character and credibility. Where there has been a relationship history, the defence has a greater pool of information about the complainant to draw on in reconstructing a version of events set on undermining what she alleges happened. At best, the approach is designed to raise a reasonable doubt about her veracity in the minds of the jury. At worst, she will be exposed to a gruelling process of cross-examination that will remain

61 In P. Easteal and L. McOrmond-Plummer, *Real Rape, Real Pain*, Melbourne: Hybrid, 2006, p. 177, secondary wounding is described as occurring when people and/or institutions 'significantly disrupt a survivor's healing' by compounding the trauma.

62 *R v C* [2003] QCA 561, [3].

63 Easteal and Feerick, 'Sexual Assault by Male Partners', above n. 51; D. Lievore, 'Intimate Partner Sexual Assault: The Impact of Competing Demands on Victims' Decisions to Seek Criminal Justice Solutions' (paper presented at the 8th Australian Institute of Family Studies Conference, Melbourne, 12–14 February 2003); D. Lievore, 'Prosecutorial Decisions in Adult Sexual Assault Cases', *Trends and Issues in Crime and Criminal Justice* 291, Canberra: Australian Institute of Criminology, 2005.

> transfixed on the detail of previous consensual sexual activity she once engaged in with her partner – the man she now accuses of rape.[64]

The focus of defence cross-examination may be on past consensual sexual activities. As noted in Chapter 9, evidence of a complainant's sexual reputation is not admissible and evidence of the complainant's sexual activities is not admissible in a sexual offence proceeding, without leave of the court. However, this does not usually apply to evidence of specific sexual activities between the victim and the accused in sexual offence proceedings:[65]

> The aim of defence barristers in these cases was unashamedly directed at suggesting that consensual sex was more likely to have occurred on the occasion in question, just as it had in the past. Across the five trials, women were asked how often they had sex, when they started having sex, and whether they could speak to the general health of their sexual relationships. They were challenged about their versions of the regularity of sex, their alleged refusals to engage in sex, and their claims to often appease their male partners through submitting to sex.[66]

Accordingly, in at least one appellate matter, a conviction was quashed and 'a miscarriage of justice' declared since 'this is a case where the jury's view of ABC's credibility in her account of how the assault took place is of great importance'.[67] The crux of the appeal was that evidence about a continuing sexual relationship had not been admitted.

Furthermore, legislative provisions restricting the admission of previous sexual activity between the accused and the complainant have been subjected to problematic judicial interpretation. As highlighted in Chapter 9, in England and Wales the House of Lords in *R v A*[68] maintained that previous sexual activity between the accused and the complainant was relevant to the issue of consent and therefore should be more readily admissible. This decision has significant ramifications for cases involving partner rape, as there is more likely to have been previous sexual activity between the partners.

As Ellison notes, however, the underlying reasoning of the House of Lords 'remains unsatisfactorily obscure'.[69] Beyond notions of 'common sense'[70] and the

64 Heenan, 'Just "Keeping the Peace"', above n. 60, p. 7.

65 For Australian examples, see Evidence (Miscellaneous Provisions) Act 1991 (ACT), s. 51(2) and Criminal Procedure Act 1986 (NSW), s. 293.

66 Ibid.

67 *Taylor v The Queen* [2009] NSWCCA 180, [73].

68 [2002] 1 AC 45.

69 L. Ellison, 'Commentary on R v A (No 2)', in R. Hunter, C. McGlynn and E. Rackley, *Feminist Judgments: From Theory to Practice*, Oxford: Hart Publishing, 2010, 206–210, p. 208.

70 *R v A* [2001] UKHL 25, [2002] 1 AC 45, 61 (Lord Steyn).

perspectives of the 'man and woman in the street',[71] very little substantiation is provided as to why previous sexual activity between the two parties is relevant to, and probative of, consent. For example, Lord Steyn merely contemplated that such evidence might 'throw light on the complainant's state of mind'.[72] In a similar vein, Lord Hutton commented that 'evidence of such a relationship will show the complainant's specific mindset towards the defendant, namely her affection for him'.[73] With reference to the opinion of Dean Wigmore, Lord Hutton noted that evidence of a previous sexual relationship 'shows an emotion towards the particular defendant tending to allow him to repeat the liberty'.[74]

These perspectives fail to recognise that consent is given anew each time and is a 'decision', as opposed to 'an emotion or a mind-set'.[75] Moreover, assuming that previous sexual activity between the parties is relevant to the issue of consent presupposes that the complainant has a disposition to consent to sexual intercourse with the accused. This, arguably, contradicts the official rejection of the use of sexual history evidence to suggest that, due to her previous sexual activity, a woman is more likely to consent to sexual intercourse, and 'reinforces patterns of discriminatory fact-finding which legitimate presumptive sexual access'.[76] This disposition perspective also 'invites the inference that women are less likely to be raped by their sexual partners rather than others'[77] and 'tends toward reintroducing the historical marital rape exemption and also toward expanding it to all cases in which women have had similar sexual interactions'.[78] Consequently, it can be seen that the decision in *R v A* not only maintains and perpetuates notions of stranger rape as 'real rape', but also limits a woman's right to say 'no' to sexual intercourse with her partner and restricts her right to legal protection.[79]

In *R v A*, therefore, we can see an interpretation which reintroduces a judicial discretion that was significantly restricted by an Act of Parliament. While the decision maintains that further scope to permit evidence of sexual activity between the parties is necessary to protect the defendant's right to a fair trial, the judgment fails to provide a substantiated explication as to why such evidence is not only relevant and probative, but also not so prejudicial that it should be excluded. Arguably, this amounts to an unethical interpretation of the Youth Justice and

71 Ibid., p. 55 (Lord Steyn).
72 Ibid., p. 61.
73 Ibid., p. 102.
74 Ibid.
75 Ellison, 'Commentary on R v A (No 2)', above n. 69, p. 208; citing C. Boyle and M. MacCrimmon, 'The Constitutionality of Bill C-49: Analyzing Sexual Assault Law as if Equality Really Mattered', *Criminal Law Quarterly* 41(2), 1998, 198–237, p. 230.
76 Boyle and MacCrimmon, 'The Constitutionality of Bill C-49', above n. 75, p. 229.
77 Ibid.
78 L. Levanon, 'Sexual History Evidence in Cases of Sexual Assault: A Critical Re-Evaluation', *University of Toronto Law Journal* 62(4), 2012, 609–651, p. 644.
79 See also G. Firth, 'The Rape Trial and Sexual History Evidence – R v A and the (Un)Worthy Complainant', *Northern Ireland Legal Quarterly* 53(3), 2006, 442–464.

Criminal Evidence Act 1999 ('YJCEA') by the House of Lords in paying insufficient regard to the suffering of women in light of the marital rape exemption and the atrocious ordeal of being cross-examined on previous sexual activity.

McGlynn, in her feminist rewriting of *R v A*, suggests that legislatures in England and Wales take guidance from the Canadian regime.[80] While adopting more of a discretionary regime, as opposed to the exclusionary/categories approach contained in the YJCEA, the Canadian legal framework is interesting in that it explicitly rejects the use of sexual history evidence to support an inference of consent. The Canadian Criminal Code states:

> evidence that the complainant has engaged in sexual activity, whether with the accused or with any other person, is not admissible to support an inference that, by reason of the sexual nature of the activity, the complainant: (a) is more likely to have consented to the sexual activity that forms the subject matter of the charge; or (b) is less worthy of belief.[81]

If sexual history evidence is admitted as being deemed relevant to some other issue in the trial, the judge must warn the jury not to draw inappropriate inferences regarding consent and credibility.[82]

This regime is not without its criticisms. Courts are still given considerable discretion regarding the perceived relevancy of sexual history evidence, and research demonstrates the negative and prejudicial impact such evidence has upon jury members. Thus, judicial warnings regarding inappropriate inferences may have little effect.[83] It has also been argued that the exclusion relates only to general sexual activity as opposed to specific or distinctive sexual encounters.[84] Nevertheless, the Canadian approach does not appear to support the decision in *R v A (No. 2)*, which is noteworthy[85] in light of the extent to which some of the Law Lords drew upon the Canadian case of *R v Seaboyer*[86] in their judgment.[87]

80 C. McGlynn, 'R v A (No 2) Judgment', in R. Hunter, C. McGlynn and E. Rackley, *Feminist Judgments: From Theory to Practice*, Oxford: Hart Publishing, 2010, 211–227, pp. 222–223, 225.
81 Criminal Code, RSC, 1985, c. C-49, s. 276(1)
82 *R v Seaboyer* [1991] 2 SCR 577, 636.
83 R.A. Schuller and P.A. Hastings, 'Complainant Sexual History Evidence: Its Impact on Mock Jurors' Decisions', *Psychology of Women Quarterly* 26(3), 252–261; R.A. Schuller and M.A. Klippenstine, 'The Impact of Complainant Sexual History Evidence on Jurors' Decisions: Consideration From a Psychological Perspective', *Psychology, Public Policy, and Law* 10(3), 2004, 321–342.
84 See also: S.M. Chapman, 'Section 276 of the *Criminal Code* and the Admissibility of "Sexual Activity" Evidence', *Queen's Law Journal* 25(1), 1999, 121–176, pp. 142–145; H. Schwartz, 'Sex with the Accused on Other Occasions: The Evisceration of Rape Shield Protection', *Criminal Reports* 31(4th), 1994, 323–252.
85 McGlynn, 'R v A (No 2) Judgment', above n. 80, p. 222.
86 [1991] 2 SCR 577.
87 See, e.g., *R v A* [2001] UKHL 25, [2002] 1 AC 45, 59–64 (Lord Steyn).

The decision of the Supreme Court of Canada in *R v Seaboyer* precedes and informs the current regime contained in the Criminal Code, s. 276. The case caused consternation among feminist legal scholars in particular,[88] as the Supreme Court declared unconstitutional the previous rape shield provision, which adopted an exclusion/exceptional categories approach with respect to the complainant's sexual history with third parties.[89] While the decision is problematic in this regard, the court nevertheless set down the principles regarding inappropriate inferences. Madam Justice McLachlin stated:

> The reality is in 1991 that evidence of sexual conduct and reputation in itself cannot be regarded as logically probative of either the complainant's credibility or consent. Although they may still inform the thinking of many, the twin myths which section 276 sought to eradicate are just that – myths – and have no place in a rational and just system of law. It follows that the old rules which permitted evidence of sexual conduct and condoned invalid inferences from it solely for these purposes have no place in our law.[90]

This statement further supports the contention that the decision in *R v A* amounts to an unethical interpretation in its failure to recognise the suffering of female rape victims.

Sentencing

Within parent-child relationships breach of trust is now treated as an aggravating variable in sentencing, but it is not often so weighted in Australian marital rape cases.[91] In fact, instead of considering the violation of the trust in an intimate relationship as aggravating, the tendency may be the opposite – constructing a spousal relationship as mitigating the penalty:

> The Australian cases are littered with continual reference to the existence of the prior relationship while few statements as to its irrelevance for sentencing purposes are to be found. More likely, the Australian courts will observe that there is some mitigatory sentencing relevance to be attached to the offender's prior relationship with his victim, though no foundation in sentencing principle is cited for such an approach.[92]

88 See, e.g., M. Shaffer, 'Seaboyer v R: A Case Comment', *Canadian Journal of Women and the Law* 3(2), 1992, 592–601; E.A. Sheehy, 'Feminist Argumentation Before the Supreme Court of Canada in *R v Seaboyer; R v Gayme*: The Sound of One Hand Clapping', *Melbourne University Law Review* 18(2), 1991, 450–468.

89 *R v Seaboyer* [1991] 2 SCR 577.

90 Ibid., p. 630.

91 S. Kift, 'That All Rape is Rape Even if Not by a Stranger', *Griffith Law Review* 4(1), 1995, 60–111, pp. 83–86.

92 Ibid., p. 86.

If the woman has willingly had sex with the rapist at some point in the recent past, this may affect the judge's construction of the offence, perhaps viewing the defendant as having a genuine but unreasonable belief in consent.[93] For instance, in *Ramage*, the Court of Criminal Appeal noted: 'about a month [after the rape] consensual intercourse of the normal vaginal type again took place'.[94]

The 'on/off' nature of the relationship also appeared to be regarded as relevant in another appellate matter:

> Given that the last of those occasions [reconciliation with consensual sex] was only a month or so before this offence took place, it might not be possible to say that the relationship was then obviously at an end. The respondent probably hoped to repair the rupture and resume living with his wife . . . However, the fact was that the parties were living apart, and this cannot be explained as the case of a husband losing his self-control during the continuance of the cohabitation.[95]

In *Goodall*, the fact that there had not been recent consensual sex was mentioned almost as an aggravating factor:

> Nor do I consider the head sentence of eight years' imprisonment for the rape here in question was manifestly excessive. That crime, too, was attended by circumstances of aggravation. *It is true, too, that Mrs W and the applicant had previously had a consensual sexual relationship, but that no longer existed.*[96]

Similar to Australian findings, in the 1990s Lees, looking at England and Wales, found that punishments meted out to estranged husbands were 'frequently lower than in other rape cases'.[97] The following extract from a Court of Appeal judgment in 1984 provides a clue as to why this might have been the case:

> . . . this was not a rape of a strange woman or a woman hardly known, but the rape of a woman with whom the appellant had lived as man and wife – initially no doubt very happily – for upwards of 10 years. This does

93 In *R v B* (1996) 88 A Crim R 91, the defendant's 12-month sentence was successfully appealed by the Crown. Malcolm CJ criticised the sentencing judge's finding that the respondent was attempting a reconciliation because this finding contradicted the facts at hand: p. 95.

94 *R v Ramage* (Unreported, Victoria Court of Criminal Appeal, 15 September 1993, Crockett, Vincent and Cummins JJ), p. 1. Although divorced, occasionally during access visits, the accused and his ex-wife had intercourse; thus the three rapes (with tearing and bleeding) were interspersed both by time and by consensual sex.

95 *DPP v Cowey* (1995) 182 LSJS 345, 346.

96 *R v Goodall* [2000] VSCA 106, [24] (Batt JA) (emphasis added).

97 S. Lees, *Ruling Passions: Sexual Violence, Reputation and the Law*, Buckingham: Open University Press, 1997, p. 123.

> add a different dimension to the case and puts the sentence at the lowest end of the bracket.[98]

This perspective has, however, shifted over time. Recognition of relationship rape commenced with Sentencing Council guidance provided to the Court of Appeal in *R v Millberry*.[99] Subsequently, the 2007 Sentencing Guidelines acknowledged that '[a]ny rape is a traumatic and humiliating experience and, although the particular circumstances in which the rape takes place may affect the sentence imposed, the starting point for sentencing should be the same'.[100] Accordingly, there should be no differentiation between relationship rape, acquaintance rape, or stranger rape.[101] Thus, following *Millberry* and the 2007 Guidelines, prima facie in England and Wales stranger and partner rapes were to be treated with equal severity. However, Rumney's close reading of *Millberry* suggests that this was not always the case.[102] While in *Millberry* 'non-stranger' rape was accorded the equivalence of stranger rape, this was only on the basis that it involved a breach of trust. Consequently, it was not in and of itself seen to be as serious. Whereas a breach of trust operated to aggravate a 'stranger rape', it did not do so in cases involving 'non-strangers'.[103] Of further note was the manner in which the Court of Appeal considered that a victim of stranger rape may be more fearful, due to the fact that the rapist is an 'unknown quantity'.[104] The victim may wonder, '[i]s he a murderer as well as a rapist?'.[105] At the same time, however, the court failed to acknowledge the heightened fear suffered by a victim of partner rape. Fear may well permeate her life and repeat victimisation is highly probable. In addition, many partner rapes can lead to pregnancy, thus giving rise to fears for the safety of the unborn child. The woman is also likely to suffer physical violence. As Rumney notes, 'the Court of Appeal would also do well to recognize the link between marital rape, domestic violence and homicide'.[106]

The Court of Appeal also speculated that partner rape may be subject to unique forms of mitigation due to 'the ongoing nature of the relationship between the offender and the victim'.[107] As an example of mitigation, the court considered a scenario in which a partner rape occurs after both parties had consumed alcohol and, because of the intoxication, the offender 'failed to show the restraint he should

98 *R v Stockwell* (1984) 6 Cr App R (S) 4, as discussed in Temkin, *Rape and the Legal Process*, above n. 10, p. 17.

99 [2003] 2 All ER 939 ('*Millberry*').

100 Sentencing Guidelines Council, *Sexual Offences Act 2003*, 2007, p. 19.

101 Ibid.

102 Rumney, 'Progress at a Price', above n. 49.

103 *Millberry*, p. 947. See Rumney, 'Progress at a Price', above n. 49, pp. 881–883.

104 *Millberry*, p. 944. See Rumney, 'Progress at a Price', above n. 49, pp. 873–875.

105 *Millberry*, p. 944.

106 Rumney, 'Progress at a Price', above n. 49, p. 874.

107 *Millberry*, p. 947.

have'.[108] In such a situation it was stated to be 'contrary to common sense to treat such a category of rape as equivalent to stranger rape'.[109] It is not clear, however, why on any 'common sense' perspective this situation should reduce the offender's sentence. The court failed to substantiate any link – whether experiential and/or on a public policy basis – between intoxication and a reduced ability to control one's sexual urges.[110] Neither was a reason presented as to why intoxication may mitigate a partner rape, but not a stranger rape.[111] The most recent sentencing guidelines, which have remedied some of these issues, will be considered in further detail at p. 227.

In Scotland it is still explicitly accepted by the judiciary that a relationship operates in mitigation to partner rape. In *HM Advocate v Ramage* the court reduced a sentence of five years to one of three-and-a-half years, with Lord Caplan stating:

> there are factors in this case which could perhaps justify treating the case as being less serious than would normally be the case with a rape offence. The appellant and the complainer were not in any sense strangers. They had been in an intimate relationship before and, indeed, at one point they had been in a sexual relationship.[112]

An appeal court in Scotland followed *Ramage* in perceiving the domestic relationship as a mitigating factor:

> Whilst the element of breach of trust involved in any domestic assault is an important factor in determining penalty, the significance of an ongoing sexual relationship in determining the penalty in a case such as this where the gravest feature is that there was penile penetration and the conviction is for rape, is a much more complex issue. The fact of the relationship is one of a complex host of facts and circumstances that have to be taken into account in determining appropriate sentence. In this case we consider that the trial judge gave insufficient weight to the fact that the couple had regularly engaged in sexual intercourse over a period of two years up to the night of the offence.[113]

The issue arose once again in the 2013 Scottish case of *HM Advocate v Cooperwhite*,[114] in which the court rejected the Attorney General's argument that a sentence of six years was unduly lenient. The facts are of particular note, given that the case involved the rape of two partners, both involving arguably aggravating features. In

108 Ibid.
109 Ibid.
110 Rumney, 'Progress at a Price', above n. 49, pp. 878–879.
111 Ibid.
112 *HM Advocate v Ramage* [1999] SCCR 592, 594.
113 *HM Advocate v Petrie* [2011] HCJAC 1, [7].
114 [2013] HCJAC 88.

relation to victim MD, the rape occurred while she was pregnant *and* following medical advice that sexual intercourse could be harmfully and potentially fatal to both the mother and unborn child. In the second case the conviction related to various occasions in which the offender attempted to engage in sexual intercourse with the victim while she was asleep and, when she awoke, continued against her explicit non-consent. While rejecting the argument that the sentence was unduly lenient, Lord Carloway called for the production of general sentencing principles, and noted the 'radically different approach'[115] adopted in England and Wales. However, as discussed at p. 223, the guidelines in England and Wales were not without their difficulties.

Not all judges regard relationship or prior relationship as a mitigating variable. Indeed, there have been some decisions in England and Wales and in Australia which have stressed both the specific trauma of a woman being raped by an estranged partner and the fact that the parameters of aggravation should be defined the same in marital rape as in other types of sexual assault:[116] 'Indeed it might be said that to rape the mother of your children makes the offence that much worse'.[117]

The trial judge in the Scottish case of *HM Advocate v Petrie*,[118] with reference to domestic abuse cases, held that a relationship should *aggravate* a sentence, as the rape involved a breach of trust – an approach which appears to go further than *Millberry*. Further, in an early Australian case, in expressing the view that the law had never countenanced the use of violence in sexual relations between any man and woman, Slicer J held that prior sexual relationship was not a mitigating factor nor was the fact that marital rape had only recently been made a crime.[119] More recently, in a case of partner rape that involved the insertion of a wine bottle into his partner's vagina, the appellate court stated that '[t]he fact that the complainant and the appellant were in an existing sexual relationship cannot mitigate the offence in this case'.[120] The trial judge had emphasised that the 'community will not tolerate persons who deal with their sexual partners in the manner in which the offender dealt with his partner whilst she was either asleep, drunk or in an unconscious state'.[121]

Unlike this last example, other case law shows that perceptions of relationship as a mitigator may vary at different levels of adjudication. In *Dungay*, for instance, the Court of Criminal Appeal increased the sentence – noting that the trial judge had accepted the submission of counsel for the appellant that the offence 'is at the lower end of the range', stating:

115 Ibid., [22].
116 Kift, 'That All Rape is Rape Even if Not by a Stranger', above n. 91.
117 *R v Hutchinson* (1994) 15 Cr App R (S) 134, 136.
118 [2011] HCJAC 1.
119 *R v S (No. 2)* [1991] Tas R 273, 280.
120 *Gillies v DPP (NSW)* [2008] NSWCCA 339, [129].
121 Ibid., [120].

> Even if, as appears to have influenced the judge, the complainant remained with the appellant after the offence and during the next day, that non-parole period does not adequately mark the seriousness of him forcing himself upon her in demanding a tear, with punches and hitting with a broom.[122]

Down the path less travelled

It is evident that marital immunity may have been a fiction without the backing of case law or a legal foundation, but it was a fiction that has had a potent impact on the attitudes and actions of the courts and the community. Although legislation has been enacted to negate the immunity, one wonders, looking at the issues of reporting, prosecutorial discontinuances and sentencing, whether fictions, like attitudes, are so easily eradicated. This is certainly not surprising given the cultural context, as discussed in Chapter 2.

Despite these holistic hurdles, there are cases getting through the system, which is an improvement. At least some members of the judiciary are recognising that marriage does not provide a licence to rape, and some are no longer trivialising its effects. For instance, in a recent Australian Capital Territory case, a husband was sentenced to almost five years' jail for raping his wife of 22 years. Penfold J, in sentencing, stated: 'This was a particularly nasty sexual assault in the sense that it appears to have involved [the man] using a sexual violation to assert his power over his wife'. The marriage had previously broken down, and the two were talking in the defendant's car. 'The victim suffered bruising, four loose teeth, swollen lips, cut and abrasions as a result of the attack'.[123] This case illustrates that injury and separation continue to appear to be more conducive to seeing consent as negated. Indeed, as we have described, part of the resistance to an effective implementation of the law derives from persistent views of consent as irrevocable with matrimony, and its negation as requiring physical force.

Further legal reform might help. Sexual assault provisions could be amended to state that consent is not relevant when actual bodily harm is involved. In cases of assault and even indecent assault, the courts affirm that view.[124] Additionally, vitiation of consent could be defined more broadly to include the type of intimidation that can be generated in a marital relationship.[125]

122 *R v Dungay* [2010] NSWCCA 82, [123].

123 *R v TN* [2013] SCC 64 (10 September 2013). Transcript of proceedings available online at www.courts.act.gov.au/supreme/sentence/view/1501/title/r-v-tn.

124 See S. Bronitt, 'Rape and Lack of Consent', *Criminal Law Journal* 16(5), 1992, 289–310. Further, in the Canadian case of *R v Welsh* (1995) 86 OAC 200, it was held that a person cannot consent to a sexual act causing bodily harm.

125 Crimes Act 1900 (ACT), s. 67(1)(h), Criminal Code Act 1899 (Qld), Sch. 1, s. 348(2)(d) and Criminal Code Act 1924 (Tas), Sch. 1, s. 2A(2)(e) contain statutory definitions of consent that provide that there is no consent when the accused is in a position of authority or trust. However, the Australian Law Reform Commission, *Family Violence*, above n. 28, p. 1158, recommends that all jurisdictions should include that consent is negated if there is 'abuse of

In addition to legislative amendment, perhaps new sentencing guidelines or improving existing ones would reduce the potential for biases or ignorance in the construction of relative harm, and of victim and perpetrator blameworthiness. Recently, in England and Wales, the Sentencing Council undertook a consultation of sentencing in sexual offence cases and produced a definitive guideline, and herein lies the potential for a more ethical recognition of the harm caused by partner rape and sexual assault.[126] The consultation guideline commences by acknowledging the rarity of stranger rape, noting that '[m]ost rapes are carried out by someone the victim knows'.[127] It is also states 'that all rape is extremely harmful to the victim. The approach taken is therefore to assume that there is *always* a baseline of harm'.[128] This perspective leads the Sentencing Council to advocate a different approach to that utilised previously in relation to assault and burglary, in which 'the formulation of harm and culpability has set out factors that indicate greater or lesser harm and those that indicate greater or higher culpability'.[129] The adoption of a new approach is significant, especially when set in a context in which the harmfulness of partner rape has frequently been diminished/ignored. Consequently, it is noted that rape amounts to 'inherently serious harm'[130] and, as such, the existence of additional features is not required to establish that the rape was 'harmful or serious'.[131]

The establishment of a baseline of harm, however, does not exclude the proposals from explicating further 'principal harm factors that a sentence should take into account',[132] and consequently the guideline sets out three categories of harm.[133] As expected, 'use of violence or threats of violence' is identified.[134] It is significant that the focus is on *violence* rather than the presence of *injuries*, to acknowledge the fact that 'the fear of violence often limits women's resistance'.[135] Moreover, the Sentencing Council emphasises that many of the factors are in no way limited to stranger rape. For example, the additional harm factor of abduction/detention 'is not intended to cover only the scenario where a victim is abducted from the street by a stranger but also to include, for example, the victim being prevented from leaving their home

a position "of authority *or trust*"; and to threats against the "complainant *or any other person*"' (emphasis in original).

126 Sentencing Council, *Sexual Offences Guideline Consultation*, 2012; Sentencing Council, *Sexual Offences Definitive Guideline*, 2013, effective 1 April 2014.

127 Sentencing Council, *Sexual Offences Guideline Consultation*, above n. 126, p. 15, citing Baroness Stern, *The Stern Review: A Report by Baroness Vivien Stern CBE of an Independent Review into How Rape Complaints are Handled by Public Authorities in England and Wales*, London: Government Equalities Office and the Home Office, 2010, p. 11.

128 Sentencing Council, *Sexual Offences Guideline Consultation*, above n. 126, p. 15 (emphasis in original).

129 Ibid.

130 Ibid., p. 16.

131 Ibid.

132 Ibid.

133 Sentencing Council, *Sexual Offences Definitive Guideline*, above n. 126, p. 10.

134 Ibid, p. 10.

135 Sentencing Council, *Sexual Offences Guideline Consultation*, above n. 126, p. 18.

during an attack'.[136] Likewise, forced entry into the victim's home 'has been deliberately worded to capture both the stranger who breaks into the victim's home and the offender who is known to the victim, for example, an ex-partner who enters the victim's home uninvited'.[137]

The next step in the guidelines relates to determining the culpability of the offender. As with the approach to harm, a baseline is established in which committing rape demonstrates 'a high degree of culpability'.[138] Consequently, the factors identified are considered to 'go beyond the culpability inherent in the act of rape itself',[139] and also encompass factors which are deemed to pertain to non-stranger rape cases, such as stalking, harassment and previous violence. The Council comments that 'it is important the factors considered are not just weighted towards rape by someone unknown to the victim but also recognise the reality that rape is more often committed by someone known to the victim'.[140] This positive approach is also adopted in its discussion of aggravating factors which include: 'victim compelled to leave their home'; 'failure to comply with current court orders'; 'offence committed whilst on licence'; 'exploiting contact arrangements with a child to commit an offence'; and 'presence of others, especially children'.[141] All of these factors 'have their roots' in domestic violence sentencing guidelines.[142]

Of further note is the acknowledgement that the presence of alcohol will only exacerbate the crime. Using intoxicants to facilitate the offence and targeting an intoxicated victim are held to increase an offender's culpability, as is his own inebriation. Thus, in contrast to the excusatory approach in *R v Millberry*,[143] the Sentencing Council contends that intoxication may 'mean that the offender has made himself insensible to the effect on his victim'.[144]

The guidelines demonstrate a better understanding of the harm of rape, and particularly partner rape, and thus have the potential to improve the sentencing in rape cases. However, difficulties remain. Rape Crisis and Rights for Women expressed concern regarding the adoption of three categories of harm, as the 'harm cannot be differentiated by the method of the rapist',[145] along with the need to avoid reinforcing a 'hierarchy of rape'.[146] Further, while an abuse of a position of trust is held to increase the culpability of the offender, the examples provided explicitly relate to those who are in a 'position of responsibility', as outlined in *R v Billiam*.[147]

136 Ibid., p. 17.
137 Ibid., p. 18.
138 Ibid., p. 19.
139 Ibid., p. 16.
140 Ibid., p. 21.
141 Sentencing Council, *Sexual Offences Definitive Guideline*, above n. 126, p. 11.
142 Sentencing Council, *Sexual Offences Guideline Consultation*, above n. 126, p. 21.
143 [2002] EWCA Crim 2891.
144 Sentencing Council, *Sexual Offences Guideline Consultation*, above n. 126, p. 24.
145 Sentencing Council, *Sexual Offences Responses to Consultation*, above n. 126, p. 10.
146 Sentencing Council, *Sexual Offences Guideline Consultation*, above n. 126, p. 24.
147 [1986] 1 WLR 349.

This fails to recognise that a breach of trust in a partner rape should also operate as an exacerbating factor. Perhaps this occurred due to the guidelines' problematic conflation of 'trust' and 'responsibility'. Trust is, arguably, a wider-reaching concept than responsibility and therefore should be held to encompass the reality that relationship rape can have a further-reaching and longer-lasting trauma.

In addition to sentencing guidelines and provisional reform, another way of assisting the court to understand the specific effects and harms of partner rape is to include expert reports by people who work in the area of violence against women as a normative part of the trial/sentencing process. These experts could also help judges and jurors to better understand what types of behaviour are coercive and what could constitute negation of consent from the victim's perspective.

Chapter 11

Violence against 'other' women

Legal systems may be insensitive not just to differences based on sex but also to variations in race, disability, ethnicity, sexual affinity and 'others'. In this chapter we look at a number of these issues, including the reasons why indigenous women, immigrant women (including those in forced marriages), lesbians and women with disabilities may remain silenced and 'trapped' in violent relationships.[1] We also discuss how access to assistance, including legal remedies, can prove particularly problematic.

Intersectionality

Feminists, in looking at violence, frequently have not informed their work with the diversity of ethnicity, race, disability and sexuality.[2] Although being female does translate into some commonalities in oppression, marginalisation and exclusion, there are many other socio-demographic factors that constitute the 'dominants' in western industrial culture, such as ethnicity, age, sexuality and physical and mental ability. Women's experiences of violence and their ability to access justice are therefore not homogeneous. Kimberlé Crenshaw coined the term 'intersectionality' to describe this juncture of marginality.[3] Her theory accounts for the experiences of individuals who are deviant in more than one way from the dominant standard:

1 Due to limitations of space, other intersections, such as age and social class, are not discussed here.

2 J. Stubbs, 'Teaching About Violence Against Women: An Interdisciplinary Project', *Legal Education Review* 6(2), 1995, 229–240; J. Stubbs, 'Violence Against Women: The Challenge of Diversity for Law, Policy and Practice' (paper presented at the Second National Outlook Symposium: Violence Crime, Property Crime and Public Policy, Canberra, Australian Institute of Criminology, 1997); J. Tolmie, 'Pacific-Asian Immigrant and Refugee Women Who Kill Their Batterers: Telling Stories that Illustrate the Significance of Specificity', *Sydney Law Review* 19(4), 1997, 472–513; J. Stubbs and J. Tolmie, 'Race, Gender and the Battered Woman Syndrome', *Canadian Journal of Women and the Law* 8(1), 1995, 122–158.

3 K. Crenshaw, 'Mapping the Margins: Intersectionality Identity Politics and Violence Against Women of Colour', *Stanford Law Review* 43(6), 1991, 1241–1300.

> Scholars adopting these approaches have challenged the primacy of gender as an explanatory model of domestic violence and have emphasized the need to examine how other forms of inequality and oppression, such as racism, ethnocentrism, class privilege, and heterosexism, intersect with gender oppression.[4]

Intersectionality theorists question gender inequality as the only explanation of domestic violence and look at how both homogeneous definitions and measurements of prevalence may be inappropriate – as will be discussed throughout this chapter.[5]

This focus on intersectionality also connects to debates regarding the relevance, or otherwise, of culture within the legal system, with some authors arguing for the adoption of a cultural defence in cases involving ethnic minority defendants.[6] Others, however, have highlighted the difficulties that multiculturalism may bring for women. For example, Okin has expressed concern that:

> 'respecting cultural differences' has increasingly become a euphemism for restricting or denying women's rights. As feminist activist-scholars have been making clear, the relevance and even the sanctity of 'cultural practices' is most often claimed when issues of sexuality, marriage, reproduction, inheritance, and power over children are concerned (issues that play a larger part in women's lives than they do in most men's).[7]

From a slightly different perspective, Volpp has argued that the use of culture in courts has led to the adoption of essentialised and static ethnic minority identities, which in turn leads to the construction of violence against women as a cultural phenomenon among minority groups.[8] In contrast, the dominant culture represents

4 N. Sokoloff and I. Dupont, 'Domestic Violence at the Intersections of Race, Class and Gender', *Violence Against Women* 11(1), 2005, 38–64, p. 39.

5 Ibid., pp. 41–45.

6 See, e.g.: M. Foblets and A. Renteln (eds), *Multicultural Jurisprudence*, Oxford: Hart Publishing, 2009; A. Renteln, *The Cultural Defense*, Oxford: Oxford University Press, 2005; Note 'The Cultural Defense in the Criminal Law', *Harvard Law Review* 99(6), 1986, 1293–1311. See also the empirical exploration of the use of the 'cultural defense' in the United States by C. Braunmühl, *Colonial Discourse and Gender in the U.S. Criminal Courts: Cultural Defenses and Prosecutions*, New York: Routledge, 2012.

7 S.M. Okin, 'Feminism, Women's Human Rights, and Cultural Differences', *Hypatia* 13(2), 1998, 32–52, p. 36. See also S.M. Okin, 'Is Multiculturalism Bad For Women?', in S.M. Okin et al. (eds), *Is Multiculturalism Bad For Women?*, Princeton: Princeton University Press, 1999, 7–26.

8 L. Volpp, '(Mis)Identifying Culture: Asian Women and the "Cultural Defense"', *Harvard Women's Law Journal* 17, 1994, 57–101; L. Volpp, 'Blaming Culture for Bad Behaviour', *Yale Journal of Law and the Humanities* 12(1), 2000, 89–116; L. Volpp, 'Feminism Versus Multiculturalism', *Columbia Law Review* 101(5), 2001, 1181–1218. Note that this perspective does not lead Volpp to reject completely the relevance of cultural evidence, but rather she calls for the adoption of a careful and nuanced recognition, which avoids perpetuating racial stereotypes. See also the

itself to be non-sexist, non-violent and protective of women. Furthermore, within the dominant group, violence against women is not presented as an aspect of culture, but rather due to personal failings.[9] This, however, does not acknowledge the extent to which violence against women is normalised in western cultures and the failure of western states to respond effectively to abused women.

Such a construction of ethnic minorities has intensified following on from 9/11. For example, in England and Wales, the increased focus on 'honour crimes' and 'honour killings' by both the state and the media has involved a process by which Asian Muslim culture, in particular, is 'Othered' and the notion of the 'dangerous Muslim male' is created.[10] At the same time, the western world is constructed as civilised and protective of women. This has also included a problematic appropriation of feminism in order to support the war following 9/11. As Butler notes:

> The sudden feminist conversion on the part of the Bush administration, which retroactively transformed the liberation of women into a rationale for its military actions against Afghanistan, is a sign of the extent to which feminism, as a trope, is deployed in the service of restoring the presumption of first world impermeability. Once again we see the spectacle of 'white men, seeking to save brown women from brown men' as Spivak once described the culturally imperialist exploitation of feminism.[11]

There has been an increasing 'racialisation of immigration laws',[12] which of course has negative ramifications for many vulnerable women. It can be argued that state policies pertaining to responses to violence against women increasingly

detailed analysis of the difference in approaches by M. Deckha, 'Is Culture Taboo? Feminism, Intersectionality, and Culture Talk in Law', *Canadian Journal of Women and the Law* 16(1), 2004, 14–53.

9 A. Gill, 'Violence Against Women in South Asian Communities in the UK: A Culture of Silence', in C. McGlynn and V.E. Munro (eds), *Rethinking Rape Law: International and Comparative Perspectives*, London: Routledge, 2010, 308–321, p. 309; S. Merry, *Human Rights and Gender Violence: Translating International Law into Local Justice*, Chicago: Chicago University Press, 2006.

10 V. Meetoo and H.S. Mirza, 'There is Nothing "Honourable" about "Honour Killings": Gender, Violence and the Limits of Multiculturalism', *International Forum* 30(3), 2007, 187–200. See also A. Carline, 'Honour and Shame in Domestic Homicide: A Critical Analysis of the Provocation Defence', in M. Idriss and T. Abbas (eds), *Honour, Violence, Women and Islam*, London: Routledge, 2011, 80–95.

11 J. Butler, *Precarious Life: The Powers of Mourning and Violence*, London: Verso, 2004, p. 41, drawing upon G.C. Spivak, 'Can the Subaltern Speak?', in C. Nelson and L. Grossberg (eds), *Marxism and the Interpretation of Culture*, Chicago: University of Illinois Press, 1988, 271–313.

12 K. Sharma and A. Gill, 'Protection for All? The Failures of the Domestic Violence Rule for (Im)migrant Women', in R. Thiara and A. Gill (eds), *Violence Against Women in South Asian Communities: Issues for Policy and Practice*, London: Jessica Kingsley Publishers, 2012, 211–231, p. 211.

display a conflict between a human rights perspective and an immigration control approach – with the latter seeming to take precedence.[13]

The answer is not to ignore culture and expect assimilation, nor uncritically to accept differing cultural practices. Neither approach offers effective solutions to the precariousness of women's lives, and both construct western culture as universal. Rather, the recognition of intersectionality requires a critical reflection upon the myriad of factors which construct (but are not determinative of) identity and experience, and how these factors interact with law, policy and society.

Differing definitions and risks of violence

Indigenous women

An unusually high proportion of indigenous women are victims of violent crime, particularly family violence.[14] In one survey, indigenous women were 2.5 times more likely to report having experienced family violence than their non-indigenous counterparts.[15] If domestic homicide is the tip of the domestic violence iceberg, it is important to note that aboriginal women account for 15 per cent of all female homicide victims in Australia, despite making up only two per cent of the total female population.[16] Additionally, there appears to be a 'normalisation of sexual violence' that is widespread and 'endemic'.[17]

Immigrants

Across countries, immigrant women may also be particularly susceptible to partner rape.[18] American research has found that immigrant women are especially vulnerable

13 H. Voolma, 'The Private is International: Domestic Violence Against Immigrant Women', *Addressing Inequalities: the Heart of the Post-2015 Development Agenda and the Future we Want for All; Global Thematic Consultation*, 2012. Available online at www.worldwewant2015.org/node/283326.

14 See Wirringa Baiya: Aboriginal Women's Legal Centre, *Statistics*, 2011. Available online at http://wirringabaiya.org.au/Information/Statistics.

15 Australian Health Ministers' Advisory Council, *Aboriginal and Torres Strait Islander Health Performance Framework Report 2010*, 2011, p. 100.

16 J. Mouzous, 'New Statistics Highlight High Homicide Rate for Indigenous Women', *Indigenous Law Bulletin* 4(25), 1999, 16–17.

17 L. Thorpe, R. Solomon and M. Dimopoulos, *From Shame to Pride: Access to Sexual Assault Services for Indigenous People*, Melbourne: Elizabeth Hoffman House, 2004, p. 22.

18 Discussed by B. Sabri, V. Barcelona de Mendoza and J. Campbell, 'Prevalence of Intimate Partner Sexual Violence Among Immigrant Groups', in L. McOrmond-Plummer, P. Easteal and J. Levy-Peck (eds), *Intimate Partner Sexual Violence: A Multidisciplinary Guide to Improving Services and Support for Survivors of Rape and Abuse*, London: Jessica Kingsley Publishers, 2014, 246–258.

to various types of violence in the home.[19] For example, financial abuse, such as deprivation of food and clothing, may be more common among migrant women since they may have no knowledge of government allowances and their lack a proficiency in the English language prevents them from gaining access to such information.[20]

Migrant women may also be at increased risk of violence because of familial subordination, fear of ostracism by community members if they leave their abuser, religious beliefs, economic dependence or a lack of familiarity with the legal provisions available in the country to which they have migrated.[21] On top of all of these factors, '[i]mmigration can cause social and cultural dislocation and intensify domestic violence'.[22]

Another type of violence that continues to take place for some young migrant women is forced marriage. By definition, this is a marriage without full and free consent involving physical, psychological, sexual, financial or emotional duress.[23] Concerns relating to forced marriage can be seen to fall within a context of what is generally referred to as 'honour crimes', which involves committing violence against women, from assault to murder, in order to restore the perceived honour of the family. These occur when the behaviour of a woman is considered to bring shame upon the family, for instance when she has become too 'westernised', has engaged in extra-marital affairs, or even when she has been raped.

Women with disabilities

Devalued in our society, women with disabilities have a relatively powerless status and may be isolated and dependent – all contributors to being the targets of violence:[24]

> Disabled women are at greater risk of abuse such as institutional abuse, chemical restraint, drug use, forced/coerced sterilisation, medical exploitation,

19 F.Y. Wong et al., 'Intimate Partner Violence, Depression, and Alcohol Use Among a Sample of Foreign-Born Southeast Asian Women in an Urban Setting in the United States', *Journal of Interpersonal Violence* 26(2), 2011, 211–229.

20 See: P. Easteal, 'Double Jeopardy: Violence Against Immigrant Women in the Home', *Family Matters* 45, 1996, 26–30; P. Easteal, 'Broken Promises: Violence Against Immigrant Women in the Home', *Alternative Law Journal* 21(2), 1996, 53–57.

21 J. Mindlin et al., *Dynamics of Sexual Assault and the Implications for Immigrant Women*, New York: Legal Momentum, 2010.

22 N. Ghafournia, 'Battered at Home, Played Down in Policy: Migrant Women and Domestic Violence in Australia', *Aggression and Violent Behavior* 16(3), 2011, 207–213.

23 Attorney-General's Department, Criminal Justice Division, *Forced and Servile Marriage*, Discussion Paper, 2011, p. 3.

24 See S. Plummer and P. Findley, 'Women with Disabilities' Experience with Physical and Sexual Abuse: Review of the Literature and Implications for the Field', *Trauma Violence Abuse* 13(1), 2012, 15–29, for a thorough review of the US literature.

humiliation, and harassment. A number of factors increase the vulnerability of disabled women to violence. These may include their impairment (such as inability to communicate using conventional means), dependence on others, fear of disclosure, and lack of economic independence, knowledge of their rights and services and support. They may also experience low self-esteem and lack assertiveness.[25]

Lesbians

A report drawing on data from the US National Violence Against Women Survey found that 11 per cent of women in a lesbian relationship reported being raped, physically assaulted and/or stalked by their female intimate partner.[26] In the United Kingdom, lesbians in the age group 20–25 were the most likely to report having experienced domestic abuse.[27] As in heterosexual relationships, the violence escalated at separation. Respondents in same sex relationships reported more emotional and sexual abuse than physical abuse in comparison to those suffering heterosexual domestic violence.[28] Emotional violence included abusers threatening to 'out' their partners and convincing them that the legal system would not provide them with assistance given its homophobic character.[29]

Obstacles to accessing assistance

> Culture and background play a role in how survivors experience the impact of violence. While a survivor's culture and social system may offer resources for safety and healing, they can also be the source of messages that can be misused to further isolate a survivor and condone a perpetrator's behavior . . . Cultural taboos against discussing issues related to sex, sexuality, and sexual abuse are widespread and act as barriers to disclosure across many cultures. It should be

25 L. Dowse, C. Frohmader and H. Meekosha, 'Intersectionality: Disabled Women', in P. Easteal (ed.), *Women and the Law in Australia*, Sydney: LexisNexis, 2010, 249–268, p. 253. See also G. Hague, R. Thiara and A. Mullender, 'Disabled Women and Domestic Violence: Making the Links, a National UK Study', *Psychiatry, Psychology and Law* 18(1), 2011, 117–136.

26 P. Tjaden, and N. Thoennes, *Full Report of the Prevalence, Incidence, and Consequences of Violence Against Women: Findings from the National Violence Against Women Survey*, Washington, DC: US Department of Justice, 2000.

27 M. Hester and C. Donovan, 'Researching Domestic Violence in Same Sex Relationships – A Feminist Epistemological Approach to Survey Development', *Journal of Lesbian Studies* 13(2), 2009, 161–173.

28 Ibid.; C. Donovan and M. Hester, 'I Hate the Word "Victim": An Exploration of Recognition of Domestic Violence in Same Sex Relationships', *Social Policy and Society* 9(2), 2010, 279–289.

29 C. Chan, 'Domestic Violence in Gay and Lesbian Relationships: An Overview', Sydney: Australian Domestic and Family Violence Clearinghouse, 2005, p. 3.

> remembered though that not every person from a given culture or background adheres to the predominant cultural norms to the same degree.[30]

All women who are multiply marginalised from the dominants face added obstacles in accessing help. They may be especially isolated for a range of reasons, explored below.

For some indigenous and immigrant women, domestic violence may be considered as a family matter; disclosure to outsiders could be perceived as bringing shame on the family.[31] Thus, extended family members may encourage the woman to remain in an abusive relationship because of their cultural or religious beliefs.[32] Other obstacles include: linguistic barriers; economic dependence; and lack of understanding of support services.[33] Further, for some sponsored migrant women, the threat of deportation by the violent partner-sponsor may be used to stop the woman leaving the violent home.[34]

Disabled women may have specific issues, which have not been encompassed within generic violence prevention policies and are not part of the broader responses to the issue of women and violence.[35] Consequently, 'Women with disabilities who want to reach out for services are met with a lack of accessible resources'.[36]

Access to many of the services available for battered women in Australia is particularly problematic for this group for the same reasons as immigrants and indigenous women: many do not identify what has happened to them as a crime, or they do not know about the services and options available to them and/or lack the physical means or the requisite self-confidence to access these services.[37]

The same is true for women in same sex relationships who may not view their relationship as abusive, associating the concept of domestic violence with

30 M. Winters and I. Morgan, 'Cross-Cultural Perspectives on Intimate Partner Violence', in L. McOrmond-Plummer, P. Easteal and J. Levy-Peck (eds), *Intimate Partner Sexual Violence: A Multidisciplinary Guide to Improving Services and Support for Survivors of Rape and Abuse*, London: Jessica Kingsley Publishers, 2014, 234–245, p. 241.

31 Ibid.

32 Family Law Council, *Improving the Family Law System for Clients from Culturally and Linguistically Diverse Backgrounds*, 2012, p. 35.

33 Easteal, 'Double Jeopardy', above n. 20, pp. 26–27; S. Rees, 'Human Rights and the Significance of Psychosocial and Cultural Issues in Domestic Violence Policy and Intervention for Refugee Women', *Australian Journal of Human Rights* 10(1), 2004, 97–119.

34 S. Anitha, 'Legislating Gender Inequalities: The Nature and Patterns of Domestic Violence Experienced by South Asian Women with Insecure Immigration Status in the United Kingdom', *Violence Against Women* 17(10), 2011, 1260–1285.

35 Women with Disabilities Australia, Submission to the South Australian Government's Discussion Paper, *Valuing South Australia's Women: Towards A Women's Safety Strategy For South Australia*, 2004. See also: Hague, Thiara and Mullender, above n. 25; R. Thiara, G. Hauge and A. Mullender, 'Losing Out on Both Counts: Disabled Women and Domestic Violence', *Disability & Society* 26(6), 2011, 757–771.

36 Plummer and Findley, 'Women with Disabilities', above n. 24, p. 24.

37 Dowse, Frohmader and Meekosha, 'Intersectionality: Disabled Women', above n. 25, p. 254.

heterosexuals.[38] This may arise particularly in identifying sexual assault coercion by their partner.[39] Even if they are able to identify an act as violence, disclosure may be particularly problematic for women in lesbian relationships:

> While many advances have been made over the last 30 years in terms of human rights and social gains for lesbian, gay, bisexual, and transgender (LGBT) people, homophobia, transphobia, and heterosexism still exist and create contexts where people are stigmatized and marginalized.[40]

Awareness that many in the community are homophobic can make it difficult for women to talk about abuse or sexual violence in their lesbian relationships or to seek any kind of support services. They might be anticipating negativity and/or discrimination.[41]

Legal obstacles

> Policies and procedures, created by law or through regulation, often include hidden biases against women of color and other marginalized groups. This can take the form of required documents of identification, eligibility requirements, and possible legal remedies available. The judicial system delivers a set of responses and consequences based on a certain set of goals and values.[42]

As well as 'covert, institutionalised discrimination' that is 'endemic and permeate[s] our institutions and our subconscious',[43] members of intersected groups may not be aware of the help available to them or how to access such help. They may mistrust and fear police or the legal system. In addition, many may have very limited access to public funds.

38 Hester and Donovan, 'Researching Domestic Violence in Same Sex Relationships, above n. 27; J. Ristock, *Relationship Violence in Lesbian/Gay/Bisexual/Transgender/Queer [LGBTQ] Communities: Moving Beyond a Gender-Based Framework*, Minnesota Center Against Violence and Abuse: Violence Against Women Online Resources, 2005. Available online at www.mincava.umn.edu/documents/lgbtqviolence/lgbtqviolence.html.

39 L. Girshick, *Woman-to-Woman Sexual Violence: Does She Call it Rape?*, Boston: Northeastern University Press, 2002; Y. Wang, 'Voices from the Margin: A Case Study of a Rural Lesbian's Experience with Woman-to-Woman Sexual Violence', *Journal of Lesbian Studies* 15(2), 2011, 166–175.

40 J. Ristock, 'Sexual Assault in Intimate Same Sex Relationships', in L. McOrmond-Plummer, P. Easteal and J. Levy-Peck (eds), *Intimate Partner Sexual Violence: A Multidisciplinary Guide to Improving Services and Support for Survivors of Rape and Abuse*, London: Jessica Kingsley Publishers, 2014, 259–269, p. 259.

41 Ibid.

42 Winters and Morgan, 'Cross-Cultural Perspectives on Intimate Partner Violence', above n. 30, p.235.

43 P. Easteal, 'Setting the Stage: The "Iceberg" Jigsaw Puzzle', in P. Easteal (ed.), *Women and the Law in Australia*, Sydney: LexisNexis, 2010, 1–20, p. 13.

Indigenous women

Indigenous victims are less likely to seek a family violence order and may not contact the police in part due to concern about their partners' well-being in the custody of police and prisons; fear of having their children removed; fear of causing divisiveness within the community; fear or empathy for the offender; and a view that criminal justice staff lack cultural sensitivity.[44] Additionally, western legal remedies, with their formality of process and structure, may conflict with the traditional indigenous legal system, which is more informal – emphasising reconciliation and the use of third party go-betweens.[45]

For some Aboriginal women, there is also a lack of awareness about mainstream services, gender segregation of experience and disclosure[46] and isolation. There is also a history of institutional racism and a lack of appropriate culturally sensitive services.[47]

Another issue may be the time constraints inherent in the legal system: lawyers need to have sufficient time to develop trust and rapport with clients.[48] In addition, there exists an Anglo cultural insensitivity to the fact that for Aboriginal women, sexual matters are private and their style of communication is more indirect. These factors can result in less than adequate legal representation. Thus, Robyn Kina, whose case is discussed in Chapters 2 and 7, was found guilty of murder in part due to her defence team's unawareness of the fact that she had been subjected to anal rape, which abuse led her to kill her de facto partner.[49]

For these reasons, indigenous rape victims may suffer tremendous mental and emotional distress when testifying at trial.[50] In addition, a dominant legal system that is adversarial in nature, with few periods of silence and often requiring answers merely of 'yes' or 'no' conflicts with the traditional indigenous communication style punctuated by long periods of silence, no direct eye-contact and answers that may not necessarily relate to the questions asked.[51] Therefore,

44 C. Cuneen, *Alternative and Improved Responses to Domestic and Family Violence in Queensland Indigenous Communities*, Queensland Government: Department of Communities, 2011.

45 Australian Law Reform Commission, *Recognition of Aboriginal Customary Laws*, Report No. 31, 1986.

46 There is traditionally a gendered separation of knowledge and experience within Indigenous cultures: 'women's business' and 'men's business'.

47 M. Willis, 'Non-Disclosure of Violence in Indigenous Communities', *Trends and Issues in Crime and Criminal Justice* 405, Canberra: Australian Institute of Criminology, 2011; P. Easteal, *Less Than Equal: Women and the Australian Legal System*, Sydney: Butterworths, 2001.

48 C. Norrington, 'Intersectionality: Indigenous Women', in P. Easteal (ed.), *Women and the Law in Australia*, Sydney: LexisNexis, 2010, 228–248, p. 241.

49 *R v Kina* (Unreported, Supreme Court of Queensland, Court of Appeal, 29 November 1993, Fitzgerald P, Davies and McPherson JJA).

50 Department for Women [NSW], *Heroines of Fortitude: The Experiences of Women In Court As Victims of Sexual Assault*, 1997, p. 101.

51 D. Eades, 'Understanding Aboriginal Silence in Legal Context', in H. Kotthoff and H. Spencer-Oatey (eds), *Handbook of Intercultural Communication*, Berlin: Mouton de Gruyter, 2007, 285–302.

Aboriginal women can be particularly vulnerable to the aggressive and intimidating style of speech used at trials and the overly complex nature of questions typical of cross-examination:[52]

> They face an elaborate structure of sexual and racial ideology that discredits and devalues their testimony. The evidence rules regulating the conduct of the adversary trial, while perhaps not directly constituting this ideology, create a space in which racist and sexist stereotypes can be deployed and reinforced.[53]

Aboriginal women may react to cross-examination by not answering, answering incorrectly or responding affirmatively when that might not have been their intention.[54] They may also answer 'yes' out of politeness. This 'gratuitous concurrence' has been recognised by the courts as a reason for restricting leading questions in the cross-examination of witnesses from a cultural background that uses such styles of speech.[55]

Immigrant women

Even if they do reach out to the law for help, immigrant women may be confronted with racism or ethnocentrism. Rosemary Hunter's research in Victorian magistrates' courts, for instance, confirmed that magistrates responded differently to non-English speaking women who were applying for family violence orders: magistrates were more likely to be either good-natured or condescending and patronising, with the women thus receiving 'special treatment at either end of the spectrum'.[56] Some immigrant or refugee women may have difficulty producing paperwork, paying for a lawyer or obtaining childcare. Language barriers, low levels of literacy and limited social networks may also cause further complications.[57]

Abused immigrant women and legal leave to remain

Further difficulties may arise for women whose immigration status is dependent upon their spouse/partner. In many countries, an individual who moves to a new country to be with her spouse/partner must wait a certain amount of time before

52 L. Ellison, 'The Mosaic Art?: Cross-Examination and the Vulnerable Witness', *Legal Studies* 21(3), 2001, 353–375.

53 K. Mack, 'An Australian Perspective of Feminism, Race and Evidence', *Southwestern University Law Review* 28(2), 1999, 367–388, p. 381.

54 Department for Women [NSW], *Heroines of Fortitude*, above n. 50, p. 105.

55 *Stack v Western Australia* (2004) 29 WAR 526, cited in Norrington, 'Intersectionality', above n. 48, p. 243.

56 R. Hunter, 'Professorial Lecture – Border Protection in Law's Empire: Feminist Explorations of Access to Justice', *Griffith Law Review* 11(2), 2002, 263–285.

57 Sabri, Barcelona de Mendoza and Campbell, 'Prevalence of Intimate Partner Sexual Violence', above n. 18.

she is allowed to apply for indefinite leave to remain. Thereafter, usually the application must be made by the couple jointly. For example, in England and Wales, a non-European Economic Area ('EEA')[58] immigrant woman who joins her spouse has temporary leave to remain, and cannot apply for indefinite leave until after a five-year probationary period.[59] Such restrictions, while instigated with the aim of reducing immigration and 'sham marriages',[60] may trap immigrant women in abusive relationships in that they face a stark choice between remaining in the relationship or leaving it and being subject to deportation. For many immigrant women the latter is not a real or safe option. Thus, the law effectively places the fate of an abused immigrant woman in the hands of her abusive husband/partner. This, it has been argued, demonstrates the ongoing influence of the doctrine of coverture, whereby a woman loses her legal identity upon marriage.[61] For example, historically, in the United States, the right to petition for permanent residency for a spouse was limited to the husband.[62] In contrast, American women who married a non-US citizen 'automatically lost their US citizenship since their identities had been merged with their [non-citizen] husbands'.[63] However, while immigration provisions are now generally gender neutral, they nevertheless remain premised on 'the concept of one dominant spouse controlling the immigration status of a subservient spouse',[64] and are thus reminiscent of the doctrine of coverture, particularly given the gendered nature of immigration.[65] This has led to concerns that the immigration laws may have the effect of 'fostering domestic violence against female immigrants'.[66]

Due to such concerns, many nations have developed exceptions to probationary time periods and many also permit an immigrant spouse to self-petition for

58 Different rules apply for EEA (EU Member States plus Iceland, Norway and Liechtenstein) nationals. The right of an EEA national to remain falls under European, as opposed to immigration, law. For further detail, particularly with regards to non-EEA family members of EEA nationals, see Rights of Women, *Silenced Voices Speak: Strategies for Protecting Migrant Women from Violence and Abuse*, 2011.

59 This has recently been increased from a two-year probationary period. See M. Gower, *Changes to Immigration Rules for Family Members*, House of Commons, Commons Library Standard Note 6353, 2013. *Immigration Rules* (HC 395 of 1993–94 as amended) are available on the UKBA website at www.ukba.homeoffice.gov.uk/policyandlaw/immigrationlaw/immigrationrules/.

60 Gower, *Changes to Immigration Rules*, above n. 59, p. 6.

61 See J. Calvo, 'A Decade of Spouse-Based Immigration Laws: Coverture's Diminishment, But Not Its Demise', *Northern Illinois University Law Review* 24(2), 2004, 153–210.

62 For an overview of the early US immigration law, see J. Calvo, 'Spouse-Based Immigration Laws: The Legacies of Coverture', *San Diego Law Review* 28(3), 1991, 593–644, pp. 601–603.

63 I.K. Balram, 'The Evolving, Yet Still Inadequate, Legal Protections Afforded Battered Immigrant Women', *University of Maryland Law Journal, Race, Religion, Gender and Class* 5(2), 2005, 387–410, p. 393.

64 Ibid., p. 394.

65 As Calvo notes, '[w]omen make up the majority of immigrating spouses': 'A Decade of Spouse-Based Immigration Laws', above n. 61, p. 156.

66 Balram, 'The Evolving, Yet Still Inadequate, Legal Protections', above n. 63, p. 397.

citizenship (as opposed to relying on her abusive partner), in cases involving domestic violence.[67] While these steps are positive, the implementation and eligibility requirements of such exceptions remain fraught with difficulties and exclusions. A good example of the difference between intent and practice of such legislative provisions can be seen in the Australian migration law regulations. Originally enacted in 1989 to ameliorate the plight of women who migrated to Australia as (potential) spouses of Australian citizens who then abused them and acted to have them denied permanent residency if they left the violent home,[68] the family violence exception has been amended several times, as described below, to make the provisions more user-friendly and accessible to overseas women victims of family violence.[69]

Until 1995, eligibility to invoke the exception was limited to applicants who could show a restraining order, a Family Law Act injunction, or a court conviction or finding of guilt against the sponsor for assault. To broaden the means of establishing that violence had taken place, in 1995 the family violence provision was changed to add 'acceptable evidence that violence has been suffered' to the other means of proof. Such evidence had to include a statutory declaration by the person who had experienced the violence and two statutory declarations by 'competent people' (or one declaration by a 'competent' person and a police record of assault).

From 1995 until 2012, competent persons for the purpose of violence against an adult included practitioners, such as doctors and psychologists, as well as women's service staff, such as the coordinator of a woman's refuge. The two competent people had to be from different categories or occupations. Their role was to determine whether violence had occurred, as opposed to the departmental or tribunal decision-maker making that determination.[70] Accordingly, it was found in *Du v Minister of Immigration and Multicultural Affairs* that the competent person must not only express an opinion that the past acts of violence had occurred, but also an opinion about the state of mind of the alleged victim.[71] The need for the latter was a reflection of the stipulation in the Regulations that the alleged victim must

67 For the UK see: Immigration Rules (HC 395 of 1993–94 as amended), para 289A–D. In relation to the US, see Violence Against Women Act of 2000 and Violence Against Women Reauthorization Act of 2013. For Australia, see Migration Regulations 1994 (Cth), div 1.5.

68 Migration (1989) Regulations and Migration. The domestic violence provisions were formally inserted into the Migration Regulations by the Statutory Rules 1995 No. 117 Migration Regulations 1994 (Cth), div 1.5.

69 These rounds of amendments are discussed by M. Crock, 'Women and Migration Law', in P. Easteal (ed.), *Women and the Law in Australia*, Sydney: LexisNexis, 2010, 328–349, pp. 334–337.

70 J. Vrachnas et al., *Migration and Refugee Law: Principles and Practice in Australia*, Cambridge: Cambridge University Press, 2nd edn, 2008.

71 [2000] FCA 1115, [18]–[19]. This was approved in *Alin v Minister of Immigration and Multicultural Affairs* [2002] FCA 979.

'reasonably fear for, or to be reasonably apprehensive about, his or her own wellbeing or safety'.[72]

Problems continued for some migrant women victims of violence in accessing this remedy since they were unable to obtain either judicial or non-judicial evidence due to their fear, shame and/or lack of access to services.[73] There were also 'legislated pedantry' related issues, which pointed to the need for legal assistance/translation:

> As is so common in immigration law, attempts to 'clarify' the law (so as to prevent abuse) have produced unconscionable rigidities in the law – to the point where the family violence provisions have been described as a 'triumph of form over substance' . . . In other words, concessions for victims of family violence will not be made unless the applicant complies with the letter of the law both in terms of the qualifications of the experts attesting to the violence and the words used by the experts to describe what has occurred.[74]

Consequently, applications were rejected 'because the statutory declarations were sworn using State rather than Federal forms; or before the wrong mix of "competent persons"'.[75]

In 2012 the Australian Law Reform Commission recommended that the statutory declaration process be streamlined and advocated that evidence in lieu of these forms should be accepted – with regulation 1.26, which governed the competent person process, being repealed.[76] In late 2012 the Commonwealth government did amend the regulations in the ways suggested, allowing applicants

72 Migration Regulations 1994 (Cth), div 1.5.

73 P. Easteal, *Less Than Equal*, above n. 46, p. 195. See also, K. Hoang, 'ALRC Inquiry Into Family Violence and Commonwealth Laws', *Australian Domestic and Family Violence Clearinghouse Newsletter* 49, 2012, p. 5.

74 M. Crock, 'Women and Migration Law', in P. Easteal (ed.), *Women and the Law in Australia*, Sydney: LexisNexis, 2010, 328–349, pp. 335–336, citing *Ibrahim v Minister for Immigration and Multicultural and Indigenous Affairs* [2002] FCA 1279; *Cakmak v Minister for Immigration and Multicultural and Indigenous Affairs* (2003) 135 FCR 183, [14]–[15]; and *Isse v Minister for Immigration and Multicultural and Indigenous Affairs* [2006] FMCA 253.

75 Crock, 'Women and Migration Law', above n. 74, p. 336. Crock cites *Mohamed v Minister for Immigration and Citizenship* [2007] FCA 1004 and *Morgan v Minister for Immigration and Multicultural Affairs* [1999] FCA 1059 as examples of cases rejected because of the use of incorrect forms. Crock explains that the use of two medical practitioners instead of substituting one for another type of expert led to the rejection of the application in *Mardini v Minister for Immigration and Multicultural and Indigenous Affairs* [2005] FMCA 1409. On appeal, see *Mardini v Minister for Immigration and Multicultural and Indigenous Affairs* [2006] FCA 488, [41].

76 Australian Law Reform Commission, *Family Violence and Commonwealth Laws – Improving Legal Frameworks*, Report No. 117, 2012. The Commission also made recommendations to broaden the eligibility for the exemption and include those on other visas such as prospective marriage visas and secondary holders of a temporary visa. The 2012 amendments did not address this issue.

to use records of previous contact with support services or government agencies.[77] Although the arguably pedantic provision was repealed, the type of evidence now required and what it needs to contain could be similarly problematic given the specificity and complexity of the new requirements, which are not easily accessible by a layperson.[78]

Similarly, in England and Wales, concerns exist regarding the high level of proof needed to show domestic violence, which includes a civil court undertaking or injunction; a caution or conviction; or a medical report or letter from a hospital, general practitioner, the police, social services or women's refuge.[79] In addition, many further eligibility requirements must be fulfilled. For example, in both the United Kingdom and the United States, the woman must still be with her spouse/partner, or, if not, must demonstrate that the relationship breakdown was due to the domestic violence.[80]

Ideal notions of victimhood are also maintained and perpetuated throughout immigration laws, and thus in the United States an abused woman must demonstrate not only that the marriage was entered into in good faith, but that she is of good moral character.[81] As noted by Bhuyan, '[f]or VAWA [Violence Against Women Act] applicants, proving good moral character converges with the performance of being a good enough victim'.[82] Notions of being a 'good enough victim' also permeate the provisions in England and Wales. In order to be eligible to apply for indefinite leave to remain, it was mandatory that an individual has no unspent convictions.[83] Of concern here was the potential for this requirement to trap women in an abusive relationship, as victims may be criminalised by acting in self-defence or being coerced into criminal activity by their abuser, or be the victim of false allegations.[84] In the United States, exceptions were introduced to the 'good moral character' rule in cases where the victim could demonstrate that there was a connection

77 Migration Legislation Amendment Regulation 2012 (No. 5) (Cth).

78 Migration Regulations 1994 (Cth), reg. 1.24(b) states that the evidence required to be shown is: 'the type and number of items of evidence specified by the Minister by instrument in writing for this paragraph'. That instrument is Minister for Immigration and Citizenship (Cth), *Evidentiary Requirements*, IMMI 12/116, 24 November 2012.

79 S. Anitha, 'Neither Safety Nor Justice: The UK Government Response to Domestic Violence Against Immigrant Women', *Journal of Social Welfare and Family Law* 30(3), 2008, 189–202, p. 191.

80 Immigration Rules (HC 395 of 1993–94 as amended), para. 289A(iv) (UK); Violence Against Women Act of 2002, s. 1503(b)(1)(A)(iii)(II)(CC)(ccc) (US).

81 Violence Against Women Act of 2002, s. 1503(b)(1)(A)(iii)(II)(CC)(ccc) (US); Sabri, Barcelona de Mendoza and Campbell, 'Prevalence of Intimate Partner Sexual Violence', above n. 18.

82 R. Bhuyan, 'The Production of the "Battered Immigrant" in Public Policy and Domestic Violence Advocacy', *Journal of Interpersonal Violence* 23(2), 153–170, p. 163.

83 *Statement of Changes in Immigrations Rules* (HC 863 of 2010–12) as amended by *Statement of Changes in Immigration Rules* (HC 908 of 2010–12).

84 House of Commons, *Immigration: Domestic Violence*, 2012, p. 3

between the conviction and the abuse.[85] While this is still onerous and problematic, it was nevertheless an improvement on the situation in England and Wales. This requirement has, however, since been abolished in cases involving domestic violence.[86]

In addition to these concerns, many vulnerable women fall outside the domestic violence exceptions. Although other avenues to apply for indefinite leave to remain may exist, such as asylum, the existing provisions currently fail to provide sufficient protection for immigrant victims of abuse.

No recourse to public funds

A further difficulty facing immigrant victims of domestic abuse is the lack of access to public funds while they only have temporary leave to remain. In England and Wales, campaign groups have argued that the 'no recourse to public funds' rule has made it very difficult for an abused woman to leave her partner while she applies for indefinite leave to remain. Without access to housing or welfare benefits, it is unlikely that a woman would be able to access a refuge,[87] and thus a victim potentially faces the consequence of either remaining with the abuser or becoming homeless. Although local authorities are able to provide some level of assistance under various legislative provisions, these are subject to varying interpretations.

Following a sustained campaign by women's groups and a subsequent pilot project, the 'Destitution Domestic Violence Concession' was established in 2012.[88] Under this concession, victims who intend to apply for indefinite leave to remain on the grounds that their relationship has broken down due to domestic violence, and who do not have the means to access accommodation or support themselves and need financial help, can apply to UK Visas and Immigration (UKVI) for a variation in their immigration status.[89] This enables them to apply to the Department of Work and Pensions for three months of financial assistance while they make an application under the domestic violence immigration rules.

This is a positive step, but considerable difficulties remain. Monitoring of the pilot project demonstrated that 65 per cent of women were ineligible for help and thus 'were either dependent on limited support elsewhere or destitute'.[90] Furthermore, as the Campaign to Abolish No Recourse to Public Funds has noted:

85 Violence Against Women Act of 2002, s. 1505(b)(1).

86 House of Commons, *Immigration Provisions for Victims of Domestic Violence*, 2013, p. 3.

87 Ibid. See also S. Anitha, 'No Recourse, No Support: State Policy and Practice towards South Asian Women Facing Domestic Violence in the UK', *British Journal of Social Work* 40(2), 2010, 462–479.

88 House of Commons, *Immigration Provisions for Victims of Domestic Violence,* above n. 86, p. 4.

89 Ibid.

90 Southall Black Sisters, 'Campaign to Abolish No Recourse to Public Funds: Home Office Concession for Destitute Victims of Domestic Violence and a Call to Save the Lives of all Women and Children (Press Release, 30 March 2012). Available online at www.southallblacksisters.org.uk/campaign-celebrates-victory-for-victims-of-domestic-violence/.

there are many other vulnerable victims who remain without a safety net. These include women in the UK on other visas, overstayers, and overseas domestic workers, who experience gender based violence or abuse and exploitation by their employers. Women who have been trafficked into the country are also not adequately protected.[91]

Issues with legal remedies and forced marriages

In theory, a forced marriage that takes place overseas will not be recognised under Australian law since it breaches at least one subsection (and possibly two) of the Marriage Act 1961 (Cth), s. 88 ('Marriage Act'), i.e. that one of the parties at the time of the marriage was domiciled in Australia and either party was not of marriageable age[92] and if the consent of either party was not real consent.[93] For those married in Australia, the marriage is void for the same reasons as if contracted outside of Australia, i.e. if there was a lack of real consent or either party is not of marriageable age.[94] In practice, however, to have the marriage not recognised as valid or nullified would probably require the individual(s) who did not consent to prove as such, to disclose and to apply to the Family Court of Australia. As discussed at p. 236, however, the cultural hurdles, pressure from the extended family and lack of information faced by such individuals would be formidable.

The Family Court in Australia has the power to grant an injunction stopping a child under the age of 18 from being taken out of Australia for the purposes of marriage.[95] The court can place the child on the airport watch list and require the parents to hand the child's passport into the Court Registry.[96]

Further, under the Marriage Act, s. 95, marrying a person who is not of marriageable age is a criminal offence, unless there is a court order.[97] The section does not provide criminal law protection for victims of forced marriages that are solemnised outside Australia. However, in 2013, *all* forced marriages were criminalised by amendment to the Criminal Code 1995 (Cth).[98] This addition to the Code was prompted by some Australian citizens using marriages to recruit women into Australia to exploit them as 'domestic servants and wives'.[99]

91 Ibid. See also House of Commons, *Immigration Provisions for Victims of Domestic Violence*, above n. 86 p. 7.

92 Marriage Act 1961 (Cth), ss 88D(2)(b), 88E(2)

93 Marriage Act 1961 (Cth), s 88D(2)(d).

94 Marriage Act 1961 (Cth), s. 23B(1)(d)–(e). For a discussion of forced marriages and relevant legislation, see Attorney-General's Department, Criminal Justice Division, *Forced and Servile Marriage*, above n. 23.

95 Family Law Act 1975 (Cth), s. 68B.

96 *Madley v Madley* [2011] FMCAfam 1007.

97 Marriage Act 1961 (Cth), s. 95.

98 Introduced in March 2013 by the Crimes Legislation Amendment (Slavery, Slavery-like Conditions and People Trafficking) Bill 2012 (Cth).

99 S. Lyneham, 'Forced and Servile Marriage in the Context of Human Trafficking', *Research in Practice* 32, Canberra: Australian Institute of Criminology, 2013.

Similarly, in England and Wales, a forced marriage is voidable due to the lack of consent,[100] and a vulnerable individual may apply for a forced marriage protection order, a breach of which is now a criminal offence.[101] Furthermore, the Anti-social Behaviour, Crime and Policing Act 2014 introduced an offence of forced marriage.[102] The development of the law in this area has been subject to criticism.[103] With regards to the civil injunction, a major incongruity exists in that the victim is frequently returned to the care of the perpetrators. As Sangher noted:

> I am not aware of any other injunction in this country under which the individual is returned to the perpetrators. In these cases, forced marriage protection orders are issued to our victims, in the main minors, then those victims are returned to multiple perpetrators in that house. Once that front door closes, I am not aware of who is monitoring the implementation of that order because the named people may not be intimidating them but, believe me, there are many other family members that are. Then our victim is put under great pressure and that is a huge concern to us.[104]

The adoption of a criminal offence in England and Wales has also received a mixed reception, with Gill expressing disquiet that a 'legalistic approach . . . does little to address the conditions in which FM [forced marriage] thrive, especially the context of gender inequality which leads to and legitimises FM'.[105] Concerns have also been expressed that increased criminalisation may deter victims from coming forward for help, due to fear of criminalising their families or any repercussions which may flow from a failed prosecution.[106] While there is an important symbolic value in the creation of a dedicated criminal offence, authorities need to ensure that the law is implemented in a manner which affords the most protection and support for those

100 Matrimonial Causes Act 1973, s. 12(c): marriage is voidable if 'either party to the marriage did not validly consent to it, whether in consequence of duress, mistake, unsoundness of mind, or otherwise'.

101 Forced Marriage (Civil Protection) Act 2007, s. 1 and Anti-Social Behaviour, Crime and Policing Act 2014, s. 120.

102 Anti-social Behaviour, Crime and Policing Act 2014, s. 121(1) states: 'A person commits an offence under the law of England and Wales if he or she – (a) uses violence, threats or any other form of coercion for the purpose of causing another person to enter into a marriage, and (b) believes, or ought reasonably to believe, that the conduct may cause the other person to enter into the marriage without free and full consent'.

103 See A. Gill and S. Anitha, 'Forced Marriage Legislation in the UK: A Critique', in A. Gill and S. Anitha (eds), *Forced Marriage: Introducing a Social Justice and Human Rights Perspective*, London: Zed Books, 2011, 137–157.

104 House of Commons and Home Affairs Committee, *Forced Marriage*, Eighth Report of Session 2010–12, 2011, p. 6.

105 A. Gill, 'The Illusion of Protection? An Analysis of Forced Marriage Legislation and Policy in the UK', *Journal of Social Welfare and Family Law* 31(3), 2009, 257–269, p. 262.

106 Home Office, *Forced Marriage Consultation*, 2011, p. 12.

who are vulnerable,[107] and that a wide range of causal factors are acknowledged. As Chantler et al. comment, 'poverty, sexuality, gender inequalities, violence, child marriages, and immigration and asylum featured strongly in survivor accounts as conduits into forced marriage'.[108]

In 2008, and ostensibly in order to prevent forced marriages, the UK government increased the minimum age for applying for a spouse or partner visa from 18 to 21.[109] The rule was successfully challenged in the case of *R (Quila and another) (FC) v Secretary of State for the Home Department*,[110] on the grounds that it amounted to a disproportionate interference with the respondent's right to a family life, under Art. 8 of the European Convention of Human Rights.[111] While this rule reverted back to the age of 18 in 2011,[112] it is disconcerting that there was little, if any, evidence to support the Home Office's argument that the increase would be effective in preventing forced marriages.[113] To the contrary, concerns had been expressed that more harm than good could flow from the change. As discussed by Chantler et al., this includes:

> the possibility of young British women being taken abroad to marry and kept there forcibly until they were old enough to sponsor their spouses; entering the UK with false documentation; and implications for mental health, particularly attempted suicide and self-harm.[114]

Although the Home Office declared that its intention was not to further restrict immigration, but rather to prevent forced marriages, one has to wonder, as does Yeo, 'whether in fact there was another agenda underlying the changes'.[115]

107 Gill and Anitha, 'Forced Marriage Legislation in the UK', above n. 103, p. 151.

108 K. Chantler, G. Gangoli and M. Hester, 'Forced Marriage in the UK: Religious, Cultural, Economic or State Violence?', *Critical Social Policy* 29(4), 2009, 587–612, p. 607.

109 Immigration Rules (HC 395 of 1993–1994 as amended by HC 113 of 2008–2008). See also the critical analysis of how Denmark and Norway have utilised immigration law to prevent forced marriage by A. Bredal, 'Border Control to Prevent Forced Marriages: Choosing Between Protecting Women and Protecting the Nation', in A. Gill and S. Anitha (eds), *Forced Marriage: Introducing a Social Justice and Human Rights Perspective,* London: Zed Books, 2011, 90–111.

110 [2011] UKSC 45.

111 Convention for the Protection of Human Rights and Fundamental Freedoms, opened for signature 4 November 1950, 213 UNTS 221 (entered into force 3 September 1953).

112 Immigration Rules (HC 395 of 1993–1994 as amended by HC 1622 of 2010–2012).

113 C. Yeo, 'Raising the Spouse Visa Age', *Journal of Immigration Asylum and Nationality Law* 23(4), 2009, 365–370. See also Chantler, Gangoli and Hester, 'Forced Marriage in the UK', above n. 108.

114 Chantler, Gangoli and Hester, 'Forced Marriage in the UK', above n. 108, p. 602.

115 Yeo, 'Raising the Spouse Visa Age', above n. 113, p. 370.

Legal issues for women with disabilities and women in same sex relationships

Like indigenous and immigrant victims of family violence, access to legal assistance can be extremely problematic for lesbians and women with disabilities. For instance, in Australia, in relation to the latter:

> Many of the current laws do not contain definitions that specifically encompass the range of settings in which disabled women may live, such as group or nursing homes. Because these experiences may not fit either traditional or contemporary definitions, violence often goes unidentified or unaddressed. It is possible for disabled women who experience violence to take measures such as apprehended or personal violence orders. However, in practice, for women with intellectual impairments who live in group homes, recognition of their specific support needs is limited. Access to effective protection is dependent on mediation and intervention by others such as staff or carers, who may also be the perpetrators of the violence of abuse.[116]

One study of 70 lesbian and bisexual women found that they faced homophobia and discrimination in trying to access criminal justice assistance. They had difficulty pressing charges because of the language of rape laws that assumed male perpetrators, and suffered emotionally (including depression, post-traumatic stress disorder and suicidality) from the negative impact of their assaults.[117]

Isolated because of homophobia and discrimination, there may be concern that, like indigenous women, disclosure will reinforce negative stereotypes.[118] A further issue is the lack of access many abused lesbian women may have to civil law remedies. It was not until the Domestic Violence Crimes and Victims Act 2004 that the government in England and Wales extended the availability of non-molestation and occupation orders to those in same sex relationships. In the United States, there are still some states that explicitly excluded same sex couples from the domestic violence protections,[119] and in many other states their availability is ambiguous at best, due to the adoption of gender-neutral language.[120]

116 Dowse, Frohmader and Meekosha, 'Intersectionality: Disabled Women', above n. 25, p. 254.

117 Girshick, *Woman-to-Woman Sexual Violence*, above n. 39.

118 Chan, 'Domestic Violence in Gay and Lesbian Relationships, above n. 29.

119 Louisiana, Montana and South Carolina. See American Bar Association, Commission on Domestic Violence, *Domestic Civil Protection Orders (CPOs) By State*, 2008.

120 Ibid. See also M.B. Collins, 'Same-Sex Domestic Violence: Addressing the Issues for the Proper Protection of Victims', *The Journal of Law in Society* 4(1), 2003, 99–120; C. DeJong and A. Burgess-Proctor, 'A Summary of Personal Protection Order Statutes in the United States', *Violence Against Women* 12(1), 2006, 69–88; K.M. Hodges, 'Trouble in Paradise: Barriers to Addressing Domestic Violence in Lesbian Relationships', *Law & Sexuality* 9, 2000, 311–331; T.R. Pfeifer, 'Out of the Shadows: The Positive Impact of *Lawrence v Texas* on Victims of Same-Sex Domestic Violence', *Penn State Law Review* 109(4), 1251–1277.

Further, it was only in 2013 that the US Federal Government extended the provisions contained in the Violence Against Women Act,[121] which provides resources for victims of domestic violence, to include those within the LGBT community. Prior to this, it was not illegal for shelters and other support services to discriminate against those in same sex relationships, and nor was funding for specialised services provided. The 2013 amendments also made other significant extensions in order to improve the plight of immigrant and Native American women.[122] Republicans in the House of Representatives initially rejected the bill and passed their own reauthorisation bill, which omitted many of the reforms.[123] Eventually the more inclusive bill was signed.[124] Nevertheless, it is exceptionally disconcerting that in 2013 a political party can argue against provisions which aim to protect some of the most vulnerable members of society.

Conclusion

In previous chapters we have seen how being female and therefore how being 'other' in a masculine-defined society and legal system may result in some commonalities in oppression, marginalisation and exclusion. In this chapter we have seen that in addition to sexism, there are other forces such as heterosexism, homophobia, racism, ableism and ethnocentrism that can further deter those who are multiply 'other' from self-identification, disclosure and accessing assistance and legal remedies.

Indeed, the police station, solicitor's office and courtroom could be conceptualised as microcosms of mainstream society with gendered, heterosexist, racist and ableist norms, expectations and stereotypes. As argued by Kline 25 years ago, unless all women 'can speak and be heard in law, hegemonic forces will continue to operate largely unchecked to enforce women's silence ... [It is] not enough that a plurality of voices be heard in law. Diverse voices must intersect and interact'.[125]

Accordingly, lawyers and other criminal and civil justice practitioners need to be attuned to the potentially different voices and experiences of women in these groups. Sensitivity to differences and awareness is a critical step, which can then be translated into practice and legislative reform to more effectively meet domestic violence survivors' needs.

121 Violence Against Women Reauthorization Act of 2013. See National Network to End Domestic Violence, *The Violence Against Women Reauthorization Act of 2013: Summary of Changes*, 2013.

122 Ibid. See also J.A. Finken, 'An Overview of the Violence Against Women Reauthorization Act as Applied to Indian Country', *Nebraska Lawyer* 16(4), 2013, 5–9.

123 HR4970 Violence Against Women Reauthorization Act of 2012. See further R.R. Runge, 'The Evolution of a National Response to Violence Against Women', *Hastings Women's Law Journal* 24(2), 2013, 429–456.

124 See further Runge, 'The Evolution of a National Response', above n. 123.

125 M. Kline, 'Race, Racism and Feminist Legal Theory', *Harvard Women's Law Journal* 12, 1989, 115–150, p. 149.

Indeterminacy of legislation and strict application of the law are important issues when looking at obstacles for these women in accessing justice. Interestingly, though, in many ways, it is a relative *lack of greyness or a perceived lack* that may be contributing to some of the problems for these multiply 'other' victims. For instance, from 1995 until 2012 the requirements of the family violence exception provision of the Migration Regulations 1958 (Cth) were very 'black and white' and decision-makers did not allow for any leeway in interpretation. Family violence orders are another example where more flexibility in both the application process and the content would be helpful. For some indigenous, immigrant, disabled and lesbian women there are particular variables that may dissuade them from applying for an order. Similar factors lessen the chances that they will contact the police, who in some jurisdictions could or would apply for the order. And, even when there is a potential for the inclusion of non-standard provisions, those orders made to protect indigenous victims are less likely to do so, with one report strongly recommending that they be in plain English and provide some examples.[126] Aboriginal victims are more apt to want to retain some contact with their abuser, and there is also a failure to understand specific conditions of life in remote indigenous communities.[127]

The move towards recognising the complexity of women's lives and their experiences of violence is therefore vital. This relates not only to feminist intersectional analysis of identity, but also entails an understanding of how different aspects of state policy and law intersect and impact upon women. While vulnerability to violence is an inescapable factor of being a social body,[128] it is important to recognise that vulnerability and precarity are unevenly distributed, with some populations more vulnerable than others.[129] Moreover, and as we have demonstrated in this chapter, various factors, including state policy, operate to maintain and perpetuate the increased vulnerability of certain 'others', and at the same time restrict their access to legal protections. In the development of law and policy, it is therefore vital that the diversity of experience is acknowledged, while at the same time tackling state tendencies to utilise female vulnerability in order to bolster cultural imperialistic notions of the civilised west. Without doubt, this is not an easy task. The exclusionary tendencies of law and policy, and how they operate in practice, need to be subject to continual scrutiny. As will be discussed in the next and final chapter, feminist law reform is a constantly evolving and contingent project.

126 Cuneen, *Alternative and Improved Responses*, above n. 44, p. 127.
127 Ibid., p. 87.
128 J. Butler, *Frames of War: When is Life Grievable?*, New York: Verso, 2009, p. 33.
129 Ibid., pp. 2–3.

Chapter 12

Conclusion

Throughout the preceding pages, we have documented the plethora of law reform enacted over the past few decades to better address violence against women. The magnitude of legislative change has been, at least in part, the consequence of global and national programmes and organisations with mandates that have included improving the legal response to victims. For example, on an international level, both the Convention on the Elimination of All Forms of Discrimination Against Women[1] ('CEDAW') and the Declaration on the Elimination of Violence Against Women[2] ('DEVAW') set down actions that states should adopt in order to protect women and bring about an end to gender-based violence.[3] At the European level, the Council of Europe's Convention on Preventing and Combating Violence Against Women 2011 places duties on signatory states, of which the United Kingdom is one, to adopt a range of legislative and policy measures.

In Australia a number of Commonwealth task forces have, over the past quarter of a century, spearheaded national and local anti-violence campaigns. The National Council to Reduce Violence against Women and their Children is the most recent iteration. It produced a national plan of action for 2010–2022.[4] In addition to the Council, there are currently two Australian research centres dedicated to gathering evidence-based research to assist policymakers, survivors and the community: the Australian Domestic and Family Violence Clearinghouse[5] (Sydney-based) and

1 Opened for signature 1 March 1980, 1249 UNTIS 13 (entered into force 3 September 1981).

2 GA Res 48/104, UN GAOR, 48th Session, 85th Plenary Meeting, Supp No. 49, UN Doc A/RES/48/104 (23 February 1994).

3 Difficulties, however, exist regarding the enforceability of these international documents. DEVAW is not legally binding, and while enforcement measures are applicable to CEDAW, they are limited in scope, and adoption of the Protocol is optional. See, e.g. J. Murdoch, 'Unfulfilled Expectations: The Optional Protocol to the Convention on the Elimination of All Forms of Discrimination Against Women', *European Human Rights Law Review* 1, 2010, 26–46.

4 See Australian Government, Department of Social Services, *The National Plan to Reduce Violence against Women and their Children*, 2010. Available online at www.fahcsia.gov.au/our-responsibilities/women/programs-services/reducing-violence/the-national-plan-to-reduce-violence-against-women-and-their-children.

5 Australian Domestic and Family Violence Clearinghouse ('ADFVC'). Available online at www.austdvclearinghouse.unsw.edu.au/home.html. Note, however, that in January 2014, due

the Australian Centre for the Study of Sexual Assault (in Melbourne).[6] Community education, prevention programmes, services for victims and lobbying for law reform are not just the province of the federal government. In Australia, each state and territory has a peak body or council, as well as crisis services with their own domestic violence phone lines, refuges[7] and sexual assault services.[8] Similarly, in the United Kingdom, successive governments have produced action plans setting out their commitment to eliminate violence, to protect and support victims, and detailing the steps that need to be taken at both national and local level.[9]

Law reform interpretation: unwritten social sub-texts and grey laws

All of these positive initiatives and the substantive legal provisions function within a larger social context, as described in Chapters 1 and 2. As noted in the latter, at the societal level, there appears to be an unconscious gendered filtering of 'reality', which can militate against successful translation of legal remedies:

> Feminism has a theory of power: sexuality is gendered as gender is sexualized. Male and female are created through the erotization of dominance and submission. The man/woman difference and the dominance/submission dynamic define each other. . . . Each sex has its role, but their stakes and power are not equal. If the sexes are unequal, and perspective participates in situation, there is no ungendered reality or ungendered perspective.[10]

The existence of unwritten social sub-texts has been evident in our findings concerning women as defendants in intimate homicide matters, as victim witnesses of family violence, rape and stalking, and as parties in family law matters. Legal gatekeepers' educational and occupational sub-cultures often act to reinforce these gender-biased beliefs and (mis)understandings about violence.[11] As a consequence,

to funding changes, the ADFVC lost staff and some research dissemination services. A new organisation, Australia's National Research Organisation for Women's Safety (ANROWS), was set up in 2014.

6 See the Australian Centre for the Study of Sexual Assault database to learn more about the sexual assault training, research and other programming currently available in Australia. Available online at www.aifs.gov.au/acssa/clearinghouse.

7 In the ACT, for example, see Domestic Violence Crisis Service ACT, *Other Useful Contacts*. Available online at www.dvcs.org.au/contacts.php.

8 See Sexual Assault Support Service, *Sexual Assault Services Throughout Australia*. Available online at: www.sass.org.au/directory/.

9 See, e.g., HM Government, *A Call to End Violence against Women and Girls*, 2013.

10 C. MacKinnon, *Toward a Feminist Theory of State*, Boston: Harvard University Press, 1989, pp. 113–114.

11 There is heterogeneity by individual gatekeepers in response to these sorts of myths and in measurement of credibility and gender-sensitive understanding. See, e.g., P. Easteal and K. Judd,

in civil and criminal remedies, police, prosecutors, magistrates and judges may invoke stereotypes in applying the law. Accordingly, research with mock jurors in England and Wales demonstrates that the reforms to the wording of the offence of rape have not affected the influence of stereotypical thinking.[12]

In previous chapters we have seen numerous instances of misunderstanding about the victim's 'reality': legal system personnel tend to focus on one incident and ignore the context and dynamics of domestic violence – equating violence in the private sphere with assaults in the public. This perception can affect the implementation and/or interpretation of laws. For example, in stalking legislation, there is a need to prove that the stalker *intended to cause harm*. Thus, to charge and to prosecute for that offence requires an interpretation of the stalker's actions that reflects the complexities and control elements of domestic violence.

Similarly, in arguing and proving self-defence, the belief that one's life is in danger and using *force as reasonable in the circumstances* tend to be interpreted through the gender-biased lens of the common law. The courts often appear to see the battered woman's belief in serious harm as unreasonable or mistaken when she has killed her batterer. Likewise, the subjective requirement of a loss of self-control in provocation embodies the masculine reaction to violence. In the same way, notions of *reasonableness* in sexual assault have long been assessed from a male perspective and permit stereotypes with regards to how rape victims should respond – that the sexual assault complaint has to be made as soon as could be *reasonably* expected.

The English and Welsh and Australian laws we have examined in this book are riddled with indeterminate concepts like 'reasonableness', culminating in an indeterminate meaning of the sum of the parts. In the context of rape laws, consent and negation of consent are obvious examples. What is considered an 'improper' question is open to subjective assessment, as is the question of who is the 'vulnerable' or the 'special' rape victim witness. 'Unacceptable risk', 'apprehension' or 'fear', 'adverse impact', 'best interest', 'arduousness', 'reasonable grounds' and 'inequitable to disregard' are all terms in family law open to interpretation. That interpretation is of course very much affected by the capacity of mediators, lawyers and judicial officers to 'walk in the shoes' of the victim; whether they believe violence has taken place; and their perception of its seriousness.

Relevant to the issue of seriousness, unfortunately, violence against women continues consistently to be minimised by many in the criminal justice system. For instance, some judges and jurors are still unable to understand why the battered woman did not simply leave her partner and how she became a veritable hostage in the home. We have also noted the persistent resistance to constructing coercive sex

'"She Said, He Said": Credibility and Sexual Harassment Cases in Australia', *Women's Studies International Forum* 31(5), 2008, 336–344.

12 See, e.g.: E. Finch and V. Munro, 'The Demon Drink and the Demonized Woman: Socio-Sexual Stereotypes and Responsibility Attribution in Rape Trials Involving Intoxicants', *Social and Legal Studies* 16(4), 2007, 591–614; E. Finch and V. Munro, 'Breaking Boundaries? Sexual Consent in the Jury Room', *Legal Studies* 26(3), 2006, 303–320.

as injurious unless perpetrated by a stranger with physical force. Mythology persists, which constructs marital rape as even less damaging or not as part of the dynamic of violence in the home. Other illustrations of minimising have also been evident, including judicial officers in family law matters seeing domestic violence as 'situation specific', or as not affecting the children.

Minimising may correlate with beliefs that reduce offenders' culpability and deflect, at least in part, the responsibility for the violence to the victims. Myths about false reporting/allegations, provocation and credibility of victims are evident both in family violence and sexual assault. For example, in England and Wales, sentence for a breach of an order can be reduced if there is perceived provocation by the victim. Further, corroboration warnings are still given in sexual assault trials in jurisdictions around the world. A 'Madonna/whore' dichotomy continues both in the perception of women who kill a violent partner and in construction of the *good* rape victim. The latter affects attrition and the outcome of arrests, prosecutions and sentencing.

The (im)possibility of feminist law reform?

Despite the high volume of reform, violence against women remains a major cause for concern. Reporting and convictions rates are low, and attrition is high. Throughout their involvement with the criminal justice system, many victims/survivors face a significant battle and are far too frequently disempowered and/or re-traumatised. Accordingly, the ability of the law to deal effectively with violence against women remains somewhat dubious and the effectiveness of feminist-inspired law reforms has been questioned. Carol Smart, in her groundbreaking book *Feminism and the Power of the Law*,[13] argued in 1989 that feminists should decentre law, lamenting the fact that: 'The feminist movement (broadly defined) is too easily "seduced" by law and even where it is critical of law it too often attempts to use law pragmatically in the hope that new law or more law might be better than the old law'.[14] Smart also argued that feminist legal theory was 'immobilised in the face of the failure of feminism to affect law and the failure of law to transform the quality of women's lives'.[15] Likewise, Martha Fineman has commented: 'I have lost faith. Feminism, it seems, has not – and perhaps cannot – transform the law. Rather, the law, when it becomes the battleground, threatens to transform feminism'.[16]

In addition, there is a real concern that feminist arguments are frequently appropriated by the state and used in ways that are contrary to feminist aims. Martin, for example, notes that 'the dark irony at the core of feminist law reform efforts' is

13 C. Smart, *Feminism and the Power of the Law*, London: Routledge, 1989.

14 Ibid., p. 160.

15 Ibid., p. 5.

16 M. Fineman, 'Feminist Legal Scholarship and Women's Gendered Lives', in M. Cain and C. Harrington (eds), *Lawyers in a Postmodern World*, Buckingham: Open University Press, 1994, 229–246, p. 233.

that the criminal justice 'system does little to serve goals of equality and security. It dispenses punishment and preserves state authority so that existing power relations are legitimated and replicated'.[17] Increasingly, punitive approaches tend to impact disproportionately on already marginalised members of society. This includes criminalising victims of violence through the adoption of strict mandatory arrest policies,[18] along with the growing popularity of 'failure to protect' offences.[19] As Smart notes, 'while some law reforms may indeed benefit some women, it is certain that all law reform empowers law'.[20] This disillusionment has given rise to an 'abstentionist' approach, which argues against turning to the law and for the exploration and adoption of alternative, and what some consider to be potentially more female-centric, forms of justice.[21]

Is the law simply too patriarchal to be used productively to bring about positive change? Are feminist reform efforts futile, or, even worse, damaging? Given the focus of this book, it is clear that we see a benefit in engaging with the law and reform endeavours in order to tackle violence against women. It is contended that there is both a symbolic and material importance in highlighting the law's failure to recognise and respond appropriately to the plight of women, and demanding that it does otherwise. Moreover, significant improvements to both the substantive and procedural law have been made. It is perhaps, therefore, more appropriate to conceptualise feminist engagement with the law as consisting of simultaneous successes and failures, as suggested by Nourse.[22] While improvements have been made, Nourse contends that 'feminist law reforms have a kind of built-in, albeit unpredictable, capacity for failure',[23] which flows from the power of social norms 'to overwhelm the best-intentioned of reforms'[24] and the structural nature of law reform – as '[l]egislatures cannot survive without the compromises and ambiguities that nurture reform's future failures'.[25] Nourse notes that '[o]ld norms do not die; they are resurrected in empty spaces, deliberate ambiguities, and new rhetorics'.[26] The norms of the past haunt the reforms of the present and future. This inevitability

17 D.L. Martin, 'Retribution Revisited: A Reconsideration of Feminist Criminal Law Reform Strategies', *Osgoode Hall Law Journal* 36(1), 1998, 151–188, p. 155.

18 See, e.g., D. Coker, 'Crime Control and Feminist Law Reform in Domestic Violence Law: A Critical Review', *Buffalo Criminal Law Review* 4(2), 2001, 801–860.

19 See, e.g., J. Herring, 'Familial Homicide, Failure to Protect and Domestic Violence: Who's the Victim?', *Criminal Law Review*, 2007 (December), 923–933.

20 Smart, *Feminism and the Power of the Law*, above n. 13, p. 161.

21 For a (critical) overview of such perspectives, see S.M. Armstrong, 'Is Feminist Law Reform Flawed? Abstentionists & Sceptics', *Australian Feminist Law Journal* 20, 2004, 43–63, pp. 45–50; R. Lewis et al., 'Law's Progressive Potential: The Value of Engagement with the Law for Domestic Violence', *Social and Legal Studies* 10(1), 2001, 105–130, pp. 112–144.

22 V. Nourse, 'The "Normal" Successes and Failures of Feminism and the Criminal Law', *Chicago-Kent Law Review* 75(3), 2000, 951–978.

23 Ibid., p. 952.

24 Ibid.

25 Ibid., pp. 952–953.

26 Ibid., p. 952.

of failure, however, does not lead Nourse to embody an abstentionist philosophy; rather, it leads her to argue that 'it makes the need for continued law reform equally "normal"',[27] a point to which we will return to in the concluding section of this chapter.

Problematic stereotypes, myths and misconceptions continue to influence the law, and this may well flow from the legal structure itself. However, the structure, the interpretability and the 'greyness' of the law also provides a potential space for more auspicious transformations. As we explored in Chapter 3, drawing upon Cornell, 'that which never was' always remains a possibility, and places an ethical responsibility on legal practitioners to 'remember the future', and to heed the suffering of others.[28] This should not be taken to suggest that a more radical transformation of the legal and social structure is not necessary. It is. However, while we await the possibility of such a moment, there is an ethical responsibility to respond to those within the present, to try to find ways within the existing system to bring about some level of justice, however difficult that may be.

A model more conducive to justice

Our comparative analysis thus indicates that the state's legal response to violence against women needs more work. From a holistic perspective (see Figure 1), we do recognise however that law is only a cog in the societal wheel and, as we have seen, its ability to effect change is therefore limited by society's institutions and values: 'changing the words on statutory pages alone will never be sufficient to overcome the competing, powerful, though unwritten social and legal sub-text which continues to be revealed in struggles over rape law reform'.[29]

To address and improve the legal response to violence against women it is necessary not only to reconceptualise and in some cases redraft the laws, but also to radically redesign the cultural landscape. In fact, to remove or alter the gender bias in interpretation of law, the culture itself must become less gender biased. It is not only the gatekeepers and the legislators who need to better understand and to reconceptualise domestic violence and sexual assault, but the community as a whole.

Trying to effect macro level changes

Accordingly, the move towards a more holistic model of change requires the adoption of a range of social and cultural change measures in addition to law

27 Ibid., p. 953.

28 See D. Cornell, 'Institutionalization of Meaning, Recollective Imagination and the Potential for Transformative Legal Interpretation', *University of Pennsylvania Law Review* 136(4), 1988, 1135–1229.

29 M. Heath, 'Disputed Truths: Australian Reform of the Sexual Conduct Elements of Common Law Rape', in P. Easteal (ed.), *Balancing the Scales: Rape, Law Reform and Australian Culture*, Sydney: Federation Press, 1998, 13–25, p. 25.

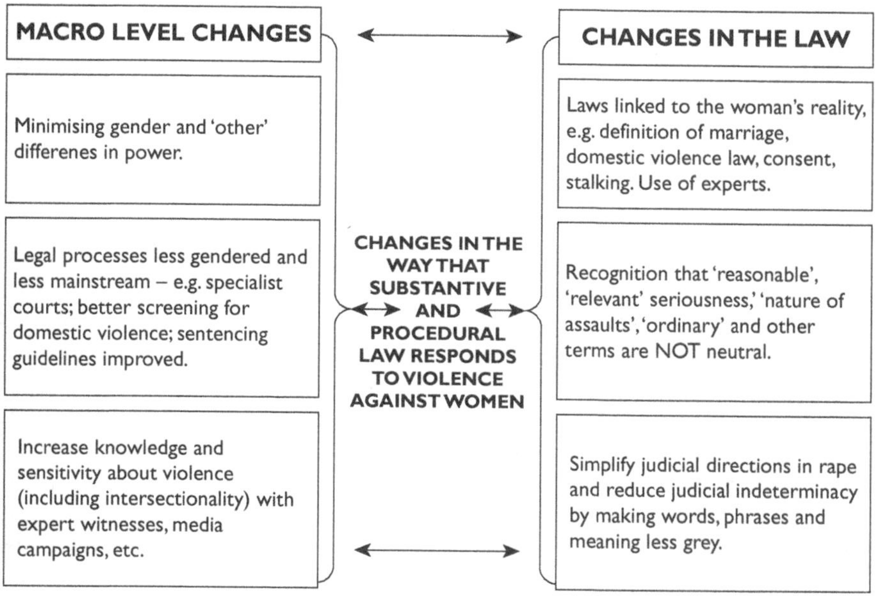

Figure 1 An holistic model for changing the legal responses to violence against women

reform. This is reflected in the international conventions on violence against women. For example, CEDAW stipulates that signatory states should:

> Adopt all appropriate measures, especially in the field of education, to modify the social and cultural practices of conduct of men and women and to eliminate prejudices, customary practices and all other practices based on the idea of the inferiority or superiority of either of the sexes and on stereotyped roles of men and women.[30]

While the issue of bringing about positive social and cultural change is undoutedly complex, and beyond the scope of this book, two particularly pertinent themes relating to the media will be briefly highlighted. First, over the years we have seen an increased use of media campaigns which broadly aim to educate the public as to the realities of abuse, reduce violence against women and support victims. One good example is the Zero Tolerance campaign, which originated in Scotland in the 1990s.[31] The campaign employed 'posters, adshells, billboad, bus and cinema

30 CEDAW, Art. 5(a).

31 For details of the campaign and imagery, see: E. Gillian and E. Samson, 'The Zero Tolerance Campaigns', in J. Hanmer and C. Itzin (eds), *Home Truths About Domestic Violence: Feminist Influences on Policy and Practice*, London: Routledge, 2000, 340–355; Zero Tolerance. Available online at www.zerotolerance.org.uk.

advertising to challenge the norms, beliefs and values which give rise to and sustain male violence'.[32] It aimed to empower women and challenge stereotypes by depicting comfortable, domestic settings of women and children, followed by the phrase: 'Male Abuse of Power is a Crime'.[33] As Gillian and Samson noted, the imagery was 'visually appealing and reflect[ed] people's notions of comfort and security', which was a sharp contrast to the 'message of the text'.[34]

Unfortunately, however, over the years some campaigns have tended towards informing women on how to avoid being a victim of male violence, particularly when they are in public,[35] an approach that arguably gains support from neoliberal politics of individual responsibilisation.[36] Such messages obscure the reality that the vast amount of abuse women suffer takes place within the home; constructs violence (or the avoidance of) as the responsibility of women, as opposed to perpetrators; and, even if unwittingly, perpetuates and promotes victim-blaming attitudes. As Brooks observes, these safety campaigns 'inadvertently compound the normalization of male violence and harassment experienced by women by presenting it as an innate aspect of male behaviour alongside the presentation of safekeeping strategies for women as "commonsense"'.[37] Care needs to be taken to ensure that educational messages do not reify stereotypical conceptions of masculinity and femininity, as such will do little to bring about positive social and cultural change. On a more positive note, recent prevention campaigns at national and local levels in the United Kingdom have focused on educating and raising the awareness of men.[38] However, more work is needed.

Concern has also been expressed by both feminist groups and the government regarding the manner in which the press maintains and perpetuates sexist attitudes and objectifies women and girls.[39] It has been argued that:

32 Gillian and Samson, 'The Zero Tolerance Campaigns', above n. 31, p. 340.

33 Ibid., pp. 351–354.

34 Ibid., p. 346.

35 See, e.g., O. Brooks, '"Guys! Stop Doing It!" Young Women's Adoption and Rejection of Safety Advice when Socializing in Bars, Pubs and Clubs', *British Journal of Criminology* 51(4), 2011, 635–651; A. Campbell, 'Keeping the "Lady" Safe: The Regulation of Femininity through Crime Prevention Literature', *Critical Criminology* 13(2), 2005, 119–140.

36 D. Garland, *The Culture of Control: Crime and Security in Contemporary Society*, Oxford: Oxford University Press, 2001; P. O'Malley, 'Risk and Responsibility', in A.B.T. Osborne and N. Rose (eds), *Foucault and Political Reason: Liberalism, Neo-Liberalism and Rationalities of Government*, Chicago: University of Chicago Press, 1996, 189–208.

37 Brooks, '"Guys! Stop Doing It!"', above n. 35, p. 646.

38 For example, Liverpool City Council ran a media campaign which aimed to educate young men that sexual intercourse with a woman who is too drunk to consent is rape. See A. Carline and G. Gunby, '"She Looks too Drunk to Consent to a Cup of Tea, Never Mind Sex": Evaluating a Sexual Consent Campaign Aimed at Young Men' (paper presented at the Rape and the Criminal Justice System: Issues from Research for Practice Conference, University of Bristol, Centre for Gender and Violence Research, 28 June 2013). Available online at www.bris.ac.uk/sps/news/2013/295.html.

39 See: End Violence Against Women Coalition, *FINAL Submission to the Leveson Inquiry*, January 2012; Eaves, End Violence Against Women Coalition, Equality Now and OBJECT,

> much current newspaper reporting about crimes of violence against women promotes and reinforces myths and stereotypes about abuse (such as 'real' and 'deserving' victims, 'provoked' or 'tragic' perpetrators etc); is often inaccurate; and does not give context about the true scale of violence against women and girls (VAWG), or the culture in which it occurs.[40]

Such representations can be seen to have an 'immediate and cumulative effect'[41] on how perpetrators and the wider community perceive violence against women. This, in turn, may reinforce a woman's reluctance to report a crime, and retraumatise a survivor/victim because of the 'continuing implication that what happened to them was in some way their fault'.[42] Accordingly, more ethical reporting on behalf of the media is needed in order to support the moves necessary to change for the better the gendered cultural landscape in which we live. Reforms to the law should be supported by wider public messages about the reality of violence against women and aim to empower survivors/victims. The law does not exist and operate in a vacuum.

Nevertheless, one cannot discount law as an important cog in the wheel, and also potentially an instrument of societal change. The legal system has traditionally contributed to forming and perpetuating men's dominance over women, the acceptability of violence in the home and women's responsibility for men's sexuality. Perhaps it is because of *this* role and its power that, over time, law can challenge social norms and myths that populate the social landscape:

> feminism needs to engage with law for purposes other than law reform . . . it is law's power to define and disqualify which should become the focus of feminist strategy rather than law reform as such. It is in its ability to redefine the truth of events that feminism offers political gains. Hence feminism can (re)define harmless flirtation into sexual harassment, misplaced paternal affection into child sexual abuse, enthusiastic seduction into rape, foetal rights into enforced reproduction, and so on.[43]

Redrafting legislation

Figure 1 shows that in addition to renovating the landscape, laws and legal processes can be improved. Through a less biased reinterpretation of its key concepts and

'Just the Women': An Evaluation of Eleven British National Newspapers' Portrayal of Women Over a Two Week Period in September 2012, Including Recommendations on Press Regulation Reform in Order to Reduce Harm to, and Discrimination Against, Women, Joint Report, 2012.

40 Eaves et al., *'Just the Women'*, above n. 39, p. 3. See also Eaves for Women, *Justice Representation? Press Reporting and the Reality of Rape*, 2002; Zero Tolerance, *Handle with Care: A Guide to Responsible Media Reporting of Violence Against Women*, 2011.

41 End Violence Against Women Coalition, *FINAL Submission to the Leveson Inquiry*, above n. 39, p. 5

42 Ibid.

43 Smart, *Feminism and the Power of the Law*, above n. 13, pp. 164–165.

better integration of the victims' reality, law does have a definite place in facilitating a more just response for those who have been abused and/or assaulted by an intimate.

Some redrafting may be necessary. For example, reformulated provisions need to reflect an understanding that a purely 'objective' standard is inadequate in today's society. Our research has shown, however, that a purely 'subjective' test is also potentially misinformed and prejudiced. One possibility would be legislative wording that reflects a two-tiered test with both objective and subjective components.

Additionally, wherever possible, added specifications could reduce the indeterminacy of the law and the possibility for ambiguity and (mis)interpretation. In Australian sexual harassment legislation, for example, the focus is on the individual's perception of the experience rather than the intention behind it. As we have seen, intention remains an important element in other types of crimes against women, such as rape – where the perpetrator can argue 'mistaken belief'.

Another example of possible legislative reform relates to the notion of consent in the law of rape and sexual assault. As we noted in Chapters 8 and 10, (mis) understandings concerning consent play a pivotal role in rape/sexual assault cases:

> [consent] creates difficulties for the jury (in interpreting its meaning), for the victim (in focusing the trial on her behaviour) and for the Crown (in endeavouring to overcome the stereotyped notions of consenting sexual relations from which the jury is likely to derive its interpretation of consent).[44]

Vitiation of consent could be defined more broadly in relation to partner rape to include the type of intimidation that can be generated in a (violent) domestic relationship, or a separate offence could be enacted for marital rape. Sexual assault provisions could be amended to make clear that consent is simply not relevant when actual bodily harm is involved. In cases of assault and even indecent assault, the courts affirm that view.

As an alternative to defining, or redefining, consent, attention has been given to the development of offences in which the notion of consent is not so pivotal.[45] Such an approach, for example, has been adopted by some of the jurisdictions that operate a gradation scheme.[46] For instance, the law in Michigan outlines three degrees of sexual conduct offences and in none of these is the complainant's lack of consent mentioned. Rather, the law stipulates that in certain circumstances sexual activity is an offence, such as if the defendant is armed with a weapon, causes personal injury

44 Criminal Law and Penal Methods Reform Committee of South Australia, *Rape and Other Sexual Offences*, Special Report, 1976, p. 24. See also J. Temkin, *Rape and the Legal Process*, Oxford: Oxford University Press, 2002, p. 166.

45 See, e.g., V. Tadros, 'Rape without Consent', *Oxford Journal of Legal Studies* 26(3), 2006, 515–543.

46 See Temkin, *Rape and the Legal Process*, above n. 44, pp. 166–172.

or uses force or coercion.[47] The focus is on violence, and rape/sexual assault is accordingly acknowledged to be a crime of violence. The prosecution, however, does not have to prove the absence of consent and the focus is on the conduct of the defendant, as opposed to the complainant. However, the presence of consent can be raised by the defence;[48] hence, the difficulties and 'shades of grey' regarding what amounts to consent may still impact upon the legal proceedings, and we can see how a space is provided for the resurrection of 'old norms'.[49] Moreover, disquiet has been expressed that gradation schemes such as in Michigan fail to acknowledge that non-consensual sexual activity is in and of itself a harm, which should be criminalised. While this may be remedied with the inclusion of an offence of non-consensual sexual conduct, as is the case in NSW,[50] this brings us full circle with how to deal with the problematic of consent.

It may well be, however, that there would be little practitioner support in England and Wales to develop the offences of rape and sexual assault 'without consent'. When questioned whether they could imagine reformulating the offence of rape in a manner which did not rely so heavily on consent, counsel invariably answered in the negative.[51] While barristers recognised that consent is difficult to define, reconceptualising rape in a manner which moves away from focusing upon the complainant's lack of consent was considered illogical. For example, one barrister asserted: 'But I mean that's what rape is, isn't it?'; and another queried: 'Well, what are you left with?'.[52] Thus, feminist law reformers frequently face a difficult struggle in order to unsettle and disrupt legal constructs which are often problematically assumed to embody common-sense and gender-neutral ways of being.

Reinterpreting existing laws

Laws already on the books and current practices can be made more effective by recognising that gender, violence and other specific life history variables are potential obstacles in accessing 'justice'.[53] Interpretation of any of these legal provisions must be underpinned with a better understanding of the victims' reality of domestic violence and rape. Expert witnesses can prove invaluable in helping

47 Mich Comp Laws § 750–520b(1) (1974). See Temkin, *Rape and the Legal Process*, above n. 44, p. 163.

48 Temkin, *Rape and the Legal Process*, above n. 44, p. 172.

49 Nourse, 'The "Normal" Successes and Failures of Feminism', above n. 22, p. 952.

50 Crimes Act 1990 (NSW), s. 61(D).

51 A. Carline and C. Gunby, '"How an Ordinary Jury Makes Sense of it is a Mystery". Barristers' Perspectives on Rape, Consent and the Sexual Offences Act 2003', *Liverpool Law Review* 32(3), 2011, 237–250.

52 Ibid, p. 242.

53 Post-egalitarian feminists reject equality as the only goal of feminist legal theory and call for a more explicit focus on diversity. See M. Fineman, *The Neutered Mother, the Sexual Family, and Other Twentieth Century Tragedies*, New York: Routledge, 1995.

decision-makers to provide this understanding.[54] By showing the court exactly how an action or inaction which intuitively seems alien does in fact fit within someone else's reality, the expert can redefine the following (and more) from the 'multi-faceted shoes of the accused',[55] and of the victim: *reasonable* or *ordinary* behaviour; *relevant* or *irrelevant* evidence; *proper* and *improper* questions; and (negation of) consent.

Expert evidence has been provided to assist tribunals and courts in Australia, for instance, in understanding how a person of '*ordinary* firmness of mind' would respond to the experiential context of domestic violence – that is, the *objective* element of the test for duress.[56] In several social security fraud prosecutions, the expert voice has argued that a victim of domestic violence could be subject to enough duress to constitute unconscionable conduct,[57] which might impair the person's capacity to agree to a marriage-like relationship.[58] By describing the effects of violence and why battered women may remain in the 'home', the expert can help to argue that the attributes of a couple as defined in the legislation no longer pertain.[59] Without that expert perspective, judicial and administrative interpretation of the Social Security Act 1991 has not reflected an understanding of the dynamics of domestic violence. This is evidenced in most of the case law involving battered women who obtained a pension or benefit as a single person

54 One example of a lack of understanding of both is eligibility for refugee status as a victim of domestic or sexual violence. See Australian Law Reform Commission, *Family Violence and Commonwealth Laws – Immigration Law*, Issues Paper 37, 2011, p. 95: 'Historically, applicants whose asylum claims are based on family violence have faced difficulties meeting the definition of a refugee in art 1A(2) of the Refugees Convention, both internationally, and in Australia'.

55 P. Papathanasiou and P. Easteal, '"The Ordinary Person" in Provocation Law: Is the "Objective" Standard Objective?', *Current Issues in Criminal Justice* 10(3), 1999, 53–73, p. 64.

56 Discussed in C. Doyle, P. Easteal and D. Emerson-Elliott, 'Domestic Violence and Marriage Like Relationships: Have We Begun to Emerge from the Dark Ages?', *Alternative Law Journal* 37(2), 2012, 91–95; P. Easteal, K. Hughes and J. Easter, 'Defences: Battered Women and Duress', *Alternative Law Journal* 18(3), 1993, 139–140.

57 Family violence was held in *Moreno v Moreno* [2009] FMCAfam 1109 to constitute unconscionable conduct sufficient to set aside an agreement. Ms Moreno (who had limited English skills) came to Australia from Russia to marry Mr Moreno. She was abused physically and verbally by her husband and signed an agreement that was unfavourable to her, with the belief that if she did not sign it, her marriage would end and her visa would be cancelled. The court held that these circumstances constituted duress significant enough to amount to unconscionable conduct as per Family Law Act 1975 (Cth), s. 90K. The agreement was set aside.

58 Social Security Act 1991 (Cth), s. 24 allows that 'for a special reason in the particular case' a person may on occasion not be treated as a member of a couple.

59 In a few cases, Administrative Appeals Tribunals have decided that there was a 'marriage-like relationship' but that there was a special reason in the particular case for the exercise of the discretion in Social Security Act 1991 (Cth), s. 24(2). See: P. Easteal and D. Emerson-Elliott, 'Marriage-like Relationships: Can Battered Woman Syndrome or Reality Be Pleaded in Social Security Law?', *Alternative Law Journal* 34(3), 2009, 159–178; Doyle, Easteal and Emerson-Elliot, 'Domestic Violence and Marriage Like Relationships', above n. 56.

while *technically* being in a marriage-like relationship, and considered as a member of a couple.[60]

Final pieces of the model: the contingent and conditional nature of feminist law reform

'For reformers, there is no time to pause as if we are at the "end of history". There simply is too much "unfinished business" in the criminal law.'[61] So concludes Nourse in her discussion of the 'normal' successes and failures of feminist-inspired criminal law reform. Throughout this book, we have engaged in a detailed and critical analysis of how the law has, over the years, responded to violence against women. We have explored the many successes: the numerous hard-fought reforms to both the substantive and procedural laws in order to recognise the reality of violence against women, to provide a more effective legal response and to ameliorate the plight of victims. At the same time, however, we have seen how the law frequently fails to provide justice, how old norms and stereotypical ways of thinking continue to inform and impact upon the law and work to exclude women's experiences, and how discretion – even when it appears to have been limited by Parliament – is frequently read back into the law. More work is necessary, but this is not a failure; more work will always be necessary.

The feminist law project aimed at responding to violence against women is an inevitably ongoing endeavour. All reforms are necessarily contingent and fallible, often involving compromise and frequently precarious consensus. Moreover, reforms can only ever reflect a particular political and historical moment in time. No reform can either fully anticipate or encapsulate the future, and nor is it possible to predict in advance how provisions will be interpreted and work in practice, how they will affect the lives of others and how a range of social and cultural factors will impede their implementation and effectiveness. This does not mean that we cannot or should not agitate for further reforms. Indeed, quite the opposite: we must press for improvements, but at the same time also remain critical and vigilant,[62] which requires an acceptance that the future is always unknown and unknowable. To this end, as conceptualised by Van Marle, feminist engagement with law is 'complex, and always tentative, constantly questioning, standing in the guise of an ethics of discomfort'.[63]

60 Social Security Act 1991 (Cth), s. 4(3) gives statutory determinants of a marriage-like relationship. Without expert evidence, there does not seem to be much acknowledgment of how violence may affect those determinants.

61 Nourse, 'The "Normal" Successes and Failures of Feminism', above n. 22, p. 978.

62 Ibid., p. 978.

63 K. Van Marle, '"We Exist, but Who Are We?": Feminist and the Power of Sociological Law', *Feminist Legal Studies* 20(2), 2010, 149–159, p. 158.

Index

Printed in the USA/Agawam, MA
February 12, 2015
608503.027